PRACTICE MAKES PERFECT®

Spanish Verb Tenses

PREMIUM FIFTH EDITION

Dorothy Richmond

Mc
Graw
Hill

New York   Chicago   San Francisco   Athens   London   Madrid
Mexico City   Milan   New Delhi   Singapore   Sydney   Toronto

1 2 3 4 5 6 7 8 9   LHS   28 27 26 25 24 23

ISBN   978-1-265-09794-3
MHID   1-265-09794-1

e-ISBN   978-1-265-09885-8
e-MHID   1-265-09885-9

Interior design by Village Bookworks, Inc.

McGraw Hill products are available at special quantity discounts to use as premiums and sales promotions or for use in corporate training programs. To contact a representative, please visit the Contact Us pages at www.mhprofessional.com.

McGraw Hill is committed to making our products accessible to all learners. To learn more about the available support and accommodations we offer, please contact us at accessibility@mheducation.com. We also participate in the Access Text Network (www.accesstext.org), and ATN members may submit requests through ATN.

McGraw Hill Language Lab App
Audio recordings, flashcards, and a digital glossary are all available to support your study of this book. Go to www.mhlanguagelab.com to access the online version of this application, or to locate links to the mobile app for iOS and Android devices. Alternatively, search "McGraw Hill Language Lab" directly in the iTunes app store, or the Google Play store for Android devices. (Note: Internet access is required to access audio via the app.)

Other titles by Dorothy Richmond:
Practice Makes Perfect: Basic Spanish
Practice Makes Perfect: Spanish Pronouns and Prepositions
Practice Makes Perfect: Spanish Vocabulary
Practice Makes Perfect: Spanish Vocabulary Building with Suffixes

Para Mary Batinich y Michael Skorich, una pareja de tortolitos

Contents

Acknowledgments ix

Introduction xi

 THE PRESENT TENSE 1

1 **Conjugation of regular verbs** 3

    The basics of verbs 3

    Conjugating verbs 4

    Regular **-ar** verbs 5

    Negative sentences 7

    Regular **-er** verbs 9

    Regular **-ir** verbs 11

    Asking questions 14

2 **Ser and estar** 19

    Using **ser** 20

    Using **estar** 25

3 **Hay** 31

4 **Tener** 35

    Possession 35

    Age 37

    Idiomatic expressions with **tener** 37

    Obligation 39

5 **The personal a** 43

6 **Common irregular verbs** 47

    Phrases with two verbs—**querer, poder, deber** 49

    Describing the weather—**hacer, estar** 50

    Playing games—**jugar** 51

    Expressing future action—**ir** + **a** + INFINITIVE 52

7 **Saber** and **conocer** 57

   Saber 57

   Conocer 60

8 **Stem-changing verbs** 65

   o > ue 65

   e > ie 67

   e > i 69

9 **Irregular verb groups** 73

   Infinitives ending with **-cer** preceded by a vowel 73

   Infinitives ending with **-ucir** 75

   Infinitives ending with **-cer** or **-cir** preceded by a consonant 77

   Infinitives ending with **-ger** or **-gir** 78

   Infinitives ending with **-aer** 80

   Infinitives ending with **-uir** not preceded by **g** 81

   Infinitives ending with **-guir** 83

10 **Reflexive verbs** 87

11 **Gustar** and **similarly formed verbs** 93

12 **The present progressive** 99

   Formation of the present progressive 99

   Object pronouns with the present progressive 104

 THE PAST TENSES, THE FUTURE TENSE, THE CONDITIONAL TENSE, AND THE PRESENT AND PAST PERFECT TENSES 107

13 **The preterite tense** 109

   Regular verbs in the preterite 110

   Irregular verbs in the preterite 117

   Verbs that change meaning in the preterite 132

14 **The imperfect tense** 135

   Regular verbs in the imperfect 136

   Irregular verbs in the imperfect 136

   When to use the imperfect 137

15 **The future tense** 159

   Regular verbs in the future 159

   Irregular verbs in the future 164

16 **The conditional tense** 171

    Regular verbs in the conditional 171

    Irregular verbs in the conditional 174

17 **The present perfect tense** 179

    Formation of the present perfect 179

18 **The past perfect tense** 187

    Formation of the past perfect 187

THE IMPERATIVE, THE SUBJUNCTIVE, THE FUTURE AND CONDITIONAL PERFECT TENSES, AND THE PASSIVE VOICE 195

19 **The imperative** 197

    tú commands 197

    usted commands 202

    ustedes commands 204

    vosotros commands 205

    nosotros commands 207

    Notable characteristics of commands 207

20 **The present subjunctive** 211

    Formation of the present subjunctive 212

    Uses of the present subjunctive 214

21 **The imperfect subjunctive** 233

    Formation of the imperfect subjunctive 233

    Uses of the imperfect subjunctive 234

22 **The future perfect tense** 245

    Formation of the future perfect 245

    Uses of the future perfect 245

23 **The conditional perfect tense** 251

    Formation of the conditional perfect 251

    Uses of the conditional perfect 252

24 **The present perfect subjunctive** 257

    Formation of the present perfect subjunctive 257

    Uses of the present perfect subjunctive 258

25 **The pluperfect subjunctive** 263

Formation of the pluperfect subjunctive 263

Uses of the pluperfect subjunctive 264

26 **The passive voice** 271

Incomplete passive voice 271

Complete passive voice 277

APPENDIX A Verb conjugation charts 281

APPENDIX B Verbs that take a preposition 285

Answer key 291

Spanish-English glossary 311

English-Spanish glossary 325

Acknowledgments

As this book goes into its fifth edition, nearly thirty years after its initial publication, the first person to acknowledge – then, now, and always – is Gilmore T. Schjeldahl, a former private student. His intelligence and endless curiosity, matched only by his kind heart, inspired me to write a book on Spanish verbs that covers not just the what and how, but also the why and when of verb usage. I will always be grateful to Mr. Schjeldahl for all he taught me.

In the same spirit, I thank all the students who chose and worked through the previous four editions of this book. Their curiosity, intelligence, and number were great enough to generate another edition. This is a great honor.

I was fortunate to work once again with Christopher Brown, publisher, who oversaw the production of this book at McGraw Hill. For over twenty-five years I have considered Christopher a great editor and friend.

Finally, and always, I thank my daughters, Daisy and Lily, who have grown to become good and honorable women. The joy and pride they have brought to me is beyond measure.

Introduction

More than any other aspect of learning a foreign language, verbs challenge the learner. *Practice Makes Perfect: Spanish Verb Tenses* is a systematic, logical approach to the study of Spanish verbs, including their tenses, moods, and special uses. This information is provided in workbook format, with clear explanations of each use of a verb. Each section contains a variety of exercises that relate directly to the material just covered and that also include previously covered material for constant review.

This fifth edition of *Practice Makes Perfect: Spanish Verb Tenses* retains the structure and format of the fourth edition. The changes are mainly in its content: There are many new paragraphs for translation, and cultural references have been brought into the 21st century.

Practice Makes Perfect: Spanish Verb Tenses takes you far beyond the rote memorization so commonly associated with studying verbs and tenses, and enables you to fully grasp the important as well as the subtle role that verbs play in every sentence we utter, write, read, or think.

The verb is the engine of the sentence. Without a verb, the sentence technically and figuratively goes nowhere. Thus, a careful, systematic study of verbs in any language is crucial to communication in any form.

Yet this careful study of the verbs need not be the drudge work so commonly associated with verbs, namely, memorizing a zillion conjugations. If you think of working with verbs as creating a scaffold for the language, which is really what verbs provide, the task at hand can seem far more meaningful and less daunting.

You may have seen several Spanish verb books already, and you may be wondering what, if anything, another verb book on the market could add. What sets *Practice Makes Perfect: Spanish Verb Tenses* apart from other Spanish verb books is its scope and its intent to teach the full picture with regard to verbs.

Many books devoted to Spanish verbs provide you with conjugations and little else. Sometimes exercises are provided, but the emphasis is nearly always on the mechanical aspect of conjugating the verb, rendering these books more verb dictionaries than actual teaching or reviewing texts. While correctly conjugating a verb is an extremely important aspect of speaking and writing well, it is still pure mechanics unless you understand the implications of the use of one verb form over another and why you choose a particular use.

Practice Makes Perfect: Spanish Verb Tenses offers you not only hundreds of verbs with their particular conjugations, but also lets you know both *when* and *why* a particular verb should be used: You are given social, philosophical, and linguistic reasons and applications for the use of verbs.

The Spanish word for *tense*, in the grammatical sense, is **tiempo**, which is also the Spanish word for "time." The philosophical and psychological aspects of time, so central to working with the tenses, unfortunately are often overlooked. To take something so rich as language—the vehicle of thought—and pare it down to its technical particulars is to take something that is beautiful and diminish it.

My experience with students of Spanish has taught me that the difficulty of the task before them is rarely what determines either the level of interest or the degree of success. What I have learned is that a step-by-step, logical approach—one that includes clear explanations and reasons for learning Spanish well—intrigues the learner. Interest and secure understanding—not ease and surface performance—are the genuine guarantors of success.

There are three main parts to this book:

◆ **Part I: The present tense**   The 12 chapters in Part I thoroughly cover verb usage in the present tense: basic conjugation of regular verbs, formation of questions, detailed information on the challenging verbs **ser** and **estar** (the verbs "to be"), use of the personal **a**, reflexive verbs, a host of irregular verbs along with their uses and nuances, and the present progressive mood.

◆ **Part II: The past, future, conditional, and perfect tenses**   Part II covers the six most basic indicative tenses (after the present): preterite, imperfect, future, conditional, present perfect, and past perfect. Their conjugations and various applications are discussed, and ample exercises are included.

◆ **Part III: The imperative, the subjunctive, and the passive voice**   This final section of the text begins with the imperative (command form), which establishes a foundation for the next chapter, the present subjunctive. These are followed by the imperfect subjunctive, future perfect, conditional perfect, present perfect subjunctive, pluperfect subjunctive, and, finally, the passive voice, which covers all tenses in this special use.

In the exercises in this text, you should assume that the English "you" is both singular and informal—translated by the Spanish **tú**—unless it carries the notation "[pl.]" or "[formal]." English "you all" is translated by the informal plural form **vosotros** unless it carries the notation "[formal]." Exercise items with ambiguity of gender carry the notation "[m.]" or "[f.]" as clarification.

Following the text are two appendixes: verb conjugation charts for all the tenses except the present, and a helpful list of verbs that require a preposition before a following word for specific usages. A complete answer key for all of the exercises follows the appendixes. Also included are contextual glossaries, both Spanish-English and English-Spanish.

Practice Makes Perfect: Spanish Verb Tenses will be helpful to motivated high school and college students, as well as to adults who are either starting fresh or returning to study Spanish. It is an excellent companion to any Spanish language basic text and is a superb review workbook. *Practice Makes Perfect: Spanish Verb Tenses* is also a sound reference source for both teachers and students of Spanish.

It is my sincere hope that this book will help those studying Spanish—at any level—to achieve their goals of speaking, writing, and reading this beautiful language with greater competence, confidence, and enjoyment.

Dorothy Richmond

THE PRESENT TENSE

TENSE	Present
TIME	Refers to both the specific *now* (at this moment) and the general *now* (these days, this time period)
KEY PHRASES	"Now," "today," "these days"—any word group that expresses the specific or general *now*
STRUCTURE	Simple tense: VERB BASE + VERB ENDING

The present tense is used to report what is happening and what is true now. The present tense can be pin-point specific or it can cover vast amounts of time. Whether the action expressed is true only at this very moment or includes a truth that sweeps over eons, the key is that—at its core—it is true *now*. Consider four kinds of "present" below.

The specific present—"right now"

> It ***is*** 10:32:44 P.M.
> At this very moment I ***see*** a shooting star.
> I now ***pronounce*** you husband and wife.

The broader, yet enclosed present

> I ***go out*** to dinner two or three times a week.
> Every Friday, Mitch ***brings*** doughnuts to the office.
> We ***go*** to Mexico three or four times a year.

The progressive present

> I ***am eating*** a bagel.
> You ***are studying***.
> He ***is reading*** a book.

The general, ongoing present

> Nearly all countries ***have*** some form of organized government.
> The president of the United States ***lives*** in Washington, D.C.
> The pope ***is*** the head of the Catholic Church.

1

Conjugation of regular verbs

The basics of verbs

As you begin your study of verb tenses in Spanish, it is important to understand the basic terminology relating to verbs and their formation.

CONJUGATION   The word *conjugation* has two related meanings in Spanish grammar: (1) one of the three groups of verbs classified by the infinitive ending (-**ar**, -**er**, and -**ir** verbs); (2) the set of verb forms consisting of the verb base plus verb endings that correspond to the subject pronouns.

INFINITIVE   The verb in its pure form—the idea of the verb, without any expression of action. In English, all infinitives include the word "to": "to sing," "to eat," "to live." In Spanish, all infinitives belong to one of three conjugations, which is determined by the infinitive ending: -**ar**, -**er**, or -**ir**. The infinitive is like a hand grenade before you pull the pin—no real action, but a lot of potential.

INFINITIVE ENDING   The -**ar**, -**er**, or -**ir** ending that identifies the verb conjugation to which the verb belongs, for example, -**ar**: **cantar** ("to sing"), -**er**: **comer** ("to eat"), -**ir**: **vivir** ("to live").

VERB BASE   The unique part of the infinitive that distinguishes the meaning of the verb. When the infinitive ending -**ar**, -**er**, or -**ir** is removed, what remains is the verb base. The verb base of **cantar** is **cant**-, the base of **comer** is **com**-, and the base of **vivir** is **viv**-. The verb base is also called the stem or root of the verb.

VERB ENDING   Specific endings added to the verb base in order to conjugate the verb. The verb endings for -**ar** verbs, for example, are -**o**, -**as**, -**a**, -**amos**, -**áis**, -**an**, and each ending corresponds to a subject pronoun.

CONJUGATED VERB FORM   The verb form that consists of the verb base and an appropriate verb ending to correspond to the subject of the verb. These conjugated forms express action with reference to the subject, for example, **Mary canta** ("Mary sings"). In this sentence, "sings" is a conjugated verb. When you conjugate a verb, you pull the pin from the hand grenade and release its action.

REGULAR VERB   A verb whose verb base remains intact, with regular -**ar**, -**er**, or -**ir** endings attached to it when conjugated.

IRREGULAR VERB   A verb whose verb base does not remain intact, or one that when conjugated does not take regular -**ar**, -**er**, or -**ir** endings.

SUBJECT   The actor(s) in the sentence. For example, the sentences "Mary sings," "We eat," and "I live" have as their subjects "Mary," "We," and "I," respectively.

3

Conjugating verbs

In English, not a lot of conjugation goes on: "I speak," "you speak," "he speaks," "she speaks," "we speak," "they speak." Only the third-person singular makes a change in the present tense of most English verbs, taking on the ending "-s."

In Spanish, there are six different verb endings for each verb tense, corresponding to the six subject pronoun groups—the singular and plural of first-person, second-person, and third-person subject pronouns. Each conjugated verb form in Spanish indicates who is performing the action (expression of person and number), as well as when the action occurred (verb tense).

Subject pronouns

In English, there are seven subject pronouns: "I," "you," "he," "she," "it," "we," and "they." Spanish has the same basic set of subject pronouns, but with additional forms that express gender. In Spanish, "we," "they," and the second-person plural form of "you" have both masculine and feminine forms. In addition, there are four words that express "you" in Spanish—singular and plural forms of both a formal and an informal "you."

Subject pronouns

SINGULAR		PLURAL	
yo	*I*	nosotros	*we* (masc., masc. & fem.)
		nosotras	*we* (fem.)
tú	*you* (informal)	vosotros	*you* (informal, masc., masc. & fem.)
		vosotras	*you* (informal, fem.)
él	*he*	ellos	*they* (masc., masc. & fem.)
ella	*she*	ellas	*they* (fem.)
usted	*you* (formal)	ustedes	*you* (formal)

It is important to note that the informal plural **vosotros** form is used primarily in Peninsular Spanish (that is, in Spain), while throughout most of Latin America **ustedes** is used in both formal and informal situations. For the most part, the word "it" is an understood subject in Spanish, and thus Spanish has no specific word for "it" as a subject pronoun.

Principles of conjugation

1 To conjugate a verb in Spanish, begin with the infinitive.

   EXAMPLE **cantar** ("to sing")

2 Find the verb base, which is what remains when the infinitive ending is removed from the infinitive.

   EXAMPLE **cantar** minus **-ar** equals **cant-**, the verb base

3 Add the verb ending that corresponds to the subject of the verb directly to the verb base.

   EXAMPLE For the subject "I" (**yo**): **cant-** (verb base) + **-o** (verb ending) = **canto** ("I sing")

Regular -ar verbs

Regular -ar endings

yo	-o	nosotros	-amos
		nosotras	-amos
tú	-as	vosotros	-áis
		vosotras	-áis
él	-a	ellos	-an
ella	-a	ellas	-an
usted	-a	ustedes	-an

NOTE Common abbreviations are **Ud.** for **usted**, and **Uds.** for **ustedes**. Both are commonly used in writing and always capitalized.

Below is the fully conjugated verb **hablar**.

hablar *to speak, talk*

yo hablo	*I speak*	**nosotros hablamos**	*we speak (masc., masc. & fem.)*
		nosotras hablamos	*we speak (fem.)*
tú hablas	*you speak*	**vosotros habláis**	*you all speak (masc., masc. & fem.)*
		vosotras habláis	*you all speak (fem.)*
él habla	*he speaks*	**ellos hablan**	*they speak (masc., masc. & fem.)*
ella habla	*she speaks*	**ellas hablan**	*they speak (fem.)*
Ud. habla	*you speak*	**Uds. hablan**	*you all speak*

Below are several common regular **-ar** verbs, followed by exercises in which you can practice conjugating the verbs and creating simple sentences.

VOCABULARIO

amar	to love	**hablar**	to speak, talk
andar	to walk	**llegar**	to arrive
bailar	to dance	**llevar**	to wear, carry
buscar	to look for, search for	**mirar**	to watch, look at
caminar	to walk, stroll	**pagar (por)**	to pay (for)
cantar	to sing	**practicar**	to practice
comprar	to buy	**preparar**	to prepare
entrar (en)	to enter (into)	**tocar**	to touch, play (*an instrument*)
escuchar	to listen (to)	**tomar**	to take
esperar	to hope, wait (for)	**trabajar**	to work
estudiar	to study	**viajar**	to travel

NOTE When translating some Spanish verbs, the English equivalent may include a preposition after the verb form, for example, **escuchar** ("to listen to"): **yo *escucho* la radio** ("I *listen to* the radio").

EJERCICIO

1·1

Traducción *Traduce las frases siguientes.*

1. *I sing.* _____

2. *You sing.* _____

3. *He sings.* _____

4. *We sing.* _____

5. *They [m.] sing.* _____

6. *I pay.* _____

7. *We pay for the house.* _____

8. *You pay.* _____

9. *They [f.] pay.* _____

10. *She studies.* _____

11. *He studies.* _____

12. *I study.* _____

13. *We study.* _____

14. *You walk.* _____

15. *We walk.* _____

16. *I work.* _____

17. *He works.* _____

18. *They work.* _____

19. *We work.* _____

20. *He dances.* _____

21. *I love.* _____

22. *You love.* _____

23. *She loves.* _____

24. *We love.* _____

25. *They love.* _____

26. *I practice.* _____

27. *He practices.* _____

28. *They enter.* _____

29. *I watch the house.* _____

30. *I look at the garden.* _____

31. *They watch the car.* _____

32. *She listens.* _____

33. *They [f.] listen.* _____

34. *I listen.* _____

35. *He buys the car.* _____

36. *I buy the dog.* _____

37. *You buy the house.* _____

38. *I speak with Miguel.* _____

39. *She pays for the books.* _____

40. *We study Spanish.* _____

¿Cuál es verdadero o falso para ti? (Which is true or false for you?)
*Escribe la respuesta—una **V** (verdadero) o una **F** (falso)—en el espacio en blanco.*

1. _____ Yo hablo inglés.

2. _____ Yo trabajo en un banco.

3. _____ Yo estudio español en la escuela.

4. _____ Yo canto muy bien.

5. _____ Yo bailo muy bien.

6. _____ Yo toco el piano.

7. _____ Yo compro la ropa en Target.

8. _____ Yo miro la televisión en el dormitorio.

9. _____ Yo preparo café en la mañana.

10. _____ Mi amigo/amiga habla español.

11. _____ Mi amigo/amiga viaja mucho.

12. _____ Mi amigo/amiga toca el clarinete.

Negative sentences

To make an affirmative sentence negative, simply add **no** directly before the verb.

Yo no hablo portugués.	*I don't speak Portuguese.*
Nosotros no trabajamos aquí.	*We don't work here.*
Tú no escuchas la radio.	*You don't listen to the radio.*
Vosotros no estudiáis francés.	*You all don't study French.*
Él no canta con el coro.	*He doesn't sing with the choir.*
Ellos no esperan el autobús.	*They don't wait for the bus.*

¿Cuál es verdadero o falso para ti?

1. _____ Yo no estudio italiano.

2. _____ Yo no viajo por el Antártico.

3. _____ Yo no camino a la escuela.

4. _____ Yo no llevo uniforme a la escuela.

5. _____ Yo no hablo con mis amigos por teléfono.

6. _____ Yo no canto en la iglesia.

7. _____ Mis amigos y yo no estudiamos español.

8. _____ Mis amigos y yo no miramos la televisión.

9. _____ Mi mejor (best) amigo/amiga no trabaja en un restaurante.

10. _____ Mi mejor amigo/amiga no toca el violín.

EJERCICIO 1·2

Traducción

VOCABULARIO	el arpa	*harp*	la mañana	*morning*
	bien	*well*	el nombre	*name*
	especial	*special*	rápidamente	*fast*
	la guitarra	*guitar*	el restaurante	*restaurant*
	la lección	*lesson*	también	*also*

Hello. My name is Paco. I study Spanish in the morning and I work in a restaurant in the afternoon. My friends speak Spanish. I practice my lessons with my friends. They speak fast. I do not speak fast. My teacher speaks Spanish and English. She also plays the guitar, and sometimes (aveces) we sing and sometimes we dance the flamenco. I practice the flamenco in my house in the evening with a friend or with my cousins. They dance very well. I wear special shoes when I dance. Sometimes my daughter Daisy plays the harp. She plays very well. I play the piano. I don't play the harp.

_____

_____

_____

_____

_____

_____

_____

_____

Regular -er verbs

To conjugate regular -er verbs, begin with the verb base and add the -er endings.

Regular -er endings

yo	-o	nosotros	-emos
		nosotras	-emos
tú	-es	vosotros	-éis
		vosotras	-éis
él	-e	ellos	-en
ella	-e	ellas	-en
usted	-e	ustedes	-en

Below is the fully conjugated verb **comer** ("to eat").

comer *to eat*

yo como	nosotros comemos
	nosotras comemos
tú comes	vosotros coméis
	vosotras coméis
él come	ellos comen
ella come	ellas comen
usted come	ustedes comen

Below are several common regular -er verbs, followed by exercises in which you can practice conjugating the verbs and creating simple sentences.

VOCABULARIO

aprender	to learn	deber	to owe
beber	to drink	leer	to read
comer	to eat	meter (*en*)	to put (into)
cometer (*un error*)	to make (*a mistake*)	poseer	to possess, own
comprender	to understand	romper	to break
correr	to run	temer	to fear, dread
creer	to believe	vender	to sell

EJERCICIO
1·3

Traducción

1. *I learn.* _____

2. *I drink.* _____

3. *He drinks.* _____

4. *You eat.* _____

5. *We eat.* _____

6. *I understand.* _____

7. *I don't understand.* _____

8. *They understand.* _____

9. *You understand.* _____

10. *You don't understand.* _____

11. *I run.* _____

12. *You run.* _____

13. *She runs.* _____
14. *They don't run.* _____
15. *We run.* _____
16. *I believe.* _____
17. *I don't believe.* _____
18. *He believes.* _____
19. *We owe.* _____
20. *I read.* _____
21. *You read.* _____
22. *You don't read.* _____
23. *He reads.* _____
24. *She reads.* _____
25. *We read.* _____
26. *I make a mistake.* _____

27. *I put.* _____
28. *You put.* _____
29. *He puts.* _____
30. *We put.* _____
31. *They [m.] put.* _____
32. *They [f.] put.* _____
33. *We break.* _____
34. *They [f.] break.* _____
35. *I break.* _____
36. *You sell.* _____
37. *We sell.* _____
38. *I don't sell.* _____
39. *She doesn't sell.* _____
40. *We learn.* _____

EJERCICIO

¿Cuál es verdadero o falso para ti? *Mark the following statements either true (**V**) or false (**F**). Note that when the subject is understood from the conjugated verb form (for example, **Como** = I eat), the subject pronoun is not required in Spanish.*

1. _____ Como mucho en McDonald's.

2. _____ Bebo leche cada día.

3. _____ No comprendo francés.

4. _____ Leo los libros de Ernest Hemingway.

5. _____ Aprendo mucho en mi clase de español.

6. _____ Macy's vende ropa.

7. _____ La biblioteca vende libros.

8. _____ Corro en el maratón de Londres.

9. _____ A veces (*at times*) cometo errores.

10. _____ Normalmente, el gato bebe leche o agua.

11. _____ Creo en fantasmas (*ghosts*).

12. _____ Muchas personas en los Estados Unidos comprenden español.

Traducción

VOCABULARIO	el autor, la autora	*author*	la revista	*magazine*
	el lápiz	*pencil*	usualmente	*usually*
	la librería	*bookstore*	el vaso	*(drinking) glass*
	el regalo	*gift*	a veces	*sometimes*

I read a lot of books. When I read a book, I usually eat pizza or drink a glass of milk or water. I learn a lot from my books. I also owe a lot of money to the bookstore. My parents read books and magazines, but I read more. The bookstore in my city sells books, magazines, pens, pencils, gifts, and much more. We don't eat in the bookstore, but sometimes we drink coffee there. My family and I own many books. Sometimes an author makes a mistake, but usually not.

Regular -ir verbs

To conjugate regular **-ir** verbs, begin with the verb base and add the **-ir** endings. Note that the endings, listed below, are identical to the endings for **-er** verbs except for the **nosotros** and **vosotros** forms.

Regular -ir endings

yo	**-o**	nosotros	**-imos**
		nosotras	**-imos**
tú	**-es**	vosotros	**-ís**
		vosotras	**-ís**
él	**-e**	ellos	**-en**
ella	**-e**	ellas	**-en**
usted	**-e**	ustedes	**-en**

Below is the fully conjugated verb **vivir** ("to live").

vivir *to live*

yo vivo	**nosotros vivimos**
	nosotras vivimos
tú vives	**vosotros vivís**
	vosotras vivís
él vive	**ellos viven**
ella vive	**ellas viven**
usted vive	**ustedes viven**

Below are several common regular -**ir** verbs, followed by exercises in which you can practice conjugating the verbs and creating simple sentences.

abrir	to open	**escribir**	to write
admitir	to admit	**existir**	to exist
asistir (a)	to attend	**permitir**	to permit
cubrir	to cover	**recibir**	to receive, welcome
decidir	to decide	**subir**	to climb, go up
describir	to describe	**sufrir**	to suffer
descubrir	to discover	**unir**	to unite
discutir	to discuss	**vivir**	to live

EJERCICIO
1·5

Traducción

1. *I open the windows.* _____

2. *She suffers a lot.* _____

3. *We live in the United States.* _____

4. *You write a lot of letters.* _____

5. *The child admits everything* (todo). _____

6. *John climbs the staircase* (la escalera). _____

7. *I discover a cat in the house.* _____

8. *Many people suffer.* _____

9. *We decide.* _____

10. *Unicorns* (los unicornios) *don't exist.* _____

11. *You all* [formal] *write well.* _____

12. *Mary describes the spiders* (la araña). _____

13. *We write many letters.* _____

14. *They don't attend school.* _____

15. *Mary and John discuss the book.* _____

16. *You unite the two parts* (la parte). _____

17. *The boys describe everything.* _____

18. *You all cover the tables.* _____

19. *John doesn't attend the meeting* (la reunión). _____

20. *I receive gifts* (el regalo) *for my birthday.* _____

EJERCICIO

¿Cuál es verdadero o falso para ti?

1. _____ Vivo en un apartamento.

2. _____ Escribo mucho en mi clase de español.

3. _____ Stephen King escribe libros de horror.

4. _____ Recibo regalos en diciembre.

5. _____ El presidente de los Estados Unidos vive en Washington, D.C.

6. _____ Asisto a la universidad.

7. _____ Los fantasmas no existen.

8. _____ Normalmente, no abro las ventanas de la casa en enero.

9. _____ Discuto mis problemas con mis amigos.

10. _____ Sufro mucho en mi clase de español.

11. _____ Muchas oficinas no permiten el consumo de tabaco en su interior.

12. _____ El jefe (*boss*) le describe el trabajo al empleado.

EJERCICIO

1·6

Traducción

VOCABULARIO

el aire	*air*	durante	*during*	por	*along*
el banco	*bank*	fresco	*fresh*	la semana	*week*
cada	*each*	el mar	*sea*	si	*if*
el calor	*heat*	la novela	*novel*	solamente	*only*
como	*like*	las personas	*people*	todo el mundo	*everyone*

Hi. My family and I live in Havana, Cuba. My father writes novels and my mother works in a bank. She decides if a person receives money from the bank. Everyone believes that Christopher Columbus discovers Cuba in 1492. Some people believe that Christopher Columbus discovers North America, too. I attend school five days each week. My little sister (hermanita) attends school only three days each week. We suffer a lot from the heat here during the day, but in the evening we welcome the fresh air like a friend. Every evening, my friends and I walk along (por) the Malecón and we look at the sea.

_____

_____

_____

_____

_____

_____

Conjugation of regular verbs   **13**

Asking questions

Now that you can conjugate verbs and form sentences, it's time to learn to form questions.

Asking simple questions

A simple question is one that elicits either a "yes" or a "no" for an answer. In Spanish, this involves placing the conjugated verb in front of the subject: **Tú hablas español** ("You speak Spanish") becomes **¿Hablas tú español?** ("Do you speak Spanish?"). In English, we often use the auxiliary verb "do" or "does" in front of a sentence to form a question. In this context, however, "do" and "does" are not translated into Spanish.

¿Vives tú en España?	*Do you live in Spain?*
¿Trabajáis en el banco?	*Do you all work in the bank?*
¿Come él aquí con frecuencia?	*Does he eat here often?*
¿Leen ellos el periódico cada día?	*Do they read the newspaper every day?*

EJERCICIO

1·7

Traducción

1. *Do you speak English?* _____

2. *Do you understand?* _____

3. *Do you all study a lot?* _____

4. *Does he sing well?* _____

5. *Does she sell clothing?* _____

6. *Does he work here?* _____

7. *Do they live there?* _____

8. *Do unicorns exist?* _____

9. *Does she write books?* _____

10. *Does he make many mistakes?* _____

11. *Do you read in the library?* _____

12. *Does she understand?* _____

Asking complex questions

Complex questions request more than a simple "yes" or "no." The asker is wanting specific information or an explanation.

To form complex questions, precede a simple question with one of the following interrogatives.

¿Quién?, ¿Quiénes?	*Who?*
¿Qué?	*What?*
¿Cuándo?	*When?*
¿Dónde?	*Where?*

¿Por qué?	*Why?*
¿Cómo?	*How?*

Accent marks are always used when these words serve as interrogatives.

¿**Quién** trabaja aquí?	***Who*** works here?
¿**Qué** comes tú?	***What*** are you eating?
¿**Cuándo** estudias?	***When*** do you study?
¿**Dónde** viven ellos?	***Where*** do they live?
¿**Por qué** existimos?	***Why*** do we exist?
¿**Cómo** decido yo?	***How*** do I decide?

NOTE The Spanish "who?" always takes a third-person verb.

EJERCICIO
1·8

Traducción

1. *Where do you live?* _____
2. *Where do you work?* _____
3. *When do you study?* _____
4. *When do you write?* _____
5. *Who understands?* _____
6. *Who doesn't sing?* _____
7. *Why does he dance?* _____
8. *Why do we work?* _____
9. *What are you preparing?* (*What do you prepare?*) _____
10. *What are you all* [formal] *watching?* _____
11. *How do they sell so much* (tanto)? _____
12. *How does she read so much?* _____

Asking limiting questions

A person asking a limiting question wants to know "which?" or "how much?" or "how many?" of the noun in question. In other words, the asker wants a limit placed on that noun. "*How many books* do you read?" "I read *ten books.*"

To form limiting questions in Spanish, use one of the following interrogatives. ¿**Cuál?** (or ¿**Cuáles?**) is generally followed by a verb (often with English "one" or "ones" understood). ¿**Cuánto?** (or ¿**Cuántos?**) is typically followed first by a noun and then by the appropriate conjugated verb. Study the following examples.

¿**Cuál?**	*Which?* (sing.)
¿**Cuáles?**	*Which?* (pl.)
¿**Cuánto?** (masc.), ¿**Cuánta?** (fem.)	*How much?*
¿**Cuántos?** (masc.), ¿**Cuántas?** (fem.)	*How many?*

¿**Cuál** prefieres?	*Which (one) do you prefer?*
¿**Cuáles** prefieres?	*Which (ones) do you prefer?*
¿**Cuánto pan** come él?	*How much bread does he eat?*
¿**Cuántos libros** lees?	*How many books do you read?*
¿**Cuánta leche** bebe usted?	*How much milk do you drink?*
¿**Cuántas ciudades** visitan ustedes?	*How many cities do you visit?*

NOTE The verb **preferir** is irregular. (This verb and others like it will be covered in Chapter 8, Stem-changing verbs.) It is used here because this is a very common use of this verb.

EJERCICIO 1·9

Traducción

1. *Which (one) functions (funcionar)?* _____

2. *Which (one) needs (necesitar) water?* _____

3. *Which (ones) function?* _____

4. *Which (ones) need water?* _____

5. *How much money do you [formal] pay?* _____

6. *How much Spanish do we learn?* _____

7. *How many cars do you buy?* _____

8. *How many books do you sell?* _____

9. *How much water does he drink?* _____

10. *How much truth (la verdad) does he possess?* _____

11. *How many people live in Mexico?* _____

12. *How many windows do they open?* _____

Traducción

VOCABULARIO

el cliente	*customer*	el tipo	*type*
la comida	*meal, food*	el huevo	*egg*
el escritor	*writer*	el panqueque	*pancake*
elegante	*elegant*	la sopa	*soup*
fascinante	*fascinating*	cada día	*every day*
la esposa	*wife*	la comida	*food*
los hijos	*children*	el amor	*love*

Kenny works in a restaurant in New York. He prepares many meals every day. Usually he works in the morning, but sometimes he works in the afternoon. Kenny doesn't work in the evening. His customers eat the food that Kenny prepares and then they pay the bill. Bob Dylan is his customer, also Madonna and the writer Calvin Trillin. His restaurant is not elegant. The food is not elegant. But, the restaurant is very popular because Kenny is fascinating. His wife, Eve, also works in the restaurant. His five children work in the restaurant. Kenny prepares many types of eggs and pancakes and soups every day. Kenny believes that when his customers eat his food they receive his love.

_____

_____

_____

_____

_____

_____

_____

_____

_____

_____

Ser and estar

2

Of all the verbs in the Spanish language, **ser** and **estar** seem to present the biggest hurdles for the native English speaker. However, because they are two of the most important verbs in the Spanish language, they deserve the attention required to master them.

Ser and **estar** are irregular verbs. They don't follow the nice, tidy conjugations you learned in Chapter 1. Instead, you must commit their various forms to memory.

The hurdles referred to, however, have less to do with memorizing their forms than with learning when to use which verb. **Ser** and **estar** both mean "to be." In English, we have only one verb "to be," which, when conjugated, translates as "I am," "you are," "he is," "she is," "we are," "they are." Both **ser** and **estar** are translated with these same meanings, but the two verbs express different ways of being. Thus when you learn to use **ser** and **estar**, you are in effect being asked to separate ways of being into different categories.

The simplest, but by no means all-inclusive, explanation for the difference between these verbs is to say that **ser** is used in enduring situations, while **estar** is used in situations that are short-term, that involve location, or that are the result of some action. To say "I am a human being," use the verb **ser**, but to say "I am kneeling," "I am in the library," or "The window is open," use the verb **estar**.

Below are the conjugations of **ser** and **estar**, followed by a more complete discussion of when to use these verbs.

ser *to be*			
yo soy	*I am*	**nosotros somos**	*we are* (masc., masc. & fem.)
		nosotras somos	*we are* (fem.)
tú eres	*you are*	**vosotros sois**	*you all are* (masc., masc. & fem.)
		vosotras sois	*you all are* (fem.)
él es	*he is*	**ellos son**	*they are* (masc., masc. & fem.)
ella es	*she is*	**ellas son**	*they are* (fem.)
usted es	*you are*	**ustedes son**	*you all are*

estar *to be*			
yo estoy	*I am*	**nosotros estamos**	*we are* (masc., masc. & fem.)
		nosotras estamos	*we are* (fem.)
tú estás	*you are*	**vosotros estáis**	*you all are* (masc., masc. & fem.)
		vosotras estáis	*you all are* (fem.)
él está	*he is*	**ellos están**	*they are* (masc., masc. & fem.)
ella está	*she is*	**ellas están**	*they are* (fem.)
usted está	*you are*	**ustedes están**	*you all are*

Using ser

Origin

One's origin is an unchangeable fact, one of the few truly permanent aspects of one's life. It does not matter where you live now. If you were born in Minnesota, you will always be from Minnesota.

Yo **soy** de Minnesota.	*I **am** from Minnesota.*
¿De dónde **eres** tú?	*Where **are** you from?*
Boris **es** de Transylvania.	*Boris **is** from Transylvania.*

Relationships

There are two types of relationships one can have with others: familial and selected.

Familial

These are blood relationships, such as parents, siblings, cousins, etc., and even though these relationships may sometimes be volatile, they do endure, due to their origin if nothing else.

Ellos **son** mis padres.	*They **are** my parents.*
Vosotros **sois** mis hermanos.	*You **are** my brothers.*
Ella **es** mi hermana.	*She **is** my sister.*

Selected

Friends, enemies, spouses, employers, and others achieve relationships with us by selection. And while the status of these relationships does change from time to time, a person generally operates under the assumption that these relationships will endure, at least in titular form.

Tú **eres** mi amigo.	*You **are** my friend.*
Él **es** mi esposo.	*He **is** my husband.*
Somos vecinos.	*We **are** neighbors.*

Physical attributes

Aspects of one's body are not to be taken lightly: They go everywhere with a person—they are not changed by location or how one feels. Even though hair color goes from brown to gray and beauty sometimes fades, these changes generally do not take place overnight. They are considered enduring.

Yo **soy** alto.	*I **am** tall.*
Rizitos de Oro **es** rubia.	*Goldilocks **is** blonde.*
Ellos **son** delgados.	*They **are** slim.*

Personality characteristics

Like physical attributes, personalities do change from time to time. However, people tend to behave and react to life pretty much the same one day to the next. (Don't confuse personality with moods, which can and do change quickly. Moods are covered under **estar**.)

Ella **es** amable.	*She **is** nice.*
Ustedes **son** cómicos.	*You all **are** funny.*
Eres cortés.	*You **are** polite.*

Possession

What's yours is yours and nobody can take it from you. Even as you write your will, the house and all its priceless knickknacks are still yours. Just because you can't take them with you doesn't mean they aren't yours until you go.

La casa **es** mía.	*The house **is** mine.*
El cristal **es** mío.	*The crystal **is** mine.*
Nada aquí **es** tuyo.	*Nothing here **is** yours.*

Profession

It's true that many people change jobs, and even careers, several times in their lives. However, one generally does not accept a job offer only to turn around and write a letter of resignation. A person who is employed, even part-time, takes on aspects of that position as another personality characteristic.

Judge Judy Scheindlin **es** abogada.	*Judge Judy Scheindlin **is** a lawyer.*
Kate Upton y Tyson Beckford **son** modelos.	*Kate Upton and Tyson Beckford **are** models.*
Ustedes **son** estudiantes.	*All of you **are** students.*

Identification

To identify anything—animal, vegetable, or mineral—use **ser**. Some linguistic philosophers will tell you (if you ask) that names (or identifying words) are meaningless in and of themselves. In other words, the name *is* the object, and thus it endures as long as the object itself.

Ésta **es** una frase.	*This **is** a sentence.*
Casablanca **es** una película.	Casablanca **is** a movie.
Éstos **son** calcetines.	*These **are** socks.*

Date and time

Though time seems fleeting (and therefore short-term, which is **estar** territory), it is still the case that "now" *is* "now." In other words, although it is illogical to say that the sentence "It is June 11" expresses the idea of something enduring, when you understand that "it" refers to "today" (as in "Today is June 11"), it becomes clear that giving the date is actually stating identification. With an expression of time, such as "It is 10:30," "it" refers to "now," and so giving the time is also a statement of identification.

Hoy **es** el catorce de julio.	*Today **is** July 14th.*
Mañana **es** sábado.	*Tomorrow **is** Saturday.*
¿Qué hora **es**?	*What time **is** it?*
Son las tres de la mañana.	*It's 3:00 A.M.*

Nationality

Nationality, like origin, can never be denied. However, for inhabitants of the United States—great melting pot that it is—one's origin and nationality often are different. Thus, one could say, **Yo soy de los Estados Unidos** ("I am from the United States"), indicating origin, and in the same breath, **Yo soy francés** ("I am French"), indicating nationality. Note that nationalities are not capitalized in Spanish.

Gabriel García Márquez **es** colombiano.
El rey Carlos y la reina consorte Camilla **son** ingleses.
Perez Hilton **es** cubano-americano.

*Gabriel García Márquez **is** Colombian.*
*King Charles and Queen Consort Camilla **are** English.*
*Perez Hilton **is** Cuban-American.*

Natural color

This is a bit tricky, because color can take either **ser** or **estar**, depending on the changeability of the color. Obviously, grass is green, the sky is blue, and snow is white—in the abstract. In these cases, use **ser**. However, there are times when the grass is not green (say, after a drought). And who has never seen gray skies or bright red, freshly painted toenails? (In these cases, use **estar**.) Just remember, when an object is referred to in its natural color, use **ser**.

La leche **es** blanca.
Mi casa **es** verde y amarilla.
La bandera de Japón **es** roja y blanca.

*Milk **is** white.*
*My house **is** green and yellow.*
*Japan's flag **is** red and white.*

EJERCICIO

¿Cuál es verdadero o falso para ti?

1. _____ Soy estudiante.

2. _____ Mi casa es blanca.

3. _____ Mi jefe (*boss*) y yo somos amigos.

4. _____ Mi mejor (*best*) amigo es mecánico.

5. _____ Neil deGrasse Tyson es inteligente.

6. _____ El clima de Hawaii es tropical.

7. _____ Los colores rojo y azul son mis favoritos.

8. _____ Las hamburguesas son muy populares en los Estados Unidos.

9. _____ Beethoven es famoso por su música.

10. _____ Shakespeare es famoso por sus pinturas.

11. _____ Soy arquitecto.

12. _____ No soy profesor de inglés.

EJERCICIO

2·1

Traducción *Each of the following sentences takes the verb* **ser.**

1. *I am from the United States.*

_____

2. *You are my friend.*

_____

3. *He is handsome.*

_____

4. *She is very interesting.*

_____

5. *They are astronauts* (el/la astronauta) *from another planet* (el planeta).

_____

6. *You all are American.*

_____

7. *Today is Monday.*

_____

8. *My socks* (los calcetines) *are white.*

_____

9. *Melissa McCarthy is an actress.*

_____

10. *He is tall. She is tall.*

_____

11. *They are handsome men.*

_____

12. *Where are you all from?*

_____

13. *We are from Chile.*

_____

14. *What time is it? It is ten o'clock.*

_____

15. *Who are you? Who are they?*

_____

16. *They are not my friends.*

_____

Ser and **estar**   **23**

17. *Fido is my dog and Fufu is your cat.*

_____

18. *Hamburgers and french fries are very popular in the United States.*

_____

19. *What is this? It is a shoe.*

_____

20. *What is this? It is a flower (la flor).*

_____

Traducción *All verbs of being in this paragraph take the verb* **ser.**

VOCABULARIO

la azucena	*white lily*	maravilloso/maravillosa	*wonderful*
por ejemplo	*for example*	la margarita	*daisy*
la fe	*faith*	la mayoría	*majority*
la flor	*flower*	el mundo	*world*
el/la florista	*florist*	la parte	*part*
hermoso/hermosa	*beautiful*	la rosa	*rose*
Holanda	*Holland*	simbólico	*symbolic*
la Inglaterra	*England*	el símbolo	*symbol*
la inocencia	*innocence*	el tulipán	*tulip*

Hi. My name is Paul, and my wife is Margarita. We are florists. Our flowers are beautiful. The majority of our flowers are from England, but some of the flowers are from other parts of the world. Typically, the tulips are from Holland and the roses are from China. Some flowers are symbolic: For example, the white daisy is a symbol of innocence, and the white lily is a symbol of faith. I believe that flowers are wonderful. Some flowers are red and some are white, but all are beautiful.

_____

_____

_____

_____

_____

_____

_____

_____

Using estar

Location

To give the location of anything, use **estar.** Whether it is short-term ("I am in the shower") or permanent ("Paris is in France"), if it's location you're dealing with, your verb is **estar** (not **ser**).

Yo **estoy** en el comedor.	*I **am** in the dining room.*
¿Dónde **estás** tú?	*Where **are** you?*
¿Dónde **está** Londres?	*Where **is** London?*

Mood

A person's mood can be considered a short-term personality characteristic. Our moods reflect how we feel at any given moment. In the discussion of **ser**, we learned that personality characteristics tend to be pervasive and enduring. But your moods ride the roller coaster of life: One day you're happy, the next day you're sad. It all depends on the ever-changing circumstances of your life.

Yo **estoy** feliz.	*I **am** happy.*
Ellos **están** tristes.	*They **are** sad.*
Vosotros **estáis** enojados.	*You all **are** angry.*
Ella **está** de buen/mal humor.	*She **is** in a good/bad mood.*

Physical condition

Like your moods, how you feel physically also changes from day to day: One day you feel hale and hearty, the next day you're sick as a dog.

Ella **está** bien.	*She **is** fine.*
Estamos enfermos.	*We **are** sick.*
Ellos **están** cansados.	*They **are** tired.*

Result of action

Use **estar** to express the condition of something or someone after an action has been completed. If you have just sat down, it means that you are sitting (or seated). Soon you may stand up, which means you are standing. If you are studying this in church, you may kneel any minute now, and then you will be kneeling. Even being dead, which is about as enduring as it gets, takes **estar**, for it is the result of having lived.

Estoy sentado.	*I **am** sitting. / I **am** seated.*
Estás de pie.	*You **are** standing.*
Ella **está** de rodillas.	*She **is** kneeling.*
La mosca **está** muerta.	*The fly **is** dead.*
Estos televisores **están** rotos.	*These television sets **are** broken.*

Unnatural color or condition

When you are very sick, your face may turn green; however, unless you are from another planet, this color is unnatural (and unattractive) to you. Meat that has sat around far too long takes on an unsavory shade of gray, bananas turn black, and old newspapers turn yellow. In a nutshell, when describing things that aren't in their natural state, use **estar**.

El cielo **está** gris.	*The sky **is** gray.*
Esta nieve **está** amarilla.	*This snow **is** yellow.*
Las manos **están** sucias.	*Her hands **are** dirty.*
Él **está** feo con esos pantalones.	*He **is** ugly in those pants.*

Going from the general to the particular

If you like coffee as I do, then you would agree that **El café es la bebida de los dioses** ("Coffee is the drink of the gods"), and you would use **ser** to express this absolute truth. This does not mean, however, that every individual cup of coffee in the world is wonderful. So, when referring to a specific cup of coffee—or a plate of spaghetti or an order of fries—use **estar**.

Este café **está** muy bueno.	*This coffee **is** very good.*
Este café **está** malísimo.	*This coffee **is** horrible.*
Estas papas fritas **están** riquísimas.	*These french fries **are** delicious.*

EJERCICIO

¿Verdadero o falso?

1. _____ Estoy en la cocina de mi casa.

2. _____ Estoy interesado/interesada en apprender español.

3. _____ Mi mejor amigo/amiga probablemente está en casa.

4. _____ México está en Norteamérica.

5. _____ Madrid y Sevilla están en España.

6. _____ Mi mejor amigo/amiga y yo estamos enfermos/enfermas.

7. _____ Estoy sentado/sentada.

8. _____ A veces, una persona está de rodillas en la iglesia.

9. _____ No estoy de pie.

10. _____ Cristóbal Colón está muerto.

11. _____ Cuando miro la televisión por muchas horas, estoy aburrido/aburrida.

12. _____ Normalmente, mis amigos y yo estamos de buen humor.

Traducción *Each of the following sentences takes the verb* **estar.**

1. *I am with John. I am not with John.*

   _____

2. *She is with Marcos. She is not with Marcos.*

   _____

3. *I am fine. I am not happy.*

   _____

4. *Where are you? Where is Felipe?*

   _____

5. *John is angry. They are angry.*

   _____

6. *Jane is standing, but we are sitting.*

   _____

7. *I am sad because you are not here.*

   _____

8. *Jane is anxious because we are not ready.*

   _____

9. *He is kneeling because we are in the church.*

   _____

10. *The chairs are not in the kitchen.*

    _____

11. *Many boys are in the house.*

    _____

12. *Why are you all here?*

    _____

13. *Argentina is in South America.*

    _____

14. *Are the dogs in the living room?*

    _____

15. *The tomatoes are green.*

    _____

16. *This chicken* (el pollo) *is very good!*

_____

17. *John is depressed* (deprimido).

_____

18. *Why aren't you happy?*

_____

19. *She is embarrassed* (avergonzada).

_____

20. *They are in a bad mood because the television is broken and therefore* (por eso)
    they are bored.

_____

_____

EJERCICIO
2·4

Traducción *All verbs of being in this paragraph take the verb* **estar.**
The speaker in the sentences is female.

VOCABULARIO

la cama	*bed*	feliz (felices [pl.])	*happy*
la cara	*face*	la jeringa	*needle/syringe*
la comida	*food*	loco	*crazy*
delicioso	*delicious*	el ojo	*eye*
en realidad	*actually*	la pastilla	*pill*
el enfermero	*nurse*	la silla	*chair*

Hi. How are you? I'm fine. Actually, I'm not fine. I am in the hospital. I'm sick. My face is green and my eyes are orange. I'm not tired. The nurse [m.] is here with a big syringe. I'm scared. Oh, good! The syringe is broken, and so I take a pill. Now I am not sick. I am fine, but the nurse is angry because the needle and the bed are broken. Therefore, I am sitting on a chair. My parents are happy. (They are not happy when they receive the bill.) The food here is delicious. Am I crazy?

_____

_____

_____

_____

_____

_____

Complete each sentence with the correct form of **ser** *or* **estar**.

1. Yo _____ enfermo/enferma.

2. Yo _____ alto/alta.

3. Tú _____ en la escuela.

4. Ellos _____ americanos.

5. Juan _____ feliz.

6. Tú _____ una persona amable.

7. Nosotros _____ tristes.

8. Este pescado _____ delicioso.

9. Vosotras _____ bonitas.

10. ¿Cómo _____ tú?

11. ¿Dónde _____ Juan?

12. ¿De dónde _____ tú?

13. Martín _____ médico.

14. Mis plumas _____ rojas.

15. Ustedes _____ con Paco y José.

16. Ellas _____ amigas de Felipe.

17. Tú _____ bajo/baja.

18. Nosotros _____ bajos.

19. Nairobi _____ en Kenya.

20. ¿Quién _____ el presidente de los Estados Unidos?

21. La banana _____ negra.

22. Mi coche no _____ en el garaje.

23. ¿Qué hora _____? _____ las dos y media de la tarde.

24. Vosotros _____ cansados.

25. Yo _____ de buen humor.

Traducción *Translate the following paragraph, using the correct form of **ser**, **estar**, or a regular verb where needed.*

VOCABULARIO

el/la artista	artist	la India	India	otro	other
el café	coffee	la isla	island	la palabra	word
la costa	coast	lavar	to wash	las personas	people
el cuarto	room	limpiar	to clean	la ropa	clothing
exportar	to export	mucho	a lot of	el té	tea
la hora	hour	el océano	ocean		

When I am in a bad mood, I clean the house. I clean every room and I wash the clothing. I work for many hours because our house is big. Some people work when they are in a bad mood, and others read a book or eat a lot of food. I live with three people and a cat [f.]. Sometimes we are happy and sometimes we are sad. In other words, we are normal. We are from India, but now we live in Sri Lanka. Our house is near the coast. Sri Lanka is an island in the Indian Ocean. Sri Lanka exports a lot of tea and coffee. When my mother prepares coffee or tea, it is delicious. My father is a doctor and my mother is an artist. They are kind. My sister is very tall. Our cat is black and gray. Where are you from? Where are you now?

_____

_____

_____

_____

_____

_____

_____

_____

_____

_____

_____

Hay

The word **hay** is truly a hardworking word in Spanish. It is used to acknowledge the existence of a thing or things. For such a tiny word, it is jam-packed with meaning. **Hay** carries all of the following meanings.

There is ....
There are ....
Is there ...?
Are there ...?

Hay una mosca en mi sopa.   *There is a fly in my soup.*
Hay cincuenta y dos naipes en una baraja.   *There are 52 cards in a deck.*
¿**Hay** un médico en la casa?   *Is there a doctor in the house?*
¿Cuántos peces **hay** en el océano?   *How many fish are there in the ocean?*

When **hay** is used in the negative (**no hay**) the English word "any" is understood.

No hay gasolina en el coche.   *There isn't any gas in the car.*
No hay conejos en estas partes.   *There aren't any rabbits in these parts.*

EJERCICIO

¿Verdadero o falso?

1. _____ Hay cincuenta estados en los Estados Unidos.

2. _____ Hay muchos libros en la biblioteca.

3. _____ Hay cinco baños en mi casa.

4. _____ No hay ventanas en mi cocina.

5. _____ En mi clase de español hay más de quince estudiantes.

6. _____ Hay muchos canguros en Australia.

7. _____ Hay muchas estrellas de cine (*movie stars*) en Hollywood.

8. _____ No hay leche en mi refrigerador ahora.

9. _____ Hay ocho océanos distintos en el mundo.

10. _____ Hay más personas en México que en la República Dominicana.

11. _____ No hay azúcar en una Coca-Cola de dieta.

12. _____ Hay un portátil en mi dormitorio.

EJERCICIO
3·1

Traducción

1. *There is a dog in the car.*

_____

2. *There are three forks* (el tenedor) *on the table.*

_____

3. *Is there a bathroom in this building* (el edificio)?

_____

4. *Are there chairs* (la silla) *in the living room?*

_____

5. *There isn't any water in the glass* (el vaso).

_____

_____

EJERCICIO
3·2

Traducción

VOCABULARIO	la ayuda	*help*	la oficina	*office*
	británico	*British*	el palacio	*palace*
	casi	*almost*	la pintura	*painting*
	la ciudad	*city*	el plato	*dish*
	enorme	*enormous*	que	*who* [relative pronoun]
	el invitado	*guest*	la residencia	*residence*
	el monarca	*monarch*	el/la visitante	*visitor*
	necesitar	*to need*		

Hi. I live in Buckingham Palace, the official residence of the British monarch. The palace is in the city of Westminster. Actually, I work in Buckingham Palace. I clean the kitchen. It is a very big kitchen. There are many dishes and glasses because there are many people and parties. The palace is enormous: There are fifty-two bedrooms for the people who live here and for their guests. There are one hundred eighty-eight bedrooms for the people who work here. (Some people need a lot of help.) There are ninety-two offices and seventy-eight bathrooms. In total, there are almost six hundred rooms here. There are many paintings in the palace. There are not any paintings of Wallis Simpson where I work. There are many visitors to the palace every year.

_____

_____

_____

_____

_____

_____

_____

_____

_____

_____

_____

_____

EJERCICIO

Describe your house or apartment, beginning each sentence with **Hay...** *to describe it. Write your description below.*

_____

_____

_____

_____

_____

_____

_____

_____

_____

_____

Tener

The verb **tener** ("to have") is a very basic and frequently used verb in Spanish, partly because it is used in so many different ways—to show possession, to show age, in several idiomatic expressions, and to show obligation. We discuss all four of these uses in this chapter.

Below is the full conjugation of **tener** in the present tense. (Note that **tener** is an irregular verb.)

tener *to have*	
tengo	tenemos
tienes	tenéis
tiene	tienen

Possession

The simplest and most common use of **tener** is to show possession.

Tengo un perro.	*I have a dog.*
Tenemos cinco dólares.	*We have five dollars.*
Tienes un hermano.	*You have one brother.*
Tenéis una casa bonita.	*You all have a pretty house.*
Juan tiene un gato.	*John has a cat.*
Ellos tienen los tenedores.	*They have the forks.*

EJERCICIO

¿Verdadero o falso?

1. _____ Tengo un animal doméstico.

2. _____ El helado tiene muchas calorías.

3. _____ Mi casa tiene tres dormitorios.

4. _____ El café tiene cafeína.

5. _____ Mi familia tiene una casa de vacaciones.

6. _____ Los Estados Unidos tiene frontera con Canadá.

7. _____ En mi clase de español, tenemos mucha tarea.

8. _____ Muchas personas tienen más de un teléfono en la casa.

9. _____ No tengo coche.

10. _____ Las tiendas Harrods y Macy's tienen muchos departamentos.

Traducción

1. *I have ten dollars.*

   _____

2. *You have my books.*

   _____

3. *She has a diamond* (el diamante).

   _____

4. *He has the knives* (el cuchillo) *and the spoons* (la cuchara).

   _____

5. *We have a new house.*

   _____

6. *All of you* [informal] *have many friends.*

   _____

7. *They have many cousins.*

   _____

8. *I don't have the money.*

   _____

9. *Who has my keys* (la llave)?

   _____

10. *Why do you have a bird* (el pájaro) *in your car?*

    _____

Age

In English, we use the verb "to be" to show age: "I *am* twenty-nine years old." In Spanish, however, one *has* years: ***Tengo* veintinueve años.**

When asking the age of someone or something, you literally ask how many years a person or thing has.

¿Cuántos años **tienes** tú?   *How old **are** you?*
¿Cuántos años **tiene** Juan?   *How old **is** Juan?*
¿Cuántos años **tiene** el coche?   *How old **is** the car?*
¿Cuántos años **tienen** ellos?   *How old **are** they?*

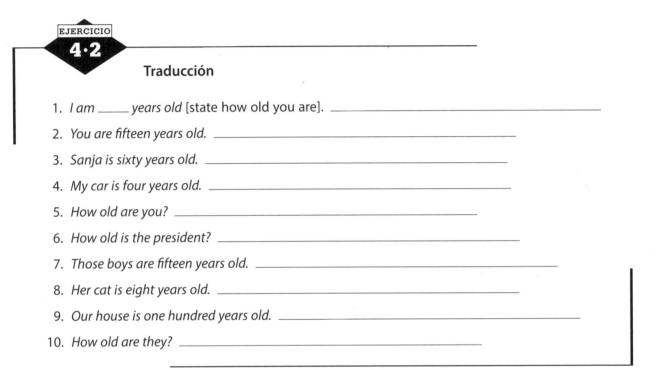

EJERCICIO
4·2

Traducción

1. *I am ____ years old* [state how old you are]. _____

2. *You are fifteen years old.* _____

3. *Sanja is sixty years old.* _____

4. *My car is four years old.* _____

5. *How old are you?* _____

6. *How old is the president?* _____

7. *Those boys are fifteen years old.* _____

8. *Her cat is eight years old.* _____

9. *Our house is one hundred years old.* _____

10. *How old are they?* _____

Idiomatic expressions with **tener**

There are several phrases in Spanish that use **tener** where we use the verb "to be" in English to express the same meaning. For example, instead of the English "being hungry" ("to be" + ADJECTIVE), one "has hunger" ("to have" + NOUN) in Spanish. Below is a list of the most common of these idiomatic expressions. Note that in the examples, **mucho** or **mucha** indicates whether a noun is masculine or feminine.

tener (mucha) hambre	to be (very) hungry
tener (mucha) sed	to be (very) thirsty
tener (mucho) frío	to be (very) cold
tener (mucho) calor	to be (very) warm
tener (mucho) miedo	to be (very) afraid
tener (mucho) orgullo	to be (very) proud
tener (mucha) suerte	to be (very) lucky
tener (mucha) prisa	to be in a (big) hurry
tener (mucho) sueño	to be (very) sleepy
tener razón	to be right
no tener razón	to be wrong

Traducción

1. *I am hungry.* _____

2. *You're thirsty.* _____

3. *He's cold.* _____

4. *We're lucky.* _____

5. *They [m.] are in a hurry.* _____

6. *I am very hungry.* _____

7. *You're very thirsty.* _____

8. *He's warm.* _____

9. *I'm very lucky.* _____

10. *You all are in a big hurry.* _____

11. *I am very proud of my daughters.* _____

12. *They [m.] are always right.* _____

Respond to each situation with a complete sentence, using an expression with **tener.**

EJEMPLOS   Elena come dos hamburguesas. *Ella tiene hambre.*

Sacas una "A" en el examen. *Tengo mucho orgullo.*

1. Tú no comes nada hoy.

   _____

2. Juan compra una Coca-Cola.

   _____

3. Juanita gana un millón de dólares.

   _____

4. Es enero y tú no tienes un suéter.

   _____

5. Jorge cree que dos y dos son cinco.

   _____

6. María corre al autobús.

   _____

7. Es julio y tú estás en Puerto Rico.

   _____

8. Un monstruo está en tu armario.

   _____

9. Tú crees que seis menos cuatro son dos.

   _____

10. Es muy tarde y Ana y Margarita están bostezando (*yawning*).

   _____

Obligation

To show obligation, use the following pattern, conjugating **tener** to correspond to the subject.

tener + **que** + INFINITIVE

Tengo que practicar el piano.	*I have to practice the piano.*
¿**Tenemos que comer** esta carne?	*Do we have to eat this meat?*
Tienes que estudiar.	*You have to study.*
Tenéis que limpiar la casa.	*You all have to clean the house.*
Juan tiene que estudiar.	*John has to study.*
Ellos tienen que bailar.	*They have to dance.*

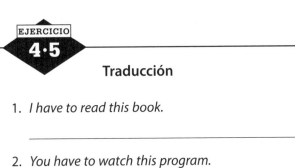

EJERCICIO
4·5

Traducción

1. *I have to read this book.*

   _____

2. *You have to watch this program.*

   _____

3. *Rudolph Nureyev has to dance.*

   _____

4. *Kenny has to open the restaurant every morning.*

   _____

5. *We have to decide now.*

   _____

6. *You all have to write thank-you letters* (la carta de agradecimiento).

   _____

7. *They [m.] have to sell their car.*

   _____

8. *I don't have to eat this soup.*

   _____

9. *You have to take the medicine.*

   _____

10. *We have to buy the wine for the party.*

   _____

EJERCICIO

¡Te toca a ti! (It's your turn!) *List five things that you have to do tomorrow. Begin each sentence with a **tener que** expression.*

1. _____

2. _____

3. _____

4. _____

5. _____

EJERCICIO
4·6

Traducción

VOCABULARIO		
	a propósito	*on purpose*
	claro	*of course*
	el arco	*arch*
	el banco	*bench*
	el espacio	*space*
	el/la gerente	*manager*
	incómodo	*uncomfortable*
	la lista	*list*
	la manga	*sleeve*
	el menú, la carta	*menu*
	el país	*country*
	las papas fritas	*french fries*
	el precio	*price*
	el uniforme	*uniform*

Hi. I work at McDonald's. I have to work every Friday and Saturday, and I have to wear a uniform. The uniform is white and orange and (of course) it has yellow arches on the sleeves. We have a new menu today, and therefore I have to study the list and the prices. I have to be in the restaurant early in the morning. We have twenty tables in our restaurant. There aren't any chairs because we have benches. The benches in "fast-food" restaurants are uncomfortable on purpose: The customers "eat and run" and, therefore, there is always room for more customers. There are McDonald's in almost every country in the world. Every McDonald's has hamburgers and french fries. I live in Dublin. Ireland has almost one hundred McDonald's. My manager is twenty years old.

The personal a

The personal **a** is unique to Spanish, and as you can see in the examples below, it has no English translation. It is used when the direct object of a verb is a specific person: An **a** is placed directly before the mention of that person, and it is known as the personal **a**. Note that the direct object—the noun that is affected directly by the verb—usually comes immediately after the verb in both English and Spanish.

Yo amo **a** Lucy.	*I love Lucy.*
Miramos **a** Jorge.	*We watch George.*
Buscas **a** mi hermano.	*You look for my brother.*
Esperáis **a** vuestro maestro.	*You all wait for your teacher.*
Él ve **a** Susana.	*He sees Susan.*
Ellos aman **a** sus padres.	*They love their parents.*

The personal **a** can be seen as a sign of respect, an acknowledgment that this person is more important than, for example, his or her car.

Veo **a** Juan.	*I see John.*
Veo el coche de Juan.	*I see John's car.*

Here are a few specific guidelines to help you know when and how to use the personal **a**.

1 You *do not* use the personal **a** with the verbs **ser** ("to be"), **tener** ("to have"), or **hay** ("there is," "there are").

Juan es (un) profesor.	*John is a professor.*
Tengo dos hermanos.	*I have two brothers.*
Hay chicos en la casa.	*There are boys in the house.*

2 You *do not* use the personal **a** when the direct object is an unspecified person.

Necesito una secretaria bilingüe.	*I need a bilingual secretary.*
Busco un amigo leal.	*I'm looking for a loyal friend.*

3 You *do* use the personal **a** when the direct object is a pet, as well as with other animals with whom you have a personal relationship. You *do not* use the personal **a** with strays, mongrels, alley cats, squirrels in your backyard, insects, cockroaches, animals you hunt or want to hunt down, or any creature of the animal kingdom you wouldn't welcome into your lovely home.

Amo **a** mi preciosa gata, Princesa.	*I love my darling cat, Princess.*
Odio las termitas.	*I hate termites.*

43

4 In a complex question that requires the personal **a**, place the **a** before the interrogative.

¿**A** quién amas?   *Whom do you love?*
¿**A** quién miras?   *Whom are you watching?*

5 When there is a series of direct objects that take the personal **a**, each one requires a personal **a**.

Veo **a** Juan, **a** María, **a** Miguel,   *I see John, Mary, Michael, Margarita, and Fido.*
   a Margarita y **a** Fido.

6 When the personal **a** precedes the definite article **el**, these contract to form **al**.

Veo **al** chico.   *I see the boy.*
Ella ama **al** hombre.   *She loves the man.*
Escuchamos **al** presidente.   *We listen to the president.*

EJERCICIO
5·1

*Insert the personal **a** where needed in the following sentences. If none is needed, put an **X** in the blank.*

1. Yo veo _____ Marta.

2. Yo veo _____ la casa blanca.

3. Tom Sawyer quiere _____ Becky Thatcher.

4. Marco tiene _____ una hermana.

5. Busco _____ mi primo.

6. Busco _____ mis zapatos.

7. Juana es _____ la presidenta del club.

8. No comprendo _____ Donald.

9. Hay _____ cinco personas en mi familia.

10. Mateo ama _____ su familia.

EJERCICIO
5·2

Traducción *Each of the following sentences requires a personal **a**.*

1. *Romeo loves Juliet.* _____

2. *I see John.* _____

3. *I don't believe Mary.* _____

4. *We listen to Jorge.* _____

5. *You look for Andrés.* _____

6. *They discover a thief* (el ladrón) *in the house.* _____

7. *Whom do you love?* _____

8. *Do you see the girl?* _____

9. *Do you believe the president?* _____

10. *We're waiting for Sylvia.* _____

11. *I watch Marcos and Teresa.* _____

12. *Timmy loves Lassie.* _____

Common irregular verbs

·6·

Below are twelve frequently used irregular verbs, together with their conjugations. It is very important to know these verbs and how to use them. In this chapter, we look at their most basic uses, as well as special features of some of these verbs.

dar *to give*

doy	damos
das	dais
da	dan

poder *to be able to*

puedo	podemos
puedes	podéis
puede	pueden

decir *to say, tell*

digo	decimos
dices	decís
dice	dicen

poner *to put*

pongo	ponemos
pones	ponéis
pone	ponen

hacer *to make, do*

hago	hacemos
haces	hacéis
hace	hacen

querer *to want*

quiero	queremos
quieres	queréis
quiere	quieren

ir *to go*

voy	vamos
vas	vais
va	van

salir *to leave*

salgo	salimos
sales	salís
sale	salen

jugar *to play*

juego	jugamos
juegas	jugáis
juega	juegan

venir *to come*

vengo	venimos
vienes	venís
viene	vienen

oír *to hear*

oigo	oímos
oyes	oís
oye	oyen

ver *to see*

veo	vemos
ves	veis
ve	ven

EJERCICIO 6·1

Traducción

1. *I give.* _____
2. *I say.* _____
3. *They [f.] hear.* _____
4. *He hears.* _____
5. *You make.* _____
6. *I play.* _____
7. *I make.* _____
8. *You all see.* _____
9. *We give.* _____
10. *She goes.* _____
11. *They [m.] come.* _____
12. *He says.* _____
13. *You put.* _____
14. *I put.* _____
15. *We see.* _____
16. *I see.* _____
17. *They [m.] want.* _____
18. *You play.* _____
19. *I leave.* _____
20. *You say.* _____
21. *I hear.* _____
22. *He wants.* _____
23. *I go.* _____
24. *They [f.] play.* _____

EJERCICIO 6·2

¡Te toca a ti! *Answer each of the following questions with a complete sentence.*

1. ¿Qué quieres para tu cumpleaños?

   _____

2. Normalmente, ¿dónde pones tu dinero?

   _____

3. Típicamente, ¿a qué hora vienes a la escuela?

   _____

4. Desde (*from*) la ventana de tu sala, ¿qué ves?

   _____

5. ¿Qué le das a tu mejor amigo/amiga para su cumpleaños este año?

   _____

6. ¿Qué dices cuando estás enojado/enojada?

   _____

7. Más o menos, ¿cuántas veces vas al cine cada año?

   _____

8. Usualmente, ¿adónde vas después de las clases?

_____

9. Generalmente, ¿a qué hora sales de casa por la mañana?

_____

10. ¿Qué haces cuando alguien te dice una mentira?

_____

Phrases with two verbs—querer, poder, deber

When two verbs operate together to form a single idea, the first verb is conjugated and the second verb remains in its infinitive form, as when a conjugated form of **tener** + **que** + INFINITIVE expresses obligation (Chapter 4).

Another way to look at this is to see that the first verb is the real action, while the second verb is proposed action. Consider the sentence, "I want to play the violin." The only thing that's really happening in this sentence is "wanting"; "playing" is merely a proposal, not the reality.

In the section on regular -**er** verbs in Chapter 1, you learned that **deber** means "to owe." When directly followed by another verb, however, **deber** means "ought," as in "I ought to study" (also translated as "I should study"). **Querer**, meaning "to want," and **poder**, meaning "to be able to, can," are also frequently used as the first verb in phrases with two verbs.

Debo salir de la oficina.	*I ought to leave the office.*
Podemos ver la luz.	*We can see the light.*
¿Puedes nadar bien?	*Can you swim well?*
¿Queréis cenar ahora?	*Do you want to eat dinner now?*
Ella quiere ser lingüista.	*She wants to be a linguist.*
Ellos no deben decirnos nada.	*They shouldn't tell us anything.*

EJERCICIO
6·3

Answer each of the following questions with a complete sentence in the present tense.

1. ¿Qué puedes hacer muy bien? _____

2. ¿Qué es lo que no puedes hacer? _____

3. ¿Qué quieres hacer mañana? _____

4. ¿Qué debes hacer cada día? _____

5. ¿Qué es lo que no debes hacer en la casa? _____

6. ¿Qué puede hacer Aretha Franklin? _____

7. ¿Qué puede hacer Isaac Stern? _____

8. ¿Qué puede hacer Babe Ruth? _____

9. ¿Qué puede hacer Pelé? _____

10. ¿Qué puede hacer F. Scott Fitzgerald? _____

11. ¿Qué puede hacer un pez? _____

12. ¿Qué pueden hacer Julia Child y Gordon Ramsey?

_____

Describing the weather—**hacer, estar**

The verbs **hacer** and **estar** are both used when talking about the weather. Because the subject in this context is the ambiguous "it," both **hacer** and **estar** are conjugated only in the third-person singular when describing weather. Note that you always use **hace** + NOUN and **está** + ADJECTIVE or GERUND. You cannot mix and match these expressions, because they won't make sense if you do. In other words, memorize the expressions that follow.

VOCABULARIO

Idioms with **hacer**		Expressions with **estar**	
hace (mucho) frío	it is (very) cold	está nublado	it is cloudy
hace (mucho) calor	it is (very) warm	está lloviendo	it is raining
hace (mucho) sol	it is (very) sunny	está nevando	it is snowing
hace (mucho) viento	it is (very) windy	está lloviznando	it is drizzling
hace fresco	it is cool	está lluvioso	it is rainy/wet
hace (muy) buen tiempo	it is (very) nice out	está húmedo	it is humid
hace (muy) mal tiempo	it is (very) bad out	está seco	it is dry

---

EJERCICIO 6·4

Responde a cada una de las preguntas siguientes con una frase completa.

1. ¿Qué tiempo hace hoy?

_____

2. ¿Qué tiempo hace en diciembre?

_____

3. ¿Qué tiempo hace en abril?

_____

4. ¿Qué tiempo hace en julio?

_____

5. Normalmente, ¿qué tiempo hace en tu cumpleaños?

_____

Playing games—**jugar**

The verb **jugar** means "to play (a game)." Do not confuse **jugar** with **tocar**, which means "to play (a musical instrument)." Below is a list of several games. Note the inclusion of the word **a** and the appropriate definite article before the name of the game. In many Spanish-speaking countries, however, people also use this verb without the inclusion of **a** or the definite article (for example, **juego béisbol**).

VOCABULARIO

jugar al ajedrez	to play chess
jugar al básquetbol	to play basketball
jugar al béisbol	to play baseball
jugar al billar	to play billiards, play pool
jugar a las damas	to play checkers
jugar al fútbol	to play soccer
jugar al fútbol americano	to play football
jugar al golf	to play golf
jugar al hockey	to play hockey
jugar a los naipes	to play cards
jugar al tenis	to play tennis
jugar al voleibol	to play volleyball

Note that the phrase "to play a game" is **jugar a un juego**.

EJERCICIO
6·5

Even though some of these players are from the past, answer each of the following questions with a complete sentence in the present tense.

1. ¿Qué juega Babe Ruth?

_____

2. ¿Qué juegan Wayne Gretzky y Sidney Crosby?

_____

3. ¿Qué juega Minnesota Fats? (*You may need to look up this person.*)

_____

4. ¿Qué juegan Kylian Mbappé y Lionel Messi?

_____

5. ¿Qué juegan Bobby Fischer y Boris Spasky?

_____

6. ¿Qué juegan Venus y Serena Williams?

_____

7. ¿Qué juega Tiger Woods?

_____

8. ¿Qué juegan LeBron James y Brittney Griner?

_____

9. ¿Qué juegan Aaron Rogers y Patrick Mahomes?

_____

10. ¿Qué juegan los niños en una tabla roja y negra?

_____

Expressing future action—**ir** + **a** + INFINITIVE

Once you have learned the verb **ir** ("to go") in the present tense, you can also speak of the future—what you are "going to do" or what is "going to happen." To do this, follow the pattern shown below. Remember that the first verb (**ir**) is conjugated, and the second verb is in the infinitive form.

ir + **a** + INFINITIVE

Voy a cantar.	*I am going to sing*.
Vamos a comprar una lámpara.	*We are going to buy a lamp.*
¿Qué vas a hacer mañana?	*What are you going to do tomorrow?*
¿Cuándo vais a salir del cuarto?	*When are you all going to leave the room?*
Va a llover.	*It's going to rain.*
Ellos no van a estar aquí.	*They aren't going to be here.*

EJERCICIO
6·6

Traducción

1. *I'm going to practice.*

_____

2. *You're going to work.*

_____

3. *She is going to watch television.*

_____

4. *We're going to sell the car.*

_____

5. *They [m.] are going to drink the milk.*

_____

6. *I'm not going to do anything.*

_____

7. *What are you going to do?*

   _____

8. *Are you going to study or watch TV?*

   _____

9. *We are not going to buy candy* (los caramelos).

   _____

10. *When are you all going to play tennis?*

    _____

| VOCABULARIO |

Some phrases of future time

this afternoon	**esta tarde**	next week	**la semana que viene**
tonight	**esta noche**	next month	**el mes que viene**
tomorrow	**mañana**	next year	**el año que viene**

EJERCICIO
6·7

¡**Te toca a ti!** *Responde a cada una de las preguntas siguientes con una frase completa.*

1. ¿Qué vas a hacer esta noche?

   _____

2. ¿Qué ropa vas a llevar mañana?

   _____

3. ¿Qué vas a comer esta tarde?

   _____

4. ¿Vas a tener una fiesta la semana que viene?

   _____

5. En tu opinión, ¿quién va a ser el próximo presidente de los Estados Unidos?

   _____

6. ¿Dónde vas a vivir el año que viene?

   _____

7. ¿Adónde vas a ir el verano que viene?

   _____

8. ¿Cuándo vas a ver a tu mejor amigo/amiga?

   _____

EJERCICIO

¿Verdadero, falso o probable?

1. _____ Voy a leer una revista esta noche.

2. _____ Mi mejor amigo/amiga va a darme un regalo para mi cumpleaños.

3. _____ Hace frío hoy.

4. _____ Voy a comprar un coche el año que viene.

5. _____ Hace calor, hace sol y hace buen tiempo hoy.

6. _____ No voy a comer nada hoy.

7. _____ Voy a votar en las elecciones presidenciales.

8. _____ Mi familia y yo vamos a vivir en otro estado el año que viene.

9. _____ Mi mejor amigo/amiga va a vender su casa este mes.

10. _____ Nunca voy a cometer otro error.

11. _____ No voy a salir de casa mañana.

12. _____ Nadie va a venir a mi casa esta noche.

Traducción

VOCABULARIO

ahora	*now*
ahora mismo	*right now*
algo	*something*
después	*afterward*
emocionado/emocionada	*excited*
especial	*special*
la limonada	*lemonade*
maravilloso/maravillosa	*wonderful*
más	*more*
el parque	*park*
el regalo	*gift*
la torta	*cake*

Tomorrow is my birthday. I want to do something special. I'm going to have a big party. All my friends are coming to the party at two o'clock. I have a lot of friends. Each friend gives me a gift and tells me, "Happy Birthday." I say to them, "Thank you very much." My mother is going to make a chocolate cake for the party. She makes the best cakes—she puts lots of chocolate on top of the chocolate cake! I hear my mother in the kitchen now, but I don't see her. During my party, we're going to play soccer in the park. I can see the park from my house. Afterward, we're going to eat pizza and drink lemonade. I am very excited. I want to have the party right now! It's going to be a wonderful party.

Saber and conocer

The verbs **saber** and **conocer** both mean "to know." On closer inspection, however, these two verbs perform two very different functions. **Saber** means "to know information," while **conocer** means "to know or be familiar with a person, place, or thing."

Saber

Saber means "to know facts and information." It implies full knowledge. Think "S is for skull": the knowledge is in your head.

saber *to know (information)*	
sé	sabemos
sabes	sabéis
sabe	saben

Note that **saber** is irregular only in the **yo** form.

Saber: to know information

When dealing with facts and information, use **saber**.

Sé tu dirección.	*I **know** your address.*
Sabemos el número de teléfono.	*We **know** the telephone number.*
Él no sabe dónde trabajo.	*He **doesn't know** where I work.*

EJERCICIO
7·1

Traducción

1. *I know your name.*

   _____

2. *You know the answer.*

   _____

3. *She knows where you live.*

   _____

4. *We don't know why he is angry.*

_____

5. *Do you know who has the money?*

_____

6. *They [m.] don't know anything about me.*

_____

7. *Does he know where María is?*

_____

8. *You all know a lot.*

_____

Saber que... to know that ...

In English, we have the option of saying either "I know *that* he's here somewhere" or, simply, "I know he's here somewhere." In Spanish, we do not have that option. We must include the conjunction **que** ("that"), which is always followed by a complete sentence.

Sé que su nombre es Juan.	*I know that his name is John.*
¿Sabes que ella está embarazada?	*Do you know that she is pregnant?*
Ellos no saben que los vemos.	*They don't know that we see them.*

EJERCICIO
7·2

Traducción

1. *I know that John is tall.*

_____

2. *You know that I'm hungry.*

_____

3. *She knows that you're thirsty.*

_____

4. *Do you know that I'm twenty-nine years old?*

_____

5. *We know that he is in a hurry.*

_____

6. *They [m.] don't know that I'm here.*

_____

7. *Do you all know that there are snakes* (la culebra) *in the garden* (el jardín)?

_____

8. *He doesn't know that you're in the garden.*

_____

Saber + INFINITIVE: to know how to do something

To say that you know how to do something in Spanish, simply use the second verb's infinitive immediately after the conjugated **saber**. Do not add **cómo** ("how"). In this context, **saber** expresses the meaning "to know how."

Sé leer.	*I know how to read.*
No sé cocinar.	*I don't know how to cook.*
Sabemos esquiar.	*We know how to ski.*
Él sabe escribir bien.	*He knows how to write well.*

EJERCICIO 7·3

Traducción

1. *I know how to sing.*

_____

2. *You know how to speak Spanish.*

_____

3. *She knows how to cook very well.*

_____

4. *He doesn't know how to speak French.*

_____

5. *Gene Kelly and Misty Copeland know how to dance.*

_____

6. *You all know how to play the piano.*

_____

7. *Do you know how to ski?*

_____

8. *Who knows how to open this door?*

_____

Traducción

VOCABULARIO

aparcar	*to park*
cierto	*true*
conducir	*to drive*
enfrente de	*in front of*
la estación de bomberos	*fire station*
la gente	*people* (in general)
llenar	*to fill*
el mecánico	*mechanic*
saber de	*to know about*
el tanque de gasolina	*gas tank*

John is my mechanic. He knows a lot about cars, and I am happy because I don't know anything about cars. No, it's not completely true. I know where the gas tank is and I know how to fill it. I know how to drive and I know that I can't park in front of a fire station. John knows that he has to know about cars and about people, because many people know very little about cars.

_____

_____

_____

_____

_____

_____

_____

Conocer

Conocer is used to express familiarity with a person, a place, a thing, or a particular field of learning. The key word here is *familiarity,* for one can never know another person, place, thing, or body of knowledge completely. Think "*C* is for corazón": the knowledge is in your heart.

conocer *to know (be familiar with)*

conozco	conocemos
conoces	conocéis
conoce	conocen

Note that **conocer** is irregular only in the **yo** form.

Conocer + a: to know a person

When talking about knowing another person (or someone's pet—but not a stray), a conjugated form of **conocer** is followed by the personal **a**, except when the object is a pronoun.

Conozco a Gaylord.	*I know Gaylord.*
Lo **conocemos**.	*We know him.*

Tú conoces a Rita.	*You know Rita.*
La **conocéis.**	*You know her.*
María conoce a Eduardo.	*Mary knows Edward.*
María y Jorge lo **conocen.**	*Mary and George know him.*

EJERCICIO
7·5

Traducción

1. *I know Antonia.* _____

2. *You know Isabel.* _____

3. *He knows his father-in-law* (el suegro). _____

4. *We know you.* _____

5. *You all know Juan.* _____

6. *She knows Juana and Paco.* _____

7. *Do you know my cats Fifi and Fufu?* _____

8. *He doesn't know me.* _____

9. *I know her.* _____

10. *You know her.* _____

11. *He knows him.* _____

12. *You know us.* _____

13. *You all know him.* _____

14. *She knows them* [m.]. _____

15. *Yes, I know them* [m.]. _____

16. *Nobody here knows me.* _____

Conocer + location: to know a place

To visit a place is to become familiar with that place. Whether you know a location inside out (for example, your hometown) or hardly at all (such as wherever it was you went on a sixth-grade field trip), use **conocer**. To emphasize how well you know a place, use **muy bien** ("very well") or **muy poco** ("hardly at all").

Conozco Puerto Rico.	*I am familiar with Puerto Rico.*
Ella conoce Londres.	*She has been to London.*
Las arañas conocen bien mi sótano.	*Spiders know my basement well.*
La actriz conoce muy bien Hollywood.	*The actress knows Hollywood very well.*
Él conoce muy poco Melbourne.	*He hardly knows Melbourne at all.*

Traducción

1. *I (don't) know Chicago.* _____

2. *The president knows Washington, D.C. well.* _____

3. *The mayor knows the city well.* _____

4. *Dorothy knows Oz.* _____

5. *They [m.] haven't been to Paris.* _____

6. *Do you know Uganda?* _____

7. *George knows the jungle* (la selva). _____

8. *The bird knows its tree* (el árbol). _____

Conocer + NOUN: to know (be familiar with) a thing, be well versed in an area

Virtually everybody has significant knowledge or talent in at least one area—history, cooking, politics, or changing a tire. Perhaps you have read all of Shakespeare's plays or Ezra Pound's poetry. Whatever your area of expertise, you know that field; to say so, use **conocer**.

Mi mecánico conoce bien los motores alemanes.	*My mechanic knows German engines well.*
El fotógrafo conoce las cámaras japonesas.	*The photographer knows Japanese cameras.*
Juanito conoce los libros del Dr. Seuss.	*Johnny knows Dr. Seuss's books.*

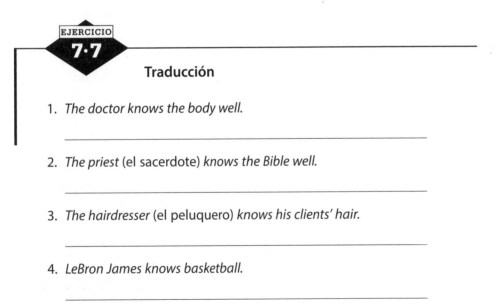

Traducción

1. *The doctor knows the body well.*

_____

2. *The priest* (el sacerdote) *knows the Bible well.*

_____

3. *The hairdresser* (el peluquero) *knows his clients' hair.*

_____

4. *LeBron James knows basketball.*

_____

5. *The manicurist knows her clients' fingernails* (la uña).

   _____

6. *The cook knows the food of Mexico.*

   _____

7. *The architect knows the architecture of Chicago.*

   _____

8. *The farmer knows the land.*

   _____

Traducción

Various uses of *saber* and *conocer* are found throughout this passage.

VOCABULARIO		
	organizar	*to arrange*
	el cocinero	*chef*
	conocer	*to meet*
	la esposa	*wife*
	maravilloso	*wonderful*
	la presentación	*introduction*
	pues,…	*well, …*
	ruso	*Russian*

I don't know why, but I believe that I know you. Do you know my cousin, Enrique? Yes?
Well, then you know that his wife knows how to speak Russian—but she can't read it.
She has lots of wonderful parties, because she knows everybody and because she knows
how to cook like a professional chef. I know that you want to meet her. I'm going to arrange
the introduction.

_____

_____

_____

_____

_____

_____

_____

_____

Stem-changing verbs

In Chapter 1, we discussed the two parts of the infinitive: (1) the infinitive ending (-**ar**, -**er**, or -**ir**), and (2) the verb base (what remains when the infinitive ending is removed). Another word for the base is the *stem*. With regular verbs, the stem or base always stays the same.

The verbs covered in this chapter show changes in the verb stem. Some of these verbs also show irregularities in the verb ending. There are three groups of stem-changing verbs: **o** > **ue**, **e** > **ie**, and **e** > **i**.

o > ue

The first group of stem-changing verbs involves changing the **o** in the verb stem to **ue** in all the conjugated forms except **nosotros** and **vosotros**. The verb endings in the conjugation remain regular.

contar *to count*		mover *to move*		dormir *to sleep*	
cuento	contamos	**muevo**	movemos	**duermo**	dormimos
cuentas	contáis	**mueves**	movéis	**duermes**	dormís
cuenta	**cuentan**	**mueve**	**mueven**	**duerme**	**duermen**

One of the features of stem-changing verbs is that the change takes place in the first-, second-, and third-person singular, and the third-person plural. If you were to draw a line around these changed verb forms, you would come up with something resembling a boot. This shape is often referred to as the "boot of irregularity."

Many people wonder, Why all this bother? Why not just conjugate these verbs using the regular pattern covered in Chapter 1? The answer has to do with sound: Spanish is nothing if not mellifluous. Without the stem change, we would have forms such as **almorzo**, **moro**, and **dormo**. It's easy to hear how deficient these sounds are compared to their correct counterparts of **almuerzo**, **muero**, and **duermo**. It's well worth the effort to learn to conjugate these verbs, and after a bit, you will be conjugating them correctly based on sound alone. *Not* making the stem change will be painful to your delicate ears!

On the following page are several common **o** > **ue** stem-changing verbs.

almorzar	to eat lunch	**mostrar**	to show
aprobar	to approve	**mover**	to move (*an object*)
colgar	to hang (up)	**probar**	to prove, test, sample, taste
contar	to count	**recordar**	to remember
costar	to cost	**resolver**	to solve
devolver	to return (*an object*)	**rogar**	to beg, pray
dormir	to sleep	**sonar**	to sound, ring
encontrar	to find	**soñar (con)**	to dream (about)
envolver	to wrap (up)	**tostar**	to toast
morder	to bite	**volver**	to return
morir	to die	**volar**	to fly

EJERCICIO

¿Cuál es verdadero o falso para ti?

1. _____ Yo duermo en un dormitorio.

2. _____ Yo cuento mi dinero cada día.

3. _____ El héroe Superhombre vuela.

4. _____ Cada mañana tuesto el pan.

5. _____ Normalmente, sueño cuando duermo.

6. _____ Típicamente, almuerzo en casa.

7. _____ A veces mis amigos y yo almorzamos en un restaurante.

8. _____ Mis amigos me muestran sus casas.

9. _____ A veces encuentro dinero en el sofá.

10. _____ Un anillo de oro con diamantes cuesta mucho.

11. _____ Después de hablar por teléfono, lo cuelgo.

12. _____ Después de leer un libro de la biblioteca, lo devuelvo.

EJERCICIO
8·1

Traducción

1. *I eat lunch.* _____

2. *You eat lunch.* _____

3. *The dog bites.* _____

4. *We approve.* _____

5. *You all beg.* _____

6. *They [m.] count the money.* _____

7. *You show the house.* _____

8. *She sleeps.* _____

9. *We solve the problem.* _____

10. *She wraps the gift.* _____

11. *I hang up the telephone.* _____

12. *You return the shirt.* _____

13. *He dies.* _____

14. *The telephone rings.* _____

15. *I find the money.* _____

16. *We return.* _____

17. *Dumbo flies.* _____

18. *Jane toasts the bread.* _____

19. *We pray for peace.* _____

20. *He dreams about a tiger.* _____

21. *I don't remember anything.* _____

22. *The book costs ten dollars.* _____

23. *You move the chairs.* _____

24. *I taste the coffee.* _____

e > ie

The second group of stem-changing verbs involves changing the **e** in the verb stem to **ie** in all the conjugated forms except **nosotros** and **vosotros**. The verb endings in the conjugation remain regular.

cerrar *to close*	
cierro	cerramos
cierras	cerráis
cierra	**cierran**

perder *to lose*	
pierdo	perdemos
pierdes	perdéis
pierde	**pierden**

hervir *to boil*	
hiervo	hervimos
hierves	hervís
hierve	**hierven**

Below are several common **e** > **ie** stem-changing verbs. Note that a few have both an **o** and an **e** in the stem (**comenzar, confesar, consentir, convertir**). You can be sure that these are **e** > **ie** stem-changing verbs (and not **o** > **ue**), because the vowel closest to the verb ending is the vowel that changes.

VOCABULARIO

advertir	to advise, warn	**mentir**	to lie, tell a lie
cerrar	to close, shut	**negar**	to deny
comenzar	to begin, commence	**pensar (en)**	to think (about)
confesar	to confess	**perder**	to lose
consentir	to consent	**preferir**	to prefer
convertir	to convert	**querer**	to want, wish
defender	to defend	**referir**	to refer
empezar	to begin	**sentir**	to feel sorry, regret
encender	to light, kindle	**sugerir**	to suggest
entender	to understand	**temblar**	to tremble
fregar	to scrub (*dishes*), wash (*dishes*)	**tropezar (con)**	to stumble, bump into
hervir	to boil		

EJERCICIO

¿Cuál es verdadero o falso para ti?

1. _____ Yo pierdo muchas cosas en mi casa.

2. _____ Entiendo español.

3. _____ Mi clase de español comienza a las diez de la mañana.

4. _____ Pinocho miente mucho.

5. _____ Para preparar el café, una persona hierve el agua.

6. _____ Cerramos la boca para hablar.

7. _____ Un buen abogado defiende a sus clientes.

8. _____ Cierro las ventanas cuando hace frío.

9. _____ Pienso mucho en mi familia.

10. _____ Mis amigos piensan en mí.

11. _____ Cada noche friego los platos.

12. _____ Entre el café y el té, yo prefiero el café.

EJERCICIO 8·2

Traducción

1. *I close the door.* _____

2. *You lose the game.* _____

3. *He washes the dishes.* _____

4. *We advise you.* _____

5. *They [m.] deny the truth.* _____

6. *He regrets it a lot.* _____

7. *You all begin.* _____

8. *She defends me.* _____

9. *You boil the water.* _____

10. *George Santos lies a lot.* _____

11. *You all consent.* _____

12. *She suggests.* _____

13. *We tremble.* _____

14. *I prefer water.* _____

15. *He wants a dog.* _____

16. *Do you understand?* _____

17. *He loses the magazine.* _____

18. *She bumps into the sofa.* _____

19. *They [m.] confess the crime* (el delito). _____

20. *The program begins.* _____

21. *I think about the war.* _____

22. *You light the candle.* _____

23. *We convert the money to dollars.* _____

24. *I refer the case to the professor.* _____

e > i

The third group of stem-changing verbs involves changing the **e** in the verb stem to **i** in all the conjugated forms except **nosotros** and **vosotros**. The verb endings in the conjugation remain regular. All of the verbs in this group are -**ir** verbs.

seguir *to follow*	
sigo	seguimos
sigues	seguís
sigue	**siguen**

repetir *to repeat*	
repito	repetimos
repites	repetís
repite	**repiten**

Below are several common **e > i** stem-changing verbs. This is the smallest of the three stem-changing verb groups. You will revisit several of these verbs in the next chapter; some of the verbs listed here show other irregular verb patterns.

VOCABULARIO

bendecir	to bless	**gemir**	to groan, moan
colegir	to deduce	**impedir**	to impede, hinder
competir	to compete	**maldecir**	to curse
conseguir	to obtain, get	**medir**	to be long, measure
corregir	to correct	**pedir**	to request, ask for
decir	to say, tell	**reír**	to laugh
despedir	to fire	**repetir**	to repeat
elegir	to elect	**seguir**	to follow, continue
freír	to fry	**servir**	to serve

NOTE The **yo** forms of **bendecir** and **decir** are, respectively, **bendigo** and **digo**. All other forms follow the pattern shown on page 69.

EJERCICIO

¿Cuál es verdadero o falso para ti?

1. _____ En un restaurante bueno, el mesero me sirve la comida.

2. _____ Muchos atletas compiten en las olimpiadas.

3. _____ Frío huevos cada mañana para el desayuno.

4. _____ Cada cuatro años, elegimos al presidente de mi país.

5. _____ Un metro mide cien centímetros.

6. _____ Pinocho siempre dice la verdad y yo siempre digo la verdad también.

7. _____ Un profesor corrige muchos exámenes.

8. _____ El papa en el Vaticano bendice a la gente con frecuencia.

9. _____ Esta semana pido un aumento a mi jefe.

10. _____ Cuando quiero información del mundo, consigo un periódico.

11. _____ Cuando compro un aparato nuevo, siempre sigo las instrucciones antes de usarlo.

12. _____ Muchas veces los padres repiten las instrucciones a los niños.

EJERCICIO

8·3

Traducción

1. *I compete.* _____

2. *You correct the test.* _____

3. *He asks for help.* _____

4. *She laughs a lot.* _____

5. *He gets a job.* _____

6. *We elect the winner.* _____

7. *We fry the potatoes.* _____

8. *You all tell the truth.* _____

9. *You fire the employee.* _____

10. *We ask for more money.* _____

11. *She groans.* _____

12. *He impedes the progress.* _____

13. *They [m.] tell us the truth.* _____

14. *I follow you.* _____

15. *You all serve us.* _____

16. *Who says this?* _____

17. *She is five feet tall.* _____

18. *They [m.] curse.* _____

19. *He deduces the truth from the facts.* _____

20. *You compete against him.* _____

21. *They [m.] laugh a lot because they are happy.* _____

22. *All of you [formal] repeat the lesson.* _____

23. *The priest blesses you.* _____

24. *What are you asking for?* _____

Traducción

VOCABULARIO

el avión	*airplane*	la comida	*food, a meal*
el/la azafato/a	*flight attendant*	las instrucciones	*instructions*
la bebida	*drink*	esta noche	*tonight*
el cacahuate	*peanut*	el pañuelo	*handkerchief*
la ciudad	*city*	viajar	*to travel*

I am on an airplane. I fly a lot because I prefer to travel fast. We are going to leave in five minutes. The flight attendant closes the door and refers us to the instructions for emergencies. Some people sleep on the airplane and others bite their handkerchiefs when the airplane trembles. No one eats lunch because the flight attendants don't serve us a meal. They [m.] serve us drinks and peanuts. Are we elephants!? When my mother flies, she thinks about her family. I prefer to think about the elegant hotel and the city that I am going to visit. Tonight I'm going to sleep in São Paulo.

_____

_____

_____

_____

_____

_____

_____

_____

_____

_____

Irregular verb groups

Many verbs are irregular in Spanish. Fortunately, there are several groups of verbs that have similar patterns when conjugated. These verbs can be grouped by the last letters of their infinitive form. In this chapter, we discuss these groups and their patterns to help you recognize and use them.

Infinitives ending with -cer preceded by a vowel

The following verbs all end with **-cer**, and in this group the **-cer** is always preceded by a vowel. All such verbs are irregular only in the **yo** form, where a **z** appears before the final **c**. All other conjugated forms are regular in the present tense.

As with stem-changing verbs, the reason for this change is how it sounds: Consider the now familiar verb **conocer**. Without the **c > z** change, its **yo** form would be **conoco** (as opposed to the lovely **conozco**). I hope at this point the "regular" formation sounds silly to you, because that is how it sounds to the native Spanish ear. Onward and upward!

conocer *to know, be familiar with*	
conozco	conocemos
conoces	conocéis
conoce	conocen

parecer *to seem*	
parezco	parecemos
pareces	parecéis
parece	parecen

Below are several common verbs in this group, along with their respective **yo** forms.

VOCABULARIO		
agradecer	to appreciate; be grateful (for)	**yo agradezco**
aparecer	to appear	**yo aparezco**
conocer	to know (*a person*)	**yo conozco**
crecer	to grow	**yo crezco**
desaparecer	to disappear	**yo desaparezco**
establecer	to establish	**yo establezco**
merecer	to deserve, merit	**yo merezco**
nacer	to be born	**yo nazco**
obedecer	to obey	**yo obedezco**
ofrecer	to offer	**yo ofrezco**
parecer	to seem	**yo parezco**
pertenecer (a)	to belong (to/on)	**yo pertenezco**
placer	to please, gratify	**yo plazco**
reconocer	to recognize	**yo reconozco**
yacer	to lie down	**yo yazco**

EJERCICIO
9·1

Write the correct form of the verb in parentheses.

1. Yo _____ (conocer) a Juan.

2. Yo _____ (pertenecer) a un club.

3. Este programa me _____ (parecer) absurdo.

4. Estos libros me _____ (pertenecer).

5. Yo no _____ (reconocer) a nadie aquí.

6. Cada día muchos bebés _____ (nacer) en el mundo.

7. Yo _____ (ofrecer) cien dólares al ganador.

8. Yo _____ (merecer) un aumento (*raise*).

9. Si un bebé no come bien, no _____ (crecer) bien.

10. A veces un fantasma _____ (aparecer) en los sueños de los supersticiosos.

Traducción

VOCABULARIO

la celebridad	*celebrity*	la idiotez	*idiocy*
el estreno	*opening, premiere*	la ley	*law*
la fama	*fame*	si	*if*
hecho/hecha por	*made by*	el talento	*talent*

I am a celebrity. I appear at lots of parties and openings for movies made by other people. I know a lot of people, but it's more important if they recognize me. I believe that I belong on the "A-list." I have no talent and I offer nothing to the world. I believe that I deserve money and fame simply because I exist. I obey all the laws of idiocy.

_____

_____

_____

_____

_____

_____

Infinitives ending with **-ucir**

Verbs that end with **-ucir** are similar to verbs ending with **-cer** in that a **z** is inserted before the final **c** in the **yo** form. All other conjugated forms are regular in the present tense.

producir *to produce*	
produzco	producimos
produces	producís
produce	producen

traducir *to translate*	
traduzco	traducimos
traduces	traducís
traduce	traducen

Below are several common verbs in this group, along with their respective **yo** forms.

VOCABULARIO		
conducir	to conduct, drive	**yo conduzco**
deducir	to deduce	**yo deduzco**
deslucir	to tarnish, spoil	**yo desluzco**
inducir	to induce, persuade	**yo induzco**
introducir	to introduce, insert, put	**yo introduzco**
lucir	to light up, display	**yo luzco**
producir	to produce	**yo produzco**
reducir	to reduce	**yo reduzco**
traducir	to translate	**yo traduzco**

Responde a cada una de las preguntas siguientes con una frase completa.

1. ¿Conduces un coche automático o de marchas (*stick shift*)?

   _____

2. ¿Produces mucho trabajo?

   _____

3. ¿Traduces muchas frases en este libro?

   _____

4. ¿Qué produce el panadero?

   _____

5. ¿Introduces una moneda en el parquímetro (*parking meter*)?

   _____

6. ¿Normalmente, reducen los impuestos los políticos?

   _____

Traducción

VOCABULARIO	el guante	*glove*
	la guantera	*glove compartment*
	el idioma	*language*
	lleno/llena	*full*
	la mayoría	*majority*
	la propina	*tip*

I drive a taxi in New York City. Usually I obey the laws of the city, but sometimes I have to drive very, very fast (you understand me, don't you?). Then I deserve a very, very big tip (I appreciate this; thank you) and I put it into the glove compartment. I never put gloves in the glove compartment, because there isn't room—it's full of money. The majority of my customers speak English, but sometimes they tell me things in other languages, and then I translate what (lo que) *they say to me.*

_____

_____

_____

_____

_____

_____

Infinitives ending with -cer or -cir preceded by a consonant

When a verb ending with **-cer** or **-cir** is preceded by a consonant, **z** replaces **c** in the **yo** form only. All other conjugated forms are regular in the present tense.

ejercer *to exert, exercise*

ejerzo	ejercemos
ejerces	ejercéis
ejerce	ejercen

zurcir *to mend*

zurzo	zurcimos
zurces	zurcís
zurce	zurcen

Below are several common verbs in this group, along with their respective **yo** forms.

VOCABULARIO

convencer	to convince, persuade	**yo convenzo**
ejercer	to exert, exercise	**yo ejerzo**
esparcir	to scatter, spread	**yo esparzo**
vencer	to conquer, defeat	**yo venzo**
zurcir	to mend, darn	**yo zurzo**

EJERCICIO
9·5

Traducción

1. *I scatter seeds* (la semilla) *in the garden.*

   _____

2. *I conquer the enemy* (el enemigo).

   _____

3. *I darn the socks* (el calcetín).

   _____

4. *I exert a lot of energy* (la energía) *when I play soccer.*

   _____

5. *The warriors* (el guerrero) *conquer their enemies.*

   _____

Traducción

VOCABULARIO	la alabanza	*praise*	la mosca	*fly*
	la fruta	*fruit*	el mosquito	*mosquito*
	el jardín	*garden*	la semilla	*seed*
	el jardinero, la jardinera	*gardener*	el vecino, la vecina	*neighbor*
	las malas hierbas	*weeds*	el vegetal	*vegetable*

I am a gardener. Every morning, I scatter seeds in the garden. Then I conquer the weeds and I convince the flies and the mosquitoes that they need to fly to my neighbor's garden. My garden produces lots of vegetables and many fruits. I deserve a lot of praise for my beautiful garden.

_____

_____

_____

_____

_____

_____

Infinitives ending with -ger or -gir

In Spanish, a **g** before **e** has a soft **g** sound (sounds like /h/). Because the infinitives in this group end with a soft **g** sound, that same sound must be retained in their conjugated forms. The **yo** form, however, would have a **g** before **o**, which in Spanish has a hard **g** sound (as in "go"). Therefore, in this group of verbs, the **g** in the **yo** form changes to **j**, so that the soft **g** sound (/h/) is retained. All other conjugated forms are regular in the present tense, except for changes required in stem-changing verbs.

coger *to catch, seize, grab*		**corregir (e > i)** *to correct*	
cojo	cogemos	**corrijo**	corregimos
coges	cogéis	corriges	corregís
coge	cogen	corrige	corrigen

On the following page are several common verbs in this group, along with their respective **yo** forms.

coger	to catch, seize, grab	**yo cojo**
colegir (e > i)	to deduce	**yo colijo**
corregir (e > i)	to correct	**yo corrijo**
dirigir	to direct	**yo dirijo**
elegir (e > i)	to elect, choose	**yo elijo**
escoger	to select, choose	**yo escojo**
exigir	to demand, require	**yo exijo**
fingir	to pretend	**yo finjo**
proteger	to protect	**yo protejo**
recoger	to pick up, gather	**yo recojo**
sumergir	to submerge, immerse	**yo sumerjo**
surgir	to surge, spurt	**yo surjo**

EJERCICIO
9·7

Traducción

1. *I protect my daughters.*

   _____

2. *I correct my problems.*

   _____

3. *The teacher* (el maestro) *corrects many papers* (el trabajo).

   _____

4. *Sometimes I pretend to be happy when I am sad.*

   _____

5. *I choose my friends with a lot of care* (el cuidado).

   _____

6. *Every four years, we elect a new leader* (el líder).

   _____

7. *I pick up my socks from the floor* (el suelo).

   _____

8. *I catch a taxi for the airport* (el aeropuerto).

   _____

9. *I demand a lot from my employees* (el empleado).

   _____

10. *I submerge the sweater in cold water.*

    _____

Traducción

VOCABULARIO

el/la astronauta	astronaut	la duquesa	duchess
el autobús	bus	la esquina	corner (exterior)
la avenida	avenue	la mochila	backpack
el duque	duke	la nave	spaceship

Every morning, I take the bus to school. I catch the bus at the corner of Duke and Duchess avenues. Before leaving (Antes de salir) for school, I select my clothing for the day and then I gather my books and my backpack. My backpack protects my books. Sometimes I pretend to be an astronaut, and the bus is a spaceship. Other times I pretend to be sick, because then I don't have to go to school.

_____

_____

_____

_____

_____

_____

_____

Infinitives ending with -aer

When an infinitive ends with **-aer**, its **yo** form ends with **-aigo**. All other conjugated forms are regular in the present tense.

caer *to fall*	
caigo	caemos
caes	caéis
cae	caen

traer *to bring*	
traigo	traemos
traes	traéis
trae	traen

Below are several common verbs in this group, along with their respective **yo** forms.

VOCABULARIO

atraer	to attract	**yo atraigo**
caer	to fall	**yo caigo**
contraer	to contract	**yo contraigo**
raer	to scrape, rub off	**yo raigo**
retraer	to bring back	**yo retraigo**
sustraer	to remove, subtract	**yo sustraigo**
traer	to bring	**yo traigo**

EJERCICIO 9·9

Complete each sentence with the correct form of the verb in parentheses.

1. Usualmente yo _____ (traer) algo a una fiesta.

2. El pintor _____ (raer) la vieja pintura del lienzo (*canvas*).

3. El azúcar _____ (atraer) a las moscas.

4. Juan _____ (contraer) matrimonio con María el próximo mes.

5. Los estudiantes de matemáticas _____ (sustraer) la cantidad mínima de la cantidad máxima.

EJERCICIO 9·10

Traducción

VOCABULARIO			
la abeja	*bee*	el girasol	*sunflower*
el aster	*aster*	el miembro, la miembra	*member*
la belleza	*beauty*	el otoño	*fall*
exacto/exacta	*exact*	plantar	*to plant*
la flor	*flower*	el verano	*summer*

I am a flower. I am an aster, (in order) to be exact. My gardener plants me because I attract bees. I bring a lot of beauty to the garden. I grow tall and beautiful in the summer and in the fall. Many people think that I am a daisy, but I am not what (lo que) I appear to be. I am actually a member of the sunflower family.

_____

_____

_____

_____

_____

Infinitives ending with -uir not preceded by g

Up to this point, the groups of irregular verbs discussed in this chapter have shown a changed or irregular form only in the **yo** form of the present tense. The infinitives ending with **-uir** not preceded by **g** show changes or irregularities in all of the conjugated forms except **nosotros** and **vosotros**. In each of these forms, a **y** is added to the stem before the verb ending is attached.

huir *to flee, run away*	
huyo	huimos
huyes	huís
huye	**huyen**

destruir *to destroy*	
destruyo	destruimos
destruyes	destruís
destruye	**destruyen**

Below are several common verbs in this group, along with their respective irregular forms.

VOCABULARIO

concluir	to conclude	concluyo, concluyes, concluye, concluyen
constituir	to constitute	constituyo, constituyes, constituye, constituyen
construir	to build, construct	construyo, construyes, construye, construyen
contribuir	to contribute	contribuyo, contribuyes, contribuye, contribuyen
destruir	to destroy	destruyo, destruyes, destruye, destruyen
fluir	to flow	fluyo, fluyes, fluye, fluyen
huir	to flee, run away	huyo, huyes, huye, huyen
incluir	to include	incluyo, incluyes, incluye, incluyen
influir	to influence	influyo, influyes, influye, influyen

EJERCICIO
9·11

Complete each sentence with the correct form of the verb in parentheses.

1. Yo _____ (construir) una casa de madera.

2. Yo nunca _____ (contribuir) dinero a un político.

3. El río _____ (fluir) al oeste.

4. El plato _____ (huir) con la cuchara (*spoon*).

5. Los libros de H. L. Mencken me _____ (influir) mucho.

6. La bomba _____ (destruir) el edificio.

7. Tú _____ (concluir) la reunión a las ocho de la noche.

8. El homicidio _____ (constituir) un crimen grave.

9. El novelista siempre _____ (incluir) varios personajes en los libros.

10. Las bibliotecas _____ (contribuir) mucho a la sociedad.

EJERCICIO 9·12

Traducción

VOCABULARIO	el bloque	*block, cube*	de madera	*wooden*
	la casa de muñecas	*dollhouse*	el monstruo	*monster*
	el closet	*closet*	los muebles	*furniture*
	al fin	*at the end*		

I'm five years old. I build many houses from the wooden blocks that are in my bedroom. Some days my sister contributes furniture from her dollhouse to the wooden houses. At the end of the day, when it's time to sleep, I destroy them. If I believe that there is a monster in my closet, I run away from the room.

_____

_____

_____

_____

_____

_____

Infinitives ending with -guir

Earlier we discussed the need to retain the soft **g** in conjugated forms for infinitives ending with -**ger** or -**gir**. Here, with infinitives ending with -**guir**, we must retain the hard **g** sound throughout the conjugation. The **u** is merely a hard sound marker in the -**gu** combination; without it, the **g** would be soft. Because **g** before **o** naturally has a hard sound, the **u** is no longer necessary in the **yo** form. Thus for this group of verbs, the **u** that appears in the infinitive is dropped in the **yo** form only. All other conjugated forms are regular in the present tense, except for changes required in stem-changing verbs.

distinguir *to distinguish*		**seguir (e > i)** *to follow*	
distingo	distinguimos	**sigo**	seguimos
distingues	distinguís	sigues	seguís
distingue	distinguen	sigue	siguen

Below are several common verbs in this group, along with their respective **yo** forms.

VOCABULARIO

conseguir (e > i)	to get, obtain	**yo consigo**
distinguir	to distinguish, pick out	**yo distingo**
erguir (e > i)	to erect, lift up	**yo irgo**
extinguir	to extinguish	**yo extingo**
perseguir (e > i)	to pursue, persecute	**yo persigo**
seguir (e > i)	to follow	**yo sigo**

Note that in **erguir**, as in other **e > i** stem-changing verbs, the stressed **e** changes to **i**: **irgo**, **irgues**, **irgue**, **erguimos**, **erguís**, **irguen**.

Complete each sentence with the correct form of the verb in parentheses.

1. Yo _____ (distinguir) entre lo bueno y lo malo.

2. La policía _____ (seguir) al criminal.

3. Yo _____ (extinguir) las velas (*candles*).

4. Yo _____ (conseguir) trabajo en la compañía telefónica.

5. Los líderes _____ (erguir) un monumento a la libertad.

6. En el verano los mosquitos me _____ (perseguir).

7. Mary _____ (conseguir) toda su ropa por catálogo.

8. Mis clases de matemáticas e inglés _____ (seguir) a mi clase de español.

9. Muchas personas no _____ (distinguir) el rojo del verde.

10. Yo te _____ (seguir) a la fiesta.

11. Ustedes no _____ (conseguir) nada de esta oficina.

12. Los bomberos (*firefighters*) _____ (extinguir) el incendio.

Traducción

VOCABULARIO

aburrido	*boring*
el aparato	*appliance*
correcto	*correct, right*
la cosa	*thing*
demasiado	*too*
las direcciones	*directions*
entre	*among*
funcionar	*to work* (appliance/machine)
el incendio	*fire* (unwanted)
la pieza	*piece*
la senda	*path*
tarde o temprano	*sooner or later*

When I get a new appliance, I never follow the directions. It's too boring. I pick out the things that I need among the many pieces, and I follow what (lo que) seems right to me. Sometimes I am wrong, and then I have to follow another path. For example, if there is a fire, I extinguish it. Sooner or later, the appliance works. (Or I return it to the store.) I'm not going to pursue a job as a mechanic.

_____

_____

_____

_____

_____

_____

_____

Reflexive verbs

10

A verb is reflexive when the subject (the performer of the action) and the object (the receiver of that action) are the same.

For example, the verb in the sentence "I see you" is not reflexive because "I" (the subject) and "you" (the object) are not the same person. However, if I look in the mirror and see myself, the verb is reflexive because "I" (the subject) and "myself" (the object) are the same person. Another way of looking at reflexive verbs is to say that *the action doesn't go anywhere.*

In English, the object of a reflexive verb is usually one of the following pronouns: "myself," "yourself," "himself," "herself," "itself," "ourselves," and "themselves." In Spanish, reflexive verbs require reflexive object pronouns.

If there is one verb in the clause, the object pronoun precedes the verb.

Me veo.   *I see **myself.***

If there are two verbs in the clause, the object either precedes the first verb or is attached directly to the second verb. Either structure is acceptable; however, adding the object pronoun to the infinitive is more common (see the second Spanish example below).

Me quiero ver.   *I want to see **myself.***
Quiero ver**me**.

In English, our use of the reflexive pronoun is quite restricted and generally involves the person as a whole: "I love myself," "you know yourself," "he hates himself," and so on.

In Spanish, however, the notion of reflexive is far more expansive. A verb is considered reflexive as long as the action is going back to the actor. For example, "I wash my hair," "you take a bath," and "we brush our teeth" all are examples of sentences that require reflexive pronouns in Spanish.

Spanish reflexive pronouns

me	nos
te	os
se	se

bañarse *to take a bath*

me baño	nos bañamos
te bañas	os bañáis
se baña	se bañan

sentarse (e > ie) *to sit down*

me siento	nos sentamos
te sientas	os sentáis
se sienta	se sientan

Note that **sentarse** is an **e** > **ie** stem-changing verb. It means literally to "seat oneself."

There are some important things to know before working with reflexive verbs.

1 Many reflexive verbs are stem-changing (these are noted in the list below), and they are conjugated like their nonreflexive counterparts.

2 Many reflexive verbs involve the mention of a body part or parts, for example, **cepillarse** ("to brush"). In Spanish, the definite article rather than the possessive adjective is typically used before the name of a body part (the reflexive pronoun makes it obvious whose body is being discussed).

Me cepillo **el** pelo.	*I brush **my** hair.*
Ella se cepilla **los** dientes.	*She brushes **her** teeth.*
Te lavas **el** pelo.	*You wash **your** hair.*

3 Nearly all verbs in the language can be either reflexive or nonreflexive: "I scratch myself" (reflexive) or "I scratch my cat" (nonreflexive). Therefore, the list below is far from exhaustive. However, certain actions are usually reflexive due to the nature of the action (bathing, shaving, brushing teeth, etc.). For the most part, these are the verbs found below.

4 In the list below, **irse** ("to go away") is a verb that differs from the general usage of a reflexive verb, in that this is not a case where the subject and object are the same. Instead, the reflexive pronoun intensifies the action. Two other reflexive verbs with distinctive meanings are **comerse** ("to gobble up"), which does not mean "to eat oneself," and **morirse** ("to pass away"), which softens the message, rather than changes the meaning, of **morir** ("to die").

Below are several common reflexive verbs.

VOCABULARIO

acostarse (o > ue)	to go to bed	**levantarse**	to stand up, get up
afeitarse	to shave oneself	**llamarse**	to call oneself
bañarse	to bathe oneself	**mirarse**	to look at oneself
casarse (con alguien)	to marry (someone); to get married	**morirse (o > ue)**	to pass away
		peinarse	to comb one's hair
cepillarse	to brush oneself, brush one's (*hair, teeth*)	**ponerse**	to become, get
		ponerse (la ropa)	to put on (clothing)
comerse	to gobble up, eat hastily	**preocuparse (por)**	to worry (about)
despertarse (e > ie)	to wake up	**probarse (o > ue)**	to try on (*clothing*)
desvestirse (e > i)	to undress oneself	**quitarse**	to take off (*clothing*), remove (*clothing*)
dormirse (o > ue)	to fall asleep		
ducharse	to take a shower	**secarse**	to dry oneself
enfermarse	to get sick	**sentarse (e > ie)**	to sit down, seat oneself
enojarse	to get angry, get mad	**sentirse (e > ie)**	to feel (*emotionally, physically*)
irse	to go away	**verse**	to see oneself
lavarse	to wash oneself	**vestirse (e > i)**	to get dressed

Me quito el sombrero.	*I take off my hat.*
Nos vestimos en la mañana.	*We get dressed in the morning.*
Te acuestas a las once.	*You go to bed at eleven o'clock.*
Os llamáis Brígida y Pancho.	*Your names are Brigida and Pancho.*
Romeo se casa con Julieta.	*Romeo marries Juliet.*
Ellas se ponen nerviosas.	*They become nervous.*

EJERCICIO

¿Cuál es verdadero o falso para ti?

1. _____ Me acuesto a las diez de la noche.

2. _____ Me despierto a las seis y media de la mañana.

3. _____ Me lavo el pelo cada día.

4. _____ Me ducho cada mañana.

5. _____ Me siento enfermo/enferma ahora.

6. _____ Me pongo feliz cuando recibo un regalo para mi cumpleaños.

7. _____ Me preocupo mucho por el dinero.

8. _____ Me cepillo los dientes tres veces cada día.

9. _____ Me enfermo más en el invierno que en el verano.

10. _____ Me llamo Mitch.

11. _____ Después de ducharme, me visto.

12. _____ Antes de acostarme, me quito la ropa y me pongo el pijama.

EJERCICIO
10·1

Traducción

1. *I go to bed.* _____

2. *You wash your hair.* _____

3. *He shaves every morning.* _____

4. *She shaves her legs.* _____

5. *You all wake up.* _____

6. *They [m.] sit down.* _____

7. *She goes away.* _____

8. *My name is Rex.* _____

9. *You take a shower.* _____

10. *We get dressed.* _____

11. *You all fall asleep.* _____

12. *She takes a bath.* _____

13. *I worry about the future.* _____

14. *You all [formal] wake up.* _____

Reflexive verbs   **89**

15. I get undressed at night. _____

16. Your name is Alicia. _____

17. He takes off his shirt. _____

18. You all [formal] see yourselves in the mirror. _____

19. I feel sick. _____

20. You comb your hair. _____

21. We brush our teeth. _____

22. She falls asleep. _____

23. Do you take a shower? _____

24. His name is Horatio. _____

25. The pig gobbles up the corn. _____

EJERCICIO
10·2

Traducción

VOCABULARIO	la alondra	lark	el mediodía	noon
	el búho	owl	sucio/sucia	dirty
	el despertador	alarm clock	tipo	kind
	el espejo	mirror	el trabajo	job
	el guarro	slob		

There are two kinds of people: There are larks (morning people) and owls (night people). I am a lark. I wake up—with or without an alarm clock—at five o'clock in the morning. I get up immediately, brush my teeth, take a shower, wash my hair, dry my hair, get dressed, and go off to work. My brother is completely different. He doesn't wake up until noon and he doesn't get up until one o'clock in the afternoon. He is a slob. He doesn't brush his teeth, doesn't wash his hair, and doesn't take a shower. When he sees himself in the mirror, I think he really sees a monster. He never combs his hair. He gets sick a lot, and he gets angry because he can't get a job when he's so dirty.

_____

_____

_____

_____

_____

_____

_____

_____

Describe your morning and evening routines, using as many reflexive verbs as you can.

_____

_____

_____

_____

_____

_____

_____

_____

Gustar and similarly formed verbs

11

There are several verbs in Spanish (and in English as well) that are commonly used only in the third-person singular or plural, together with an indirect object pronoun. The most common of these verbs is **gustar** ("to be pleasing to").

While in English one says, "I like the cat" ("I" = SUBJECT and "the cat" = DIRECT OBJECT), in Spanish you say, literally, "The cat is pleasing to me" ("The cat" = SUBJECT and "me" = INDIRECT OBJECT).

The key to the verbs in this section is remembering that they are typically seen only in their third-person singular and plural forms. The subjects of these verbs (the things being discussed) have an effect on people—"frogs fascinate me," "noise bothers you," "recipes for chili interest him"—rather than people having an effect on them. To negate a sentence, simply put **no** before the indirect object pronoun.

To work with these verbs, follow this pattern.

INDIRECT OBJECT PRONOUN + THIRD-PERSON VERB + NOUN(S)

Singular subject

Me gusta el gato.	*I like the cat.*
No te gusta el libro.	*You don't like the book.*
Le gusta la casa.	*He likes the house.*
No nos gusta el perro.	*We don't like the dog.*
Os gusta la luz.	*You all like the light.*
Les gusta la revista.	*They like the magazine.*

Plural subject

Me gustan los gatos.	*I like the cats.*
No te gustan los libros.	*You don't like the books.*
Le gustan las casas.	*He likes the houses.*
No nos gustan los perros.	*We don't like the dogs.*
Os gustan las luces.	*You all like the lights.*
Les gustan las revistas.	*They like the magazines.*

When mentioning the name of a person (or persons), place the name (or pronoun) between the preposition **a** and the indirect pronoun. This adds clarity and emphasis.

A Juan le gusta bailar.	*John likes to dance.*
A los chicos les gusta hablar.	*The boys like to talk.*
A ella le encanta el café.	*She loves coffee.*
A ellos no les falta nada.	*They don't need anything.*

93

Below are several common verbs that are used like **gustar**. In some cases, a more common way of expressing this meaning in English follows in brackets.

VOCABULARIO

aburrir	to be boring (to/for someone)
bastar	to be enough (to/for someone)
disgustar	to be repugnant (to someone) [to hate]
doler (o > ue)	to be painful (to someone) [to hurt, to ache]
encantar	to be enchanting (to someone) [to love]
faltar	to be lacking/missing (to someone)
fascinar	to be fascinating (to someone)
gustar	to be pleasing (to someone) [to like]
importar	to be important (to someone)
interesar	to be interesting (to someone)
molestar	to be bothersome (to someone) [to bother]
parecer	to seem/appear (to someone)
sobrar	to be left over or extra (to someone)

EJERCICIO

¿Cuál es verdadero o falso para ti?

1. _____ Me interesa la historia de los Estados Unidos.

2. _____ No me molestan las arañas.

3. _____ Me importan mucho mis estudios.

4. _____ Muchos programas en la televisión me parecen absurdos.

5. _____ No me duelen los pies ahora.

6. _____ Los libros de J. K. Rowling me fascinan.

7. _____ Me encanta la música de Taylor Swift.

8. _____ Me falta un botón en mi camisa ahora.

9. _____ No me interesan los políticos.

10. _____ A veces me duele la espalda.

11. _____ Ahora me duelen mucho los ojos.

12. _____ Normalmente, me sobra dinero.

13. _____ Muchos políticos me aburren.

14. _____ Muchos políticos me molestan.

EJERCICIO

11·1

Traducción

1. *Truth is important to me.* _____

2. *I don't like spiders.* _____

3. *My stomach aches.* _____

4. *I have too many books.* _____

5. *She likes the autumn.* _____

6. *It seems ridiculous to me.* _____

7. *I love your dress!* _____

8. *We have ten dollars left over.* _____

9. *I hate your attitude.* _____

10. *I love ice cream.* _____

11. *You are missing a button* (el botón). _____

12. *These photos are fascinating to us.* _____

13. *The movie is interesting to them.* _____

14. *What is important to you?* _____

15. *His manners* (los modales) *disgust me.* _____

16. *He seems egotistical to me.* _____

17. *This movie bores me.* _____

18. *She bothers me.* _____

EJERCICIO

¿Cuál es verdadero o falso para tu mejor amigo/amiga?

1. _____ A él / A ella le gusta ir al cine.

2. _____ A él / A ella le importa el dinero.

3. _____ A él / A ella le encantan los dramas de William Shakespeare.

4. _____ A él / A ella le duele la cabeza con frecuencia.

5. _____ A él / A ella le duelen los dientes a veces.

6. _____ A él / A ella le fascinan las teorías de Albert Einstein.

7. _____ A él / A ella le interesa cocinar.

8. _____ A él / A ella le molestan los mentirosos (*liars*).

¡Te toca a ti! *Responde a cada una de las preguntas siguientes con una frase completa.*

1. ¿Qué comida te gusta más?

   _____

2. ¿Qué tienda te encanta?

   _____

3. ¿Qué cosas te interesan mucho?

   _____

4. ¿Qué te interesa mucho?

   _____

5. ¿Te falta dinero para comprar un avion?

   _____

6. ¿Qué te molesta mucho?

   _____

7. ¿Qué estación del año te encanta? ¿Por qué?

   _____

8. ¿Qué aspectos de otras personas te fascinan?

   _____

Para estos personajes de la literatura, ¿es verdadero o falso?

1. _____ A Romeo le fascina Julieta.

2. _____ A Harry Potter y Ron Weasley les disgusta la escuela.

3. _____ A Don Quijote le gusta quedarse en casa.

4. _____ A Mary Poppins le encantan los niños.

5. _____ A Caperucita Roja le molesta el lobo.

6. _____ A Gulliver el mundo le parece muy pequeño.

7. _____ A Rapunzel le sobra mucho pelo.

8. _____ A Pinocho le encanta la verdad.

9. _____ A la Bruja Mala del Oeste le faltan los zapatos de rubí.

10. _____ A la Bella Durmiente le falta un beso del príncipe.

11. _____ Al Rey Midas no le importa ni le interesa el oro.

12. _____ A las malas hermanastras, les duelen los pies cuando se ponen los zapatos de la Cenicienta.

Traducción

VOCABULARIO	el botiquín	*medicine cabinet*	(estar) sano	*(to be) healthy*
	la cabeza	*head*	el secreto	*secret*
	la medicina	*medicine*	la vida	*life*
	la salud	*health*		

I have a headache and it bothers me a lot. My health is important to me. I don't like it when I'm sick. I love it when I feel well. I should take medicine, but I hate what (lo que) I have in the medicine cabinet. It seems like old milk to me, and it disgusts me. I'm fascinated by people who are always healthy. They love life and they are interested in many things. Who are they? Where are they from?

_____

_____

_____

_____

_____

_____

_____

_____

The present progressive　·12·

The use of the present progressive is easy to spot in English. The time is in the present, and "-ing" is attached to the verb, for example, "I am studying (now)." The addition of "-ing" to a verb indicates that the action is in progress.

It is important to note that the present progressive is used less frequently in Spanish than in English. In English, we use the present progressive very broadly, often to describe what is going on in our lives in general: "I am living in New York," "I am working in a bank," "I am taking a course in Voodoo rituals."

In Spanish, however, the use of the present progressive is more restricted. It is used primarily to indicate what a person is doing *right now*. In other words, in Spanish, use the present progressive to describe what you are doing or what is happening at the time you report it. The rest of the time you use the simple present tense: "I live in New York," "I work in a bank," "I study Spanish."

Formation of the present progressive

As in English, there are two parts to the present progressive: (1) the auxiliary "to be" and (2) the present participle, which is the base verb with "-ing" attached. In Spanish, the auxiliary is **estar: estoy, estás, está, estamos, estáis, están**. The conjugated **estar** is then followed by the present participle.

Regularly formed present participles

Nearly all present participles are formed regularly. To form these, do the following.

-**ar** VERBS　　Drop the -**ar** and add -**ando** (**hablando, estudiando, trabajando, pensando**).

-**er** VERBS　　Drop the -**er** and add -**iendo** (**comiendo, bebiendo, vendiendo, poniendo**).

-**ir** VERBS　　Drop the -**ir** and add -**iendo** (**abriendo, sufriendo, escribiendo, viviendo**).

Note that -**er** verbs and -**ir** verbs share the same present participle ending.

Estoy **hablando**.	*I am **speaking**.*
Estamos **estudiando**.	*We are **studying**.*
Estás **comiendo**.	*You are **eating**.*
Estáis **bebiendo** leche.	*You all are **drinking** milk.*
Él está **abriendo** la puerta.	*He is **opening** the door.*
Ellos están **escribiendo** una carta.	*They are **writing** a letter.*

For most verbs, the verb stem does not change: **hablar/hablando**, **comer/comiendo**, **abrir/abriendo**. However, with stem-changing -**ir** verbs, the present participle shows a stem change as well, for example, **mentir/mintiendo**, **dormir/durmiendo**, **pedir/pidiendo**.

EJERCICIO

In the course of an average day, which of the following things might you say you are doing? Put an X by those things.

1. _____ Estoy trabajando.

2. _____ Estoy estudiando español.

3. _____ Estoy practicando mi risa falsa (*my fake laugh*).

4. _____ Estoy vendiendo ropa.

5. _____ Estoy escribiendo una carta.

6. _____ Estoy pensando en mi familia.

7. _____ Estoy comprando comida.

8. _____ Estoy cocinando.

9. _____ Estoy contando el dinero.

10. _____ Estoy confesando un crimen.

11. _____ Estoy moviendo los muebles (*furniture*) en la casa.

12. _____ Estoy resolviendo mis problemas.

13. _____ Estoy lavando los platos.

14. _____ Estoy conduciendo el coche.

15. _____ No estoy haciendo nada.

16. _____ Estoy mintiendo a mis amigos.

17. _____ Estoy durmiendo en mi cama.

18. _____ No estoy pidiendo nada.

EJERCICIO

12·1

Traducción

1. *I am looking for a good book.*

   _____

2. *You are watching the television.*

   _____

3. *He is playing the piano.*

_____

4. *We are eating pizza and drinking lemonade.*

_____

5. *You all are receiving many gifts.*

_____

6. *You all [formal] are covering the furniture.*

_____

7. *We are eating lunch.*

_____

8. *I am thinking about my best friend.*

_____

9. *What are you doing?*

_____

10. *What is she eating?*

_____

11. *They are sleeping.*

_____

12. *She is lying to me.*

_____

Irregularly formed present participles

-Er and -ir verbs whose stem ends in a vowel (for example, **leer** or **influir**) require a slight twist when forming the present participle. With these verbs, the participle ending is -**yendo**: the *y* replaces the *ie*, to avoid having three vowels in a row. Several of these verbs, along with their respective present participles, are listed below.

-er verbs			**-ir verbs**		
atraer	to attract	atrayendo	construir	to construct	construyendo
caer	to fall	cayendo	contribuir	to contribute	contribuyendo
contraer	to contract	contrayendo	destruir	to destroy	destruyendo
creer	to believe	creyendo	fluir	to flow	fluyendo
leer	to read	leyendo	huir	to flee	huyendo
poseer	to possess	poseyendo	incluir	to include	incluyendo
raer	to scrape	rayendo	influir	to influence	influyendo
releer	to reread	releyendo	instituir	to institute	instituyendo
retraer	to bring back	retrayendo	ir	to go	yendo
sustraer	to remove	sustrayendo	oír	to hear	oyendo
traer	to bring	trayendo	sustituir	to substitute	sustituyendo

Note that the present participle for the verb **ir** is **yendo**.

*Think of one of your friends. Which of the following statements could you make about him or her in the course of an average day? Put an **X** by those things that he or she might be doing.*

1. _____ Está leyendo el periódico.

2. _____ Está contribuyendo dinero a la iglesia.

3. _____ Está trayendo los libros a la escuela.

4. _____ Está construyendo una casa.

5. _____ Está huyendo de la policía.

6. _____ Está releyendo un buen libro.

7. _____ Está destruyendo una casa.

8. _____ Está sustituyendo a un profesor en la escuela.

9. _____ Está oyendo mucho ruido (*noise*).

10. _____ Está influyendo mucho a otro amigo / otra amiga.

EJERCICIO

12·2

Traducción

1. *The river is flowing to the south.*

   _____

2. *The client is not believing the car salesman* (el vendedor de coches).

   _____

3. *We are not reading anything.*

   _____

4. *The president is not influencing the people.*

   _____

5. *Hatred* (el odio) *is destroying our society* (la sociedad).

   _____

6. *Romeo is fleeing with Juliet.*

   _____

7. *She isn't hearing anything in the basement* (el sótano).

   _____

8. *What are you reading?*

_____

9. *Who is bringing wine to the party?*

_____

10. *Why are you all* [formal] *constructing a house in the suburbs* (las afueras)?

_____

Present participles for stem-changing -ir verbs

For stem-changing -ir verbs, form the present participle as follows.

o > ue VERBS: **o > u**	**dormir > durmiendo**	sleeping
	morir > muriendo	dying
e > ie VERBS: **e > i**	**advertir > advirtiendo**	warning
	consentir > consintiendo	consenting
	hervir > hirviendo	boiling
	mentir > mintiendo	lying (telling untruths)
	preferir > prefiriendo	preferring
	referir > refiriendo	referring
	sentir > sintiendo	feeling, regretting
	sugerir > sugiriendo	suggesting
e > i VERBS: **e > i**	**competir > compitiendo**	competing
	conseguir > consiguiendo	getting
	decir > diciendo	saying, telling
	medir > midiendo	measuring
	pedir > pidiendo	requesting
	reír > riendo	laughing
	repetir > repitiendo	repeating
	seguir > siguiendo	following
	servir > sirviendo	serving

EJERCICIO
12·3

Complete each sentence with an appropriate present participle from the list above to make a meaningful sentence.

1. El gato está _____ en el sofá.

2. Pinocho está _____ a Gepetto.

3. Yo estoy _____ el agua para preparar el café.

4. La criada (*maid*) está _____ la cena.

5. Los niños se están _____ del payaso (*clown*).

6. Los Yanquis de Nueva York están _____ contra las Medias Blancas de Chicago.

7. El cómico está _____ bromas (*jokes*) al público.

8. Después de probar el insecticida, las cucarachas se están _____.

9. La policía está _____ el carro del criminal.

10. El adolescente está _____ a sus padres las llaves del carro.

Object pronouns with the present progressive

When a verb in the present progressive takes an object or objects, the object(s) are attached directly to the present participle. When there are two objects, remember the **RID** rule: **R**eflexive, **I**ndirect, **D**irect. This is the only order in which object pronouns can appear. Note the use of accents below, which are necessary to maintain the present participle's original stress.

Estoy **mirándolo**.	*I am **watching it**.*
Estamos **discutiéndolo**.	*We are **discussing it**.*
Estás **escribiéndole**.	*You are **writing to him**.*
Estáis **cantándonos**.	*You all are **singing to us**.*
Él está **duchándose**.	*He is **taking a shower**.*
Ellos están **cepillándose los dientes**.	*They are **brushing their teeth**.*
Ella está **comprándoselo**.	*She is **buying it for herself**.*
Ellos están **haciéndomelos**.	*They are **making them for me**.*

EJERCICIO

*In the course of an average morning, which of the following statements might you be saying about yourself? Put an **X** before those actions.*

1. _____ Estoy duchándome.

2. _____ Estoy cepillándome los dientes.

3. _____ Estoy acostándome.

4. _____ Estoy bañándome.

5. _____ Estoy lavándome el pelo.

6. _____ Estoy quitándome la ropa.

7. _____ Estoy durmiéndome.

8. _____ Estoy viéndome en el espejo.

9. _____ Estoy preocupándome por el peso.

10. _____ Estoy sentándome para tomar café.

11. _____ Estoy poniéndome la ropa.

Traducción

1. *I am studying it* [m.].

   _____

2. *You are singing it* [f.] *to us.*

   _____

3. *He is writing me a letter.*

   _____

4. *Are you writing to them?*

   _____

5. *Why are you all* [formal] *telling me this?*

   _____

6. *Why are you telling it* [m.] *to me?*

   _____

7. *They* [m.] *are sitting down.*

   _____

8. *We are reading it* [m.].

   _____

9. *He is lying to me.*

   _____

10. *What are you giving me?*

    _____

11. *They* [m.] *are following us.*

    _____

12. *What is Lily reading to you?*

    _____

Traducción

VOCABULARIO	la audiencia	*audience*	el filete	*steak*
	el brebaje	*concoction*	la langosta	*lobster*
	cocinar	*to cook*	el músico	*musician*
	cortar	*to cut*	el supermercado	*supermarket*
	culinario	*culinary*	vegetariano	*vegetarian*
	de hecho	*in fact*	el/la víctima	*victim*

Hi. My name is Julia. I'm twenty-one years old and I'm a student at a famous culinary school. I don't know why I'm here; I don't like to cook. In fact, almost everything in the supermarket disgusts me. I'm a vegetarian, but here I am, preparing chicken, steak, and lobster for a group of professors who know that I'm a terrible cook. I can't say who is more frightened—I or my victims (there are five professors waiting for me in the dining room) who have to taste this concoction. I know that they are going to give me an "F" after eating this meal. I'm cutting the meat, but I'm dreaming about playing my guitar in front of an audience. I want to be a musician, not a cook.

_____

_____

_____

_____

_____

_____

_____

_____

_____

_____

THE PAST TENSES, THE FUTURE TENSE, THE CONDITIONAL TENSE, AND THE PRESENT AND PAST PERFECT TENSES

We have covered the present tense, together with its many nuances and various permutations. Now it's time to describe events of the past and the future. Remember that in Spanish **el tiempo** means both "time" and "tense." When working with the tenses (in any language), you add the element of time to your message.

In this section, you will learn how to describe events that occurred (preterite), used to occur (imperfect), will occur (future), would occur (conditional), have occurred (present perfect), and *had* occurred (past perfect). If English is your first language, you probably float easily and seamlessly among these six tenses.

One of the common by-products of studying another language, especially its various tenses, is a delight in understanding the intricacies of your native language and the realization of how sophisticated a process it is to move a message from one time to another. The old phrase "Even a six-year-old could do this" holds true here, because most young children already have mastered the tenses you are about to study. Realize, though, that while a youngster apparently moves effortlessly from one tense to another, it often takes an adult's mind to appreciate what's really going on.

The preterite tense

TENSE	Preterite
TIME	Refers to specific, completed past actions
KEY PHRASES	Certain time ("last night," "yesterday at 4:00," "last July 4th") or certain number of times
STRUCTURE	Simple tense: VERB BASE + VERB ENDING

The preterite tense allows you to refer to specific past actions performed at a fixed point in time, a specific number of times, or during an enclosed span of time.

The key to the preterite tense is the quantitative nature of the action. If the action is in the past and you can pinpoint when or how many times it occurred—as though there were a frame or box around the action—use the preterite tense. Consider the following sentences.

Fixed point in time

> I **called** you at **3:00**.
> He **bought** the car on **Tuesday afternoon**.
> We **watched** the movie **last night**.

Specific number of actions

> I **called** you **five times**.
> They **ate ten sandwiches**.
> She **read** the book **twice**.

Enclosed amount of time

> I **worked** for **eight hours**.
> The meeting **lasted two and a half hours**.
> He **lived** there for **two years**.

In each of the preceding sentences, the action's time is specific and measured in some way—by the clock, the calendar, or the number of times the action occurred.

Although an obvious feature of the preterite tense is that it quantifies action, the quantity of our actions is not always stated. Sometimes it is implied. Consider these sentences:

> I **went** to John's party.
> We **ate** at McDonald's.
> The meeting **was** boring.

In the first two sentences, the implication is that the person performed the action once. In the third, the implication is that the entire meeting, from beginning to end, was boring. In all of these sentences, the action is quantified, even if only by implication.

A good test for determining if a sentence is in the preterite is to consider if it is reasonable to ask "for how long?" or "when?" the action took place. For example, if someone tells you, "John called me," you can reasonably ask, "When?" and expect a specific answer. But if this person says, "John used to call me several times a day," you probably would be wasting your time if you asked "When?" or "How many times did he call you?"

In these examples, "John called me" takes the preterite, but "John used to call me several times a day" does not. (This latter sentence is in the imperfect tense, which will be discussed in the next chapter.)

Regular verbs in the preterite

To conjugate regular verbs in the preterite, do the following:

-ar VERBS   Drop the **-ar** infinitive ending, and add the following verb endings to the stem.

-é	-amos
-aste	-asteis
-ó	-aron

Below is the full conjugation of **hablar** ("to speak, talk") in the preterite tense.

hablar *to speak, talk*	
yo hablé	**nosotros hablamos**
tú hablaste	**vosotros hablasteis**
él/ella/usted habló	**ellos/ellas/ustedes hablaron**

Note that the **nosotros** form is identical in the preterite and the present tenses for **-ar** verbs. Don't worry: the context of the conversation will carry the meaning and its time.

Yo hablé.	*I spoke.*
Hablamos con Juan anoche.	*We spoke with John last night.*
Tú miraste la película.	*You watched the movie.*
Vosotros comprasteis palomitas.	*You all bought popcorn.*
Ella me **llamó** tres veces.	*She called me three times.*
Ellos contaron el dinero.	*They counted the money.*

-er AND **-ir** VERBS   Drop the **-er** or **-ir** infinitive ending, and add the following verb endings to the stem.

-í	-imos
-iste	-isteis
-ió	-ieron

Below is the full conjugation of **comer** ("to eat") in the preterite tense.

comer *to eat*	
yo comí	**nosotros comimos**
tú comiste	**vosotros comisteis**
él/ella/usted comió	**ellos/ellas/ustedes comieron**

Below is the full conjugation of **abrir** ("to open") in the preterite tense.

abrir *to open*	
yo **abrí**	nosotros **abrimos**
tú **abriste**	vosotros **abristeis**
él/ella/usted **abrió**	ellos **abrieron**

Escribí una carta.	*I wrote a letter.*
Comimos pizza.	*We ate pizza.*
Vendiste tu casa.	*You sold your house.*
Rompisteis las ventanas.	*You all broke the windows.*
Ella **bebió** tres vasos de agua.	*She drank three glasses of water.*
Ellos **abrieron** las cajas.	*They opened the boxes.*

NOTE Most stem-changing verbs do not show the stem change in the preterite tense. For example, see the **o > ue** stem-changing verb **contar** ("to count"): **yo cuento** ("I count"), **yo conté** ("I counted"). The exceptions to this pattern are certain stem-changing **-ir** verbs, which are discussed under Irregular verbs in the preterite, page 117.

Before working with usage of the preterite, it is important to be familiar with the more common preterite "markers," or words and phrases that indicate a specific time frame. Several are listed below.

VOCABULARIO

this morning	**esta mañana**	last week	**la semana pasada**
this afternoon	**esta tarde**	last month	**el mes pasado**
yesterday	**ayer**	last year	**el año pasado**
yesterday morning	**ayer por la mañana**	two days ago	**hace dos días**
yesterday afternoon	**ayer por la tarde**	a month ago	**hace un mes**
last night	**anoche**	___ ago	**hace ___**
last Saturday	**el sábado pasado**		

EJERCICIO

Para ti, ¿cuál es verdadero o falso?

1. _____ Hablé por teléfono ayer por la tarde.

2. _____ Comí una ensalada anoche.

3. _____ Abrí las ventanas de mi casa a las siete de la mañana.

4. _____ Miré la televisión anoche.

5. _____ Bebí jugo de naranja esta mañana.

6. _____ Asistí a la escuela la semana pasada.

7. _____ Compré un coche el año pasado.

8. _____ Vendí mi casa el mes pasado.

Traducción (Note that the last three sentences employ reflexive verbs.)

1. *I bought a shirt yesterday.* _____

2. *You studied last night.* _____

3. *She worked for two hours.* _____

4. *We washed the clothing last night.* _____

5. *They [m.] sang five songs.* _____

6. *I ran to the corner.* _____

7. *You wrote a letter.* _____

8. *She opened the door.* _____

9. *We didn't open those windows.* _____

10. *They [m.] sold the car.* _____

11. *We danced the tango last night.* _____

12. *They [m.] spoke with the owner.* _____

13. *I took a shower this morning.* _____

14. *You washed your hair two hours ago.* _____

15. *They [f.] went to bed at eleven thirty.* _____

¡Te toca a ti! *Responde a cada una de las preguntas siguientes con una frase completa.*

1. ¿Hablaste por teléfono anoche?

_____

2. ¿Dónde te compraste la camisa?

_____

3. ¿Qué comiste anoche?

_____

4. ¿Qué recibiste para tu último cumpleaños?

_____

5. ¿Escuchaste la radio hoy?

_____

6. ¿Tomaste café ayer por la mañana?

_____

7. ¿Bailaste el fin de semana pasado?

_____

8. ¿Estudiaste español el año pasado?

_____

Traducción _All of the verbs in the following paragraph are regular, but you will need to use both present and preterite tenses._ **¡Ojo!** (Watch out!)

VOCABULARIO

acabarse	_to end_	inmediatamente	_immediately_
el baile	_ball, dance_	llorar	_to cry_
barrer	_to sweep_	la madrastra	_stepmother_
besar	_to kiss_	la medianoche	_midnight_
la canción	_song_	el palacio	_palace_
conocer	_to know, meet_	el príncipe	_prince_
cruel	_cruel_	quitar el polvo	_to dust_
de repente	_all of a sudden; suddenly_	regalar	_to give (a gift)_
enamorarse	_to fall in love_	el rey	_king_
entrar en	_to enter_	el suelo	_floor_
el hada madrina	_fairy godmother_	todo el día	_all day long_
la hermanastra	_stepsister_	volverse loco/loca	_to go crazy_

My name is Cinderella. I live with my stepmother and my two stepsisters. They are very cruel. Two days ago, all day long, I worked: I cleaned the house, washed the clothes, prepared the meals, dusted the furniture, and swept the floors. They watched TV and ate all day long. Then, at six o'clock they left for the ball at the king's palace. I cried for ten minutes, and I sang a song. All of a sudden, my fairy godmother appeared in the living room. She gave me a dress and shoes, and I left for the ball. I entered the palace and met the prince. Immediately we fell in love. We danced until midnight, and I ran from the palace because my special night ended. I lost (perder) one of my new shoes. This afternoon, the prince arrived with my shoe. We kissed and then we flew to Las Vegas and got married. My stepmother and stepsisters went crazy.

_____

_____

_____

_____

_____

_____

_____

Orthographic changes in regular verbs

There are three standard orthographic, or spelling, changes in Spanish that affect verbs in the preterite, as well as in other tenses. In the preterite, these changes occur only in the first-person singular (**yo**) form. All other conjugated forms are regular in the preterite. These orthographic changes are as follows.

VERBS ENDING WITH **-gar**   The **g** changes to **gu** before **e**: **yo llegué** ("I arrived").

VERBS ENDING WITH **-car**   The **c** changes to **qu** before **e**: **yo practiqué** ("I practiced").

VERBS ENDING WITH **-zar**   The **z** changes to **c** before **e**: **yo empecé** ("I began").

The reason for the first two orthographic changes is to retain the sounds present in the infinitives. In order to retain the hard **g** sound in those infinitives ending with -gar, the letter **g** must become **gu** before the **e** in the **yo** form. Likewise, in order to retain the hard **c** sound in those infinitives ending with -car, the letter **c** must be replaced by the **qu** combination before the **e** in the **yo** form. (The letters **g** and **c** naturally have soft sounds before the vowels **e** and **i**.) The reason for the third orthographic change is that the letter **z** never immediately precedes the letter **e** in Spanish (except in a very few cases that are borrowed from other languages). Replacing the **z** with the letter **c** retains the soft sound present in the infinitive.

Below are several common verbs with orthographic changes in the preterite, along with their respective **yo** forms.

VOCABULARIO

g > gu

llegar	to arrive	yo llegué
jugar	to play (*a game*)	yo jugué
pagar	to pay (for)	yo pagué
regar	to water (*a plant*)	yo regué
segar	to mow (*grass, etc.*)	yo segué
tragar	to swallow	yo tragué
vagar	to wander	yo vagué

c > qu

aparcar	to park	yo aparqué
buscar	to look for, search	yo busqué
clarificar	to clarify	yo clarifiqué
clasificar	to classify	yo clasifiqué
destacar	to stand out	yo destaqué
empacar	to pack	yo empaqué
justificar	to justify	yo justifiqué
practicar	to practice	yo practiqué
sacar	to take out, take (*a picture*)	yo saqué
tocar	to touch, play (*an instrument*)	yo toqué

z > c

autorizar	to authorize	yo autoricé
comenzar	to commence, begin	yo comencé
empezar	to begin	yo empecé
organizar	to organize	yo organicé
rezar	to pray	yo recé
simbolizar	to symbolize	yo simbolicé
trazar	to trace	yo tracé
tropezarse (con)	to bump into	yo me tropecé

NOTE Although the verbs showing these orthographic changes do not follow exactly the regular pattern of forming the preterite tense, they are still considered regular verbs in the preterite, because these are standard orthographic changes that occur at all times in all tenses.

EJERCICIO
13·4

Traducción

1. *I practiced the piano for an hour.*

   _____

2. *I arrived at two o'clock.*

   _____

3. *I organized the party.*

   _____

4. *I began to dance on the table.*

   _____

5. *I played the guitar for two hours at the reception.*

   _____

6. *I played tennis with the pro* (el jugador profesional).

   _____

7. *I took twenty pictures of my cat.*

   _____

8. *I authorized the purchase a week ago.*

   _____

9. *I classified the information.*

   _____

10. *I bumped into your house's step* (el peldaño).

    _____

11. *I parked the car in the parking garage (el estacionamiento) three hours ago.*

   _____

12. *I never stood out in English class for my pronunciation.*

   _____

13. *I swallowed the medicine without thinking.*

   _____

14. *I paid the gas bill.*

   _____

15. *I watered my friend Lola's plants.*

   _____

Traducción

VOCABULARIO	el borrador	*eraser*	la mascota	*pet*
	la cuenta	*bill*	la planta	*plant*
	deshacerse de	*to get rid of*	sacar fotos	*to take photos*
	después de eso	*after that*	los trastos	*junk*

Yesterday I played for one hour and worked for ten hours. I played cards with my friends in the morning. After that, I paid all my bills, watered the plants, practiced the piano, took photos of my pets, organized the junk in the garage, justified the possession of the junk, and prayed for a giant eraser in order to get rid of everything.

_____

_____

_____

_____

_____

_____

Irregular verbs in the preterite

There are several irregular verbs in the preterite. While patterns do emerge and the endings are similar, it is important to understand the various types of conjugations.

Verbs with irregular stems and a special set of endings

Below is a set of endings that are used with several common irregular verbs in the preterite.

-e	-imos
-iste	-isteis
-o	-ieron

Fortunately, the irregular stems that take these endings follow three recognizable patterns:

+ **Andar**, **estar**, and **tener** have the letters **uv** in the irregular preterite stem.
+ **Caber**, **haber**, **poder**, **poner**, and **saber** have a **u** in the irregular preterite stem.
+ **Hacer**, **querer**, and **venir** have an **i** in the irregular preterite stem.

Below are eleven verbs that take these endings, along with their conjugated forms in the preterite.

VOCABULARIO

Verbs that have uv in the irregular preterite stem

andar	to walk	anduv-	anduve, anduviste, anduvo, anduvimos, anduvisteis, anduvieron
estar	to be	estuv-	estuve, estuviste, estuvo, estuvimos, estuvisteis, estuvieron
tener	to have	tuv-	tuve, tuviste, tuvo, tuvimos, tuvisteis, tuvieron

Verbs that have u in the irregular preterite stem

caber	to fit	cup-	cupe, cupiste, cupo, cupimos, cupisteis, cupieron
haber	to have (*auxiliary*)	hub-	hube, hubiste, hubo, hubimos, hubisteis, hubieron
poder	to be able to	pud-	pude, pudiste, pudo, pudimos, pudisteis, pudieron
poner	to put, place	pus-	puse, pusiste, puso, pusimos, pusisteis, pusieron
saber	to know, find out	sup-	supe, supiste, supo, supimos, supisteis, supieron

Verbs that have i in the irregular preterite stem

hacer	to make, do	hic-	hice, hiciste, hizo, hicimos, hicisteis, hicieron
querer	to want	quis-	quise, quisiste, quiso, quisimos, quisisteis, quisieron
venir	to come	vin-	vine, viniste, vino, vinimos, vinisteis, vinieron

---

NOTES

1 The only exception in these patterns is found in the third-person singular of **hacer**, which is **hizo**. (The **c** changes to **z** to avoid the hard **c** sound.)

2 There are no accent marks on these irregular endings.

Para ti, ¿cuál es verdadero o falso?

1. _____ Tuve una fiesta hace dos semanas.

2. _____ Anduve a la escuela esta mañana.

3. _____ Anoche no pude dormir.

4. _____ No hice nada ayer.

5. _____ El fin de semana pasado, alguien vino a mi casa.

6. _____ Puse los zapatos en el armario anoche.

7. _____ Estuve increíblemente enfermo/enferma ayer.

8. _____ No pude dormir anoche.

Traducción

1. *I walked through the park.*

_____

2. *He came to my party.*

_____

3. *Last night I couldn't sleep.*

_____

4. *They [m.] had an accident last Tuesday.*

_____

5. *We made the beds this morning.*

_____

6. *When did you know the answer?*

_____

7. *You all were here for no more than ten minutes.*

_____

8. *I put the clothes in the closet.*

_____

9. *What did you do last night?*

_____

10. *They [f.] had to work for ten hours yesterday.*

_____

11. *I put on my shoes.*

_____

12. *We were there for half an hour.*

_____

13. *Who made the beds?*

_____

14. *She didn't come to the meeting, because she had an accident.*

_____

15. *I was in the store for twenty minutes and then I came here.*

_____

EJERCICIO

¡Te toca a ti! ¿Qué hiciste ayer? *Write ten sentences to tell what you did yesterday. Use the first-person singular form of the verb in the preterite tense.*

1. _____

2. _____

3. _____

4. _____

5. _____

6. _____

7. _____

8. _____

9. _____

10. _____

Traducción

VOCABULARIO la acera   *sidewalk*
el bolsillo   *pocket*
el cerrajero *locksmith*
la llave   *key*

*I was very sad last night. I had a horrible day at work. I was so bored! I arrived home at 10 P.M.
I know that I put my keys in my pocket, but I couldn't find them. I had to call a locksmith. He went
to my house and didn't arrive until midnight. I fell asleep on the sidewalk.*

_____

_____

_____

_____

_____

Ser and ir

The preterite conjugations for **ser** and **ir** are identical. But don't worry—you'll be able to tell by the
context which verb is required. **Ser** is used far less often than **ir** in the preterite.

ser *to be*		**ir** *to go*	
fui	fuimos	fui	fuimos
fuiste	fuisteis	fuiste	fuisteis
fue	fueron	fue	fueron

Below are several example sentences using **ser** and **ir** in the preterite. Note that the conjugated
verb forms are identical in Spanish, but context and usage make clear that two different verbs are
involved. Conjugated forms of **ir** are nearly always followed by the preposition **a** ("to").

ser

Yo **fui** presidente del club por dos años.	*I **was** president of the club for two years.*
Tú **fuiste** principal de la escuela por cinco años.	*You **were** principal of the school for five years.*
Nelson Mandela **fue** prisionero político por veintisiete años.	*Nelson Mandela **was** a political prisoner for twenty-seven years.*
Nosotros **fuimos** universitarios por cuatro años.	*We **were** university students for four years.*
Fuisteis generales en el ejército por diez años.	*All of you **were** generals in the army for ten years.*
Ellos **fueron** jueces por cuarenta años.	*They **were** judges for forty years.*

ir

Yo **fui** a México el año pasado.
Tú **fuiste** al cine anoche.
Dan Harris **fue** al Centro de Meditación.
Fuimos a Ámsterdam para nuestra
　luna de miel.
¿**Fuisteis** a la luna con un mono?
Ellos **fueron** a Cuba tres veces el año
　pasado.

I **went** to Mexico last year.
You **went** to the movies last night.
Dan Harris **went** to the Meditation Center.
We **went** to Amsterdam for our honeymoon.

Did all of you **go** to the moon with a monkey?
They **went** to Cuba three times last year.

EJERCICIO
13·8

Traducción

1. *I went to the game.*

　_____

2. *I was president of the club for one year.*

　_____

3. *He went to the store (in order) to buy eggs.*

　_____

4. *Why did you go away?*

　_____

5. *They [f.] didn't go yesterday because they went last week.*

　_____

6. *We didn't go to the wedding.*

　_____

7. *Did you all go to school today?*

　_____

8. *Who was the big winner yesterday?*

　_____

9. *The party was terrible.*

　_____

10. *The meeting went well.*

　_____

11. *Anita and Pepe were girlfriend and boyfriend* (los novios) *for two years, but they never went
to the movies.*

　_____

12. *He was my best friend for ten years.*

　_____

13. *We went separately (por separado) to the same store.*

_____

14. *Where did you all [formal] go last night?*

_____

15. *How was the party? It was a disaster!*

_____

Decir and traer

The verbs **decir** ("to say, tell") and **traer** ("to bring") are conjugated in the preterite as follows.

decir *to say, tell*		**traer** *to bring*	
dije	dijimos	traje	trajimos
dijiste	dijisteis	trajiste	trajisteis
dijo	dijeron	trajo	trajeron

Below are verbs related to, and conjugated in the same manner as, **traer**.

VOCABULARIO

atraer	to attract	**atraje, atrajiste, atrajo, atrajimos, atrajisteis, atrajeron**
distraer	to distract	**distraje, distrajiste, distrajo, distrajimos, distrajisteis, distrajeron**
retraer	to bring back, dissuade	**retraje, retrajiste, retrajo, retrajimos, retrajisteis, retrajeron**
sustraer	to remove, take away	**sustraje, sustrajiste, sustrajo, sustrajimos, sustrajisteis, sustrajeron**

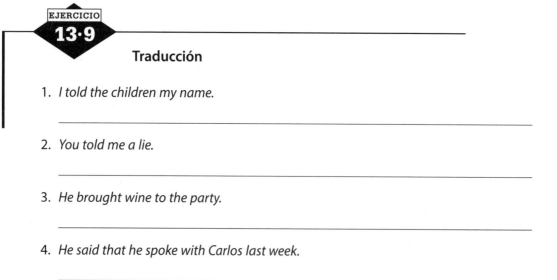

EJERCICIO
13·9

Traducción

1. *I told the children my name.*

_____

2. *You told me a lie.*

_____

3. *He brought wine to the party.*

_____

4. *He said that he spoke with Carlos last week.*

_____

5. We said that we didn't eat the cookies.

_____

6. The television distracted me.

_____

7. What did you all [formal] say to Mary?

_____

8. What did you tell her?

_____

9. His manners (los modales) attracted me.

_____

10. What did he say when you told him that you wrote the letter?

_____

11. I didn't tell them anything.

_____

12. What did you bring us?

_____

13. They [m.] didn't tell me the truth.

_____

14. Did he tell you what (lo que) he told me yesterday?

_____

15. The sugar attracted the flies.

_____

Dar and ver

Because the verbs **dar** and **ver** are very similar in their preterite conjugations, they are easy to learn together. While **dar** is clearly irregular, **ver** is irregular only in that the accent marks on the first- and third-person singular are omitted. Below are the full conjugations for **dar** and **ver** in the preterite.

dar _to give_		**ver** _to see_	
di	**dimos**	**vi**	vimos
diste	**disteis**	viste	visteis
dio	**dieron**	**vio**	vieron

Traducción

1. *I gave John a package yesterday.*

   _____

2. *I saw John yesterday.*

   _____

3. *She gave me a book.*

   _____

4. *She saw us at the movies.*

   _____

5. *What did you give him for his birthday?*

   _____

6. *Which movie did you all see last night?*

   _____

7. *When they saw me, they gave me the money.*

   _____

8. *You all* [formal] *didn't give us anything.*

   _____

9. *Did you see the cat that Miguel gave me?*

   _____

10. *I didn't see the present that they gave us.*

   _____

Traducción

VOCABULARIO			
el/la agente de viajes	*travel agent*	el pájaro	*bird*
la arena	*sand*	la playa	*beach*
¡ay!	*alas!*	la pulgada	*inch*
al día siguiente	*the next day*	relajarse	*to relax*
la diversión	*fun*	sacar	*to take out*
nevar	*to snow*	la selva tropical	*rain forest*
ofrecer	*to offer*	el traje de baño	*bathing suit*

I went to Puerto Rico last January. It was wonderful! A friend of mine is a travel agent, and when she offered me the opportunity to go to the Caribbean for a week of sun and fun—for very little money—I said to her, "When do we go?" The day we left, it snowed six inches here. When we arrived in San Juan, sun, heat, and sand greeted us. We took a taxi to our hotel, I took my bathing suit out of my suitcase, and we went to the beach. The next day we went to El Yunque, the rain forest, where we walked for hours and saw many beautiful birds and trees. I couldn't believe it—it was so beautiful! The next day we went to Luquillo Beach and swam and read and relaxed. We did this every day until—alas!—we had to return to reality.

Stem-changing -ir verbs

Most stem-changing verbs change only in the present. However, stem-changing **-ir** verbs make small changes in the preterite as well. There are three groups of stem-changing **-ir** verbs in the present tense, and each one has a specific stem change in the preterite, but only in the third-person singular and plural.

In verbs with the **o** > **ue** stem change in the present, the preterite shows an **o** > **u** stem change in the third-person forms.

dormir *to sleep*	
dormí	dormimos
dormiste	dormisteis
durmió	**durmieron**

In verbs with the **e** > **ie** stem change in the present, the preterite shows an **e** > **i** stem change in the third-person forms.

mentir *to lie*	
mentí	mentimos
mentiste	mentisteis
mintió	**mintieron**

In verbs with the **e > i** stem change in the present, the preterite shows an **e > i** stem change in the third-person forms.

pedir *to request, ask for*

pedí	pedimos
pediste	pedisteis
pidió	**pidieron**

Below are several common verbs in each of these groups of stem-changing **-ir** verbs.

VOCABULARIO

o > ue verbs in the present tense

dormir	to sleep
morir	to die

e > ie verbs in the present tense

advertir	to advise, warn
mentir	to lie
preferir	to prefer
sentir(se)	to feel

e > i verbs in the present tense

medir	to measure, be long
pedir	to request, ask for
repetir	to repeat
seguir	to follow, continue
servir	to serve

EJERCICIO
13·12

Traducción

1. *She slept for ten hours.*

_____

2. *They [m.] lied to me.*

_____

3. *He requested more coffee.*

_____

4. *The cockroaches died.*

_____

5. *Our lawyer warned us of the danger* (el peligro).

_____

6. *At that moment, she preferred not to say anything.*

_____

7. *Did they advise you of your rights?*

_____

8. *Dorothy followed the yellow brick* (el ladrillo) *road.*

_____

9. *They [m.] repeated the question twice.*

_____

10. *He asked his boss for a raise* (el aumento).

_____

Verbs that change i to y in the preterite

For those -**er** and -**ir** verbs with a vowel immediately preceding the infinitive ending, the verb ending for the preterite forms follows this pattern: The third-person singular verb ending changes from -**ío** to -**yó**, and the third-person plural verb ending changes from -**ieron** to -**yeron**, and in all other conjugated forms in the preterite (instead of only the first-person singular form), the i becomes **í** (with a written accent).

creer *to believe*	
creí	creímos
creíste	creísteis
creyó	**creyeron**

Below are several common verbs with the **i > y** change in the preterite, together with their third-person singular and plural forms showing the change.

VOCABULARIO

caer	to fall	cayó	cayeron
caer(se)	to fall down	se cayó	se cayeron
creer	to believe	creyó	creyeron
leer	to read	leyó	leyeron
oír	to hear	oyó	oyeron
poseer	to possess	poseyó	poseyeron
proveer	to provide	proveyó	proveyeron

There are a few exceptions to this pattern.

1 The verb **traer** and its compound verbs **atraer** and **distraer** follow a different pattern for their conjugations in the preterite. See page 122.

2 Verbs ending with -**guir** (for example, **seguir**) simply follow the pattern for stem-changing -**ir** verbs, because the **u** is not pronounced.

3 Verbs ending with **-uir** not preceded by **g** (for example, **destruir**) make the change **i > y** in the third-person conjugated forms, but all the other conjugated forms follow the regular pattern.

destruir *to destroy*

destruí	destruimos
destruiste	destruisteis
destruyó	**destruyeron**

Below are several common verbs that are conjugated like **destruir** in the preterite, together with their third-person forms.

VOCABULARIO

construir	to build, construct	**construyó**	construyeron
contribuir	to contribute	**contribuyó**	contribuyeron
destruir	to destroy	**destruyó**	destruyeron
fluir	to flow, run	**fluyó**	fluyeron
huir	to flee, run away, escape	**huyó**	huyeron
incluir	to include	**incluyó**	incluyeron
influir	to influence	**influyó**	influyeron

EJERCICIO
13·13

Traducción

1. *John didn't hear me.*

   _____

2. *They [f.] read my book twice.*

   _____

3. *The trees fell down during the storm.*

   _____

4. *Three inmates (el preso) escaped from the prison (la cárcel) last night.*

   _____

5. *The caterers (el abastecedor) didn't provide enough bread.*

   _____

6. *The thieves (el ladrón) destroyed our house.*

   _____

7. *Did you read my newspaper?*

   _____

8. *They [m.] contributed one hundred fifty dollars last year.*

_____

9. *The dish ran away with the spoon.*

_____

10. *Humpty Dumpty fell down.*

_____

11. *The tears flowed from my eyes.*

_____

12. *The branch fell from the tree.*

_____

13. *They fled from the scene of the crime.*

_____

14. *They constructed an enormous house.*

_____

15. *Why didn't he include us?*

_____

Verbs ending with -ucir

All verbs ending with **-ucir** are conjugated like **producir**, where the **c** changes to **j**, and the endings are **-e, -iste, -o, -imos, -isteis, -eron**.

producir *to produce*	
produje	produjimos
produjiste	produjisteis
produjo	produjeron

Below are several common verbs that are conjugated like **producir**.

VOCABULARIO			
conducir	to drive, lead	condujo	condujeron
deducir	to deduce, infer	dedujo	dedujeron
inducir	to induce, lead	indujo	indujeron
introducir	to introduce	introdujo	introdujeron
producir	to produce	produjo	produjeron
reducir	to reduce, cut down	redujo	redujeron
traducir	to translate	tradujo	tradujeron

Traducción

1. *I produced a movie last year.*

   _____

2. *You translated the document well.*

   _____

3. *We drove to the theater.*

   _____

4. *The magician produced a rabbit from the hat.*

   _____

5. *You all drove twenty miles.*

   _____

6. *I translated this sentence from English to Spanish.*

   _____

7. *We led the boys to the cafeteria.*

   _____

8. *They drove us to the wedding.*

   _____

9. *How many pages did you translate?*

   _____

10. *How far* (hasta dónde) *did you drive?*

    _____

11. *I deduced the answer.*

    _____

12. *The president didn't reduce taxes* (el impuesto) *last year.*

    _____

¿Verdadero o falso?

1. _____ En el cuento de Ricitos de Oro (*Goldilocks*), la chica durmió en la cama del osito.

2. _____ Un árbol se cayó en mi casa anoche.

3. _____ Bollywood produjo muchas películas el año pasado.

4. _____ Romeo y Julieta huyeron a Las Vegas para casarse.

5. _____ Durante su vida R. Buckminster Fuller construyó varios cúpulas geodésicas.

6. _____ El mejor taxista en Londres probablemente condujo miles de kilómetros ayer.

7. _____ Muchas personas creen que la presidencia de Richard Nixon (Estados Unidos, 1969–1974) fue un desastre.

8. _____ Yo fui a la luna la semana pasada.

9. _____ Millones de personas pidieron hamburguesas en McDonald's el año pasado.

10. _____ Pinocho nunca mintió, ni una sola vez.

11. _____ El cantante Michael Jackson y la actriz Farrah Fawcett murieron el mismo día en 2009 (el 25 de junio).

12. _____ No más de cien personas durmieron en hoteles anoche.

Traducción

VOCABULARIO	la clase	class, type	el idioma	language (particular)
	el credo	ethic	el lenguaje	language (general)
	la cuestión	issue	nacer	to be born
	el ensayo	essay	la política	politics
	el escritor	writer	la riqueza	richness

H. L. Mencken was a great writer. He was born in Baltimore in 1880, where he lived his entire life, and he died in 1956. He wrote many essays on politics and social issues, but his principal interest, I believe, was language—in particular, the English of the United States. One of his most famous books is The American Language, in which Mencken discussed the richness of the United States and how many other languages influenced this language. He also produced a series of autobiographies and diaries. He read all types of literature and possessed a very strict personal ethic. He believed that a person should work hard, play hard, and, above all, think.

Verbs that change meaning in the preterite

Because the preterite tense implies that an action occurred either at a specific time or over a specific period of time, certain verbs change meaning in this tense. Note that the action of the following verbs is more mental or emotional than physical.

	PRESENT	PRETERITE
conocer	*to know (a person/place)*	*to meet* **Conocí** a Juan la semana pasada. *I met John last week.*
poder	*to be able (to do something)*	*to manage (to do something)* **Ella pudo** encontrarlo. *She managed to find it.*
no poder	*not to be able (to do something)*	*to fail (to do something)* **No pudimos** encontrarlo. *We couldn't find it.* OR *We failed to find it.*
querer	*to want*	*to try* **Quise** salir. *I tried to leave.*
no querer	*not to want*	*to refuse* **Él no quiso** comer. *He refused to eat.*
saber	*to know (a fact/information)*	*to find out, learn about* ¿Cuándo lo **supiste**? *When did you find (it) out?* OR *When did you learn about it?*
sentir	*to feel*	*to regret, be sorry* **Sentí** llamarla. *I regretted calling her.* OR *I was sorry I called her.*
tener	*to have*	*to have (at a certain time)* **Ella tuvo** un bebé ayer. *She had a baby yesterday.*

EJERCICIO

Para ti, ¿cuál es verdadero o falso?

1. _____ No pude dormir anoche.

2. _____ Conocí a mi mejor amigo/amiga hace más de cinco años.

3. _____ Tuve un accidente de coche el año pasado.

4. _____ Pude pagar los impuestos el año pasado antes del quince de abril.

5. _____ Leí el periódico esta mañana y supe mucho de los dilemas políticos.

6. _____ En mi cumpleaños pasado no quise comer nada.

7. _____ Una amiga mía tuvo un bebé este año.

8. _____ Mis padres se conocieron en una cita a ciegas (*blind date*).

9. _____ Muchos políticos no pudieron cumplir la palabra este año.

10. _____ Mi mejor amigo/amiga tuvo una fiesta en su casa el sábado pasado.

EJERCICIO
13·17

Traducción

1. *I met Lisa twenty-five years ago.*

_____

2. *He failed to see my point of view.*

_____

3. *They [m.] didn't find (it) out until fifteen years ago.*

_____

4. *My niece had a baby last December.*

_____

5. *Why did you all refuse to leave?*

_____

6. *He regretted winning the money.*

_____

7. *She tried to leave but couldn't find her keys.*

_____

8. *I managed to pay the bills on time this month.*

_____

9. *We met each other on an elevator.*

_____

10. *I found out that Jane managed to forge* (falsificar) *my signature.*

_____

EJERCICIO
13·18

Traducción

VOCABULARIO

el ataque de corazón	*heart attack*	levantarse	*to stand*
caerse	*to fall down*	rendirse	*to give up*
el cuarto	*quarter*	tacklear	*to tackle*
el estado de coma inducido	*medically induced coma*	tomar lugar	*to take place*
		tratar	*to treat*

The world met Damar Hamlin on Monday, January 2, 2023, during a football game between the Cincinnati Bengals and the Buffalo Bills (of New York). The game took place in Cincinnati, Ohio. Damar (of the Bills), only 24 years old, tackled Tee Higging (of the Bengals) in the first quarter at 8:55 p.m. Everything was normal, but suddenly Damar couldn't stand, and he fell down. Several doctors entered the field and treated him. He went to the hospital by ambulance. Shortly after, viewers found out that Damar had a heart attack and almost died. But he refused to give up, and after three days in a medically-induced coma, Damar woke up. His progress continued, and he was able to leave the hospital nine days later.

The imperfect tense

TENSE	Imperfect
TIME	Refers to nonspecific, continuous past actions
KEY PHRASES	"Used to," "was + _____-ing," "would," "always"
STRUCTURE	Simple tense: VERB BASE + VERB ENDING

We use the imperfect tense when referring to actions that took place in the past, either repeatedly or over an extended period of time. It also indicates that an action in the past took place during an unspecified span of time. This differs significantly from the preterite, which is used to specify an action either at a particular point in time or for a specific number of times.

In fact, the element of time, though certainly in the past, is necessarily *not* specific for actions expressed in the imperfect. In these situations, it is simply irrelevant. Therefore, for situations expressed in the imperfect, one cannot determine when the action began or ended, the exact time it occurred, or the number of times it occurred.

Consider the following sentences.

> *I used to live in St. Louis.*
> *John always ate cereal for breakfast.*
> *Abby was a good conversationalist.*

In the first sentence, the message clearly states that I lived in St. Louis in the past; however, *when* or *for how long* is not mentioned. While this action could be quantified (for example, I lived in St. Louis *for four years*), in this sentence the speaker has chosen not to do so. Thus, in this case, the length of time is irrelevant.

In the second sentence, we know that in the past John ate cereal for breakfast. The addition of the word *always*, however, indicates both that he did so many, many times and that it would be virtually impossible to find out exactly how many times he did eat cereal for breakfast. In this case, the number of times cannot be determined.

The last sentence is a description of something that was ongoing. In fact, there is no real action involved other than being good at something. The time involved most likely would be "most of Abby's life." As in the first sentence, the exact amount of time is irrelevant in this context and, as in the second example, it would be impossible to determine exactly how long she was able to keep up her end of a conversation.

The essence of the imperfect tense is that the specific elements of time are missing. Messages in the imperfect do not tell us *when specifically*, but rather *when in general*. To summarize, the imperfect tense is used to refer to past actions in the following situations.

- The length of time over which the action occurred is irrelevant.
- The number of times the action occurred cannot be determined.
- The action is one of "being" in the past in a situation that was ongoing.

Regular verbs in the imperfect

Nearly all verbs in the imperfect are regular. To form the imperfect, follow the patterns below.

-ar VERBS   Drop the **-ar** infinitive ending and add the following verb endings.

-aba	-ábamos
-abas	-abais
-aba	-aban

Below are the full conjugations of **hablar** and **estudiar** in the imperfect tense.

hablar *to speak, talk*		**estudiar** *to study*	
hablaba	hablábamos	estudiaba	estudiábamos
hablabas	hablabais	estudiabas	estudiabais
hablaba	hablaban	estudiaba	estudiaban

-er AND **-ir** VERBS   Drop the **-er** or **-ir** infinitive ending and add the following verb endings.

-ía	-íamos
-ías	-íais
-ía	-ían

Below are the full conjugations of **comer** and **vivir** in the imperfect tense.

comer *to eat*		**vivir** *to live*	
comía	comíamos	vivía	vivíamos
comías	comíais	vivías	vivíais
comía	comían	vivía	vivían

Irregular verbs in the imperfect

There are only three verbs that are irregular in the imperfect—**ser**, **ir**, and **ver**. Their full conjugations in the imperfect are below.

ser *to be*		**ir** *to go*		**ver** *to see*	
era	éramos	iba	íbamos	veía	veíamos
eras	erais	ibas	ibais	veías	veíais
era	eran	iba	iban	veía	veían

Note that for all verbs—regular and irregular—the first- and third-person singular forms are identical in the imperfect tense.

When to use the imperfect

Habitual or continuous action in the past

In English, we often use the phrase "used to," as in "I used to live in Texas" or "They used to eat in that restaurant." In these cases, there is no indication of when or how many times this action occurred or how long it lasted.

EJERCICIO

¿Cuál es verdadero o falso para ti?

1. _____ Vivías en Nueva York.

2. _____ Jugabas con muñecas.

3. _____ De niño/niña, tenías un perro.

4. _____ Mirabas *Barrio Sésamo* (*Sesame Street*).

5. _____ Trabajabas en un restaurante.

6. _____ Leías la revista *Highlights*.

7. _____ Masticabas chicle en la escuela.

8. _____ Montabas en triciclo.

9. _____ Almorzabas en una cafetería.

10. _____ Ibas a la escuela en autobús.

11. _____ Saltabas en la cama.

12. _____ Tomabas vitaminas.

EJERCICIO
14·1

Traducción

1. *I used to study with John.*

   _____

2. *He used to work in a bank.*

   _____

3. *We used to live in an apartment.*

   _____

4. *They [m.] used to write notes to their friends in class.*

   _____

5. You used to read lots of magazines.

_____

6. You all used to open the windows in January.

_____

7. I used to make my bed every morning.

_____

8. Mickey Mantle used to play baseball for the Yankees.

_____

9. They [f.] used to call us every night.

_____

10. Where did you used to work?

_____

11. Where did you all [formal] used to live?

_____

12. He used to swim in our pool (la piscina).

_____

13. Mark used to be president of our club.

_____

14. I used to go to Ravello, Italy, every winter.

_____

15. We used to invite everybody to our parties.

_____

Simple description

Many times sentences in the imperfect simply describe how things were. Whereas the preterite often emphasizes physical action, the imperfect frequently focuses on background description. It references what things were like, rather than what happened. The verb **ser**, which is used for description, origin, and time, and the verb **estar**, used to denote location, short-term conditions, and the result of an action, are both used frequently in such situations. Consider the following sentences.

Compré un coche.	PRETERITE (specific action)	I **bought** a car.
El coche **era** rojo.	IMPERFECT (description)	The car **was** red.
Ana **se casó**.	PRETERITE (specific action)	Ana **got married**.
Ana **estaba** casada.	IMPERFECT (description)	Ana **was** married.

Descriptions involving a person's profession or role in the past are in the imperfect, because they refer to what the person "used to" be or do. In addition, it would often be difficult, if not impossible, to pinpoint when this "being" or "doing" began and ended.

¿Qué era? *Complete each of the following sentences with the appropriate profession. Choose from the selections that follow, using the plural form where appropriate.*

filósofo	arquitecto	bailarín	explorador
psiquiatra	payaso	político	escritor
detective	pianista	antropóloga	pintor

1. Winston Churchill era _____.

2. Frank Lloyd Wright era _____.

3. Emmett Kelly y Bozo eran _____.

4. Margaret Mead era _____.

5. Sherlock Holmes y Hercule Poirot eran _____.

6. Leo Tolstoy era _____.

7. Vladimir Horowitz y Jerry Lee Lewis eran _____.

8. Aristóteles era _____.

9. Pablo Picasso era _____.

10. Sigmund Freud era _____.

11. Rudolf Nureyev y Anna Pavlova eran _____.

12. Cristóbal Colón era _____.

Traducción

1. *My father was a farmer* (el granjero).

_____

2. *Mary had a little lamb* (el corderito).

_____

3. *We wore uniforms to school.*

_____

4. *I was embarrassed* (avergonzado).

_____

5. *The store didn't have the shirt that I wanted.*

_____

6. *The windows were open, but the door was closed.*

_____

7. *Susana was pregnant* (embarazada).

_____

8. *You all were wearing silly hats.*

_____

9. *George was tall and handsome.*

_____

10. *The cat was in the attic* (el desván).

_____

11. *My pen didn't work* (funcionar).

_____

12. *Where was the money?*

_____

13. *I had lots of friends at camp* (el campamento).

_____

14. *The cat was black and white.*

_____

15. *The monster had two heads.*

_____

Traducción

VOCABULARIO	la ciencia	science
	el científico, la científica	scientist
	la clase	class
	diferente	different
	la explosión	explosion
	fingir	to pretend
	el laboratorio	laboratory
	loco/loca	mad, crazy
	el médico, la médica	doctor
	menor	younger
	mezclar	to mix
	soñar con + INFINITIVE	to dream of (being/doing something)

When I was younger, I liked school a lot. My favorite class was science, and I always dreamed of being a doctor. I had a "laboratory" in my house. I used to mix different things and I hoped for an explosion. Whenever I did this, my mother was angry. She liked the house as it was. My friends and I pretended that we were mad scientists.

_____

_____

_____

_____

_____

_____

_____

"-ing" in the past

The addition of "-ing" to a verb in English indicates an action in progress, for example, "I am working." References to such actions in the past ("I was working") generally omit mention of a specific length of time, and thus are conjugated in the imperfect. We often use this format to describe two actions going on at the same time, for example, **Yo *tocaba* la guitarra y Juan *cantaba*** ("I *was playing* the guitar and John *was singing*"). See also The progressive in the past, page 155.

EJERCICIO
14·5

Traducción

1. *I was washing* (fregar) *the dishes.*

   _____

2. *Nobody was listening while the politician was speaking.*

   _____

3. *He was walking and I was running.*

   _____

4. *They [m.] were listening to the radio while they were studying.*

   _____

5. *We were trying to sleep, but the baby was crying* (llorar).

   _____

6. *Why were you watching television when I was studying?*

   _____

7. *The children were playing in the garden.*

   _____

8. *We were living in a glass house.*

   _____

9. *You all were selling T-shirts* (la camiseta) *on the corner* (la esquina).

   _____

10. *I was suffering from a cold* (el resfriado).

   _____

11. *The frogs* (la rana) *were jumping* (saltar) *near the lake.*

   _____

12. *I was taking a shower while they [f.] were eating breakfast.*

   _____

13. *Carmen was preparing dinner.*

   _____

14. *We were thinking about you a lot.*

   _____

15. *While she was explaining the theory* (la teoría), *everybody was leaving.*

   _____

Mental or emotional action or physical sensation

Feelings and mental actions are usually not bound by either time or number of occurrences. These actions are not physical. Rather, they describe a state of being, and thus they are continuous. In fact, several of the verbs listed below change meaning significantly when used in the preterite (see The preterite tense, page 109).

Yo esperaba el autobús.	*I was waiting for the bus.*
	OR *I waited for the bus.*
No creíamos el cuento.	*We didn't believe the story.*
Estabas cansado.	*You were tired.*
Queríais ir al cine.	*You wanted to go to the movies.*
Romeo amaba mucho a Julieta.	*Romeo loved Juliet a lot.*
Ellos tenían veinte dólares esta mañana.	*They had twenty dollars this morning.*
Hacía buen tiempo.	*It was nice out.*
Me dolían los oídos.	*My ears hurt.*

Below are several common verbs that are often used in the imperfect.

VOCABULARIO

amar	to love	**molestar**	to be bothersome to
conocer	to know a person/place	**odiar**	to hate
creer	to believe	**pensar (e > ie) (en)**	to think (about)
doler	to be painful to	**poder (o > ue)**	to be able to
esperar	to hope, wait (for)	**querer (e > ie)**	to want
estar	to be	**saber**	to know
gustar	to be pleasing to	**sentir (e > ie)**	to regret, feel sorry
llevarse bien con	to get along with	**sentirse (e > ie)**	to feel

EJERCICIO 14·6

¿**Verdadero o falso?** *Some of the following sentences contain both an imperfect and a preterite clause.*

1. _____ Esta mañana nadie comió nada porque no tenía hambre.

2. _____ Dumbo podía volar porque tenía unas orejas enormes.

3. _____ Muchas personas fueron al cine la semana pasada porque querían ver una película.

4. _____ Elvis Presley era un cantante muy popular que también actuó en treinta y una películas.

5. _____ John Lennon tocaba la guitarra para los Beatles y también escribió muchas canciones.

6. _____ De niño, Mahatma Gandhi tenía un televisor en su dormitorio y lo miraba mucho.

EJERCICIO 14·7

Traducción

1. *I knew the answer.*

_____

2. *Jane hated the color red.*

_____

3. *Did you know him?*

_____

4. *They [m.] didn't believe me.*

_____

5. *My family loved me a lot.*

   _____

6. *We were very sad for a long time.*

   _____

7. *He hated his new boss.*

   _____

8. *I liked the photo of your family.*

   _____

9. *I liked the flowers in their garden.*

   _____

10. *Even though he bothered me, I loved him.*

    _____

11. *She worried about you a lot.*

    _____

12. *Were you thinking about me?*

    _____

13. *What were you thinking about?*

    _____

14. *How did you feel during the trial* (el juicio)*?*

    _____

15. *She didn't get along with* (llevarse bien con) *her mother-in-law* (la suegra)*.*

    _____

EJERCICIO
14·8

Traducción *This paragraph contains verbs in the present, preterite, and imperfect tenses.*

VOCABULARIO

enorme	*enormous*
la experiencia	*experience*
extraño	*strange*
la mariposa	*butterfly*
por un rato	*for a while*
la raya	*stripe*

Yesterday, when I was walking to school, I saw a butterfly. It was enormous. At first I was afraid, but only for a while, because I knew that butterflies are not monsters. It was red and orange and had yellow stripes. It was beautiful and it had big eyes that seemed purple to me. This experience was very strange.

_____

_____

_____

_____

_____

_____

"Would" and "could" in the past

The words "would" and "could" are markers for two different tenses in English—the imperfect and the conditional. Because of this, they often present problems for English speakers who are learning another language. Consider the following sentences.

> ***I would go to the movies**, but I don't have time.*
> ***I would go to the movies** every weekend as a child. (**I used to go to the movies....**)*

The first sentence is in the conditional tense (which will be covered in Chapter 16), because it refers to an action that *would* take place in the future if a certain condition were met, namely, my having more time. The second sentence is in the imperfect, because it refers to an action that took place many times in the *past*. In the imperfect, "would" is the equivalent of "used to."

The same holds true for "could." Consider the following sentences.

> *I'm so hungry, **I could eat three hamburgers**.*
> *When I was younger, **I could eat three hamburgers** without gaining weight.*

The first sentence is conditional because it refers to an uncompleted action that might (or might not) take place in the future. The second, however, refers to what the person "used to be able to" do. In the imperfect, "could" is equivalent to "was able to" or "were able to."

Additional examples illustrate these differences.

Cuando yo era joven, **jugaba** al béisbol cada fin de semana.	*When I was young, **I would play** baseball every weekend. (used to)*
Cuando yo vivía en Florida, **podía** nadar todo el año.	*When I lived in Florida, **I could** swim all year long. (was able to)*
Juan **no estudiaba** porque no le gustaba la clase.	*John **wouldn't study** because he didn't like the class. (didn't used to)*

Traducción

1. *As a child, John would watch TV every day after school.*

   _____

2. *When we lived in France, we would drink wine with every meal.*

   _____

3. *Last year they [m.] couldn't speak Spanish.*

   _____

4. *Why couldn't you go to the movies with me?*

   _____

5. *When I was young, I would look under the bed every night before turning out (apagar) the light.*

   _____

6. *Barry Bonds could play baseball better than Pete Rose.*

   _____

7. *When Jane used to work at the bank, she would drink fifteen cups (la taza) of coffee every day.*

   _____

8. *When you [formal] were younger, you could remember the capitals of every state.*

   _____

9. *When John Smith worked for the CIA, he would never tell anybody his real name.*

   _____

10. *They [m.] couldn't vote because they didn't have identification.*

    _____

11. *You were never home. Where would you go those nights?*

    _____

12. *We couldn't call you because the telephone wouldn't work.*

    _____

13. *For every party that we had, Lisa would bring french fries and I would bring ketchup.*

    _____

14. *The bread was moldy (mohoso). I couldn't eat it.*

    _____

15. *As a girl, Vicky would have to make her bed every morning before leaving for school.*

    _____

Key words and phrases

Certain words or phrases, when used to describe frequency of a past action, imply repetitive, uncounted occurrences of that action. When one of these words or phrases appears in a sentence describing an ongoing past action, use the imperfect tense. Several of these words and phrases are listed below.

VOCABULARIO

all day long	**todo el día**	from time to time; once in a while	**de vez en cuando**
all one's life	**toda la vida**		
all the time	**todo el tiempo**	many times	**muchas veces**
always	**siempre**	never	**nunca**
at times, sometimes	**a veces**	often	**a menudo, con frecuencia**
every day	**cada día**	so many times	**tantas veces**
every year	**cada año**	various/several times	**varias veces**
for a while	**por un rato**	whenever	**cuando**
frequently	**frecuentemente, con frecuencia**		

EJERCICIO
14·10

Traducción

1. *I always studied before a test.*

   _____

2. *He frequently called me after 10:00 P.M.*

   _____

3. *I always wanted to have a piano.*

   _____

4. *They [m.] always cheated* (engañar) *us whenever we played cards.*

   _____

5. *You ate there frequently.*

   _____

6. *You all often wrote long letters.*

   _____

7. *From time to time we sent money to the organization.*

   _____

8. *Sometimes he didn't earn as much money as his wife.*

   _____

9. *All the time that I was there, you all never said anything.*

_____

10. *He always sent a thank-you note after receiving a gift.*

_____

11. *She never bought anything without a coupon* (el cupón).

_____

12. *He frequently lied to us, but we never said anything to him.*

_____

13. *I always wondered* (preguntarse) *why she washed her hands so many times every day. She was strange* (raro).

_____

14. *She was never happy. She complained* (quejarse) *every day, all day long.*

_____

15. *At times we read, and at times we wrote in our diaries. Once in a while we watched movies* (ver películas) *on Netflix.*

_____

EJERCICIO

¡Te toca a ti! *Cuando eras menor, ¿cuál era verdadero* (**V**) *o falso* (**F**) *para ti?*

1. _____ Cada día me cepillaba los dientes dos o tres veces.
2. _____ Jugaba a las damas con mis amigos.
3. _____ Todo el día robaba bancos y varias tiendas.
4. _____ Con frecuencia dormía hasta las tres de la tarde.
5. _____ Siempre me llevaba bien (*got along*) bien con mis padres.
6. _____ A veces nadaba en un lago y otras veces nadaba en el océano.
7. _____ Con frecuencia recibía una "F" en la clase de matemáticas.
8. _____ Siempre me llevaba bien con mis amigos.
9. _____ Cada día tenía una manicura y una pedicura.
10. _____ Casi cada día hablaba por teléfono.

Complete each sentence with the appropriate preterite or imperfect form of the verb in parentheses. Look for the markers. For example, **anoche** *(last night) indicates the preterite, while* **con frecuencia** *(frequently) indicates the imperfect.*

1. Yo _____ (hablar) con Jorge esta mañana.

2. De niño, Felipe _____ (vivir) en México.

3. Anoche, Marcos _____ (comer) tres tacos.

4. De niña, Lilia _____ (comer) tacos cada noche.

5. Ayer, nosotros _____ (ir) al cine.

6. Yo _____ (comprar) esta camisa en Harrods.

7. Nosotros _____ (llegar) aquí a las dos de la tarde.

8. Juanita _____ (llegar) a la una.

9. María siempre _____ (estudiar) en la cocina.

10. Ayer María _____ (estudiar) por una hora.

11. A veces los señores Molino _____ (comer) en el patio.

12. El jueves pasado, los Yankees de Nueva York _____ (jugar) al béisbol contra los Twins de Minnesota.

13. Mi tío siempre _____ (ser) más alto que yo.

14. Tú nunca _____ (ser) tan alto como yo.

15. Ellos _____ (ir) al cine tres veces el fin de semana pasado.

Clock time and age in the past

When referring to the time of day or one's age in the past, always use the imperfect. There are only two verbs involved here: **ser** (for clock time) and **tener** (for age). Note that references to time and age are often made with regard to other actions, and that these actions often (but not always) are in the preterite.

Era la una cuando **llegué.** IMPERFECT + PRETERITE	*It was one o'clock when **I arrived.***
Eran las ocho y media cuando **me desperté.** IMPERFECT + PRETERITE	*It was eight thirty when **I woke up.***
Yo tenía diez años cuando **conocí** a Juan. IMPERFECT + PRETERITE	*I was ten years old when **I met** John.*
No conocía a Juan cuando **tenía** ocho años. IMPERFECT + IMPERFECT	*I didn't know John when I was eight.*

Traducción

1. *It was two thirty when you called me.*

   _____

2. *Mary was twenty-two when she bought her first car.*

   _____

3. *It was a quarter after four when I found the money.*

   _____

4. *They [f.] were eighteen years old when they graduated (graduarse) from high school.*

   _____

5. *It was five to five when the tree fell down.*

   _____

6. *We worked hard when we were fifteen.*

   _____

7. *When I got up, it was six fifteen.*

   _____

8. *I learned how to ride a bike when I was six years old.*

   _____

9. *It was a quarter to four in the morning when the telephone rang.*

   _____

10. *She had her first baby, a girl, when she was forty-one, and she had her second daughter when she was forty-four.*

    _____

11. *We didn't know that it was twelve thirty.*

    _____

12. *It was three o'clock in the morning when they left.*

    _____

13. *Where did you live when you were fourteen years old?*

    _____

14. *What time was it when you finished the book?*

    _____

15. *How old was John when he got married (casarse)?*

    _____

EJERCICIO
14·13

¡**Te toca a ti!** *Responde a las preguntas siguientes con una frase completa.*

1. ¿Qué hora era cuando te acostaste anoche?

   _____

2. ¿Qué hora era cuando te levantaste esta mañana?

   _____

3. ¿Cuántos años tenías cuando comenzaste la escuela?

   _____

4. ¿Cuántos años tenías cuando aprendiste a montar en bicicleta?

   _____

5. ¿Qué hora era cuando saliste de tu casa esta mañana?

   _____

6. ¿Qué hora era cuando volviste a tu casa anoche?

   _____

7. ¿Cuántos años tenías cuando comenzaste a estudiar español?

   _____

8. ¿Cuántos años tenías cuando aprendiste a nadar?

   _____

Había—hay in the past

Just as **hay** in the present is both singular and plural ("there is," "there are"), the imperfect form **había** (from the verb **haber**), means both "there was" and "there were." Because **había** as an imperfect form is used to express existence, not action, it is typically used to express **hay** when referring to the past.

Había leche en el refrigerador.	*There was milk in the refrigerator.*
Había tres hombres y un bebé en la película.	*There were three men and a baby in the movie.*
No había dinero en el banco.	*There wasn't any money in the bank.*
No había hojas en el árbol.	*There weren't any leaves on the tree.*

NOTE In the preterite, **hay** becomes **hubo**. Due to **hay**'s primary function of expressing existence (a usage most often requiring the imperfect tense in the past), the preterite form of **hay** is used only rarely—for example, **Hubo un ataque nuclear anoche** ("There was a nuclear attack last night").

Traducción *Remember that the English word "any" is understood in negative expressions with* **hay.**

1. *There was a spider under my bed this morning.*

_____

2. *There were twenty people at the party.*

_____

3. *There was a fly in my soup.*

_____

4. *There were one hundred questions on the test.*

_____

5. *There was a lot of noise during the storm.*

_____

6. *There were five hundred pages in the book.*

_____

7. *There wasn't any gasoline in the tank.*

_____

8. *There weren't any leaves* (la hoja) *on the trees.*

_____

9. *There wasn't enough time for questions.*

_____

10. *There were more women than men at the meeting.*

_____

11. *There was garbage* (la basura) *on the table.*

_____

12. *There was so much fog* (la niebla) *that I couldn't drive.*

_____

13. *In January, it was so cold that there wasn't anybody outside.*

_____

14. *In the summer, there were lots of people in the streets.*

_____

15. *There weren't any women in that restaurant.*

_____

Traducción

VOCABULARIO

la docena	*dozen*	puré de arañas	*mashed spiders*
el edificio	*building*	el resfriado	*cold*
el entomólogo	*entomologist*	el ser humano	*human being*
la exposición	*exhibit*	solo	*just*
la libra	*pound*	verdaderamente	*really*
la mariposa	*butterfly*	volando de un lado a otro	*flying around*

When I was young, there was an exhibit of insects at the zoo every summer. My family and I always went. There was a building just for butterflies, and there were ten kinds of butterflies flying around. There was also a building that had dozens of insects. I never knew that there were so many insects. There was information everywhere. I found out that for every pound of humans, there are twelve pounds of insects. I also read that Little Miss Muffet really existed. Her father, Thomas Muffet, was an entomologist who gave his daughter mashed spiders when she was sick. This was a common remedy for colds 200 years ago!

_____

_____

_____

_____

_____

_____

_____

_____

_____

"Going to" do something in the past

An expression of intent, such as stating that one is "going to" do something, is a mental expression. In the **ir** + **a** + INFINITIVE expression **Voy a comprar un carro** ("I am going to buy a car"), there is no physical action taking place. Such sentences referring to the past, therefore, will be in the imperfect tense.

Yo iba a comprar un carro.	*I was going to buy a car.*
Íbamos a comer.	*We were going to eat.*
¿Ibas a llamarme?	*Were you going to call me?*
Ibais a darme dinero.	*You all were going to give me money.*
Él iba a cantar.	*He was going to sing.*
Ellos iban a contar las ovejas.	*They were going to count the sheep.*

Traducción

1. *I was going to eat.*

   _____

2. *Were you going to tell me something?*

   _____

3. *He was going to wear his white shirt, but it was dirty.*

   _____

4. *We were going to shovel* (quitar) *the snow.*

   _____

5. *They [m.] were going to spend the day in the country, but the weather was bad.*

   _____

6. *When were you all* [formal] *going to sit down?*

   _____

7. *I was going to go to bed at ten thirty, but there was a good program on television.*

   _____

8. *How were you going to do this?*

   _____

9. *Why was she going to build a house in the woods?*

   _____

10. *Who was going to fix this faucet* (el grifo)*?*

    _____

11. *We were going to brush our teeth, but there wasn't any toothpaste* (la pasta de dientes)*.*

    _____

12. *I was going to give him money for his birthday.*

    _____

13. *Where were you all going to send this package?*

    _____

14. *When were you going to bring us the flowers?*

    _____

15. *Why wasn't he going to fill the glasses with water?*

    _____

The progressive in the past

There are two ways to show the progressive (that is, English "-ing" expressions) in the past in Spanish: You can use the imperfect tense (see "-ing" in the past on page 141), or you can use **estar** + PRESENT PARTICIPLE, where **estar** is conjugated in the imperfect. This latter construction is identical to the present progressive as covered in Chapter 12, except that in referring to the past, the conjugated form of **estar** is in the imperfect tense.

Yo estaba hablando.	*I was speaking.*
Estábamos comiendo.	*We were eating.*
Estabas leyendo un libro.	*You were reading a book.*
Estabais arreglando el coche.	*You were fixing the car.*
Él estaba cepillándose los dientes.	*He was brushing his teeth.*
Ellas estaban mirándose.	*They were looking at each other.*

EJERCICIO

¿Qué estabas haciendo anoche? *Escribe una X delante de las cosas que estabas haciendo anoche.*

1. _____ Yo estaba estudiando español.

2. _____ Yo estaba jugando a los naipes.

3. _____ Yo estaba cepillándome los dientes.

4. _____ Yo estaba escribiendo una carta.

5. _____ Yo estaba pagando las cuentas.

6. _____ Yo estaba limpiando la casa.

7. _____ Yo estaba cocinando.

8. _____ Yo estaba contando el dinero.

9. _____ Yo estaba durmiendo.

10. _____ Yo estaba pensando en mis amigos.

11. _____ Yo estaba sirviendo una comida especial a mi familia.

12. _____ Yo estaba viendo la televisión.

Traducción

1. *I was eating.* _____

2. *You were studying.* _____

3. *Dumbo was flying.* _____

4. *She was eating lunch.* _____

5. *We were drinking milk.* _____

6. *You all were telling the truth.* _____

7. *They [m.] were going to bed.* _____

8. *You all* [formal] *were brushing your hair.* _____

9. *I was taking a bath.* _____

10. *John was shaving.* _____

11. *Sophia was playing the piano.* _____

12. *Serena was playing tennis.* _____

EJERCICIO
14·18

Traducción *This paragraph includes verbs in the present, preterite, and imperfect tenses.*

VOCABULARIO		
	afirmar que	*to claim that*
	el celular	*cell phone*
	celular	*cellular*
	el chanchullero, la chanchullera	*scammer*
	la culpa	*fault*
	el demandado, la demandada	*defendant*
	el/la demandante	*plaintiff*
	demandar	*to sue*
	el episodio	*episode*
	fallar a favor de	*to rule in favor of*
	incluso si	*even if*
	el/la juez/a	*judge*
	mientras	*while*
	la onza	*ounce*
	el pedazo	*piece*
	pesar	*to weigh*
	poner un anuncio	*to place an ad*
	el programa	*program, show*
	según	*according to*

This afternoon I saw the best episode of Judge Judy *while I was eating lunch. I love that show. The plaintiffs (Shannon and Karen Ann Davenport) were suing the defendant (Kelli Filkins) because Filkins posted an ad on eBay for two cell phones. The Davenports wanted the cell phones and they sent Filkins the money, but when Filkins received their money, she didn't sent them cell phones. She sent them photos of the cell phones! Judge Judy was angry, very angry in this episode. Judge Judy told Kelli Filkins that she was a scammer. Kelli told Judge Judy that it wasn't her fault because the Davenports couldn't read. According to Filkins, it said "Photo only." But it also claimed that one of the cell phones weighed 4.7 ounces, and the piece of paper did not weigh 4.7 ounces (a typical piece of paper weighs .16 of an ounce). Judge Judy told Kelli that if she lives for one hundred years, she's never going to have the intelligence in her entire body that Judge Judy has in one finger, and she was right! The Davenports won the case and Kelli Filkins lost it. Judge Judy ruled in favor of the Davenports and said that Kelli had to pay them $5,000. This episode is on YouTube, and you can watch it, too!*

_____

_____

_____

_____

_____

_____

_____

_____

_____

_____

_____

_____

_____

_____

_____

_____

_____

_____

The future tense

TENSE	Future
TIME	Refers to a future, specific action
KEY PHRASES	"Will"
STRUCTURE	Simple tense: VERB INFINITIVE + VERB ENDING

We use the future tense to describe actions that *will* take place. In English, the word "will" or "shall" is the essence of the future tense. When either of these words is placed before a verb, the future tense is formed. For example, "I will go," "You will study," and "We shall dine" are all examples of the future tense in English.

In Spanish, the future tense is a simple tense, meaning that no auxiliary verb, such as "will," is required for the expression of actions in the future in Spanish. The future aspect of the action is expressed in the conjugated form of the main verb.

Most Spanish verbs are regular in the future tense. The future tense is formed by adding the appropriate future tense ending to the infinitive, which serves as the verb stem for the future tense. Below is the set of verb endings used for all verbs, whether regular or irregular, in the future tense.

-é	-emos
-ás	-éis
-á	-án

Irregular verbs in the future tense make a change in the *stem* rather than the ending. Note that all of the verb endings, except the first-person plural (**nosotros**), take a written accent.

Regular verbs in the future

hablar *to speak, talk*		**comer** *to eat*		**vivir** *to live*	
hablaré	hablaremos	comeré	comeremos	viviré	viviremos
hablarás	hablaréis	comerás	comeréis	vivirás	viviréis
hablará	hablarán	comerá	comerán	vivirá	vivirán

Iré al teatro con Marcos.	*I will go to the theater with Marcos.*
Nos levantaremos a las cinco.	*We will get up at five o'clock.*
¿Dónde **estarás** mañana?	*Where will you be tomorrow?*
Enviaréis las cartas esta noche.	*You all will send the letters tonight.*
¿**Quién será** el próximo presidente?	*Who will be the next president?*
Aquellas mujeres nos **oirán**.	*Those women will hear us.*

Below are several common expressions of future time.

EJERCICIO

En tu opinión, ¿cuál es verdadero o falso?

1. _____ Comeré una hamburguesa mañana.

2. _____ Marco Rubio será el próximo presidente de los Estados Unidos.

3. _____ Mi mejor amigo/amiga me dará un regalo para mi cumpleaños.

4. _____ Iré al cine este fin de semana.

5. _____ Los Mets de Nueva York ganarán la próxima Serie Mundial.

6. _____ Viajaré a México el año que viene.

7. _____ Celebraremos la Navidad en noviembre.

8. _____ Si una persona deja abierta la puerta en el verano, muchas moscas entrarán en la casa.

9. _____ Todos los aviones en todos los aeropuertos llegarán y partirán a su hora esta semana.

10. _____ En veinticuatro horas estaré en mi casa.

11. _____ El vampiro beberá la sangre.

12. _____ Nadie leerá el periódico mañana.

13. _____ Esta noche lavaré los platos y después los secaré.

14. _____ Mi carro no funcionará sin aceite.

15. _____ Nadaré en el océano este verano.

Complete each sentence with the appropriate future tense form of the verb in parentheses.

1. Mañana yo _____ (comprar) comida para la cena.

2. Los dos gatos _____ (correr) alrededor de la casa.

3. Vosotros _____ (abrir) las ventanas.

4. Tú _____ (ser) famoso/famosa algún día.

5. Mi primo _____ (estar) enfermo si come diez tamales.

6. Nosotros _____ (jugar) a los naipes esta noche.

7. Ella _____ (llevar) una mini-falda al baile.

8. Yo no _____ (ducharse) porque no hay agua.

9. Ellos _____ (llegar) a las ocho.

10. El perro _____ (vomitar) si come esos huesos.

11. Nunca _____ (nevar) en Costa Rica.

12. Ellos _____ (acostarse) a las once y media.

Traducción

1. *I'll speak with you tomorrow.*

   _____

2. *She'll buy a new car next year.*

   _____

3. *He will sleep until tomorrow afternoon.*

   _____

4. *We will arrive at ten o'clock tomorrow night.*

   _____

5. *What time will you go to bed?*

   _____

6. *How much money will you all need?*

   _____

7. *They [m.] will stay* (quedarse) *in a hotel next month.*

   _____

8. *It will never snow (nevar) in Panama.*

_____

9. *Where will you be tonight at eleven thirty?*

_____

10. *What time will the program begin?*

_____

11. *I don't want to give him the money, because I know that he'll lose it.*

_____

12. *I won't take off (quitarse) this sweater until next summer.*

_____

13. *We will attend the university next fall.*

_____

14. *I won't sign (firmar) this letter, because it's not true.*

_____

15. *If I buy this suit (el traje) instead of that one, I'll save (ahorrar) fifty dollars.*

_____

EJERCICIO
15·3

¡Te toca a ti! *Responde a cada una de las preguntas siguientes con una frase completa.*

1. ¿Qué comerás esta noche? _____

2. ¿Quién será el próximo presidente de los Estados Unidos?

_____

3. ¿Adónde irás el verano que viene? _____

4. ¿Hablarás español mañana? _____

5. ¿Dónde estarás en tres horas? _____

6. ¿A qué hora te acostarás esta noche?

_____

7. ¿Qué llevarás mañana? _____

8. ¿Qué programa mirarás en la televisión esta semana?

_____

9. ¿Qué país ganará la Copa Mundial el año que viene?

_____

10. ¿Colgarás tu ropa antes de acostarte esta noche?

_____

11. ¿A qué hora te levantarás mañana? _____

12. ¿Por cuánto tiempo estudiarás español mañana?

_____

Traducción _This paragraph includes verbs in the present, preterite, imperfect, and future tenses._

VOCABULARIO

adelgazar	_to lose weight_
cumplir	_to keep_ (one's resolution)
engordar	_to gain (weight)_
faltar a su palabra	_to break one's promise_
gastar	_to spend (money)_
ir de compras	_to go shopping_
la manzana, la cuadra	_city block_
montar en bicicleta	_to ride a bike_
perder el tiempo	_to waste time_
pertenecer	_to belong_
quejarse (de)	_to complain (about)_
tratar de_ + INFINITIVE	_to try to (do something)_

Tomorrow is the first of January, and therefore I will try to do all the things I wrote on my list of resolutions for next year. Last year I made ten resolutions, and for a while I kept them, but one by one I broke my promises to myself. This year, however, I will lose weight—last year I gained ten pounds. I will work harder—I wasted a lot of time last year. I will read more—I read only two books this past year. I will go to the gym more often—I belong to a club, but I never go. I will spend less money—I used to go shopping two or three times every week. I will walk or ride my bicycle instead of driving—yesterday I drove three blocks in order to buy a newspaper—how ridiculous! I will complain less—I was not a little angel this year. Finally, I will study Spanish more. I will be perfect— just like last year.

_____

_____

_____

_____

_____

_____

_____

_____

_____

Irregular verbs in the future

There are twelve very common verbs that are irregular in the future tense. Their endings are regular (-é, -ás, -á, -emos, -éis, -án), but each of these twelve verbs shows a change in the stem. They can be grouped to make learning them a bit easier, because there are patterns in how the infinitive stem changes.

Below are the twelve irregular verbs in the future tense, shown in three groups. The infinitive of each one appears with its first-person singular (yo) form in the future tense.

VOCABULARIO

Group 1
The infinitive stem drops the final vowel of its ending; the future tense verb ending is added to the modified stem.

caber	to fit, have enough room	yo cabré
haber	to have (*auxiliary*)	yo habré
poder	to be able to	yo podré
querer	to want	yo querré
saber	to know a fact, know how	yo sabré

Group 2
The infinitive stem drops the final vowel of its ending and replaces it with the letter **d**; the future tense verb ending is added to the modified stem.

poner	to put, place	yo pondré
salir	to leave	yo saldré
tener	to have, hold	yo tendré
valer	to be worth	yo valdré
venir	to come	yo vendré

Group 3
The infinitive stem is shortened; the future tense verb ending is added to the modified stem.

decir	to say, tell	yo diré
hacer	to do, make, make out (*a check*)	yo haré

Podré hacerlo mañana.	*I will be able to do it tomorrow.*
Saldremos a las cuatro.	*We will leave at four o'clock.*
Tú me lo **dirás**.	*You will tell (it to) me.*
Vendréis a nuestra fiesta.	*You all will come to our party.*
La mesa no cabrá en este cuarto.	*The table won't fit in this room.*
Estos anillos valdrán mucho.	*These rings will be worth a lot.*

Compounds of irregular verbs

Some of the irregular verbs in the future have compounds that are irregular in the same way. For example, the first-person singular (yo) form of **tener** ("to have") in the future tense is **tendré**, and for **obtener** ("to obtain, get") it is **obtendré**.

Yo tendré empleo.	*I will have work.*
Yo obtendré empleo.	*I will get work.*
Él hará la tarea.	*He will do the assignment.*
Él rehará la tarea.	*He will redo the assignment.*

Below are several common compounds of irregular verbs in the future, showing the infinitive and the first-person singular (**yo**) form in the future tense.

VOCABULARIO

abstenerse de + INFINITIVE	to abstain from (doing something)	**me abstendré de** + INFINITIVE
atenerse a	to depend on, rely on	**me atendré a**
componer	to compose	**compondré**
contener	to contain, hold	**contendré**
convenir en + INFINITIVE	to agree to (do something)	**convendré en** + INFINITIVE
deshacer	to undo, untie (*a knot*)	**desharé**
detener	to detain, stop, arrest	**detendré**
mantener	to maintain	**mantendré**
obtener	to obtain, get	**obtendré**
oponerse	to oppose	**me opondré**
ponerse	to become, put on (*clothing*), set (*sun*)	**me pondré**
rehacer	to redo, remake	**reharé**
sostener	to sustain, support, uphold	**sostendré**
suponer	to suppose, assume	**supondré**

An exception to this pattern is **bendecir** ("to bless"). The verb **decir** is one of the twelve irregular verbs in the future, with a modified stem (**dir-**). The verb **bendecir** does not share that irregularity. **Bendecir** is regular in the future tense.

El sacerdote te **dirá**.	The priest **will tell** you.
El sacerdote te **bendecirá**.	The priest **will bless** you.

EJERCICIO

Para ti, ¿cuál es verdadero o falso?

1. _____ Compondré una canción este año.

2. _____ Se pondrá el sol mañana antes de las seis.

3. _____ Me abstendré de comer chocolate este año.

4. _____ Si nadie me llama por teléfono hoy, supondré que todo el mundo está enojado conmigo.

5. _____ Un buen policía detendrá a muchos criminales durante su carrera.

6. _____ Antes de nadar, una persona se pondrá el traje de baño.

7. _____ Si cometo un error en este capítulo, reharé todos los ejercicios.

8. _____ Si hace mucho frío el invierno que viene, me pondré guantes antes de salir de casa.

Traducción

1. *I will put on my hat.*

   _____

2. *He will untie this knot.*

   _____

3. *Will you oppose the president?*

   _____

4. *All of you will abstain from smoking for two weeks.*

   _____

5. *Who will compose the music?*

   _____

6. *We'll depend on you.*

   _____

7. *Will this pail* (el balde) *hold all the paint* (la pintura)?

   _____

8. *He'll remake his bed later.*

   _____

9. *I will assume that you know the answer.*

   _____

10. *The police will detain you if you drive drunk* (borracho).

    _____

11. *She will maintain good grades in college.*

    _____

12. *Where will you get enough money (in order) to buy the new furniture?*

    _____

13. *Will you all* [formal] *agree to stay with me for a while?*

    _____

14. *These beams* (la viga) *will not support a house.*

    _____

15. *Tomorrow I will abstain from eating.*

    _____

Habrá—hay in the future

The third-person singular of **haber** in the future, **habrá**, is the future form of **hay** ("there is," "there are"). When used alone, **habrá** translates as "there will be" and is used for both singular and plural.

Habrá una fiesta en tu honor.	***There will be** a party in your honor.*
Habrá veinte personas en la fiesta.	***There will be** twenty people at the party.*

NOTE **Habrá** can also be used as an auxiliary verb; in that context, it is always used before a past participle rather than alone. This use of **habrá** will be covered in Chapter 22, *The future perfect tense.*

EJERCICIO

En tu opinión o experiencia, ¿cuál es verdadero o falso?

1. _____ Tendré una fiesta el sábado que viene.

2. _____ Saldré de mi casa en una hora y media.

3. _____ Sabré más mañana que lo que sé hoy.

4. _____ Varios amigos míos vendrán a mi casa esta noche.

5. _____ En un año podré hablar español muy bien.

6. _____ Habrá rebajas (*sales*) en Harrod's en enero.

7. _____ Los futboleros de Italia querrán ganar la Copa Mundial este año.

8. _____ No haré nada este fin de semana.

9. _____ No diré nada a nadie esta noche.

10. _____ Un anillo de oro valdrá más en veinte años que ahora.

11. _____ Una mesa y ocho sillas no cabrán en mi cocina.

12. _____ Mañana me pondré a dieta.

EJERCICIO
15·6

Complete each of the following sentences with the correct form of the verb in parentheses.

1. Nosotros _____ (hacer) las camas mañana.

2. Ellos _____ (poner) los tenedores en el cajón.

3. Ella _____ (tener) quince años en julio.

4. El sofá no _____ (caber) en la sala.

5. ¿Quién _____ (saber) la respuesta?

6. Nadie _____ (querer) vivir en esta casa.

7. Los elefantes no _____ (poder) levantar este coche.

8. Nosotros no _____ (decir) nada acerca de tus problemas.

9. Vosotros _____ (venir) en septiembre.

10. Ellos _____ (salir) a las dos de la tarde.

11. Este collar de perlas _____ (valer) cinco mil dólares en diez años.

12. _____ (haber) cuatro almohadas en la cama.

EJERCICIO
15·7

Traducción *Remember that the English word "any" is understood in negative expressions with* **hay**.

1. *I'll want to see your photos.*

   _____

2. *Where will you put the sofa? I'll put it in the living room.*

   _____

3. *Mary will make the bride's dress.*

   _____

4. *What time will they come?*

   _____

5. *You all* [formal] *won't be able to see the boat from there.*

   _____

6. *There will be three hundred stores in the new mall* (el centro comercial).

   _____

7. *John will know the answer.*

   _____

8. *How much will the car be worth next year?*

   _____

9. *There will not be any noise during the program.*

   _____

10. *Will there be time for asking questions* (hacer preguntas)?

   _____

11. *Will you be able to call me later?*

   _____

12. *These hammers* (el martillo) *will never fit into that box.*

_____

13. *This house will be worth more than two million dollars in five years.*

_____

14. *I will not tell your secret to anyone.*

_____

15. *They [m.] will make out their check for five hundred dollars.*

_____

EJERCICIO
15·8

Traducción

VOCABULARIO	la almohada	*pillow*	por primera vez	*for the first time*
	la camioneta	*van*	renunciar a	*to quit* (a job)
	conocer a	*to meet*	soñar con	*to dream of*
	el hogar	*home*	el sueño	*dream*
	iguales	*(the) same, equal*	el vehículo	*vehicle*
	el lugar	*place*	viajar	*to travel*
	un par	*a couple*	la vida	*life*

In a couple of weeks, I'll quit this job and begin a new life. I sold my house and bought a van. Last night I put food, clothing, my camera, and a pillow—everything that I'll need—into the van. I can't believe it! Soon that vehicle will be my home. During the past five years I saved enough money to live for ten years. I won't be able to go to fancy restaurants or buy Armani suits, but I will be able to travel. I'll visit new places and I'll meet new people. I always dreamed of doing this. I won't be rich, but I'll be happy. For the first time in my life, my reality and my dreams will be the same.

_____

_____

_____

_____

_____

_____

_____

_____

Traducción *The following sentences include both regular and irregular verbs in the future tense.*

1. *John will arrive at ten o'clock.*

   _____

2. *Where will you put the lawnmower (el cortacésped)?*

   _____

3. *We will eat the raisins (la pasa) from the box.*

   _____

4. *When will you find out (averiguar) if you have the job?*

   _____

5. *They [m.] will not go to bed until midnight.*

   _____

6. *I will never know how to play the violin.*

   _____

7. *From time to time, I will visit you in prison.*

   _____

8. *How much will this ring be worth in twenty years?*

   _____

9. *Will you obey the laws of this city?*

   _____

10. *It will never snow in Panama, and it will never rain in the desert.*

    _____

11. *They [m.] will tell us lies, but we will not believe anything.*

    _____

12. *Will you have to travel much? Will you be able to travel much?*

    _____

13. *My car will not fit into the garage. I'll have to leave (dejar) it on the street.*

    _____

14. *I will bury the treasure (el tesoro) tonight; otherwise (de lo contrario), it won't be here tomorrow.*

    _____

15. *The entire treasure will not fit in this trunk (el baúl); I will have to put the diamonds in my pocket.*

    _____

The conditional tense

TENSE	Conditional
TIME	Refers to the hypothetical future
KEY PHRASES	"Would"
STRUCTURE	Simple tense: VERB INFINITIVE + VERB ENDING

The conditional tense expresses the feeling of future uncertainty, generally translated as English "would" + VERB. It differs from the future tense, which expresses future certainty ("He *will be* here"), in that it suggests probability or possibility if some condition were met: "He *would be* here (but he's sick)" or "He *would be* here (if he weren't so busy)."

The inherent feature of the conditional tense is that some condition is *not* being met, but that *if* it were met, a certain action *would* take place. Sometimes this condition is stated, as in the following examples.

> *He would play pro basketball **if** he were taller.*
> *Would you call me **if** I gave you my number?*
> *I would eat in that restaurant, **but** it's too expensive.*
> *I would call her, **but** she was rude at the party.*

Note that there is often a phrase beginning with "but" or "if" to explain the reason that the action would (or would not) be completed in a sentence using the conditional tense. At times this reason is not stated explicitly, but is implied or simply understood, as in the following examples.

> *I would go.* (if I were you)
> *They wouldn't sing this song.* (because the lyrics are stupid)
> *They would spend the money.* (but you hid it)

Note that in sentences that use the conditional tense followed by a hypothetical *if*-clause (for example, "if I were," "if you had," "if we saw"), use of the subjunctive is required after the *if*-clause. Because we have not yet covered the subjunctive, none of the examples or exercises in this chapter will include sentences containing a hypothetical *if*-clause.

Regular verbs in the conditional

Most verbs are regular in the conditional tense. In fact, the future and the conditional tenses share the same irregular verbs. For conditional forms of regular verbs, the infinitive itself is the stem and the appropriate tense ending is added to the infinitive. Below are the verb endings for the conditional tense.

-ía	-íamos
-ías	-íais
-ía	-ían

Below are the full conjugations of **hablar**, **comer**, and **vivir** in the conditional tense. Note that all three verbs use the same verb endings.

hablar *to speak, talk*		**comer** *to eat*		**vivir** *to live*	
hablaría	hablaríamos	comería	comeríamos	viviría	viviríamos
hablarías	hablaríais	comerías	comeríais	vivirías	viviríais
hablaría	hablarían	comería	comerían	viviría	vivirían

Yo compraría el vestido, pero no tengo suficiente dinero.	*I would buy the dress, but I don't have enough money.*
¿Cuándo **iríamos**?	*When would we go?*
¿**Comerías** en ese restaurante?	*Would you eat in that restaurant?*
Estaríais allí a las diez, pero tenéis que estudiar.	*You all would be there at ten, but you have to study.*
Nadie dormiría allí.	*No one would sleep there.*
Ellos no cantarían esta canción.	*They wouldn't sing this song.*

◆ **EJERCICIO**

Place an X by all the things you would do if you won $100,000,000 in a lottery.

1. _____ Renunciaría al trabajo.

2. _____ Daría parte del dinero a los pobres y el resto a un candidato político.

3. _____ Viajaría por el mundo.

4. _____ Depositaría todo el dinero en el banco.

5. _____ Me mudaría a una casa enorme y muy elegante.

6. _____ Compraría regalos para mi familia y todos mis amigos.

7. _____ Celebraría el premio con mis amigos en un buen restaurante y pagaría por todos.

8. _____ Compraría un coche nuevo.

9. _____ Escribiría un libro sobre mi vida.

10. _____ No cambiaría ningún aspecto de mi vida.

Traducción

1. *I would eat the cookies, but I'm on a diet* (estar a dieta).

_____

2. *Would she marry* (casarse con) *John?*

_____

3. *Where would you go?*

_____

4. *They* [m.] *wouldn't live in that house because it's haunted* (embrujado).

_____

5. *Would you all* [formal] *deliver* (entregar) *the newspapers to our house?*

_____

6. *If I teach this class, all of you would be my students.*

_____

7. *I'm not going to give them the money because they would lose it.*

_____

8. *We would change the words of the song, but it would be too difficult.*

_____

9. *I'd get up, but my leg is sore* (my leg hurts).

_____

10. *I know they would give you the money that you need.*

_____

11. *Would you buy a used car from this man?*

_____

12. *Who would think such a thing* (tal cosa)?

_____

13. *Why wouldn't he shave* (afeitarse) *with that razor* (la navaja)?

_____

14. *Why would anybody read this?*

_____

15. *I wouldn't play the piano in front of a crowd* (la multitud).

_____

Irregular verbs in the conditional

The twelve verbs that are irregular in the future are also irregular in the conditional, and in the same way. The verb endings are regular (-ía, -ías, -ía, -íamos, -íais, -ían), but each of these twelve verbs shows a change in the stem. They are grouped to make learning them easier, because there are patterns to how the infinitive stem changes.

Below are the twelve irregular verbs in the conditional tense, shown in three groups. The infinitive of each one appears with its first-person singular (**yo**) form in the conditional tense.

VOCABULARIO

Group 1

The infinitive stem drops the final vowel of its ending; the conditional tense verb ending is added to the modified stem.

caber	to fit, have enough room	**yo cabría**
haber	to have (*auxiliary*)	**yo habría**
poder	to be able to	**yo podría**
querer	to want	**yo querría**
saber	to know a fact, know how	**yo sabría**

Group 2

The infinitive stem drops the final vowel of its ending and replaces it with the letter **d**; the conditional tense verb ending is added to the modified stem.

poner	to put, place	**yo pondría**
salir	to leave	**yo saldría**
tener	to have, hold	**yo tendría**
valer	to be worth	**yo valdría**
venir	to come	**yo vendría**

Group 3

The infinitive stem is shortened; the conditional tense verb ending is added to the modified stem.

decir	to say, tell	**yo diría**
hacer	to do, make, make out (*a check*)	**yo haría**

Yo le **diría** a Timotea cualquier cosa.	*I **would tell** Timothy anything.*
¿Qué **haríamos**?	*What **would we do**?*
¿Cuándo **saldrías**?	*When **would you leave**?*
Sabríais sus nombres.	*You all **would know** their names.*
Nuestro sofá no cabría en ese cuarto.	*Our sofa **wouldn't fit** in that room.*
Estos anillos no valdrían nada.	*These rings **wouldn't be worth** anything.*

Compounds of irregular verbs

Some of the irregular verbs in the conditional have compounds that are irregular in the same way. For example, the first-person singular (**yo**) form of **tener** ("to have") in the conditional tense is **tendría**, and for **obtener** ("to obtain, get") it is **obtendría**.

Yo tendría empleo.	*I **would have** work.*
Yo obtendría empleo.	*I **would get** work.*
Él haría la tarea.	*He **would do** the assignment.*
Él reharía la tarea.	*He **would redo** the assignment.*

Below are several common compounds of irregular verbs in the conditional, shown as the infinitive together with the first-person singular (**yo**) form in the conditional tense.

An exception to this pattern is **bendecir** ("to bless"). The verb **decir** is one of the twelve irregular verbs in the conditional, with a modified stem (**dir-**). The verb **bendecir** does not share that irregularity. **Bendecir** is regular in the conditional tense.

El sacerdote te **diría**.	*The priest **would tell** you.*
El sacerdote te **bendeciría**.	*The priest **would bless** you.*

Habría—hay in the conditional

The third-person singular of **haber** in the conditional, **habría**, is the conditional form of **hay** ("there is," "there are"). When used alone, **habría** translates as "there would be" and is used for both singular and plural.

Habría más dinero aquí, pero fuimos al casino.	*__There would be__ more money here, but we went to the casino.*
Juan perdió cinco libros; de otra manera, **habría** treinta en el estante.	*John lost five books; otherwise, __there would be__ thirty on the shelf.*

NOTE **Habría** can also be used as an auxiliary verb; in that context, it is always used before a past participle rather than alone. This use of **habría** will be covered in Chapter 23, The conditional perfect tense.

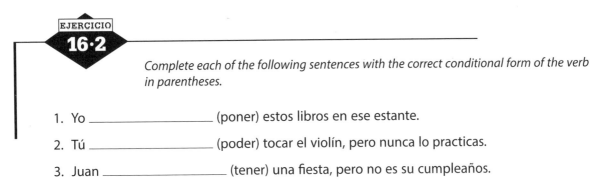

EJERCICIO 16·2

Complete each of the following sentences with the correct conditional form of the verb in parentheses.

1. Yo _____ (poner) estos libros en ese estante.

2. Tú _____ (poder) tocar el violín, pero nunca lo practicas.

3. Juan _____ (tener) una fiesta, pero no es su cumpleaños.

4. Esta pulsera _____ (valer) mucho, pero no es de oro.

5. ¿Qué _____ (hacer) Sherlock Holmes en esta situación?

6. Estas sillas _____ (caber) en la sala, pero no en el dormitorio.

7. Nosotros _____ (venir) a su fiesta, pero estamos enfermos.

8. _____ (haber) mucha comida, pero Juan estaba aquí anoche y se comió todo.

9. ¿Qué _____ (decir) tú en esta situación?

10. Yo no _____ (decir) nada.

EJERCICIO

16·3

Traducción

1. *I would come to your party, but I'm sick.*

   _____

2. *Where would you put these chairs?*

   _____

3. *This bracelet would be worth more, but it's broken.*

   _____

4. *What would you all say to that man?*

   _____

5. *We would have the reception in our house, but there isn't enough room.*

   _____

6. *Do you think that Robert would know the answer?*

   _____

7. *Who would be able to do such a thing?*

   _____

8. *I would want the car, but it isn't my choice.*

   _____

9. *There would be two dozen eggs in the refrigerator, but we ate four for breakfast.*

   _____

10. *Would these plates fit into the cabinet?*

    _____

11. *What would you do during a hurricane?*

    _____

12. *I wouldn't tell him, because he can't keep a secret* (guardar un secreto).

_____

13. *We would make out* (hacer) *the check, but there isn't enough* (suficiente) *money in the bank.*

_____

14. *I'm not going to give these shoes to Marcos, because I know that he wouldn't be able to wear them.*

_____

15. *I would put the flowers in front of the house, not in back.*

_____

EJERCICIO
16·4

Traducción

VOCABULARIO

conceder	*to grant*	el peso	*weight*
el cuento de hadas	*fairy tale*	la pobreza	*poverty*
el deseo	*wish*	por eso	*therefore*
la guerra	*war*	preocuparse por	*to worry about*
pedir	*to request, ask for*	sufrir	*to suffer*
el personaje	*character*	la tristeza	*sadness*

When I was young, I loved to read fairy tales. One of my favorite characters was Aladdin, because he was always granting people their fantasies in the form of three wishes. What would I do? First, I would ask him for a million wishes, but I know that he wouldn't do that. Therefore, these are my three wishes: 1. My cat would be able to speak, and she and I would have long conversations. 2. I would never have to worry about my weight. And the most important wish is this (one): 3. No one in the world would suffer another minute: There would be no war, there would be no hunger, there would be no poverty, there would be no sadness.

_____

_____

_____

_____

_____

_____

_____

_____

_____

_____

The present perfect tense

TENSE	Present perfect
TIME	Refers to the recent past or to past actions that are still true
KEY PHRASES	"Have," "has" ("I have eaten," "she has eaten")
STRUCTURE	Compound tense: **haber** conjugated in the present tense + PAST PARTICIPLE

The present perfect tense is a compound tense, which means that it requires an auxiliary, or helping, verb. This is also true in English, where the auxiliary verb is "have" or "has"—"I *have* spoken," "She *has* studied." In Spanish, the auxiliary verb is **haber**, which means "to have (done something)." Do not confuse **haber** with **tener**, which means "to have, possess."

We often use the present perfect tense when speaking about something that was true in the past and is still true. The sentence "I have lived here for ten years" means that starting ten years ago I lived here, I still live here, and I have lived here all the time in between.

The present perfect is also used to indicate that an action was completed recently: "I can't go out to dinner because I have eaten."

An important aspect of the present perfect tense is that the action referred to takes place in a span of time, either stated or implied, that leads up to and includes the present. However, the action referred to within this span of time took place at a time that is *not precisely specified* or implied (as in the preterite).

For example, in the sentence "I've gone to the club three times this year," the span of time includes all of this year until now. However, we do not know exactly when (that is, on which dates) the person visited the club. If you ask a person, "How have you been?" the implied span of time is "lately."

Formation of the present perfect

Because the present perfect tense is a compound tense, you will be working with two verbs, not one. To form verbs in this tense, first conjugate **haber** in the present tense.

haber *to have (auxiliary)*

he	hemos
has	habéis
ha	han

The conjugated form of **haber** is then followed by the past participle of the desired verb. Most past participles in Spanish are regular. Let's consider these first.

Regular past participles

The patterns for regular past participles are below.

-ar VERBS	Drop the **-ar** ending and replace it with **-ado**.	**hablar** > **hablado**
-er VERBS	Drop the **-er** ending and replace it with **-ido**.	**comer** > **comido**
-ir VERBS	Drop the **-ir** ending and replace it with **-ido**.	**vivir** > **vivido**

Below are the full conjugations of **hablar**, **comer**, and **vivir** in the present perfect tense.

hablar *to speak, talk*

he hablado	hemos hablado
has hablado	habéis hablado
ha hablado	han hablado

comer *to eat*

he comido	hemos comido
has comido	habéis comido
ha comido	han comido

vivir *to live*

he vivido	hemos vivido
has vivido	habéis vivido
ha vivido	han vivido

Yo he hablado con Roberto.	*I have spoken with Robert.*
Nos hemos acostado.	*We have gone to bed.*
Tú has estado aquí por diez minutos.	*You have been here for ten minutes.*
¿Habéis recibido los regalos?	*Have you all received the presents?*
Mitch ha sido mi amigo por treinta y cinco años.	*Mitch has been my friend for thirty-five years.*
No lo **han visitado.**	*They haven't visited him.*

There are two guidelines that will help you in your use of the present perfect tense.

1 The conjugated form of **haber** and the past participle are not—and cannot be—separated by any other words.

2 Object pronouns always precede the conjugated form of the verb **haber**.

◆ EJERCICIO

*Put an **X** next to each of the things that you have done today.*

1. _____ He hablado por teléfono.

2. _____ He tomado café.

3. _____ He comido una ensalada.

4. _____ He comprado una camisa.

5. _____ He almorzado.

6. _____ Me he duchado.

7. _____ He contado mi dinero.

8. _____ He recibido un regalo.

9. _____ He cometido un error.

10. _____ He escuchado la radio.

11. _____ Me he lavado el pelo.

12. _____ He lavado el coche.

EJERCICIO

17·1

Traducción

1. *I have worked.* _____

2. *You have listened.* _____

3. *She has drunk the milk.* _____

4. *We have understood.* _____

5. *They [m.] have received a present.* _____

6. *We have sold the house.* _____

7. *Have you watched television today?* _____

8. *Where have they lived?* _____

9. *I have showered.* _____

10. *He has been with me.* _____

11. *You [formal] have learned a lot.* _____

12. *Have you brushed your teeth?* _____

13. *He has called me six times.* _____

14. *I've run three miles.* _____

15. *She hasn't washed her hair.* _____

Irregular past participles

All conjugations in the present perfect tense begin with **haber** conjugated in the present tense, followed by a past participle. Most past participles are regular. However, there are several irregular past participles, and they fall into two distinct groups.

One group of irregular past participles follows a pattern, which makes them easier to learn. Most -**er** and -**ir** verbs with a vowel (other than **u**) immediately preceding the infinitive ending have past participles that end with -**ído** (note the accent over the **i** of the ending). Verbs ending with -**uir**, however, are regular. For example, the past participle of **construir** is **construido**. The second group of irregular past participles must be learned individually.

Below are several common verbs that have irregular past participles.

VOCABULARIO

Irregular past participles that end with -ído

atraer	to attract	atraído
caer	to fall	caído
creer	to believe	creído
leer	to read	leído
oír	to hear	oído
poseer	to possess	poseído
sonreír	to smile	sonreído
traer	to bring	traído

Irregular past participles that must be learned individually

abrir	to open	abierto
cubrir	to cover	cubierto
decir	to say, tell	dicho
describir	to describe	descrito
descubrir	to discover	descubierto
devolver	to return (*something*)	devuelto
disolver	to dissolve	disuelto
envolver	to wrap, wrap up	envuelto
escribir	to write	escrito
freír	to fry	frito
hacer	to make, do	hecho
morir	to die	muerto
oponer	to oppose	opuesto
poner	to put, place	puesto
proveer	to provide, furnish	provisto
pudrir	to rot, languish	podrido
resolver	to resolve	resuelto
romper	to break, break through/up	roto
ver	to see	visto
volver	to return	vuelto

He **abierto** la puerta.
No hemos **hecho** nada.

I have opened the door.
We haven't done anything.

¿No **has escrito** la carta?
¿**Habéis visto** la película?

Haven't you written the letter?
Have you all seen the movie?

Él me **ha dicho** una mentira.
Los huevos se **han podrido**.

He has told me a lie.
The eggs have rotted.

EJERCICIO

¿Qué has hecho esta semana? *Escribe una **X** delante de todo lo que has hecho durante la semana pasada.*

1. _____ He visto una película.

2. _____ He escrito una carta.

3. _____ He resuelto todos mis problemas.

4. _____ He leído un libro.

5. _____ He abierto las ventanas de mi casa.

6. _____ He dicho una mentira.

7. _____ He frito un huevo.

8. _____ He roto un plato.

9. _____ He devuelto libros a la biblioteca.

10. _____ He envuelto un regalo.

EJERCICIO 17·2

Traducción

1. *I have read twenty pages.* _____

2. *She has opened the book.* _____

3. *Where have you put the dishes?* _____

4. *The rabbit has died.* _____

5. *Have you told her the truth?* _____

6. *What have you seen?* _____

7. *The cook has fried all the eggs.* _____

8. *What have you done today?* _____

9. *The store has provided us with clothing.* _____

10. *She has broken another fingernail* (la uña). _____

11. *Has he resolved his problems?* _____

12. *We haven't said anything.* _____

13. *The politician has not told us the truth.* _____

14. *Why haven't they returned?* _____

15. *What have you made for us?* _____

Traducción *These sentences contain both regular and irregular past participles.*

1. *I have had the money for more than twenty years.*

   _____

2. *She has opened the window, and I have closed the door.*

   _____

3. *My neighbor's dog has barked* (ladrar) *all night long, and I haven't been able to sleep.*

   _____

4. *Where have you put your suitcase?*

   _____

5. *How many times have you brushed your teeth today?*

   _____

6. *Why haven't you shaved today? Why haven't you showered today?*

   _____

7. *For how many years have you known Charles?*

   _____

8. *You've arrived* (llegar) *late every day this week.*

   _____

9. *Have you all* [formal] *seen her?*

   _____

10. *The thieves have robbed our jewels and have broken all the windows.*

    _____

11. *Have the newlyweds* (los recién casados) *returned from their honeymoon* (la luna de miel)?

    _____

12. *Your manners* (los modales) *have attracted me.*

    _____

13. *They* [m.] *have demonstrated their love for Beethoven's music.*

    _____

14. *If she is as rich as you tell me, then why has she robbed the bank?*

    _____

15. *The telephone has rung twenty times. Why haven't you answered it?*

    _____

Traducción

VOCABULARIO

la cortina	*curtain*
desastre	*disaster*
el desván	*attic*
enterrar	*to bury*
el fregadero de cocina	*kitchen sink*
guardar	*to save* (things in general)
nacer	*to be born*
en ocasiones innumerables	*on countless occasions*
el patio trasero	*backyard*
el rincón	*corner* (interior)
el siglo	*century*
la tienda de departamentos	*department store*

I'm in my grandmother's attic. What a disaster! She has lived in this house for more than eighty years. She was born here, she was married here, and she buried six dogs and five cats in the backyard. She even has a kitchen sink in the corner! She has saved everything—from (desde) books and clothing to (hasta) photos, furniture, and old curtains. She has told me many times that I can have all the furniture. She has also told my sister that she can have all the furniture. I've been in this attic on countless occasions and I know that I haven't seen anything from this century. What (lo que) she has saved wouldn't fit into a department store.

The past perfect tense

TENSE	Past perfect
TIME	Refers to the remote past or to actions that occurred prior to a specific point in time
KEY PHRASES	"Had" ("I had traveled," "We had studied")
STRUCTURE	Compound tense: **haber** conjugated in the imperfect + PAST PARTICIPLE

The past perfect tense is a compound tense, which means that it requires an auxiliary verb followed by a past participle. We form the past perfect tense in the same manner in English, using the auxiliary "had," as in "You *had* written the letter" and "She *had* bought three suits," for all persons.

We use the past perfect tense (sometimes called the pluperfect tense) when referring to an action that occurred prior to something else. When using this tense, there is always a stated or implied cutoff point. Consider the following sentence.

> ***I had read three chapters*** *before realizing that I'd already read the book.*

The action, reading three chapters, stopped at the cutoff point of discovering that the book had been read. The act of reading three chapters, in a sense, is hidden behind the discovery. In this sense there is always something that stops whatever action is referred to in the past perfect tense.

The past perfect differs from the present perfect in that sentences in the present perfect are still true: In the present perfect, cutoff point is *now*. In the past perfect, the cutoff point is at some time in the past.

Formation of the past perfect

Because the past perfect tense is a compound tense, it is formed with an auxiliary verb and a past participle. To form verbs in this tense, first conjugate **haber** in the imperfect tense.

haber *to have (auxiliary)*

había	habíamos
habías	habíais
había	habían

Note that the first-person and third-person singular forms are identical. Don't worry—the context of the sentence will carry the meaning.

The formation of the past perfect tense is identical to that of the present perfect, except that the conjugation of **haber**, the auxiliary verb, is in the imperfect. The conjugated form of **haber** is then followed by the past participle of the main verb.

Regular past participles

The patterns for regular past participles can be found in Chapter 17, The present perfect tense. Below are examples of regular past participles used with the past perfect tense.

Yo había preparado la cena.	*I had prepared dinner.*
No habíamos probado ese método.	*We hadn't tried that method.*
Habías estado aquí.	*You had been here.*
Habíais trabajado duro.	*You all had worked hard.*
Él no había visitado a mi tío.	*He hadn't visited my uncle.*
¿Se habían acostado?	*Had they gone to bed?*

The following examples include a specific cutoff point. Remember that the verb after a preposition is not conjugated.

Yo había comido antes de llamarte.	*I had eaten before calling you.*
No habíamos escuchado el discurso hasta el martes.	*We hadn't listened to the speech until Tuesday.*
¿Te habías lavado las manos antes de comer?	*Had you washed your hands before eating?*
Habíais conocido a Jorge antes de la fiesta, ¿no?	*You all had met George before the party, right?*
Él **no había cerrado** la puerta antes de salir.	*He hadn't closed the door before leaving.*
Ellos **no habían manejado** el coche antes de comprarlo.	*They hadn't driven the car before buying it.*

EJERCICIO

Para ti, ¿cuál es verdadero o falso?

1. _____ Antes de comenzar este ejercicio, yo había conseguido una pluma.

2. _____ Antes de ducharme esta mañana, me había cepillado los dientes.

3. _____ Antes de comprar este libro, yo nunca había estudiado español.

4. _____ Antes de acostarme anoche, había apagado todas las luces en la casa.

5. _____ Antes de graduarme de la escuela secundaria, había conseguido trabajo para el verano.

6. _____ Me había lavado las manos antes de almorzar ayer.

7. _____ Yo había aprendido a nadar y montar en bicicleta antes de cumplir seis años.

8. _____ Antes de mi trabajo actual (*present*), había trabajado en un banco.

9. _____ Antes de tener una bicicleta, yo había montado en triciclo.

10. _____ Yo había volado en un avión antes de cumplir tres años.

EJERCICIO
18·1

Traducción

1. *I had paid the bill.*

_____

2. *She had lived in Texas.*

_____

3. *They [m.] had lost all the letters.*

_____

4. *We hadn't received an invitation.*

_____

5. *Had you worn those shoes before the wedding?*

_____

6. *I had eaten all the candy before discovering the prize.*

_____

7. *We had practiced for four hours before the concert.*

_____

8. *How long had you smoked before quitting (it)?*

_____

9. *She had lived in St. Louis before moving to St. Paul.*

_____

10. *We had dated (salir) for three years before getting married.*

_____

11. *The soldiers had suffered a lot before the end of the war.*

_____

12. *Before the party, I had cleaned the house from top to bottom* (de cabo a rabo).

_____

13. *He hadn't done anything before the party.*

_____

14. *I had never enjoyed* (disfrutar de) *the theater as much as he.*

_____

15. *Before going to bed, had you all turned off* (apagar) *the lights?*

_____

Irregular past participles

Whether the past participle is regular or irregular, using the past perfect tense requires conjugating **haber** in the imperfect (**había, habías, había, habíamos, habíais, habían**).

The past participles do not change: They will have the same form in the past perfect as in the present perfect (and in all other compound tenses)—whether regular or irregular.

Irregular past participles can be found in Chapter 17, The present perfect tense.

Yo había visto la película.	*I had seen the movie.*
Habíamos abierto todas las ventanas.	*We had opened all the windows.*
Habías vuelto del mercado.	*You had returned from the market.*
Habíais envuelto los regalos.	*You all had wrapped the gifts.*
La comida se había podrido.	*The food had rotted.*
Los científicos habían descubierto otro elemento.	*The scientists had discovered another element.*

EJERCICIO

En tu opinión o experiencia, ¿cuál es verdadero o falso?

1. _____ Antes de leer *The Hunger Games,* yo había leído los libros de Harry Potter.

2. _____ Yo había visto *El Mago de Oz* antes de ver *Casablanca.*

3. _____ Antes del año 1900, mi bisabuelo había nacido.

4. _____ Anthony Hopkins había actuado en varias películas antes de ganar un Oscar.

5. _____ Pinocho había dicho muchas mentiras y por eso su nariz estaba muy larga.

6. _____ Antes de morir, Martin Luther King, hijo, había hecho muchas cosas buenas para la gente.

7. _____ Alguien había descubierto las Américas antes que Cristóbal Colón.

8. _____ Para el año 1960, Sears había abierto muchas tiendas en los Estados Unidos.

9. _____ Antes de morir, Gandhi había descrito su visión de la paz.

10. _____ Al principio, Caperucita Roja había creído que el lobo era su abuela.

Traducción

1. *I hadn't opened the windows until May of that year.*

   _____

2. *They [m.] hadn't done anything.*

   _____

3. *She hadn't seen the movie before Saturday.*

   _____

4. *All the trees had died.*

   _____

5. *We hadn't solved the problems before the meeting.*

   _____

6. *The thieves had broken the chairs and the windows.*

   _____

7. *Had you all [formal] covered the tables before the storm* (la tormenta)?

   _____

8. *Where had you put the money?*

   _____

9. *I had written fifty letters before receiving an answer.*

   _____

10. *Had they provided you with enough information?*

    _____

11. *The food had rotted in the refrigerator.*

    _____

12. *We had fried enough potatoes for an army* (el ejército).

    _____

13. *What had you done in order to help them?*

    _____

14. *The dog hadn't discovered the bones* (el hueso) *under the bed.*

    _____

15. *The books had fallen from the shelf* (el estante).

    _____

EJERCICIO

¡Te toca a ti! *¿Qué habías hecho hoy antes de abrir este libro? Responde con una frase completa.*

1. _____

2. _____

3. _____

4. _____

5. _____

EJERCICIO

18·3

Traducción

VOCABULARIO

again and again	*una y otra vez*	nickname	*el apodo*
bestseller	*el éxito de ventas*	not anymore	*ya no*
to fall	*caer*	Prince	*el príncipe*
to give birth	*dar a luz a*	six-part series	*la serie de seis partes*
interview	*la entrevista*	subterfuge	*el subterfugio*
just the beginning	*apenas el principio*	televised	*televisado*
memoir	*la memoria*	working Royals	*los miembros activos*
misery	*la miseria*		*de la familia real*
to move (change residence)	*mudarse*		

Prince Harry and Meghan Markle were married on May 19, 2018. Meghan had been an actress and Harry was, well, a prince. Meghan gave birth to their son, Archie, on May 6, 2019, and later gave birth to their daughter, Lilibet, on June 4, 2021. Lilibet had been a nickname of Queen Elizabeth (Harry's grandmother). Even though they were happy together, Harry and Meghan did not like being part of the Royal Family, and they moved to Canada in 2019, and later moved to Montecito, California, where they now live. On March 7, 2021, they had a televised interview with Oprah Winfrey in which they revealed their misery being working Royals. The interview was explosive, but it was just the beginning. In December 2022, Harry and Meghan presented a six-part series on Netflix, again, sharing their misery. But, wait! There's more! In January 2023, Harry's memoir, Spare, was published in which he revealed even more misery and subterfuge within the Royal Family. It was immediately a bestseller, but had many critics. Many people believe that they said too much, over and over. By February 2023, Harry and Meghan's popularity had fallen dramatically. For years, Harry had been "the favorite Royal." Not anymore. What do you think?

THE IMPERATIVE, THE SUBJUNCTIVE, THE FUTURE AND CONDITIONAL PERFECT TENSES, AND THE PASSIVE VOICE

In this third and final section of the book, we cover the imperative (commands), the subjunctive mood, the compound tenses, and the passive voice.

So far, we've covered the present, the past, and the future in the indicative mood. It's time to do the same in the subjunctive: Instead of reporting events as they happen (indicative), we refer to situations that involve uncertainty, desire, ignorance, emotion, or an impersonal opinion (subjunctive).

We begin by working with the imperative, because that establishes a good foundation for working with the subjunctive. Then we'll build on that foundation by learning to speak in complete sentences of hopes and desires for outcomes over which we have little or no control—this is the essence of the subjunctive mood. The three aspects of time—past, present, and future—all exist within the subjunctive framework. However, instead of reporting situations as they occur, occurred, or will occur, we comment on situations as we'd like (or not like) to believe that they are, were, or will be.

The imperative

·19·

MOOD	Imperative
TIME	Refers to the present
KEY PHRASES	Any command
STRUCTURE	Simple: VERB BASE + VERB ENDING

The imperative deals with a single aspect of the language—giving commands. We call the imperative a mood rather than a tense, because commands do not vary according to time as the tenses do. The only time frame involved in a command is "now," as in "Clean your room *now.*"

Statements in the imperative are direct. There are no qualifiers, such as "*I want you to* clean your room" or "*You should* clean your room." The message is straightforward, often containing only one word—"Go!" "Stop!" "Look!" "Wait!" "Listen!"

The understood recipient of any command is "you." Even when admonishing yourself to do something, you are speaking to yourself as "you" (the **tú** form in Spanish). We can, however, also give "we" commands, which in English usually begin with "let's"—"Let's dance," "Let's eat," "Let's go."

This chapter covers commands in five sections: a section for each of the four forms of "you" in Spanish (**tú**, **usted**, **vosotros**, and **ustedes**), and a fifth section for "we," or **nosotros**, commands. Verbs for which the affirmative command ("Go!") differs from the negative command ("Don't go!") in Spanish will be covered, as will the use of object pronouns with commands.

One final note: Work with the imperative establishes a good foundation for working with the present subjunctive, which is introduced in the next chapter.

tú commands

Regular affirmative commands

A regular affirmative command is formed by simply dropping the **s** from the second-person singular conjugated form, as follows.

Hablas.	*You speak.*	>	**¡Habla!**	*Speak!*
Comes.	*You eat.*	>	**¡Come!**	*Eat!*
Vives.	*You live.*	>	**¡Vive!**	*Live!*

Traducción *Rewrite the following affirmative commands in Spanish, using* **tú** *commands.*

1. *Study!* _____
2. *Work!* _____
3. *Look!* _____
4. *Listen!* _____
5. *Read!* _____
6. *Run!* _____
7. *Walk!* _____
8. *Dance!* _____
9. *Write!* _____
10. *Decide!* _____

11. *Sell!* _____
12. *Pay!* _____
13. *Suffer!* _____
14. *Count!* _____
15. *Fly!* _____
16. *Begin!* _____
17. *Think!* _____
18. *Sleep!* _____
19. *Continue!* _____
20. *Confess!* _____

Regular negative commands

A regular negative command is formed as follows.

1 Begin with the present tense first-person singular (**yo**) form of the verb.

2 Remove the -**o** ending. This is called the "**yo** stem."

3 For -**ar** verbs, add -**es**. For -**er** and -**ir** verbs, add -**as**.

EXAMPLES   **habl**o   >   **habl-**   >   hables
           como   >   **com-**   >   comas
           escribo > **escrib-** >   escribas

¡No hables!	*Don't speak!*	¡No compres el pescado!	*Don't buy the fish!*
¡No comas!	*Don't eat!*	¡No vendas la casa!	*Don't sell the house!*
¡No escribas!	*Don't write!*	¡No abras la puerta!	*Don't open the door!*

NOTE   When the **yo** form ends in -**oy**, such as in **estar**, the -**oy** is removed to form the "**yo** stem."

Standard orthographic (spelling) changes

Before the letter **e**, the following orthographic changes come into play.

◆ **c** > **qu**

No tocas el piano.   >   **¡No toques el piano!**
You don't play the piano.   ***Don't play the piano!***

◆ **g** > **gu**

No juegas al béisbol.   >   **¡No juegues al béisbol!**
You don't play baseball.   ***Don't play baseball!***

◆ z > c

No comienzas.   >   ¡No comiences!
You don't begin.   ***Don't begin!***

Traducción *Rewrite the following negative commands in Spanish, using* **tú** *commands.*

1. *Don't look!* _____

2. *Don't sing!* _____

3. *Don't study!* _____

4. *Don't run!* _____

5. *Don't think!* _____

6. *Don't drink the water!* _____

7. *Don't arrive late!* _____

8. *Don't practice now!* _____

9. *Don't pay the bill!* _____

10. *Don't organize the papers!* _____

11. *Don't read my diary!* _____

12. *Don't dance on the table!* _____

13. *Don't open the windows!* _____

14. *Don't admit anything!* _____

15. *Don't believe anything!* _____

Irregular **tú** commands

There are very few verbs that have irregular commands in the **tú** form. Listed below are the most common infinitives for these verbs, with both their affirmative and negative command forms.

INFINITIVE	AFFIRMATIVE	NEGATIVE
decir	**di**	**no digas**
hacer	**haz**	**no hagas**
ir	**ve**	**no vayas**
poner	**pon**	**no pongas**
salir	**sal**	**no salgas**
ser	**sé**	**no seas**
tener	**ten**	**no tengas**
venir	**ven**	**no vengas**

EJERCICIO
19·3

Traducción *Rewrite the following irregular commands in Spanish, using* **tú** *commands.*

1. *Put the book here!* _____

2. *Tell the truth!* _____

3. *Make the bed!* _____

4. *Leave the house!* _____

5. *Come to the kitchen!* _____

6. *Be kind!* _____

7. *Go to the living room!* _____

8. *Have the money by tomorrow!* _____

9. *Don't put the shoes on the table!* _____

10. *Don't say anything!* _____

11. *Don't make the beds!* _____

12. *Don't leave now!* _____

13. *Don't come tomorrow!* _____

14. *Don't be selfish!* _____

15. *Don't go shopping today!* _____

16. *Don't have animals in the house!* _____

Affirmative commands with object pronouns

With an affirmative command, the object pronoun(s) are attached directly to the end of the verb in its imperative form.

¡Estúdialo!	*Study it!*	¡Hazme un favor!	*Do me a favor!*
¡Tráemelo!	*Bring it to me!*	¡Dinos el secreto!	*Tell us the secret!*
¡Deme el libro!	*Give me the book!*	¡Levántate!	*Stand up!*
¡Déjame en paz!	*Leave me alone!*	¡Tráigame el libro!	*Bring me the book!*

Note that the original stress pattern is retained for pronunciation. In Spanish words that end with a vowel, an **n**, or an **s**, the natural stress falls on the next-to-last syllable. When the addition of an object pronoun (or pronouns) would affect the original stress pattern, a written accent is added so that the stress remains on the originally stressed syllable. For the verb **dar**, the command form **dé** often retains its written accent with an object pronoun attached, although the original stress would be retained without it.

Habla.	*He speaks.*	¡Habla!	*Speak!*	¡Háblame!	*Speak to me!*
Mira.	*He looks.*	¡Mira!	*Look!*	¡Míralos!	*Look at them!*
Come.	*He eats.*	¡Come!	*Eat!*	¡Cómelo!	*Eat it!*

When two object pronouns are involved, remember the **RID** rule:

Reflexive, **I**ndirect, **D**irect

A reflexive pronoun precedes an indirect or direct object pronoun, and an indirect object pronoun precedes a direct object pronoun. If both the indirect and direct object pronouns begin with the letter **l**, the indirect pronoun changes to **se**, as in the last example below. (This rule for the order of object pronouns applies for all imperatives—**tú**, **usted**, **vosotros**, **ustedes**, and **nosotros** commands.)

¡Dímelo!	*Tell it to me!*	¡Cómpratelo!	*Buy it for yourself!*
¡Dámelas!	*Give them to me!*	¡Dáselo!	*Give it to him!*

EJERCICIO
19·4

Traducción *Rewrite the following affirmative commands in Spanish, using **tú** commands.*

1. *Buy it [m.]!* _____

2. *Sell it [f.]!* _____

3. *Sit down!* _____

4. *Go to bed!* _____

5. *Take a bath!* _____

6. *Tell me a story!* _____

7. *Put it [m.] here!* _____

8. *Go away!* _____

9. *Put them [f.] there!* _____

10. *Leave us alone!* _____

11. *Tell it [m.] to us!* _____

12. *Write it [f.] to me!* _____

13. *Sing it [f.] to her!* _____

14. *Buy it [m.] for me!* _____

15. *Do it [m.] for yourself!* _____

Negative commands with object pronouns

With a negative command, the object pronoun(s) precede the verb in its imperative form. The object pronoun is independent of the verb. When there are two object pronouns, the **RID** rule applies.

¡No me mires!	*Don't look at me!*	¡No lo hagas!	*Don't do it!*
¡No le des el dinero!	*Don't give him the money!*	¡No se lo digas!	*Don't tell it to him!*
¡No lo pongas allí!	*Don't put it there!*	¡No los compres!	*Don't buy them!*

Traducción *Rewrite the following negative commands in Spanish, using* **tú** *commands.*

1. *Don't read it [m.]!* _____

2. *Don't drink it [f.]!* _____

3. *Don't kiss it [m.]!* _____

4. *Don't tell me lies!* _____

5. *Don't lie to me!* _____

6. *Don't go away!* _____

7. *Don't stand up!* _____

8. *Don't take a shower!* _____

9. *Don't go to bed!* _____

10. *Don't hate me!* _____

11. *Don't give it [f.] to him!* _____

12. *Don't tell it [m.] to them!* _____

13. *Don't sell it [m.] to us!* _____

14. *Don't read it [m.] to me!* _____

15. *Don't sing it [f.] to her!* _____

usted commands

Regular commands

Regular **usted** commands have a single form for both affirmative and negative commands. They are formed as follows.

1 Begin with the present tense first-person singular (**yo**) form of the verb.

2 Remove the **-o** ending. This is called the "**yo** stem."

3 For **-ar** verbs, add **-e**. For **-er** and **-ir** verbs, add **-a**. (Remember to incorporate the standard orthographic changes.)

EXAMPLES   **hablo**   >   **habl-**   >   hable
           como   >   **com-**   >   coma
           escribo >   **escrib-** >   escriba

¡Hable!	*Speak!*	¡Ponga!	*Put!*	¡Esté!	*Be!*
¡Coma!	*Eat!*	¡Tenga!	*Have!*	¡Dé!	*Give!*
¡Escriba!	*Write!*	¡Traiga!	*Bring!*	¡Comience!	*Begin!*

NOTE When the **yo** form ends in -**oy**, such as in **estar**, the -**oy** is removed to form the "**yo** stem." Both **estar** and **dar** have third-person **usted** command forms that would be identical to other words with the same spelling. Therefore, the command forms carry an accent mark to distinguish them (**dé**, as distinct from **de** ("of, from"); **esté**, as distinct from **este** ("this")).

Traducción *Rewrite the following regular commands in Spanish, using* **usted** *commands. Assume that the object pronoun "it" is always masculine.*

1. *Sing!* _____

2. *Sell!* _____

3. *Count!* _____

4. *Pay!* _____

5. *Run!* _____

6. *Do it!* _____

7. *Play the piano!* _____

8. *Read it!* _____

9. *Bring it here!* _____

10. *Stand up!* _____

11. *Give it to me!* _____

12. *Tell it to me!* _____

13. *Don't tell me a lie!* _____

14. *Don't wait for us!* _____

15. *Don't rob the bank!* _____

16. *Give me the money!* _____

17. *Sit down!* _____

18. *Put it there!* _____

19. *Don't do it!* _____

20. *Tell him a story!* _____

Irregular commands

There are only three irregular **usted** commands.

ir	¡Vaya!	*Go!*
saber	¡Sepa!	*Know!*
ser	¡Sea!	*Be!*

Traducción *Rewrite the following irregular commands in Spanish, using* **usted** *commands.*

1. *Go away!* _____

2. *Know it [m.]!* _____

3. *Be good!* _____

4. *Don't go away!* _____

5. *Don't be bad [f.]!* _____

6. *Don't go to the party!* _____

7. *Know everything for tomorrow!* _____

8. *Go to the front of the room!* _____

ustedes commands

Ustedes commands are nearly identical to **usted** commands, the only difference being an **n** added to the end for the plural form. The same form is used for both affirmative and negative commands. This is true for all verbs, whether regular or irregular.

¡Hablen!	*Speak!*	¡Váyanse!	*Go away!*
¡No coman!	*Don't eat!*	¡Sépanlo!	*Know it!*
¡Escriban!	*Write!*	¡Sean amables!	*Be kind!*

NOTE The **ustedes** form is used in both formal and informal situations in Spanish America.

Traducción *Rewrite the following commands in Spanish, using* **ustedes** *commands.*

1. *Work!* _____

2. *Think!* _____

3. *Don't do that!* _____

4. *Don't leave!* _____

5. *Sit down!* _____

6. *Put them [m.] here!* _____

7. *Don't tell me anything!* _____

8. *Play the piano!* _____

9. *Play baseball!* _____

10. *Bring me the food!* _____

11. *Tell him the secret!* _____

12. *Don't go away angry [f.]!* _____

13. *Go to bed!* _____

14. *Wash your hands!* _____

15. *Brush your teeth!* _____

vosotros commands

Regular affirmative commands

A regular affirmative **vosotros** command is formed by simply dropping the **r** from the infinitive and adding the letter **d**. This is true for all verbs except reflexives.

¡Trabajad!	*Work!*	¡Decídmelo!	*Tell it to me!*
¡Bebed!	*Drink!*	¡Traednos la foto!	*Bring us the photo!*
¡Escribid!	*Write!*	¡Sed simpáticos!	*Be kind!*
¡Sabedlo!	*Know it!*	¡Idos!	*Go away!*

The affirmative **vosotros** command for a reflexive verb is formed by attaching the reflexive pronoun directly to the same stem (INFINITIVE minus **r**). No **d** is added to the stem before attaching the pronoun.

¡Levantaos!	*Stand up!*	¡Sentaos!	*Sit down!*
¡Acostaos!	*Go to bed!*	¡Callaos!	*Be quiet!*

NOTE The informal **vosotros** command is used only in Spain.

EJERCICIO
19·9

Traducción *Rewrite the following affirmative commands in Spanish, using* **vosotros** *commands.*

1. *Fly!* _____

2. *Return!* _____

3. *Come!* _____

4. *Stop!* _____

5. *Run!* _____

6. *Boil the water!* _____

7. *Sleep!* _____

8. *Read it [m.]!* _____

9. *Go to the store!* _____

10. *Put it [f.] in the house!* _____

11. *Do us a favor!* _____

12. *Arrive at ten o'clock!* _____

Regular negative commands

Regular negative **vosotros** commands are formed as follows.

-ar VERBS   Add **-éis** to the "**yo** stem."

-er VERBS   Add **-áis** to the "**yo** stem."

-ir VERBS   Add **-áis** to the "**yo** stem."

¡No trabajéis!	*Don't work!*	¡No me lo digáis!	*Don't tell it to me!*
¡No bebáis!	*Don't drink!*	¡No nos traigáis nada!	*Don't bring us anything!*
¡No escribáis!	*Don't write!*	¡No se lo deis!	*Don't give it to him!*

Note that the negative **vosotros** commands of **ir**, **saber**, and **ser** mirror that of the **usted** commands for these verbs.

ir	¡No vayáis conmigo!	*Don't go with me!*
saber	¡No sepáis todo!	*Don't know everything!*
ser	¡No seáis antipáticos!	*Don't be mean!*

Negative commands for stem-changing -ir verbs

For negative **vosotros** commands, stem-changing -**ir** verbs show stem changes of **e** > **i** and **o** > **u**.

pedir	**¡No pidáis!**	***Don't request!***	dormir	**¡No durmáis!**	***Don't sleep!***
servir	**¡No sirváis!**	***Don't serve!***	morirse	**¡No os muráis!**	***Don't die!***
seguir	**¡No sigáis!**	***Don't follow!***	repetir	**¡No repitáis!**	***Don't repeat!***

EJERCICIO 19·10

Traducción   *Rewrite the following negative commands in Spanish, using* **vosotros** *commands.*

1. Don't eat! _____

2. Don't speak! _____

3. Don't play here! _____

4. Don't sing! _____

5. Don't sleep in the park! _____

6. Don't boil the water! _____

7. Don't fall asleep! _____

8. Don't leave! _____

9. Don't take the money! _____

10. Don't follow me! _____

11. Don't go to bed! _____

12. Don't go away! _____

nosotros commands

Both affirmative and negative **nosotros** ("we") commands generally translate as "let's" statements in English: "Let's eat," "Let's dance," "Let's go." Regular **nosotros** commands are formed as follows.

1 Begin with the present tense first-person singular (**yo**) form of the verb.

2 Remove the **-o** ending. This is called the "**yo** stem."

3 For **-ar** verbs, add **-emos**. For **-er** and **-ir** verbs, add **-amos**. (Remember to incorporate the standard orthographic changes.)

> EXAMPLES   **habl**o   >   **habl-**   >   hablemos
>   **com**o   >   **com-**   >   comamos
>   **escrib**o >   **escrib-** >   escribamos

> ¡Hablemos!   *Let's talk!*
> ¡Comamos!   *Let's eat!*
> ¡Escribamos!   *Let's write!*

NOTE   When the **yo** form ends in **-oy**, such as in **estar**, the **-oy** is removed to form the "**yo** stem." This pattern has been presented several times in this chapter. Knowing this pattern will help greatly in the study of the present subjunctive.

Notable characteristics of commands

1 Stem-changing verbs—except stem-changing **-ir** verbs—do not change in the **nosotros** form.

> ¡Contemos el dinero!   *Let's count the money!*
> ¡Pensemos!   *Let's think!*
> ¡Movamos los muebles!   *Let's move the furniture!*
> ¡Volvamos!   *Let's return!*

2 Stem-changing **-ir** verbs show the following changes in **nosotros** commands.

o > ue VERBS	The **o** changes to **u**.	EXAMPLE	dormir	**¡Durmamos!**	*Let's sleep!*
e > ie VERBS	The **e** changes to **i**.		mentir	**¡Mintamos!**	*Let's lie!*
e > i VERBS	The **e** changes to **i**.		pedir	**¡Pidamos!**	*Let's ask!*

3 Verbs ending with **-car**, **-gar**, and **-zar** make the necessary standard orthographic changes where needed (**c > qu, g > gu, z > c**).

> ¡Toquemos el piano!   *Let's play the piano!*
> ¡Paguemos la cuenta!   *Let's pay the bill!*
> ¡Comencemos!   *Let's begin!*

4 With reflexive verbs, drop the **s** of the conjugated verb before adding **nos**. Otherwise, add all object pronouns directly to the end of the conjugated form.

> Levantemos + nos = ¡Levantémonos!   *Let's stand up!*
> Sentemos + nos = ¡Sentémonos!   *Let's sit down!*
> Acostemos + nos = ¡Acostémonos!   *Let's go to bed!*

5 To form a negative **nosotros** command, just add **no** before the verb.

¡No trabajemos!	*Let's not work!*
¡No volemos!	*Let's not fly!*
¡No nos bañemos!	*Let's not take a bath!*

EJERCICIO
19·11

Traducción *Rewrite the following regular commands in Spanish, using* **nosotros** *commands.*

1. *Let's study!* _____

2. *Let's walk!* _____

3. *Let's not study!* _____

4. *Let's not eat!* _____

5. *Let's sell the car!* _____

6. *Let's do something!* _____

7. *Let's not do anything!* _____

8. *Let's eat lunch!* _____

9. *Let's put the dog outside!* _____

10. *Let's sing to them!* _____

11. *Let's not lie!* _____

12. *Let's not begin now!* _____

13. *Let's tell the truth!* _____

14. *Let's not say anything!* _____

15. *Let's buy it* [m.]! _____

There are only three verbs with irregular **nosotros** commands (though **ir** has both reflexive and nonreflexive forms). Note that **ir** has different affirmative and negative forms.

ir	**¡Vamos!**	*Let's go!*	**¡No vayamos!**	*Let's not go!*
irse	**¡Vámonos!**	*Let's go away!*	**¡No nos vayamos!**	*Let's not go away!*
saber	**¡Sepamos!**	*Let's know!*	**¡No sepamos!**	*Let's not know!*
ser	**¡Seamos!**	*Let's be!*	**¡No seamos!**	*Let's not be!*

Traducción *Rewrite the following irregular commands in Spanish, using* **nosotros** *commands.*

1. *Let's know everything!* _____

2. *Let's be kind!* _____

3. *Let's not go to the party!* _____

4. *Let's go away tonight!* _____

5. *Let's not be cowards* (el cobarde)*!* _____

6. *Let's go to the movies tomorrow!* _____

7. *Let's be honest people!* _____

8. *Let's not go away this afternoon!* _____

The present subjunctive  ·20·

MOOD	Present subjunctive
TIME	Refers to the uncertain present and future
KEY PHRASES	Main clause of uncertainty + **que**
STRUCTURE	Simple tense: VERB BASE + VERB ENDING

The subjunctive mood can be defined in terms of the situations in which it is used, often described as fitting into these eight categories.

1 Desire
2 Ignorance
3 Emotional statement or comment
4 Impersonal opinion
5 Uncompleted action
6 Vague or indefinite antecedent
7 "Perhaps" and "maybe"
8 "Even if"

Up to this point, we have worked with sentences that are indicative, and they do what the name implies: They indicate or report something. Consider the following indicative sentence.

> *I know that you speak Spanish.*

The speaker is certain of something (that you speak Spanish) and is reporting that information.

In every subjunctive sentence, however, there is always some aspect of uncertainty—something that is not known or not controllable. Consider the subjunctive sentence below.

> *I hope that you speak Spanish.*

The second clause of this sentence is in the subjunctive, because the speaker does not *know* that you speak Spanish and is not reporting that you do. Instead, because the speaker has a *desire* that you speak Spanish rather than certain knowledge that you do, this sentence represents the first category of situations listed above for the subjunctive.

In sentences with a subjunctive clause, there is often an indicative clause that reports desire, ignorance, an emotion, or an impersonal opinion related to the action in the subjunctive clause.

Desire

*I hope **that you are happy**.*
*I suggest **that you buy the red car**.*
*We demand **that he pay in cash**.*
*He prays **that you get well**.*
*You insist **that we wash the dishes**.*

Ignorance

*I doubt **that he lives here**.*
*I don't think **that she knows my name**.*
*She doesn't believe **that you live here**.*

Emotional statements or comments

*I'm happy **that you're the president**.*
*He's sad **that I'm the principal**.*
*They're delighted **that we're here**.*

Impersonal opinion

*It's great **that you can dance so well**.*
*It's better **that we sit here**.*
*It's terrible **that we have to wait**.*
*It's advisable **that you sign your name in ink**.*

Uncompleted action

*We'll eat **after we wash our hands**.*
*I'll feel better **when I sit down**.*
*He won't work here **unless he gets a raise**.*
*I'll wear clean clothes **in case I have an accident**.*

Vague or indefinite antecedent

*I need an assistant **who is punctual**.*
*He wants a wife **who cooks as well as his mother**.*
*We want a car **that has a television**.*
*Isn't there anyone **who can read this**?*

"Perhaps" and "maybe"

***Perhaps** she'll call us tonight.*
***Maybe** he has the money.*

"Even if"

***Even if he knows**, he won't tell us.*
***Even if she is Miss America**, we won't hire her.*

Formation of the present subjunctive

Nearly all verbs in the present subjunctive are formed in the same way. There are three steps involved, which are shown below for nine common verb prototypes in Spanish. Beyond these, only six irregular verbs remain.

1   Begin with the **yo** form of the present indicative.

hablar	**hablo**
comer	**como**
vivir	**vivo**
conocer	**conozco**
tener	**tengo**
hacer	**hago**

querer	**quiero**
salir	**salgo**
ver	**veo**

2 Remove the **-o** ending.

hablar	**habl-**
comer	**com-**
vivir	**viv-**
conocer	**conozc-**
tener	**teng-**
hacer	**hag-**
querer	**quier-**
salir	**salg-**
ver	**ve-**

3 Add the following endings.

-ar VERBS	-e, -es, -e, -emos, -éis, -en
-er VERBS	-a, -as, -a, -amos, -áis, -an
-ir VERBS	-a, -as, -a, -amos, -áis, -an

Below are the full conjugations in the present subjunctive for the nine verbs listed above.

hablar	hable, hables, hable, hablemos, habléis, hablen
comer	coma, comas, coma, comamos, comáis, coman
vivir	viva, vivas, viva, vivamos, viváis, vivan
conocer	conozca, conozcas, conozca, conozcamos, conozcáis, conozcan
tener	tenga, tengas, tenga, tengamos, tengáis, tengan
hacer	haga, hagas, haga, hagamos, hagáis, hagan
querer	quiera, quieras, quiera, queramos, queráis, quieran
salir	salga, salgas, salga, salgamos, salgáis, salgan
ver	vea, veas, vea, veamos, veáis, vean

EJERCICIO

¿Cuál es tu opinión? ¿Cuál es verdadero o falso para ti?

1. _____ Es importante que yo hable cada día con mis amigos.

2. _____ Espero que la reina consorte Camilla de Inglaterra me conozca.

3. _____ Es imposible que veamos todas las películas producidas por Hollywood.

4. _____ Quiero un coche que pueda volar.

5. _____ Aunque yo salga de mi casa temprano, llego tarde al trabajo.

6. _____ Es mejor que cada persona haga su cama cada día.

7. _____ Me lavaré las manos antes de que yo coma.

8. _____ Dudo que el rey Carlos tenga poderes supernaturales.

9. _____ Busco un perro que no ladre.

10. _____ No creo que un caballo viva en tu casa.

Note that there is no stem change in the **nosotros** or **vosotros** forms of any of the verbs above.

In stem-changing **-ir** verbs, however, the present subjunctive shows the following changes in the stem of the **nosotros** and **vosotros** forms.

o > ue VERBS	The **o** changes to **u**.	EXAMPLE	dormir	**durmamos, durmáis**
e > ie VERBS	The **e** changes to **i**.		mentir	**mintamos, mintáis**
e > i VERBS	The **e** changes to **i**.		pedir	**pidamos, pidáis**

Irregular verbs in the present subjunctive

There are six verbs that do not follow the patterns described above. Below are the full conjugations in the present subjunctive for these six irregular verbs.

dar	dé, des, dé, demos, deis, den
estar	esté, estés, esté, estemos, estéis, estén
haber	haya, hayas, haya, hayamos, hayáis, hayan
ir	vaya, vayas, vaya, vayamos, vayáis, vayan
saber	sepa, sepas, sepa, sepamos, sepáis, sepan
ser	sea, seas, sea, seamos, seáis, sean

Note that accented vowels are retained.

EJERCICIO

¿Cuál es tu opinión? ¿Cuál es verdadero o falso para ti?

1. _____ Es importante que una persona sea honesta y honrada.

2. _____ Quiero que muchas personas me den regalos para mi cumpleaños.

3. _____ Es terrible que muchas personas no sepan la diferencia entre el bien y el mal.

4. _____ Espero que mis amigos estén felices hoy.

5. _____ Dudo que haya un unicornio en este mundo.

6. _____ Es bueno que muchas personas vayan a la playa cada día para tomar el sol.

7. _____ No comeré nunca en un restaurante hasta que el mesero me dé una servilleta.

8. _____ Necesito un asistente que sepa todo.

9. _____ Insisto en que los miembros de mi familia sean políticos.

10. _____ Es ridículo que muchas personas den dinero a los tele-evangelistas.

Uses of the present subjunctive

Use the subjunctive whenever there is a degree of desire, ignorance, emotion, or impersonal opinion on the part of the subject.

A sentence containing a subjunctive clause has two parts: the main clause and the subordinate clause. These two clauses are generally separated by **que** (meaning "that"). The main clause contains the statement of desire, ignorance, emotion, or opinion; this clause is in the indicative. The subordinate clause contains whatever is being considered; this clause is in the subjunctive. Consider the following sentence.

*I doubt that **he works much**.*

The main clause "I doubt" is in the indicative, because it is reporting. The subordinate clause, "he works much," is in the subjunctive because of the uncertainty expressed in the main clause. This sentence is expressed in Spanish as follows.

Yo dudo que **él trabaje mucho**.

Note that although subjunctive verb forms are identifiable by a distinct conjugated verb form in Spanish, the subjunctive is not necessarily expressed by a distinct verb form in English.

Expressions of desire

Verbs in the main clause that express a wish, a preference, a request, or similar desire set up the need for the subjunctive in the subordinate clause. In these situations, the subject tells what he or she would like to happen; whether it will actually happen is not certain.

Below are several common verbs of desire that require the use of the subjunctive.

VOCABULARIO

esperar	to hope	**preferir (e > ie)**	to prefer
exigir	to demand	**querer (e > ie)**	to want
insistir en	to insist (on)	**rogar (o > ue)**	to pray, beg
ojalá	God willing, I strongly hope	**sugerir (e > ie)**	to suggest
pedir (e > i)	to request		

Él prefiere que **yo hable**.	*He prefers that **I speak**.*
Ellos esperan que **podamos** bailar.	*They hope that **we can** dance.*
Insistimos en que **tengas** el dinero.	*We insist that **you have** the money.*
Ella pide que **sirváis** el café.	*She requests that **you all serve** the coffee.*
Quiero que **Juan estudie**.	*I want **John to study**. (literally, I want that John study.)*
Espero que **ellos vivan** en esa casa.	*I hope that **they live** in that house.*
Ojalá que **ella llegue** a tiempo.	*God willing, **she (will) arrive** on time.*

EJERCICIO

¿Cuál es verdadero o falso para ti?

1. _____ Ojalá que no tenga un examen hoy.

2. _____ Espero que haga buen tiempo mañana.

3. _____ Espero que el próximo presidente sea demócrata.

4. _____ Quiero que mis amigos sean amables.

5. _____ Prefiero que haya nieve en la Navidad.

6. _____ Espero que llueva el fin de semana que viene.

7. _____ Excepto en caso de emergencia, sugiero que nadie me llame después de las diez de la noche.

8. _____ Cuando tengo una fiesta, quiero que los invitados lleguen a tiempo.

9. _____ Pido que mis vecinos no tengan muchas fiestas ruidosas.

10. _____ Espero que no haya cucarachas en mi cocina.

11. _____ Cuando asisto a una reunión, prefiero que (yo) no tenga que preparar nada.

12. _____ Insisto en que las personas me den el mismo respeto que yo les doy a ellos.

Traducción

1. *I hope that she speaks with me tomorrow.*

   _____

2. *I want you to eat the bread.*

   _____

3. *He wants me to write a letter.*

   _____

4. *We pray that you are well.*

   _____

5. *They [m.] want us to do it.*

   _____

6. *She hopes that you can come to the party.*

   _____

7. *They [f.] suggest that you do it.*

   _____

8. *I insist that you all work.*

   _____

9. *He requests that we be here at nine o'clock.*

   _____

10. *Why do you request that I do it?*

    _____

11. *I prefer that we not leave the house until five o'clock.*

    _____

12. *She hopes that you know her.*

    _____

13. *We insist that you eat with us.*

_____

14. *Do you want me to count the money?*

_____

15. *They [m.] suggest that we put the papers in the cabinet* (el gabinete).

_____

Traducción *Verbs in **bold italic** are in the present subjunctive.*

VOCABULARIO

amable	*friendly*
cambiar	*to change*
cometer un error	*to make a mistake*
el desempeño	*performance*
el jefe, la jefa	*boss*
justo	*fair*

*Tomorrow is the first day of my new job. I hope that everything **goes** well for me. My boss seems very friendly, but I prefer that she **be** more fair than friendly. I want her **to understand** that if I make a mistake (and I'm sure that I'll make many), I want her **to tell** (it to) me directly. Before the first week **ends**, I'm going to request that she **tell** me what she thinks of my performance. If she suggests that I **change** some aspect of my work, it will be easier to do so then than after working there for a few months.*

_____

_____

_____

_____

_____

_____

_____

Ignorance

Verbs in the main clause that express ignorance or doubt set up the need for the subjunctive in the subordinate clause. In these situations, the subject acknowledges uncertainty or ignorance of the outcome of the action described in the subordinate clause.

Below are several common verbs of ignorance that require the use of the subjunctive.

Most of these verbs are used in the negative, for example, **no estar seguro que** ("to not be sure that"). Although these verbs in the negative set up the use of the subjunctive in the subordinate clause, these same verbs in the affirmative set up the indicative in the subordinate clause.

NEGATIVE/SUBJUNCTIVE **Yo no creo** que Juan **tenga** el dinero.
*I **don't think** that John **has** the money.*

AFFIRMATIVE/INDICATIVE **Yo creo** que Juan **tiene** el dinero.
*I **think** that John **has** the money.*

EJERCICIO
20·3

Traducción

1. *I doubt that she eats in that restaurant.*

   _____

2. *I don't suppose that you'll tell me the name of the murderer* (el asesino).

   _____

3. *They [m.] don't believe that he plays the piano.*

   _____

4. *She isn't sure that the coffee is ready.*

   _____

5. *We don't think that the Vikings will win the game.*

   _____

6. *He is not convinced that I need so much money.*

   _____

7. *Why don't you believe that we know him?*

   _____

8. *We aren't convinced that the moon (la luna) is made (ser) of green cheese.*

_____

9. *He doubts that they [m.] know the answer.*

_____

10. *She isn't sure that we always tell the truth.*

_____

11. *Why aren't you convinced that I am always right (tener razón)?*

_____

12. *It doesn't seem that he wants to be here.*

_____

13. *I'm not sure that you can understand this.*

_____

14. *He doesn't believe that I'm his neighbor.*

_____

15. *I don't imagine that you believe my story (la historia).*

_____

_____

EJERCICIO
20·4

Traducción *Verbs in **bold italic** are in the present subjunctive.*

VOCABULARIO			
la compañía	company	el líder	leader
de la noche a la mañana	overnight	planear	to plan
en cambio	on the other hand	salir bien	to go well
estar listo	to be ready	tampoco	not either
hacerse	to become	tan	so, such

*I doubt that John **knows** that we're planning a party for him. It doesn't seem possible that he **is** the new president of this company, and I don't imagine that he **believes** it either. I doubt that he **likes** this new position. I'm not convinced that he **is ready** for so great a responsibility; on the other hand, I don't suppose that anyone **can** become a great leader overnight. I want everything **to go well** for him.*

_____

_____

_____

_____

Emotional statement or comment

Emotions often color the truth of a situation and introduce a degree of uncertainty. A sentence that follows the pattern *emotion or personal feeling* + "that" sets up the need for the subjunctive. Consider the sentence "I'm angry that she's so evil." The person's inherent evilness, while certainly clear and true to the speaker, might not be so evident to others.

This particular pattern (*emotion* + "that") often introduces an unknown, unrealized future as well. Consider the sentence "I'm excited that our team will win the championship."

This pattern is expressed in Spanish as *emotion or personal feeling* + **que**, where **que** introduces a subordinate clause that contains a verb in the subjunctive.

EJERCICIO
20·5

Traducción

1. *I'm happy that you're so* (tan) *tall.*

   _____

2. *He's sad that she's a dishonest person.*

   _____

3. *We're delighted* (encantado) *that you can come to our party.*

   _____

4. *They [m.] are angry that their team won't win the tournament* (el torneo).

   _____

5. *You're disgusted* (indignado) *that our team will lose every game.*

   _____

6. *I'm frustrated that she's always late.*

   _____

7. *She's anxious* (ansioso) *that you'll lose the money.*

   _____

8. *I'm worried that they'll [m.] tell me more lies* (la mentira).

   _____

9. *She's worried that I'll reveal* (revelar) *the truth about her.*

   _____

10. *He's sad that she's with another man.*

   _____

Impersonal opinion

An impersonal opinion in the main clause that expresses emotion, uncertainty, unreality, or an indirect or implied command sets up the need for the subjunctive in the subordinate clause.

Several common impersonal expressions that convey this type of impersonal opinion are listed below. Each expression follows the pattern *impersonal expression* + **que** (*impersonal expression* + "that"). For each of these expressions, **que** introduces a subordinate clause that contains a verb in the subjunctive.

VOCABULARIO

conviene que	it is advisable that
es fantástico que	it is fantastic that
es importante que	it is important that
es imposible que	it is impossible that
es increíble que	it is incredible that
es (una) lástima que	it is a pity that, it is a shame that
es mejor que	it is better that
es necesario que	it is necessary that
es posible que	it is possible that
es preferible que	it is preferable that
es probable que	it is probable that
es ridículo que	it is ridiculous that
es terrible que	it is terrible that
más vale que	it is better that
ojalá (que)	I hope (that), if only he/it/they/etc. would/could/might, God willing (that)
puede ser que	it may be that

Es una lástima que **yo esté** enfermo.
*It's a pity that **I'm** sick.*

Es mejor que **comamos** el apio.
*It's better that **we eat** the celery.*
  OR *It's better **for us to eat** the celery.*

Es necesario que **te vayas** ahora.
*It is necessary that **you go** now.*
  OR *It is necessary **for you to go** now.*

Es importante que **miréis** este programa.
*It's important that **you all watch** this program.*

Ojalá que **no llueva** mañana.
*I hope **it doesn't rain** tomorrow.*

Conviene que **ellos sepan** su dirección.
*It's advisable that **they know** their address.*

EJERCICIO
20·6

Traducción

1. *It's better that we eat in the kitchen.*

   _____

2. *It's necessary for you to call them tomorrow.*

   _____

3. *It's preferable that you buy the eggs by the dozen* (por docenas).

   _____

4. *It's unlikely that they'll be ready by five o'clock.*

   _____

5. *It's advisable that you* [formal] *have an attorney* (el abogado) *with you.*

   _____

6. *It's important that no one know that secret.*

   _____

7. *It may be that Alice doesn't work here anymore* (ya no).

   _____

8. *It's ridiculous that so many politicians* (el político) *don't tell the truth.*

   _____

9. *It's impossible for me to be in two places at the same time* (al mismo tiempo).

   _____

10. *It's incredible that he speaks twelve languages* (el idioma).

    _____

11. *It's a shame that ice cream has so many calories* (la caloría).

    _____

12. *If only* (Ojalá) *Jane wouldn't sing at* (en) *the wedding* (la boda).

    _____

13. *It's fantastic that we don't have to sit next to* (al lado de) *them* [m.].

    _____

14. *It may be that Steven isn't what* (lo que) *he says he is.*

    _____

15. *It's impossible for me to remain* (quedarse) *in this room one more minute.*

    _____

222 PRACTICE MAKES PERFECT   Spanish Verb Tenses

Traducción *Verbs in **bold italic** are in the present subjunctive.*

VOCABULARIO

el cochino	slob
desordenado	messy
el folleto	pamphlet
imponer	to enforce
ordenado	neat
la regla	rule
el reglamento	regulation
la reunión	meeting
la sala de juntas	boardroom
no tener nada que ver con	to have nothing to do with
quedarse de brazos cruzados	to twiddle one's thumbs

*Last night for the first time I read the rules and regulations of the company where I have worked for six years. It's possible that I **am** the only person who has read this pamphlet. There are so many absurd rules. For example, it's ridiculous that we **should** keep our desks neat at all times. It's better that a person **have** the freedom to be a slob if that is what he/she needs in order to work well. Also, it's incredible that we **have to** attend all meetings, including the ones that have nothing to do with our own work (nobody ever goes to these meetings). It's better that we **work** at a messy desk than attend a meeting in a neat boardroom and twiddle our thumbs. If only no one would **enforce** these rules!*

Uncompleted action

When the action of the subordinate clause is pending or indefinite, the verb in the subordinate clause will be in the subjunctive. For example, in the sentence "I'll speak with John *when he arrives*," you may believe with all your heart that John will arrive, but until you see the whites of his eyes, you cannot *know* this for certain.

Below are several common connecting phrases that frequently set up the subjunctive.

VOCABULARIO

a menos que	unless	**hasta que**	until
antes (de) que	before	**mientras que**	while
con tal (de) que	provided that	**para que**	so that, in order that
cuando	when	**sin que**	without
después (de) que	after	**tan pronto como**	as soon as
en caso de que	in case		

Ella te llamará **tan pronto como yo llegue.**   *She'll call you **as soon as I arrive.***
Cocinaré **para que podamos** comer.   *I'll cook **so that we can** eat.*

Él no irá **a menos que tú vayas.**   *He will not go **unless you go.***
Tocaré el piano **con tal de que cantéis.**   *I'll play the piano **provided that you sing.***

Estudiaré **en caso de que haya** un examen.   *I will study **in case there is** a test.*
Trabajaremos **hasta que cierren** la oficina.   *We will work **until they close** the office.*

EJERCICIO 20·8

Traducción *In many of the following sentences, the main clause is in the future tense.*

1. *I won't eat until I'm hungry.*

_____

2. *I'll write you a note so that you remember to buy milk.*

_____

3. *You'll feel (sentirse) better after you take this medicine.*

_____

4. *He won't marry (casarse con) a woman unless she's intelligent.*

_____

5. *You all can't hunt (cazar) unless you have a license (la licencia).*

_____

6. *I'll dry the dishes while you wash them.*

_____

7. *The priest can't baptize (bautizar) the baby before the godparents (los padrinos) arrive.*

_____

8. *The game's not over (acabarse) till it's over.*

_____

9. *I'll believe it when I see it.*

_____

10. *He's going to read this book another time in case we have a quiz* (la prueba).

_____

11. *He won't eat anything unless he has a napkin* (la servilleta) *on his lap* (el regazo).

_____

12. *Every week, I save* (ahorrar) *fifty dollars so that I have enough money for my vacation.*

_____

13. *She'll never be happy until she knows how to conjugate* (conjugar) *verbs.*

_____

14. *You should brush your teeth before we leave for the dentist's office* (el consultorio del dentista).

_____

15. *I can't wear these pants until I lose* (perder) *ten pounds.*

_____
_____

EJERCICIO
20·9

Traducción *Verbs in **bold italic** are in the present subjunctive.*

VOCABULARIO	
prestar	to loan, lend
devolver	to repay
dentro del plazo de tres meses	within three months
pedir	to ask for, request
conseguir un puesto	to get a job
obtener un reembolso de los impuestos	to get a tax refund
el hueso	bone
la herencia	inheritance
llevar a los tribunales	to take to court
el juez	judge

*My friend needed a car, but she didn't have enough money. I told her that I would loan her five thousand dollars, and she told me she would repay me within three months. I gave her the money, she bought the car, but she didn't repay me anything. After three months, I asked her for my money and she said, "I'll pay you when I **get** a job." But, she had a job. Then, she said, "I'll pay you when I **get** my tax refund." She got (received) her tax refund. But, she still didn't pay me anything. I wanted my money. I was like a dog with a bone. Then, she said, "I'll pay you when I **get** my inheritance." But, no one died. I took her to court. She told the judge that it was a gift. The judge didn't believe her and asked her, "Are you waiting until pigs **fly**?" I finally received my money, but I've lost a friend.*

_____
_____
_____
_____

Vague or indefinite antecedent

When the object or person being referred to in the main clause is not known to exist (this is referred to as an indefinite antecedent), the subjunctive is required in the subordinate clause. The difference between a definite antecedent and indefinite antecedent can be seen in the following sentences.

DEFINITE ANTECEDENT	*I have a secretary who is efficient.*
INDEFINITE ANTECEDENT	*I want a secretary who is efficient.*

Él quiere una esposa que **gane** mucho dinero.　　*He wants a wife who **earns** a lot of money.*

No conozco a nadie que **sepa zapatear**.　　*I don't know anyone who **knows how to tap-dance**.*

Note that, with verbs of desire, the personal **a** is not used when the person may not exist.

EJERCICIO
20·10

Traducción

1. *We're looking for a house that has three bedrooms.*

   _____

2. *She wants a dog that doesn't bark* (ladrar).

   _____

3. *Is there anyone here who can play the guitar?*

   _____

4. *I need a maid* (la criada) *who washes* (limpiar) *windows.*

   _____

5. *Is there anybody in the world who knows how to express* (expresarse) *himself clearly?*

   _____

6. *I'm looking for a cat that doesn't scratch* (arañar) *the furniture* (los muebles).

   _____

7. *Where can I buy a shirt that isn't polyester* (el poliéster)?

   _____

8. *There isn't anyone here who can help you.*

   _____

9. *For his birthday this year he wants a parrot* (el loro) *that speaks three languages.*

   _____

10. *I want to live in a city where there isn't any crime* (el crimen).

    _____

Traducción *Verbs in **bold italic** are in the present subjunctive.*

VOCABULARIO

el aparcamiento	*parking space*	la muñeca	*wrist*
el artículo	*item*	nunca jamás	*never ever*
el centro comercial	*shopping mall*	parecer	*to look like*
el collar	*necklace*	la perlita	*little pearl*
la dependienta	*clerk*	el planeta	*planet*
el guante	*glove*	la puerta principal	*front door*
el gusto	*taste*	desmontable	*detachable*
ir de compras	*to go shopping*	la reina	*queen*
la joya	*jewel*	el tacón	*heel*
la manga	*sleeve*	tardar (en)	*to take time*
meterse en	*to put oneself through*	la tienda	*store*

*I went shopping with Giralda this morning. I will never ever put myself through that torture again. Giralda is impossible! First, she wants a parking space that **is** no more than ten feet from the front door of the mall. This took half an hour. Next, she wants a dress that **has** detachable sleeves so that she **can** wear it all year. She also wants a necklace that **looks like** something a queen would wear, but she also wants this necklace **to cost** less than ten dollars. She wants shoes that **have** jewels on the heels and she wants gloves that **have** little pearls at the wrists. In each store, she told the clerk exactly what she wanted, and each clerk told Giralda that there is no store in that mall, or in any mall on this planet, that **sells** such items. Giralda was furious and told me that there is no one in this world who **understands** her fabulous taste.*

"perhaps" and "maybe"

Clauses introduced by the words "perhaps" or "maybe" are usually cloaked in uncertainty, and therefore they require the use of the subjunctive. The words **acaso**, **quizá(s)**, and **tal vez** all mean "perhaps" and "maybe," and for the most part they are used interchangeably. **Acaso**, however, is generally reserved for writing, while **quizá(s)** and **tal vez** are used more in daily conversation. Both **quizá** and **quizás** can be used, though **quizá** is more common. There is no difference in meaning, but it's best for a person to choose one form and use that form consistently.

Quizá **él no te conteste.**
Perhaps he won't answer you.
OR *Maybe he won't answer you.*

Acaso **ellos no vayan de compras.**
Perhaps they won't go shopping.
OR *Maybe they won't go shopping.*

Tal vez **ella esté enferma.**
Perhaps she's sick. OR *Maybe she's sick.*

Quizá **no la conozcamos.**
Perhaps we don't know her.
OR *Maybe we don't know her.*

EJERCICIO
20·12

Traducción

1. *Maybe he has the money.*

_____

2. *Perhaps we can go.*

_____

3. *Maybe they [m.] live here.*

_____

4. *Perhaps you know him.*

_____

5. *Maybe they'll [m.] buy the house today.*

_____

6. *Perhaps we are lost (perdido).*

_____

7. *Maybe he isn't the smartest person in the world.*

_____

8. *Perhaps you all shouldn't drink this milk.*

_____

9. *Maybe the politician isn't telling the truth.*

_____

10. *Perhaps the cat has only eight lives.*

_____

EJERCICIO

20·13

Traducción *Each "maybe" appears as* **tal vez** *in the Answer key. Your answers may vary.*

VOCABULARIO

A ver	Let's see
¡Ajá!	That's it!
la basura	garbage
el césped	lawn
cortar	to mow
dar un paseo	to take a walk
el huevo	egg
ir al cine	to go to the movies
remontar una cometa	to fly a kite
sacar	to take out

Let's see. I don't have to work today. What should I do? Maybe I'll read a book. Maybe I'll buy a book. Maybe I'll write a book! Maybe I'll go to the movies. Maybe I'll study Spanish. Maybe I'll fly a kite. Maybe I'll fly to the moon. Maybe I'll mow the lawn. Maybe I'll eat an egg. Maybe I'll go for a walk. Maybe I'll take out the garbage. Maybe I'll do nothing. That's it! I'll do nothing!

_____

_____

_____

_____

_____

_____

aunque meaning "even if"

Aunque is the Spanish word for "even if," "although," and "even though." When the action *has not yet occurred* or *is not known to be occurring,* **aunque** sets up the subjunctive. For example, in the sentence **Iremos** *aunque llueva* ("We will go *even if it rains*"), the rain has not yet begun. When the action already has occurred or is occurring, use the indicative, as in the sentence **Iremos** *aunque llueve* ("We will go *even though it is raining*").

Aunque él no hable español, lo contrataré.   *Even if he doesn't speak Spanish, I'll hire him.*
Aunque no ganemos, estaremos felices.   *Although we may not win, we'll be happy.*

Traducción

1. *Even if Jane cooks, I won't stay* (quedarse).

   _____

2. *Although they [m.] may want to watch television, we won't let* (dejar) *them.*

   _____

3. *Even if you yell* (gritar) *at me, I won't change my mind* (cambiar de idea).

   _____

4. *Although he may think he's a genius* (el genio), *everyone knows that he isn't.*

   _____

5. *Even if you offer the policeman a thousand dollars, he'll still* (todavía) *give you a ticket*
   (la multa).

   _____

6. *Although we may be ignorant of* (ignorar) *the candidates, we still have the right* (el derecho)
   to vote.

   _____

7. *Even if you put the cat in the basement, Barbara will still sneeze* (estornudar).

   _____

8. *Although you all may feel sick, you still have to take the test.*

   _____

9. *Even if you wind your watch* (dar cuerda al reloj) *fifty times, it will never work.*

   _____

10. *Although he may smile* (sonreír) *all the time, inside* (en su interior) *he is evil* (malo).

    _____

11. *Even if I know the answer, I won't tell you.*

    _____

12. *Although you all [formal] may think I'm crazy, I know that I'm right.*

    _____

Traducción

VOCABULARIO

alguien	*someone*
el florista	*florist*
gigante	*giant*
el intruso	*intruder*
llamar a la puerta	*to be at the door*
mirar por la ventana	*to look through the window*
parecerse a	*to look like*
el ramo	*bouquet*
el vendedor	*salesperson*

Oh no! Someone is at the door. I'm looking at him through the window. He doesn't look like anyone that I know. It's possible that it's a politician, but it's more likely that it's a salesperson. Or maybe it's the mailman. No—he always carries packages. Even if it's the mailman, I won't open the door. Maybe it's the florist with a bouquet of flowers for me. No—florists always have flowers. I don't know who this person can be. Maybe it's a representative from Publishers Clearing House because I've won ten million dollars. No—he would have that giant check with him (consigo). I'm not going to open the door. I hope that the intruder will go away.

EJERCICIO
20·16

Traducción *The following selection includes subjunctive themes from all eight categories.*

VOCABULARIO

cambiar	*to change*	mejorar	*to improve*
cenar	*to dine, eat dinner*	o… o…	*either … or …*
el cielo	*heaven*	rara vez	*rarely*
es decir	*that is to say*	la receta	*recipe*
la delicia	*treat*	repetirse	*to repeat oneself*
la manzana	*apple*	la tarta	*tart*

There isn't anyone who can cook as well as my friend Catarina. It's great that she's having a party this weekend, because I haven't eaten a good meal in a long time (that is to say, since the last time I ate dinner at her house). I hope that she makes her famous apple tart again, but I doubt that she will make it this weekend, because she served it less than a year ago and she rarely repeats herself. Even if she prepares this treat, it won't be the same, because she always improves every recipe a little each time she uses it. I fear that I will never taste that same tart again. Maybe I'll beg her, so that she will prepare the tart for me for my birthday. I know that when I taste that tart again I will either be in heaven or in Catarina's dining room.

The imperfect subjunctive  •21•

MOOD	Imperfect subjunctive
TIME	Refers to the past
KEY PHRASES	Hypothetical "if," "as if"
STRUCTURE	Simple tense: VERB BASE + VERB ENDING

The imperfect subjunctive is used in the same situations as the present subjunctive—when there is an aspect of uncertainty, after certain expressions, and after certain words (such as "perhaps," "maybe," and "even if"). However, the time frame is in the past rather than in the present.

In the study of the indicative tenses, we distinguish between the preterite and the imperfect tenses in the past. This distinction is not an issue in the subjunctive mood, where the imperfect subjunctive refers to actions in the imagined or hypothetical past.

Consider the following two sentences.

Espero que Ricardo **tenga** el libro.	*I hope that Richard **has** the book.*
Esperaba que Ricardo **tuviera** el libro.	*I hoped that Richard **had** the book.*

In the first sentence, both verbs are in the present—**Espero** ("I hope") in the main clause and the present subjunctive **tenga** ("has") in the subordinate clause.

In the second sentence, the main clause **Esperaba** ("I hoped") is in the past (the imperfect indicative), which sets the stage for the imperfect subjunctive.

We'll look at the formation of the imperfect subjunctive tense and then at the situations in which it is used.

Formation of the imperfect subjunctive

The base of the imperfect subjunctive is what remains after the **-ron** ending is dropped from the third-person plural of the preterite tense. This is the base for all forms of the imperfect subjunctive.

THIRD-PERSON PRETERITE		IMPERFECT SUBJUNCTIVE BASE
hablaron	*they spoke*	**habla-**
comieron	*they ate*	**comie-**
abrieron	*they opened*	**abrie-**
tuvieron	*they had*	**tuvie-**
dijeron	*they said*	**dije-**
fueron	*they were*	**fue-**
fueron	*they went*	**fue-**
estuvieron	*they were*	**estuvie-**
hicieron	*they made, they did*	**hicie-**
pusieron	*they put*	**pusie-**

To this base, add either of the following sets of endings.

-ra	-ramos		-se	-semos
-ras	-rais	OR	-ses	-seis
-ra	-ran		-se	-sen

Of these two sets of endings, which may be used interchangeably, the **-ra** endings are more commonly used, and these are the endings that are shown in the examples in this book. Below is the full conjugation of **hablar** in the imperfect subjunctive.

hablar *to speak, talk*

hablara	**habláramos**
hablaras	**hablarais**
hablara	**hablaron**

Note that in the first-person plural (**nosotros**) form, the stress falls on the vowel that precedes the imperfect subjunctive ending (for example, **habláramos**, **dijéramos**, **tuviéramos**, **fuéramos**), and a written accent mark is required.

Uses of the imperfect subjunctive

Main clause in the past

When the main clause is in the past and the subjunctive is required, use the imperfect subjunctive in the subordinate clause.

Ella quería que **yo hablara** en español.	*She wanted **me to speak** in Spanish.*
Fue terrible que **estuviéramos enfermos**.	*It was terrible that **we were sick**.*
Querían que **supieras** la respuesta.	*They wanted **you to know** the answer.*
Él dudaba que **pudierais** bailar.	*He doubted that **you all could** dance.*
Yo esperaba que **no hubiera** un accidente.	*I hoped that **there wasn't** an accident.*
Comimos antes de que **ellos llegaran**.	*We ate before **they arrived**.*

Traducción

1. *I wanted John to buy the towels* (la toalla).

   _____

2. *It was a pity that you had to work last Sunday.*

   _____

3. *There wasn't anyone in the class who spoke French.*

   _____

4. *We doubted that Humpty Dumpty fell from the wall* (el muro).

   _____

5. *No one believed that Mary had a little lamb* (el corderito).

   _____

6. *Mr. Clean requested that we take off our shoes before entering his palace* (el palacio).

   _____

7. *Was it necessary that you all call me in the middle* (en medio) *of the night?*

   _____

8. *They weren't sure that I could take care of myself* (cuidarse).

   _____

9. *She prepared dinner so that we wouldn't die* (morirse) *of hunger.*

   _____

10. *We cleaned the house before they arrived.*

    _____

11. *She studied in case there was a test the next day.*

    _____

12. *He begged me not to order the lobster* (la langosta) *because it's so* (tan) *expensive.*

    _____

13. *We didn't think that anyone heard us.*

    _____

14. *Was anybody there who knew all the state capitals?*

    _____

15. *We asked that they continue without us.*

    _____

Main clause in the present with a subordinate clause in the past

When the main clause is in the present tense and requires the subjunctive, but the verb in the main clause refers to an action in the past, the subordinate clause is in the imperfect subjunctive.

Ella espera que yo no **gastara** todo el dinero.　She hopes that **I didn't spend** all the money.
Siento que **no conociéramos** a Mateo.　I'm sorry that **we didn't meet** Matthew.
Estoy contento de que él **estudiara**.　I'm happy that he **studied**.
Es absurdo que **tuvieran** que pagar.　It's absurd that **they had** to pay.

EJERCICIO 21·2

Traducción

1. They [f.] don't believe that I made these cookies (la galleta).

_____

2. It's unlikely that Francis Bacon wrote these plays (el drama).

_____

3. We're not convinced that Little Miss Muffet was afraid of the spider (la araña).

_____

4. I'm sorry that you were sick and couldn't come to our party.

_____

5. I don't suppose that you knew that she was the thief (el ladrón).

_____

6. It doesn't seem that the maid cleaned the house this morning.

_____

7. God willing, you paid the bills (la cuenta) on time this month.

_____

8. It may be that no one heard your speech (el discurso).

_____

9. He behaves (portarse) as if he were three years old.

_____

10. I don't think that he studied last night.

_____

11. He hopes that you washed your hands before eating.

_____

12. It may be that she didn't want to take (sacar) our picture.

_____

13. *It's a miracle that the airline* (la aerolínea) *didn't lose your luggage* (el equipaje).

_____

14. *Is it possible that you left* (dejar) *your keys in the car?*

_____

15. *It's incredible that you were born* (nacer) *the same day as I.*

_____

Hypothetical *if-* clauses in the past

Most *if*-clauses in the past fall under the heading "hypothetical" and are therefore, at best, presumptive, which leads straight into the domain of the subjunctive. Consider the sentence "If I were taller, I would play basketball." My being taller is clearly hypothetical, and therefore the verb "were" is in the subjunctive.

A few important points regarding this type of sentence follow.

♦ A subordinate *if*-clause in the past is very often linked with a main clause in the conditional indicative. For example, consider the sentence "If I were taller (*if*-clause in the past), I would play basketball (conditional indicative)."

*Jugaría al básquetbol, **si yo fuera** más alto.*	*I would play basketball, **if I were** taller.*
Recibirías buenas notas **si estudiaras**.	*You would get good grades **if you studied**.*
Yo no iría **si fuera** tú.	*I wouldn't go **if I were** you.*
¿Te quedarías **si hubiera** un incendio?	*Would you stay **if there were** a fire?*

♦ Only hypothetical *if*-clauses in the past are in the subjunctive. If the intent is to elicit true information (and therefore they are not hypothetical), the clause remains in the indicative. Consider the sentence **Pregunté a Juan si él sabía la respuesta** ("I asked John if he knew the answer"). There are two indications that the conjugated form of **saber** remains in the indicative: (1) The information is clearly verifiable (because all you have to do is ask John), and (2) the main clause (**Pregunté a Juan**) is in the preterite, not the conditional.

♦ *If*-clauses in the present do not take the subjunctive: **Si Juan tiene el dinero, te pagará** ("If John has the money, he will pay you"). *If*-clauses in the present are usually followed by either the present or the future indicative.

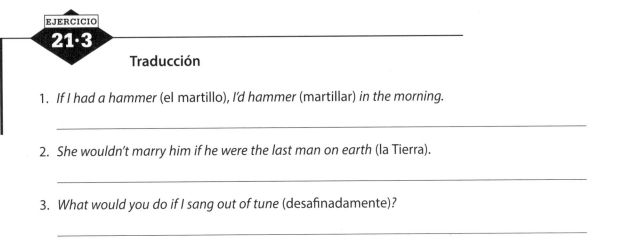

EJERCICIO
21·3

Traducción

1. *If I had a hammer* (el martillo), *I'd hammer* (martillar) *in the morning.*

_____

2. *She wouldn't marry him if he were the last man on earth* (la Tierra).

_____

3. *What would you do if I sang out of tune* (desafinadamente)?

_____

4. *If you knew the answer, would you tell us?*

_____

5. *If giraffes* (la jirafa) *didn't have long necks* (el cuello), *they couldn't eat leaves* (la hoja).

_____

6. *If it weren't for gravity* (la gravedad), *we would float* (flotar) *like bubbles* (la burbuja).

_____

7. *The bears wouldn't eat your food if you hung* (colgar) *it from a tree.*

_____

8. *If Pinocchio didn't lie so much, people would believe him once in a while* (de vez en cuando).

_____

9. *If there were no cars, there wouldn't be so much pollution* (la contaminación).

_____

10. *If he weren't so lazy* (perezoso), *I'd hire* (contratar) *him.*

_____

11. *If it weren't raining, we could take a walk in the park.*

_____

12. *If it weren't so cold, I would ride my bicycle* (ir en bicicleta) *to work.*

_____

13. *This ring* (el anillo) *would be worth* (valer) *a lot more money if the diamond were genuine.*

_____

14. *If my car started* (arrancar) *in this weather, it would be a miracle* (el milagro).

_____

15. *If pigs could fly, where would they go?*

_____

"as if" and "as though" clauses

The verb in a subordinate clause that begins with "as if" or "as though" (**como si**) is in the imperfect subjunctive. The main clause can be in the present, the past, or the conditional tense.

Te ves como si **fueras** culpable.	*You look as if **you were** guilty.*
Actuábamos como si **estuviéramos** enfermos.	*We acted as if **we were** sick.*
Él se puso el sombrero como si **fuera** el rey.	*He put on his hat as though **he were** the king.*
Hablaban como si **supieran** todo.	*They were talking as if **they knew** everything.*

Traducción

1. *He speaks as if he were the King himself* (el mismo rey).

_____

2. *In your situation, I would act* (actuar) *as if I didn't know anything.*

_____

3. *She talks as if she were the owner* (el dueño) *of this company* (la empresa).

_____

4. *We danced as if we were Fred Astaire and Ginger Rogers.*

_____

5. *He spends* (gastar) *money as though there were no tomorrow.*

_____

6. *You look* (verse) *as if you saw a ghost* (el fantasma).

_____

7. *He looks as if he lost his best friend.*

_____

8. *The critic* (el crítico) *looks as though he liked the play.*

_____

9. *You sing as though you swallowed* (tragar) *a bird.*

_____

10. *It was as if I couldn't remember anything.*

_____

11. *He felt as if he already knew her.*

_____

12. *She lived each day as though it were the last* (el último).

_____

13. *He spoke to me as though I didn't have a brain* (el cerebro).

_____

14. *She looked as though she lost* (perder) *a lot of weight.*

_____

15. *You used to smoke as if you were a chimney* (la chimenea).

_____

querer and poder

The verbs **querer** ("to want") and **poder** ("to be able to, can") operate in a unique manner within the framework of the imperfect subjunctive. Each verb takes on a special meaning when used in the main clause of a sentence. Consider the following two sentences, each spoken in a restaurant.

> *I want a cup of coffee.*
> *I would like a cup of coffee.*

The first sentence is direct and brusque and, if spoken with great emphasis, could sound rude. The second sentence, merely by changing "want" to "would like," has a softened effect and makes the speaker appear more civil.

At first glance, the second sentence appears to be in the conditional. However, the conditional tense is used to tell what would happen if a certain condition were met, for example, "I would like a cup of coffee if I hadn't already drunk ten cups this morning." But that is not the speaker's intent here. He clearly wants a cup of coffee and he also wants to appear reasonably courteous, so he changes "want" to "would like" and probably gets better service as a result! To achieve this same sort of gallantry in Spanish, you need only to use **querer** in the imperfect subjunctive.

Yo quisiera una taza de café.	*I would like a cup of coffee.*
¿Quisieras leer mi diario?	*Would you like to read my diary?*

A similar situation occurs with the verb **poder** ("to be able to, can"). Consider the following inquiries.

> *Can you wash the windows?*
> *Will you wash the windows?*
> *Could you wash the windows?* OR *Would you wash the windows?*

The first inquiry is in the present tense, and it implies that the speaker wants to know if the addressee has the talent required to wash windows. The second inquiry is in the future tense, and it is a request—spoken directly and with enough emphasis, it could be considered pushy. The third inquiry (also a request) appears to be in the conditional, and it would be in the conditional if the question were actually "Could you wash the windows if your hands weren't broken?" But this speaker isn't seeking information, but rather someone to perform an onerous task.

In English, either "could" or "would" might be used with a slightly ingratiating tone, and probably with an added "please." In Spanish, the speaker begins with **Si** ("If") plus the imperfect subjunctive form of **poder**, followed by the conditional form of the verb referring to whatever the speaker wants done.

¿Si pudieras, limpiarías las ventanas?	*Could you wash the windows? (If you could, would you wash the windows?)*
¿Si pudieras, te sentarías, por favor?	*Would you sit down, please? (If you could, would you sit down, please?)*

Traducción

1. *I would like a cold lemonade, please.*

_____

2. *What would you like to do tonight?*

_____

3. *Could you mail* (echar al correo) *these letters for me?*

_____

4. *Would you do a favor for me?*

_____

5. *We would like a room* (la habitación) *with a view of the river.*

_____

6. *Could you move* (moverse) *a little to the right* (a la derecha)?

_____

7. *Where would you like to go for your honeymoon* (la luna de miel)?

_____

8. *Where would you all like to eat tomorrow night* (mañana por la noche)?

_____

9. *The queen* (la reina) *would like to speak.*

_____

10. *Could you be quiet* (callarse), *please?*

_____

11. *What would you all* [formal] *like to do this afternoon?*

_____

12. *We would like to roller skate* (patinar sobre ruedas) *in the shopping mall* (el centro comercial).

_____

13. *Could you* [formal] *make me a cup of coffee?*

_____

14. *Could you* [formal] *take me to your leader?*

_____

15. *Would you like to eat these crickets* (el grillo) *covered* (cubierto) *with chocolate?*

_____

querer meaning "to wish"

The other specialized use of **querer** ("to want") in the imperfect subjunctive is the context in which it means "to wish." To form wish-filled sentences, use **querer** in the imperfect subjunctive in the main clause, and when there is no change of subject ("*I* wish that *I* had a million dollars"), follow the conjugated **querer** with an infinitive.

Yo quisiera tener un millón de dólares.	*I wish that I had a million dollars.*
Quisiéramos conocer a más personas.	*We wish that we knew more people.*

In such sentences, if there is a change of subject ("I wish that *you* were here"), the imperfect subjunctive form of **querer** is followed by **que** and the imperfect subjunctive form of the second verb.

Yo quisiera que **estuvieras** aquí.	*I wish that you were here.*
Quisiéramos que él nos **llamara**.	*We wish that he would call us.*
Quisieras que **no lloviera**.	*You wish that it wouldn't rain.*
Quisierais que Juan **estuviera** aquí.	*All of you wish that John were here.*
Ella quisiera que **hubiera** comida en la casa.	*She wishes that there were food in the house.*
Quisieran que **yo tuviera** un coche.	*They wish that I had a car.*

EJERCICIO

¿Estás de acuerdo? ¿Sí o no?

1. _____ (Yo) quisiera ser más alto/alta.

2. _____ (Yo) quisiera que el dinero creciera en los árboles.

3. _____ (Yo) quisiera que los políticos siempre nos dijeran la verdad.

4. _____ (Yo) quisiera tener más tiempo.

5. _____ (Yo) quisiera que la gente leyera más y mirara la televisión menos.

6. _____ (Yo) quisiera que los aviones salieran y llegaran a su hora.

7. _____ (Yo) quisiera que más personas montaran en bicicleta en vez de conducir todo el tiempo.

8. _____ (Yo) quisiera que no hubiera guerras.

9. _____ (Yo) quisiera que no tuviéramos que pagar tanto por la gasolina.

10. _____ (Yo) quisiera hacer más ejercicio y comer menos.

11. _____ (Yo) quisiera que el presidente me conociera personalmente.

12. _____ (Yo) quisiera vivir en Madrid.

13. _____ (Yo) quisiera que estuviéramos de vacaciones ahora.

14. _____ (Yo) quisiera correr en un maratón.

EJERCICIO

21·6

Traducción

1. *I wish that you weren't so nervous.*

   _____

2. *We wish that you were here.*

   _____

3. *I wish that there were a machine* (la máquina) *that could wash and dry clothes at the same time.*

   _____

4. *I wish that you didn't have to hear this.*

   _____

5. *Jane wishes that her husband didn't watch so much television.*

   _____

6. *Children always wish that they were older and adults wish that they were younger.*

   _____

7. *I wish that I spoke Spanish fluently* (con soltura).

   _____

8. *He wishes that he could drive.*

   _____

9. *He wishes that he could see through* (a través de) *walls* (la pared).

   _____

10. *I wish that we weren't behind* (detrás de) *the horses in the parade* (el desfile).

    _____

11. *I wish that I made* (ganar) *more money.*

    _____

12. *I wish that it would snow* (nevar).

    _____

13. *We wish that they would go* (irse) *home.*

    _____

14. *I wish that there weren't any calories in ice cream.*

    _____

15. *Donald wishes that he didn't have to pay taxes* (el impuesto).

    _____

Traducción

VOCABULARIO

el árbol	*tree*	el mago	*wizard*
la bruja	*witch*	el mono	*monkey*
el cerebro	*brain*	sobre todo	*most of all*
el corazón	*heart*	todo el mundo	*everybody*
desaparecer	*to disappear*	tolerar	*to tolerate*
el espantapájaros	*scarecrow*	valiente	*brave*
el estaño	*tin*	volante	*flying*
el león	*lion*		

In The Wizard of Oz, *everybody wishes that his or her life were different. The Scarecrow wishes that he had a brain. The Tin Man wishes that he had a heart. The Lion wishes that he were brave. Toto wishes that the flying monkeys would disappear. The tree wishes that people wouldn't eat his apples. The Wizard wishes that he were a wizard, and the Wicked Witch wishes two things: that she had Dorothy's shoes and that she could tolerate water better. Most of all, Dorothy wishes that she were in Kansas.*

_____

_____

_____

_____

_____

_____

_____

_____

The future perfect tense

TENSE	Future perfect
TIME	Refers to completion of future action
KEY PHRASES	"Will have"
STRUCTURE	Compound tense: **haber** conjugated in the future + PAST PARTICIPLE

The future perfect tense is indicative, and it refers to an action that will have taken place in the future at or by a specified time, for example, "I will have finished this book by Friday" or "I'll have this book finished by Friday."

The future perfect tense also can be used to express probability or conjecture, as in the sentence "He probably has left already."

Formation of the future perfect

The future perfect is a compound tense, which means that an auxiliary verb is required before the main verb. The auxiliary verb **haber** is conjugated in the future tense and is followed by the past participle of the main verb, as follows.

habré + PAST PARTICIPLE	habremos + PAST PARTICIPLE
habrás + PAST PARTICIPLE	habréis + PAST PARTICIPLE
habrá + PAST PARTICIPLE	habrán + PAST PARTICIPLE

Uses of the future perfect

To express what will have happened

The future perfect expresses an action that will have taken place by a specified time in the future. In English one can say, "I will have written this letter by three o'clock" or, more commonly, "I will have this letter written by three o'clock." In Spanish, these sentences both translate as **Habré escrito esta carta para las tres**.

Habré pintado la casa para el sábado.	*I will have the house painted by Saturday.*
Habremos leído el libro para el jueves.	*We will have read the book by Thursday.*
¿Cuándo **habrás hecho** esto?	*When will you have this done?*
Habréis comido para las siete.	*You all will have eaten by seven o'clock.*
Él no lo **habrá visto** para entonces.	*He won't have seen it by then.*
Habrán vendido su coche para mañana.	*They will have sold their car by tomorrow.*

EJERCICIO
22·1

Traducción

1. *In two weeks, I will have lived here for four years.*

_____

2. *By next year, McDonald's will have sold another billion* (mil millones) *hamburgers.*

_____

3. *She won't have prepared dinner by five thirty.*

_____

4. *When will they have the work finished* (terminar)?

_____

5. *We will have known each other for twelve years this August.*

_____

6. *Will you all have your dresses ironed* (planchar) *by this afternoon?*

_____

7. *Will you have all this clothing washed by tonight?*

_____

8. *He won't have the pharmacy* (la farmacia) *opened by then.*

_____

9. *We have to go now; if we go later, they'll* [m.] *have left already.*

_____

10. *If you give all the food to the dog, he'll have all of it eaten by tomorrow.*

_____

11. *You needn't worry: I'm sure they'll have told her everything by now* (para este momento).

_____

12. *I suppose that everyone will have gone to bed by midnight* (la medianoche).

_____

13. *At this rate* (A este ritmo), *you'll have fried more potatoes than McDonald's by the end of the week.*

_____

14. *If you lose this election, you will have lost more elections than anybody* (nadie).

_____

15. *If you win this election, you will have proven that it is possible to fool* (engañar) *all the people all the time.*

_____

To express probability

The future perfect is used to express probability or conjecture with regard to something that took place in the recent past.

It is in the conjecture aspect where the future perfect differs from the present perfect. Note the difference in the following two sentences.

PRESENT PERFECT	Él lo **ha hecho**.	*He **has done** it.*
FUTURE PERFECT	Él lo **habrá hecho**.	*He **must have done** it.* OR *He's **probably done** it.*

The first sentence simply reports an action; there is no uncertainty on the speaker's part. However, in the second sentence, although the speaker appears reasonably certain, there is still a little room left for doubt. It is this slight uncertainty that is expressed in the use of the future perfect.

Lo siento. **Me habré dormido**.	*I'm sorry. **I must have fallen asleep**.*
Nos habremos perdido.	*We **must have gotten lost**.*
Habrás estado aquí.	*You **must have been** here.*
Habréis leído el libro.	*You all **must have read** the book.*
¿Quién **habrá escrito** tal cosa?	*Who **could have written** such a thing?*
¿Adónde **habrán ido**?	*Where **could they have gone**?*

EJERCICIO
22·2

Traducción

1. *Fernando must have sent these flowers to me.*

_____

2. *He must have paid our bill. How nice!*

_____

3. *Fido must have stolen these slippers* (la zapatilla).

_____

4. *Where could my little dog have gone?*

_____

5. *Abdul looks* (verse) *pretty* (bien) *mad; Farrah must have told him everything.*

_____

6. *The kitchen stinks (oler mal)! Dorothy must have made dinner again.*

_____

7. *That is a lie! You must have heard it from Roger.*

_____

8. *How does he know these things? He must have read my diary (el diario).*

_____

9. *When could this have happened?*

_____

10. *Arthur must have known that Mary burned (quemar) all his love letters (la carta de amor).*

_____

11. *You must have known that he was married.*

_____

12. *I must have been crazy (in order) to buy vitamins (la vitamina) over the telephone (por teléfono).*

_____

13. *Bears must have eaten our food.*

_____

14. *It must have been terrible to discover that cockroaches were the real owners of your house.*

_____

15. *She must have given you a fake (falso) telephone number.*

_____

_____

EJERCICIO
22·3

Traducción

VOCABULARIO	ahorrar	*to save* (money)
	hacer un cheque	*to make out a check*
	la hipoteca	*mortgage*
	el interés	*interest*
	mudarse	*to move*
	olvidar	*to forget*
	pobre	*poor*
	tomar en consideración	*to take into account*
	último	*last*
	una vez	*ever*

I can't believe it! By the end of this month (Para finales de mes), I will have paid for this house completely. I never thought that this would happen. I thought that I would either move or die before making out that last miserable check. When I make out that last check, taking into account all the interest I've paid, I will have bought this house almost three times. A year from now, I suppose that I'll have forgotten that the bank owned (tener) more of this house than I did for many years, and the bank will have forgotten that I had ever (alguna vez) existed. I must have been crazy to think that a forty-year mortgage would make me feel as if I were a mature adult. It only made me feel poor. In two years, I'll have saved thousands of dollars and taken at least two long vacations. I wish I were in Tahiti right now.

_____

_____

_____

_____

_____

_____

_____

_____

_____

_____

The conditional perfect tense

TENSE	Conditional perfect
TIME	Refers to an uncompleted action
KEY PHRASES	"Would have"
STRUCTURE	Compound tense: **haber** conjugated in the conditional + PAST PARTICIPLE

Of all the tenses, the conditional perfect holds the dubious honor of being the only one to express no action whatsoever. It is the favorite tense of excuse makers. The conditional perfect is used to refer to an action that *would have taken place* but didn't, because something got in the way or some specified condition was not met.

In any sentence containing the conditional perfect, there will always be an "if" or a "but" lurking about, whether stated or implied. People whose verbiage contains a good deal of conditional perfect sentences most likely are those who don't get a lot done and who have a lot of excuses for everything that they don't do.

> I **would have paid** you, but I couldn't find my wallet.
> If it weren't so difficult, I **would have baked** you a pie.

The conditional perfect also expresses probability or conjecture with regard to an action either in the remote past, for example, "Where do you suppose they had been?" or with reference to time, for example, "It must have been three o'clock when he arrived."

Formation of the conditional perfect

The conditional perfect is indicative. Because it is a compound tense, the auxiliary verb **haber** is conjugated in the conditional tense and is followed by the past participle of the main verb.

habría + PAST PARTICIPLE	habríamos + PAST PARTICIPLE
habrías + PAST PARTICIPLE	habríais + PAST PARTICIPLE
habría + PAST PARTICIPLE	habrían + PAST PARTICIPLE

Uses of the conditional perfect

To express what would have happened

Conditional perfect followed by the indicative

A verb in the conditional perfect followed by a verb in the indicative expresses an action that *would have* taken place, but did not take place for a specified reason.

When the main clause is in the conditional perfect and the dependent clause is introduced with "but," the verb in the dependent clause will be in the indicative, rather than the subjunctive, mood.

Él habría trabajado, **pero estaba cansado.**   *He would have worked, **but he was tired.***
Yo habría comido, **pero no tenía hambre.**   *I would have eaten, **but I wasn't hungry.***

EJERCICIO
23·1

Traducción *In the following sentences, a clause with a verb in the conditional perfect is linked to a clause with a verb in the indicative.*

1. *I would have called you, but my cell phone (teléfono celular) wasn't working (funcionar).*

   _____

2. *He would have gone to the theater with us, but he had a headache.*

   _____

3. *Sherlock Holmes would have known who stole (robar) the diamonds, but you (f.) didn't hire (contratar) him.*

   _____

4. *We would have invited the Joneses, but the last time they came to our house, they got sick (enfermarse).*

   _____

5. *I would have gone on a diet, but I don't have much willpower (la fuerza de voluntad).*

   _____

6. *I would have prepared dinner, but I was in a bad mood.*

   _____

7. *He would have changed the lightbulb, but there was no one to turn (girar) the ladder (la escalera).*

   _____

8. *He would have turned in (entregar) his assignment (la tarea), but the dog ate it.*

   _____

9. *We would have eaten the food, but it was moldy* (mohoso).

_____

10. *They wouldn't have done anything in this situation because they are weak* (débil) *and lazy* (flojo) *people.*

_____

Conditional perfect followed by the imperfect subjunctive

A verb in the conditional perfect expresses an action that *would have* taken place were some other condition or situation met.

When the main clause is in the conditional perfect and the dependent clause is introduced with the hypothetical "if," the verb in the dependent clause will be in the imperfect subjunctive.

EJERCICIO
23·2

Traducción *In the following sentences, a clause with a verb in the conditional perfect is linked to a clause with a verb in the imperfect subjunctive.*

1. *Would you have told me the answer if you knew it?*

_____

2. *We would have given you a bigger piece* (el pedazo) *of cake if you weren't on a diet* (estar a dieta).

_____

3. *He would have hired* (contratar) *me if I spoke Spanish.*

_____

4. *Would all of you have gone to the beach if it weren't raining?*

_____

5. *What would you have done if you didn't have your debit card* (la tarjeta de débito)?

_____

6. *I would have bought the dress if it were one size* (el tamaño) *smaller.*

_____

7. *If she weren't so selfish* (egoísta), *she would have helped you.*

_____

8. *Would you have called me if I gave you my real telephone number?*

_____

9. *She wouldn't have married him if he were the last man on earth.*

_____

10. *If I thought for a moment I would like the book, I'd have read it.*

_____

To express conjecture or probability

The conditional perfect expresses conjecture or probability with regard to the following situations.

1 An action in the (relatively) remote past

Él lo **habría visto.**	*I suppose **he had seen** it.*
¿Adónde **habrían ido**?	*Where do you think **they had gone?***

NOTE In Spanish, the speaker's "I suppose" is understood in a statement, as is the "do you think?" aspect of a question. Therefore, Spanish sentences expressing this conjecture or probability do not translate these phrases explicitly.

2 The (clock) time or reference to a date of a specific action

Habría sido la una cuando él llegó.	*It **must have been** one o'clock when he arrived.*
Habrían sido las dos cuando me dormí.	*It **must have been** two o'clock when I fell asleep.*
Habría sido febrero cuando nació Fido.	*It **must have been** February when Fido was born.*
Habría sido el domingo pasado cuando se cayó.	*It **must have been** last Sunday when he fell.*

EJERCICIO
23·3

Traducción

1. *I suppose I had worn the ring only two or three times before the robbery* (el robo).

_____

2. *Where do you suppose she had hidden* (esconder) *the money?*

_____

3. *It must have been one o'clock in the morning when the telephone rang* (sonar).

_____

4. *It must have been July or August when I met you, because it was very hot.*

_____

5. *I suppose they'd never met anyone like you.*

_____

6. *It must have been November when I bought this, because I remember that there were turkeys* (el pavo) *everywhere* (en todas partes).

_____

7. *Do you suppose they had lied to us?*

_____

8. *It must have been a Tuesday when we met, because that day everybody was voting.*

_____

9. *It must have been February when I received this letter, because there was a valentine in the envelope.*

_____

10. *I don't suppose they had studied very much.*

_____

11. *It must have been four in the morning when Barbie returned from her date* (la cita) *with Ken.*

_____

12. *It must have been the Fourth of July, because I had on* (tener puesto) *a red, white, and blue T-shirt* (la camiseta).

_____

13. *It must have been a holiday* (el día de fiesta), *because the post office* (la oficina de correos) *was closed.*

_____

14. *Who do you suppose had left* (dejar) *those shoes on the highway* (la carretera)?

_____

15. *Why do you suppose Peter had put his wife inside a pumpkin* (la calabaza)?

_____

Traducción

VOCABULARIO | al principio | *at first*
| la caja | *box*
| la caridad | *charity*
| dejar solo | *to leave alone*
| donar | *to donate*
| la estación de policía | *police station*
| inmediatamente | *immediately*
| mil | *thousand*
| pues | *well*
| un rato | *a while*
| salir de | *to leave from*
| la situación | *situation*

Yesterday, while I was walking through the park, I found a box filled with money. At first I was happy, because, well, who wouldn't be happy in this situation? But after a while I began to worry, and I decided to take it to the police station. Last night, I asked some of my friends what they would have done. John said that he would have bought a car—there was at least ten thousand dollars in the box. Ana told me that she would have donated the money to charity. Roberto said he would have left the box alone and (would have) left the park immediately. What would you have done?

_____

_____

_____

_____

_____

_____

_____

_____

The present perfect subjunctive

MOOD	Present perfect subjunctive
TIME	Refers to the relatively recent past
KEY PHRASES	"Has" or "have" + PAST PARTICIPLE
STRUCTURE	Compound tense: **haber** conjugated in the present subjunctive + PAST PARTICIPLE

As its name implies, the present perfect subjunctive refers to action in the time frame of the present perfect ("John has eaten"), and in a situation that requires the subjunctive ("I hope that John has eaten"). With an understanding of the general time frame of the present perfect—completed action (often in the recent past)—and the situations in which the subjunctive is used, you will know when to use the present perfect subjunctive.

PRESENT PERFECT INDICATIVE	**Yo sé** que Juan **ha comido**. *I know that John **has eaten***.
PRESENT PERFECT SUBJUNCTIVE	**Yo espero** que Juan **haya comido**. *I hope that John **has eaten***.

Formation of the present perfect subjunctive

The present perfect subjunctive is a compound tense, which means that an auxiliary verb is required before the main verb. The auxiliary verb **haber** is conjugated in the present subjunctive and followed by the past participle of the main verb.

haya + PAST PARTICIPLE	hayamos + PAST PARTICIPLE
hayas + PAST PARTICIPLE	hayáis + PAST PARTICIPLE
haya + PAST PARTICIPLE	hayan + PAST PARTICIPLE

Uses of the present perfect subjunctive

Main clause in the present with a subordinate clause in the present perfect subjunctive

When the main clause in the present (or present perfect) tense requires the use of the subjunctive and refers to an action that *may have* taken place, the verb in that subordinate clause will be in the present perfect subjunctive.

Es posible que **yo lo haya leído**.	*It's possible that **I've read it**.*
Es improbable que **nos hayamos conocido** antes.	*It's unlikely that **we've met** before.*
Espero que **hayas comido**.	*I hope that **you have eaten**.*
Espero que **hayáis comido**.	*I hope that **you all have eaten**.*
Dudamos que **él haya estado** aquí.	*We doubt that **he has been** here.*
Podemos comenzar después que **hayan llegado**.	*We can begin after **they have arrived**.*

EJERCICIO
24·1

Traducción

1. *I hope that the cat hasn't eaten my goldfish* (la carpa dorada).

   _____

2. *It's unlikely that anyone here has driven a Rolls Royce.*

   _____

3. *I don't believe that those people in Kalamazoo have seen Elvis Presley.*

   _____

4. *You haven't lived until you've seen the Grand Canyon* (el Gran Cañón).

   _____

5. *Do you know anyone who has read all of Shakespeare's plays?*

   _____

6. *The jury* (el jurado) *doubts that the defendant* (el acusado) *has told the truth.*

   _____

7. *It's incredible that no one has found the money we buried* (enterrar) *in the backyard* (jardín de casa).

   _____

8. *You all can dance after the band* (la banda) *has begun to play.*

   _____

9. *It's a miracle that the bank has loaned* (prestar) *him money.*

   _____

10. *It may be that they [m.] have never learned to read.*

_____

11. *It's ridiculous that I've had to wait in this line* (la cola) *for more than an hour.*

_____

12. *We can't go until after everyone has voted.*

_____

13. *We hope that you [formal] have enjoyed* (gozar de) *your stay* (la estancia) *here.*

_____

14. *Is there anyone in the world who hasn't read* The Cat in the Hat?

_____

15. *I'm looking for a student who has never failed* (reprobar) *a test.*

_____

Main clause in the future with a subordinate clause in the present perfect subjunctive

When a main clause in the future tense refers to an action in the subordinate clause that *may have* or *will have* taken place (uncompleted action), the verb in that subordinate clause is in the present perfect subjunctive.

¿Te quedarás después de que **me haya ido**?	*Will you stay after **I've gone**?*
Será estupendo que **hayamos leído** tanto.	*It will be great that **we've read** so much.*
¿Qué harás cuando **hayas terminado** esto?	*What will you do when **you've finished** this?*
Volveremos después que **os hayáis ido**.	*We'll return after **you all have left**.*
Hablaremos cuando Juan **haya terminado**.	*We will speak when John **has finished**.*
Jugarán después que **hayan trabajado**.	*They will play after **they've worked**.*

EJERCICIO
24·2

Traducción

1. *I will not hire anyone who has gotten his or her diploma from the Internet.*

_____

2. *What will you do after you have conquered* (vencer) *all your fears* (el temor)?

_____

3. *After we've counted our money, we'll deposit it in the bank.*

_____

4. *The program will begin when they have arrived.*

   _____

5. *He will not tell you anything until you have paid him.*

   _____

6. *As soon as you have set the table* (poner la mesa)*, we will eat dinner* (cenar)*.*

   _____

7. *I will bring a salad to the party in case the host* (el anfitrión) *hasn't prepared enough food.*

   _____

8. *He will not go to bed until he's brushed his teeth.*

   _____

9. *You will never know true happiness until you have appeared on the* Oprah Winfrey Show.

   _____

10. *He will never be able to run a mile* (la milla) *in four minutes until he has quit* (dejar de) *smoking.*

    _____

11. *What will we do after we've spent all our money?*

    _____

12. *I will not drink milk that has been on the counter* (el mostrador) *all day long.*

    _____

13. *We will not make* (tomar) *any financial* (financiero) *decisions until we've paid this year's taxes.*

    _____

14. *Captain Kirk will go where no man has gone before.*

    _____

15. *As soon as he has taken this medicine, he will feel better.*

    _____

Traducción

VOCABULARIO

It's great	*Es formidable*
to take care of one's self	*cuidarse*
still	*todavía*
to be crowned	*ser coronado*
frenemy	*el amigo-enemigo*
delusion	*el delirio*
even bigger than	*todavía más grande(s) que*
ego	*el ego*
addled mind	*la mente confusa*
to become a movie star	*convertirse en estrella de cine*
to win	*ganar*
Nobel Prize	*el Premio Nobel*
to award	*otorgar*
stupidity	*la estupidez*
toxic relationship	*la relación toxica*
worthy	*digno*

"It's great that you've finally started to take care of yourself, but what will you do a year from now when you still haven't been crowned Miss Universe?" This is what I want to say to my frenemy, *Courtney, whose delusions are even bigger than her ego. In Courtney's addled mind, she hopes that by next month she'll have lost fifty pounds, she'll have become a movie star, and she'll have won a Nobel Prize (she'll win a Nobel Prize when they award one for stupidity). God willing, a year from now I'll have ended this toxic relationship and will have met someone worthy of my absolute perfection.*

The pluperfect subjunctive

MOOD	Pluperfect subjunctive
TIME	Refers to the relatively remote past
KEY PHRASES	"Had" + PAST PARTICIPLE
STRUCTURE	Compound tense: **haber** conjugated in the imperfect subjunctive + PAST PARTICIPLE

As its name implies, the pluperfect subjunctive (also referred to as the past perfect subjunctive) refers to action in the time frame of the pluperfect ("Mary had spoken"), and in a situation that requires the subjunctive ("I hoped that Mary had spoken" (before she left)). With an understanding of the general time frame of the pluperfect—completed action before another action occurred—and the situations in which the subjunctive is used, you will know when to use the pluperfect subjunctive.

PLUPERFECT INDICATIVE	**Yo sabía** que María **había hablado.**
	*I **knew** that Mary **had spoken**.*
PLUPERFECT SUBJUNCTIVE	**Yo esperaba** que María **hubiera hablado.**
	*I **hoped** that Mary **had spoken**.*

Formation of the pluperfect subjunctive

The pluperfect subjunctive is a compound tense, which means that an auxiliary is required before the main verb. The auxiliary verb **haber** is conjugated in the imperfect subjunctive and followed by the past participle of the main verb.

hubiera + PAST PARTICIPLE	hubiéramos + PAST PARTICIPLE
hubieras + PAST PARTICIPLE	hubierais + PAST PARTICIPLE
hubiera + PAST PARTICIPLE	hubieran + PAST PARTICIPLE

Uses of the pluperfect subjunctive

Main clause in the past with a subordinate clause in the pluperfect subjunctive

When the main clause is in the past (either preterite or imperfect) and refers to an action that *only possibly* had taken place, and the main clause requires the use of the subjunctive, the subordinate clause will be in the pluperfect subjunctive.

¿Fue posible que **yo hubiera hecho** tal cosa?

*Was it possible that **I had done** such a thing?*

Él actuaba como si **nos hubiéramos conocido** antes.

*He acted as if **we had met** before.*

Yo esperaba que **hubieras comido**.

*I hoped that **you had eaten**.*

Ella dudaba que **hubierais leído** la tarea.

*She doubted that **you all had read** the assignment.*

No había nadie que **hubiera escuchado**.

*There wasn't anybody who **had listened**.*

Fue terrible que **no hubieran pagado** la cuenta.

*It was terrible that they **hadn't paid** the bill.*

EJERCICIO

25·1

Traducción

1. *I wasn't sure that they had heard me.*

   _____

2. *John hoped that the students had studied the lesson.*

   _____

3. *It was a pity that the plumber* (el fontanero) *hadn't fixed the drain* (el desagüe).

   _____

4. *We wrote them a letter in case they hadn't understood us.*

   _____

5. *Was it possible that they [m.] had never heard of Leo Tolstoy?*

   _____

6. *They were acting as if they had never met* (conocerse) *before.*

   _____

7. *He didn't believe that I had said such a thing.*

   _____

8. *It was unlikely that she had paid for the car in cash* (al contado).

   _____

9. *There wasn't anyone at the party who had traveled around the world.*

   _____

10. *I never believed that she had been Miss America.*

_____

11. *He refused (negarse a) to speak until we had locked (cerrar) the doors.*

_____

12. *I sent him a text (el texto) in case he hadn't yet heard the good news (las buenas noticias).*

_____

13. *It was tragic that the gardener (el jardinero)—not the butler (el mayordomo)—had done it.*

_____

14. *She always doubted that he had been honest (honrado) with her.*

_____

15. *There wasn't anyone in the house who had gotten up before ten thirty.*

_____

Hypothetical *if*-clause followed by the pluperfect subjunctive

When a hypothetical *if*-clause is followed by a reference to an action that had only possibly taken place, the verb in the *if*-clause is in the pluperfect subjunctive. These *if*-clauses often appear with a main clause in the conditional perfect.

Yo no te habría preguntado
   si hubiera sabido la respuesta.

Si no me hubieras mentido, no me
   habría enojado contigo.

Si hubiera habido más tiempo,
   yo habría aprobado el examen.

¿Qué habrías hecho **si ellos no te
   hubieran encontrado**?

*I wouldn't have asked you **if I had known**
   the answer.*

***If you hadn't lied to me**, I wouldn't have gotten
   mad at you.*

***If there had been more time**, I would have
   passed the test.*

*What would you have done **if they hadn't
   found you**?*

EJERCICIO
25·2

Traducción

1. *If I had read this book earlier (antes), I wouldn't have made so many mistakes in my life.*

_____

2. *If Barbara had known the truth about Ken, would she have married him?*

_____

3. *If you had warned (advertir) us of the earthquakes (el terremoto), we wouldn't have built our house in this area (el área).*

_____

4. *It would have been nice (bueno) if you had included a photo (la foto) with this article (el artículo).*

_____

5. *If you had called me ten minutes earlier, I wouldn't have been home.*

_____

6. *I don't know where I'd be if I hadn't met you.*

_____

7. *If there had been one ounce (la onza) of truth in your speech (el discurso), somebody would have believed you.*

_____

8. *If you had been born two days earlier, we would have had the same birthday.*

_____

9. *If there hadn't been a snowstorm (la nevada) yesterday, there would have been one today.*

_____

10. *If we had known that you were in trouble (tener dificultades), we would have offered you help.*

_____

11. *If you hadn't given me these mittens (la manopla), I think that I would have frozen to death (morirse de frío).*

_____

12. *If you hadn't put another stamp (el sello) on that letter, the post office wouldn't have accepted it.*

_____

13. *If anyone had told me that, I wouldn't have believed it.*

_____

14. *If you hadn't given your goldfish so much food, it wouldn't have died.*

_____

15. *How would they have felt if you hadn't received an invitation?*

_____

querer ("to wish") in the main clause with the pluperfect subjunctive in the subordinate clause

The use of **querer**, meaning "to wish," was discussed in Chapter 21, The imperfect subjunctive. With this meaning, **querer** is often used with the pluperfect subjunctive.

Quisiera **que nunca lo hubiera conocido.**	*I wish **that I'd never met him.***
Él quisiera **que lo hubiéramos escuchado.**	*He wishes **that we had listened to him.***
Quisiera **que hubieras tenido más tiempo.**	*I wish **that you had had more time.***
Quisiera **que hubierais estado allí.**	*I wish **that you all had been there.***
Quisiéramos **que hubiera hecho más calor.**	*We wish **that it had been warmer.***
¿Quisieras **que no lo hubieran visto?**	*Do you wish **that they hadn't seen it?***

Note that in this use of **querer**, the sentence does not typically begin with the subject pronoun **yo** ("I").

EJERCICIO

Para ti, ¿cuál es verdadero o falso?

1. _____ Quisiera que hubiera nevado más el invierno pasado.

2. _____ Quisiera que yo hubiera nacido en otro siglo.

3. _____ Quisiera que yo hubiera comido menos ayer.

4. _____ Quisiera que yo hubiera estudiado más cuando era menor.

5. _____ Quisiera que yo hubiera aprendido a bailar como un/una profesional.

6. _____ Quisiera que yo hubiera tomado lecciones de cocinar.

7. _____ Quisiera que yo hubiera coniciera a la reina Isabel de Inglaterra.

8. _____ Quisiera que yo hubiera gastado menos dinero el año pasado.

9. _____ Quisiera que yo hubiera leído más este año.

10. _____ Quisiera que yo hubiera hecho más ejercicio el año pasado.

11. _____ Quisiera que yo no hubiera comprado tanto el diciembre pasado.

12. _____ Quisiera que yo hubiera recibido un caballo para mi último cumpleaños.

EJERCICIO

25·3

Traducción

1. *I wish that he had studied more in high school.*

_____

2. *Do you wish that he had kept his word* (cumplir su palabra)?

_____

3. *He wishes that he hadn't eaten so much.*

_____

4. *We wish that you had told us that this would be a formal party.*

_____

5. *I wish that we hadn't eaten lunch* (almorzar) *here.*

_____

6. *He wishes that he had saved* (ahorrar) *more money.*

_____

7. *I wish that I'd tried on* (probarse) *these pants before buying them.*

_____

8. *I wish that you hadn't fried these sausages* (la salchicha) *in lard* (la manteca).

_____

9. *Do you all wish that there had been more variety* (la variedad) *in the program?*

_____

10. *I wish that it hadn't rained on my parade* (el desfile).

_____

11. *Do you sometimes wish that you'd been born* (nacer) *in another century* (el siglo)?

_____

12. *I wish that I had turned off* (apagar) *the lights three hours ago.*

_____

13. *I wish that it hadn't been so cold.*

_____

14. *We wish that they had told us about the cockroaches in this hotel.*

_____

15. *I wish that you hadn't put so much cinnamon* (la canela) *in this tea.*

_____

EJERCICIO
25·4

Traducción

VOCABULARIO

el aparcamiento	*parking space*
aparcar	*to park*
bloquear	*to block*
el cajero	*cashier*
cuestionar	*to question*
darse cuenta de que	*to realize*
disputar	*to fight* (a ticket)
el globo	*balloon*
el letrero	*sign*
la multa de aparcamiento	*parking ticket*
prohibido estacionar	*no parking*
la suerte	*luck*
tener cuidado	*to be careful*
la vista	*view*

If I had been more careful, I wouldn't be in this office fighting this parking ticket. I thought it was strange that there was a parking space open right (directamente) in front of the theater five minutes before the play began, but who am I to question such good luck? In fact, there was a sign that said "No Parking" two feet from my car, but a very tall man was standing in front of it, blocking the view. No, nobody would believe that. There was a woman selling balloons and I couldn't see the sign through the balloons, so if anybody is going to pay this ticket, she should pay it—nobody will believe that, either. The truth is that I realize that if I had told anyone these absurd stories, I would have to pay more than I probably owe now. Where is the cashier's office?

The passive voice

26

VOICE   Passive

KEY PHRASES   "You," "they," "one," "[it] is done"

STRUCTURE   **Se** + verb in the third-person singular OR **se** + verb in the third-person plural

There are two kinds of passive voice: incomplete and complete. Both of them are discussed in this chapter. However, greater attention is paid to the incomplete passive voice, because it is far more common in everyday conversation.

Incomplete passive voice

A sentence in the incomplete passive voice indicates that an action is performed, but there is *no named agent performing the action*. In the sentence "Mary sells clothing at Bloomingdale's," "Mary" is the agent, and so the sentence is not in the passive voice. However, in the sentence "Clothing is sold at Bloomingdale's," there is no named agent (we do not know exactly who is selling the clothing). Thus, the second sentence is in the incomplete passive voice.

We often use the incomplete passive voice in English without even being aware of it. The ubiquitous "they," as in "they say …," is an example of the incomplete passive voice: "They say that cats make nice pets." Who says so? "They" do. Who are "they"? Nobody knows.

The incomplete passive voice is used in giving directions, as in the sentence "In order to get to the bank, you need to turn right at the corner." Who needs to turn right? "You" do, but so does anyone else wanting to get to the bank from here. In this case, the word "you" does not refer to *you* specifically, but rather to the collective "you," which indicates the incomplete passive voice at work.

> *They say that you shouldn't swim after eating.*
> *They don't accept applications after 4:00.*
> *One should never make a telephone call after 9:00 P.M.*
> *You should look both ways before crossing the street.*
> *Spanish is spoken here.*
> *This house was built in 1956.*

Note that in the sentences above, while there are specific actions, there are no specific agents. This demonstrates the essence of the incomplete passive voice.

Formation of the incomplete passive voice

There are only two possible conjugated verb forms in a sentence that employs the incomplete passive voice: third-person singular and third-person plural. Each conjugated verb, whether singular or plural, is preceded by **se**.

The noun that follows the conjugated verb determines if that verb is conjugated in the singular or plural form: A singular noun is preceded by a verb in its third-person singular form; a plural noun is preceded by a verb in its third-person plural form.

Se construye la casa.	*The house is built.*
Se construyen las casas.	*The houses are built.*

Note that in English, the word order of the noun and verb is reversed.

Se habla español aquí.	***Spanish is spoken** here.*
Se hablan español y francés aquí.	***Spanish and French are spoken** here.*
Se dice que la educación es la clave del éxito.	***They say that** education is the key to success.*
Se necesitan huevos para cocer una torta.	***You need eggs** in order to bake a cake.*
No se debe nadar después de una comida grande.	***You shouldn't swim** after a big meal.*
Se apagan las luces a las diez de la noche.	***The lights are turned off** at 10 P.M.*
Se dobla a la izquierda en la calle Elm.	***You turn left** on Elm Street.*
Se pagan las cuentas cada viernes.	***The bills are paid** every Friday.*

EJERCICIO 26·1

¿Verdadero o falso?

1. _____ Se habla portugués en Brasil.

2. _____ Se venden libros en la biblioteca.

3. _____ Se dice que no se debe llevar zapatos blancos después de la primera semana de septiembre.

4. _____ En los Estados Unidos, no se puede fumar en los aviones.

5. _____ Para conseguir un doctorado, no se necesita estudiar mucho.

6. _____ Para hablar en un teléfono público, se necesita introducir una moneda.

7. _____ En un hotel, normalmente se paga con tarjeta de crédito.

8. _____ Tradicionalmente, se sirven champaña y torta antes de la boda.

9. _____ Se fabrican muchos televisores y cámaras en Japón.

10. _____ Se cultivan naranjas y plátanos en Alaska.

EJERCICIO

26·2

Complete each sentence with the correct form of the verb in parentheses.

1. Se _____ (vender) pan en la panadería.

2. Se _____ (vender) zapatos en la zapatería.

3. Se _____ (jugar) al béisbol en este estadio.

4. Se _____ (jugar) los partidos de béisbol en este estadio.

5. Se _____ (mirar) la televisión demasiado estos días.

6. Se _____ (cultivar) trigo (*wheat*) en este campo (*field*).

7. Se _____ (cultivar) manzanas en esta huerta (*orchard*).

8. Se _____ (construir) caminos (*paths*) para bicicletas en muchas ciudades.

9. No se _____ (deber) comer antes de operarse.

10. No se _____ (poder) nadar afuera cuando hace mucho frío.

EJERCICIO

26·3

¿Qué se habla en...? *Responde con una frase completa. ¡No te olvides de que en Suiza y en Canadá, hay más de un idioma oficial!*

alemán	inglés	japonés	ruso
francés	italiano	portugués	suizo

1. ¿Qué se habla en Francia? _____

2. ¿Qué se habla en Japón? _____

3. ¿Qué se habla en Alemania? _____

4. ¿Qué se habla en Portugal? _____

5. ¿Qué se habla en Suiza? _____

6. ¿Qué se habla en Rusia? _____

7. ¿Qué se habla en Canadá? _____

8. ¿Qué se habla en Inglaterra? _____

Traducción

1. You can't buy a good cigar (el puro) these days (hoy en día) for less than five dollars.

   _____

2. White wine is drunk with chicken and fish.

   _____

3. They say that Colombian coffee is the best.

   _____

4. One needs to be careful (tener cuidado) when driving in a snowstorm (la tormenta de nieve).

   _____

5. How do you say "dog" in French?

   _____

6. They speak Portuguese in Brazil.

   _____

7. Where is it written that the president has to be a man?

   _____

8. If you drive like a madman (el loco), you'll get a ticket (la multa).

   _____

9. It is said that a pig is smarter than a horse.

   _____

10. They always waste (perder mucho tiempo) a lot of time in these meetings.

    _____

11. If it is maintained (mantener) properly, a car will last (durar) for twenty years.

    _____

12. One never wears white shoes after the first of September.

    _____

13. If you exercise more (hacer más ejercicio) and eat less, you'll lose weight (adelgazarse).

    _____

14. Where do you go in this town for a good hamburger?

    _____

15. If they can put a man on the moon, why can't they make (fabricar) a car that lasts more than five years?

    _____

The incomplete passive voice in other tenses

When using the incomplete passive voice in other tenses, begin with **se** and add the conjugated form of the desired verb (using the third-person singular or plural form of that verb). The formation does not vary from one verb tense to another.

PRETERITE
Se construyó esta casa en 1956.
*This house **was built** in 1956.*

IMPERFECT
Cuando yo era joven, **no se podía comer** carne los viernes.
*When I was young, **you couldn't eat** meat on Fridays.*

FUTURE
Se terminará esta casa el año que viene.
*This house **will be finished** next year.*

CONDITIONAL
Se moriría en Plutón.
*A **person would die** on Pluto.*

PRESENT PERFECT
Se ha escrito este libro para los enamorados de los gatos.
*They've **written** this book for cat lovers.*

PAST PERFECT
No se había pintado la casa hasta 1945.
*The house **hadn't been painted** until 1945.*

FUTURE PERFECT
Se habrá terminado el puente hace un año en abril.
*The bridge **will have been finished** for a year in April.*

CONDITIONAL PERFECT
Se habría repintado la casa, pero decidimos no venderla.
*The house **would have been repainted**, but we decided not to sell it.*

PRESENT SUBJUNCTIVE
Espero que **no se sirvan** perritos calientes en la recepción.
*I hope that **they don't serve** hot dogs at the reception.*

IMPERFECT SUBJUNCTIVE
Fue ridículo que **se tuviera que pagar** tanto por televisión cable.
*It was ridiculous that **you had to pay** so much for cable TV.*

PRESENT PERFECT SUBJUNCTIVE
Ella espera que **no se haya vendido** el vestido que quiere.
*She hopes that **they haven't sold** the dress she wants.*

PLUPERFECT SUBJUNCTIVE
Ella esperaba que **no se hubiera vendido** el vestido que quería.
*She hoped that **they hadn't sold** the dress she wanted.*

EJERCICIO

¿Qué piensas tú? ¿Verdadero o falso?

1. _____ Un día se podrá vivir hasta los 150 años.

2. _____ Hace dos cientos años se viajaba con frecuencia a caballo.

3. _____ Si se estudiara muchísimo, uno podría graduarse de la universidad en menos de tres años.

4. _____ Espero que no se aumenten los impuestos este año.

5. _____ Se añade el fluoruro al agua en muchas ciudades para prevenir caries.

6. _____ En el futuro, se comprará todo con tarjeta de crédito.

7. _____ Es trágico que se malgaste tanta comida cuando millones de personas tienen hambre.

8. _____ Yo creía que se podía vivir bien con una dieta de sólo chocolate y Coca-Cola.

9. _____ Se hizo mi coche en Japón.

10. _____ Se mejorarían las escuelas si hubiera más maestros y menos administradores.

11. _____ Se debe hacer ejercicio por lo menos tres o cuatro veces por semana.

12. _____ Se tenía que leer en la noche con velas y lámparas de queroseno.

EJERCICIO
26·5

Traducción *The following sentences use several different verb tenses.* **¡Ojo!**

1. *When were these pictures taken?*

_____

2. *Where was your sofa made?*

_____

3. *They used to sell bread for five cents a loaf* (la barra).

_____

4. *The house was painted* (pintar) *last year.*

_____

5. *There was so much noise* (el ruido) *in the restaurant that you couldn't think.*

_____

6. *I wanted the flowers delivered* (entregar) *by four thirty.*

_____

7. *You couldn't hear anything; everybody was talking at the same time* (al mismo tiempo).

_____

8. *The party was a disaster* (el desastre). *The living room hadn't even been cleaned.*
   [The word "even" is understood in Spanish.]

_____

9. *You used to be able to smoke anywhere; now it seems you can't smoke anywhere*
   (en ninguna parte).

_____

10. *The book will be published* (publicar) *next year.*

_____

11. *The element was discovered by accident* (por casualidad).

_____

12. *The house hadn't been painted in* (durante) *fifty years.*

_____

13. *They'll close the doors at eleven thirty.*

_____

14. *If you've seen one castle* (el castillo), *you've seen them all.*

_____

15. *You haven't lived until you've heard Van Morrison sing "Gloria."*

_____

Complete passive voice

At times, even when the agent is known and stated, the passive voice is used to lend special emphasis to the action. This is called the complete passive voice. The unstated message is that although the agent is known, the action is the more important focus. In these situations, use the following pattern.

NOUN + ser + adjectival form of the PAST PARTICIPLE (+ por + agent)

Although the mention of the agent with this format is not mandatory, it is common. When you mention the agent, you will precede his/her action with the preposition **por** ("by"). Since you are using the adjectival form of the past participle, remember that the participle must agree in gender and number with the noun.

Note the various tenses in play in the following examples.

El retrato **es visto** por todos.	*The portrait **is seen** by everyone.*
La pintura **fue vista** por todos.	*The painting **was seen** by everyone.*
Los retratos **serán vistos** por todos.	*The portraits **will be seen** by everyone.*
Las pinturas **eran vistas** por todos.	*The paintings **used to be seen** by everyone.*

EJERCICIO
26·6

¿Verdadero o falso?

1. _____ *La Mona Lisa* fue pintada por Leonardo da Vinci.

2. _____ *Tom Sawyer* y *Huckleberry Finn* fueron escritos por William Shakespeare.

3. _____ Durante el siglo diecinueve, Abraham Lincoln fue elegido presidente de los Estados Unidos.

4. _____ En la Biblia, Goliath es matado por David.

5. _____ La electricidad fue descubierta por Galileo.

6. _____ El teléfono fue inventado por Alexander Graham Bell.

7. _____ Mis zapatos fueron diseñados por Whoopi Goldberg.

8. _____ Hace muchos años, el español fue declarado el idioma oficial de España.

9. _____ La novela *Guerra y paz* fue escrita por Leo Tolstoy.

10. _____ Mi coche fue hecho en la luna.

11. _____ Todos mis problemas serán resueltos durante el año que viene.

12. _____ Cuando yo era joven, las camas en mi casa eran de plástico.

EJERCICIO
26·7

Traducción

1. *The play* (el drama) *Romeo and Juliet was written by William Shakespeare.*

   _____

2. *Many new houses were constructed after World War II* (la Segunda Guerra Mundial).

   _____

3. *The leaflets* (el folleto) *will be distributed* (repartir) *by volunteers tomorrow.*

   _____

4. *These cookies were made by elves* (el duende).

   _____

5. *The spoiled child* (el niño consentido) *was given too many toys by his parents.*

   _____

6. *The tires* (el neumático) *were slashed* (acuchillar) *by vandals.*

   _____

7. *The television will be turned on* (poner) *when John enters this house.*

   _____

8. *This quilt* (la colcha) *was sewn* (coser) *completely by hand* (a mano).

   _____

9. *The doors will be opened and closed by armed guards.*

   _____

10. *The grass was planted* (sembrar) *by Martin.*

    _____

11. *These bills would have been paid by John, but he lost the checkbook* (el talonario de cheques).

    _____

12. *When I was young, my classes were always taught by excellent teachers.*

    _____

13. *I hope that my house is bought by a nice person.*

    _____

14. *I hope that this mess (el lío) wasn't made by mice.*

_____

15. *The national anthem (el himno nacional) was sung by my neighbor before the game.*

_____

Traducción

VOCABULARIO	a bocajarro	*point-blank*	el lanzador	*quarterback*
	el compañero	*teammate*	la oportunidad	*chance*
	despertarse	*to wake up*	el reportero	*reporter*
	entrenar	*to train*	rezar	*to pray*
	entrevistar	*to ask, interview*	seguro	*sure*
	estupendo	*great*	el sueño	*dream*
	ignorar	*to ignore*	toda la situación	*the whole thing*

After the Super Bowl, the winning quarterback was interviewed by a reporter who asked him how he felt. This is what he said: "Well, you work hard all year and you train every day. Of course you hope for something like this, but you know that it's just a dream, and then you win lots of games, but only because you have great teammates, and you're really happy. But you aren't prepared for a day like this. You wake up and you know that this is the most important day of your life and you think that you have a chance to win, but you can't be too sure. So you pray. And you play your best and hope that you win. And when you win, it's the most wonderful thing you've ever felt in your life, and when you're asked point-blank how you feel, you completely ignore the whole thing and speak in the passive voice."

_____

_____

_____

_____

_____

_____

_____

_____

_____

_____

Appendix A

Verb conjugation charts

Preterite conjugations

Regular verbs

hablar	hablé	hablaste	habló	hablamos	hablasteis	hablaron
comer	comí	comiste	comió	comimos	comisteis	comieron
abrir	abrí	abriste	abrió	abrimos	abristeis	abrieron

Verbs with standard orthographic changes (first-person singular only)

llegar	**llegué**	llegaste	llegó	llegamos	llegasteis	llegaron
comenzar	**comencé**	comenzaste	comenzó	comenzamos	comenzasteis	comenzaron
practicar	**practiqué**	practicaste	practicó	practicamos	practicasteis	practicaron

Irregular verbs

andar	anduve	anduviste	anduvo	anduvimos	anduvisteis	anduvieron
caber	cupe	cupiste	cupo	cupimos	cupisteis	cupieron
dar	di	diste	dio	dimos	disteis	dieron
decir	dije	dijiste	dijo	dijimos	dijisteis	dijeron
estar	estuve	estuviste	estuvo	estuvimos	estuvisteis	estuvieron
haber	hube	hubiste	hubo	hubimos	hubisteis	hubieron
hacer	hice	hiciste	hizo	hicimos	hicisteis	hicieron
ir	fui	fuiste	fue	fuimos	fuisteis	fueron
poder	pude	pudiste	pudo	pudimos	pudisteis	pudieron
poner	puse	pusiste	puso	pusimos	pusisteis	pusieron
producir	produje	produjiste	produjo	produjimos	produjisteis	produjeron
querer	quise	quisiste	quiso	quisimos	quisisteis	quisieron
saber	supe	supiste	supo	supimos	supisteis	supieron
ser	fui	fuiste	fue	fuimos	fuisteis	fueron
tener	tuve	tuviste	tuvo	tuvimos	tuvisteis	tuvieron
traer	traje	trajiste	trajo	trajimos	trajisteis	trajeron
venir	vine	viniste	vino	vinimos	vinisteis	vinieron
ver	vi	viste	vio	vimos	visteis	vieron

Verbs with a stem change in the third person

dormir	dormí	dormiste	**durmió**	dormimos	dormisteis	**durmieron**
mentir	mentí	mentiste	**mintió**	mentimos	mentisteis	**mintieron**
pedir	pedí	pediste	**pidió**	pedimos	pedisteis	**pidieron**
creer	creí	creíste	**creyó**	creímos	creísteis	**creyeron**
destruir	destruí	destruiste	**destruyó**	destruimos	destruisteis	**destruyeron**

Imperfect conjugations

Regular verbs

hablar	hablaba	hablabas	hablaba	hablábamos	hablabais	hablaban
comer	comía	comías	comía	comíamos	comíais	comían
vivir	vivía	vivías	vivía	vivíamos	vivíais	vivían

Irregular verbs

ir	iba	ibas	iba	íbamos	ibais	iban
ser	era	eras	era	éramos	erais	eran
ver	veía	veías	veía	veíamos	veíais	veían

Future conjugations

Regular verbs

hablar	hablaré	hablarás	hablará	hablaremos	hablaréis	hablarán
comer	comeré	comerás	comerá	comeremos	comeréis	comerán
vivir	viviré	vivirás	vivirá	viviremos	viviréis	vivirán

Irregular verbs

caber	cabré	cabrás	cabrá	cabremos	cabréis	cabrán
decir	diré	dirás	dirá	diremos	diréis	dirán
haber	habré	habrás	habrá	habremos	habréis	habrán
hacer	haré	harás	hará	haremos	haréis	harán
poder	podré	podrás	podrá	podremos	podréis	podrán
poner	pondré	pondrás	pondrá	pondremos	pondréis	pondrán
querer	querré	querrás	querrá	querremos	querréis	querrán
saber	sabré	sabrás	sabrá	sabremos	sabréis	sabrán
salir	saldré	saldrás	saldrá	saldremos	saldréis	saldrán
tener	tendré	tendrás	tendrá	tendremos	tendréis	tendrán
valer	valdré	valdrás	valdrá	valdremos	valdréis	valdrán
venir	vendré	vendrás	vendrá	vendremos	vendréis	vendrán

Conditional conjugations

Regular verbs

hablar	hablaría	hablarías	hablaría	hablaríamos	hablaríais	hablarían
comer	comería	comerías	comería	comeríamos	comeríais	comerían
vivir	viviría	vivirías	viviría	viviríamos	viviríais	vivirían

Irregular verbs

caber	cabría	cabrías	cabría	cabríamos	cabríais	cabrían
decir	diría	dirías	diría	diríamos	diríais	dirían
haber	habría	habrías	habría	habríamos	habríais	habrían
hacer	haría	harías	haría	haríamos	haríais	harían
poder	podría	podrías	podría	podríamos	podríais	podrían
poner	pondría	pondrías	pondría	pondríamos	pondríais	pondrían
querer	querría	querrías	querría	querríamos	querríais	querrían
saber	sabría	sabrías	sabría	sabríamos	sabríais	sabrían
salir	saldría	saldrías	saldría	saldríamos	saldríais	saldrían

tener	tendría	tendrías	tendría	tendríamos	tendríais	tendrían
valer	valdría	valdrías	valdría	valdríamos	valdríais	valdrían
venir	vendría	vendrías	vendría	vendríamos	vendríais	vendrían

Present subjunctive conjugations

Regular verbs

hablar	hable	hables	hable	hablemos	habléis	hablen
comer	coma	comas	coma	comamos	comáis	coman
vivir	viva	vivas	viva	vivamos	viváis	vivan

Verbs with standard orthographic changes

llegar	llegue	llegues	llegue	lleguemos	lleguéis	lleguen
comenzar	comience	comiences	comience	comencemos	comencéis	comiencen
practicar	practique	practiques	practique	practiquemos	practiquéis	practiquen

Irregular verbs

dar	dé	des	dé	demos	deis	den
estar	esté	estés	esté	estemos	estéis	estén
haber	haya	hayas	haya	hayamos	hayáis	hayan
ir	vaya	vayas	vaya	vayamos	vayáis	vayan
saber	sepa	sepas	sepa	sepamos	sepáis	sepan
ser	sea	seas	sea	seamos	seáis	sean

Imperfect subjunctive conjugations

Regular verbs

hablar	hablara	hablaras	hablara	habláramos	hablarais	hablaran
comer	comiera	comieras	comiera	comiéramos	comierais	comieran
vivir	viviera	vivieras	viviera	viviéramos	vivierais	vivieran

Irregular verbs (verbs with irregular stems)

andar	anduviera	anduvieras	anduviera	anduviéramos	anduvierais	anduvieran
caber	cupiera	cupieras	cupiera	cupiéramos	cupierais	cupieran
creer	creyera	creyeras	creyera	creyéramos	creyerais	creyeran
dar	diera	dieras	diera	diéramos	dierais	dieran
decir	dijera	dijeras	dijera	dijéramos	dijerais	dijeran
destruir	destruyera	destruyeras	destruyera	destruyéramos	destruyerais	destruyeran
dormir	durmiera	durmieras	durmiera	durmiéramos	durmierais	durmieran
estar	estuviera	estuvieras	estuviera	estuviéramos	estuvierais	estuvieran
haber	hubiera	hubieras	hubiera	hubiéramos	hubierais	hubieran
hacer	hiciera	hicieras	hiciera	hiciéramos	hicierais	hicieran
ir	fuera	fueras	fuera	fuéramos	fuerais	fueran
mentir	mintiera	mintieras	mintiera	mintiéramos	mintierais	mintieran
pedir	pidiera	pidieras	pidiera	pidiéramos	pidierais	pidieran
poder	pudiera	pudieras	pudiera	pudiéramos	pudierais	pudieran
poner	pusiera	pusieras	pusiera	pusiéramos	pusierais	pusieran
producir	produjera	produjeras	produjera	produjéramos	produjerais	produjeran
querer	quisiera	quisieras	quisiera	quisiéramos	quisierais	quisieran
saber	supiera	supieras	supiera	supiéramos	supierais	supieran

ser	fuera	fueras	fuera	fuéramos	fuerais	fueran
tener	tuviera	tuvieras	tuviera	tuviéramos	tuvierais	tuvieran
traer	trajera	trajeras	trajera	trajéramos	trajerais	trajeran
venir	viniera	vinieras	viniera	viniéramos	vinierais	vinieran
ver	viera	vieras	viera	viéramos	vierais	vieran

Conjugations of the auxiliary **haber**

Present perfect

he	has	ha	hemos	habéis	han

Past perfect

había	habías	había	habíamos	habíais	habían

Future perfect

habré	habrás	habrá	habremos	habréis	habrán

Conditional perfect

habría	habrías	habría	habríamos	habríais	habrían

Present perfect subjunctive

haya	hayas	haya	hayamos	hayáis	hayan

Past perfect subjunctive

	hubiera	hubieras	hubiera	hubiéramos	hubierais	hubieran
OR	hubiese	hubieses	hubiese	hubiésemos	hubieseis	hubiesen

Appendix B

Verbs that take a preposition

Many Spanish verbs require a preposition before a following word for a specific usage. Below are several of these verbs, grouped by preposition and arranged alphabetically within groups. Following each VERB + PREPOSITION is the abbreviation for the part of speech that usually follows the verb in this usage, the verb's English equivalent, and an indicator of the usage itself. For example, the entry "**acabar de** (*v.*) to have just (*done something*)" could be illustrated by this example: **María acaba de escribir una carta** ("Mary has just written a letter").

NOTE In the entries for verbs listed under **a**, remember that the **a** following these verbs is a preposition. Be careful not to confuse the preposition **a** with the personal **a** (as discussed on pages 43–44).

Abbreviations include (*v.*) for *verb* and (*n.*) for *noun*.

a

acertar a (*v.*) to manage to (*do something*), to succeed in (*doing something*)
acostumbrarse a (*n.*) to become used to (*someone/something*)
adaptarse a (*n.*) to adapt oneself to (*something [a situation]*)
adelantarse a (*n.*) to step forward to (*someone/something*)
animar a (*v.*) to encourage to (*do something*)
animarse a (*v.*) to make up one's mind to (*do something*)
aprender a (*v.*) to learn to (*do something*)
apresurarse a (*n./v.*) to hasten to (*somewhere / do something*), to hurry to (*somewhere / do something*)
arriesgarse a (*v.*) to risk (*doing something*)
asistir a (*n.*) to attend (*something [a function]*)
asomarse a (*n.*) to appear at (*something*), to look out from (*something*)
aspirar a (*v.*) to aspire to (*do something / be someone*)
atreverse a (*v.*) to dare to (*do something*)
aventurarse a (*v.*) to venture to (*do something*)
ayudar a alguien a (*v.*) to help someone to (*do something*)
burlar a (*n.*) to make fun of (*someone*)
comenzar a (*v.*) to begin to (*do something*)
comprometerse a (*v.*) to obligate oneself to (*do something*)
condenar a alguien a (*v.*) to condemn someone to (*do something*)
consagrarse a (*n.*) to devote oneself to (*someone/something*)
contribuir a (*n.*) to contribute to (*something*)
convidar a (*n./v.*) to invite to (*something [a function] / do something*)
correr a (*n./v.*) to run to (*somewhere / do something*)

285

cuidar a (*n.*) to care for (*someone* [*a person, a pet*]), to take care of (*someone* [*a person, a pet*])

dar a (*n.*) to face (*something*)

dar cuerda a (*n.*) to wind (*something* [*a watch*])

decidirse a (*v.*) to decide to (*do something*)

dirigirse a (*n.*) to go to (*somewhere*), to address (*someone*)

disponerse a (*v.*) to prepare to (*do something*), to be disposed to (*do something*)

empezar a (*v.*) to begin to (*do something*)

enseñar a (*v.*) to teach to (*do something*)

forzar a (*v.*) to force to (*do something*)

impulsar a (*v.*) to impel to (*do something*)

incitar a (*v.*) to incite to (*do something*)

inducir a (*v.*) to induce to (*do something*)

inspirar a (*v.*) to inspire to (*do something*)

instar a (*v.*) to urge to (*do something*)

invitar a (*v.*) to invite to (*do something*)

ir a (*n./v.*) to go to (*somewhere*), to be going to (*do something*)

limitarse a (*v.*) to limit oneself to (*do something*)

llegar a (*n./v.*) to arrive at (*somewhere*), to manage to (*do something*)

meterse a (*v.*) to take up (*doing something*)

negarse a (*v.*) to refuse to (*do something*)

obligar a (*v.*) to oblige to (*do something*)

ofrecerse a (*v.*) to offer to (*do something*), to promise to (*do something*), to volunteer to (*do something*)

oponerse a (*n./v.*) to be opposite to (*something*), to oppose (*doing something*)

pararse a (*v.*) to stop (*doing something*)

parecerse a (*n.*) to resemble (*someone*)

pasar a (*n./v.*) to pass to (*something / doing something*), to proceed to (*something / doing something*)

persuadir a (*v.*) to persuade to (*do something*)

ponerse a (*v.*) to begin to (*do something*), to set about (*doing something*)

prestarse a (*v.*) to lend oneself to (*doing something*)

probar a (*v.*) to try to (*do something*)

quedarse a (*v.*) to stay somewhere to (*do something*)

rebajarse a (*n./v.*) to stoop to (*something* [*a situation*] */ doing something*)

reducirse a (*n./v.*) to reduce a situation or oneself to (*something / do something*)

rehusar a (*v.*) to refuse to (*do something*)

renunciar a (*n.*) to renounce (*something*), to give up (*something*), to quit (*something* [*a job*])

resignarse a (*n./v.*) to resign oneself to (*something / doing something*)

resistirse a (*n./v.*) to resist (*something / doing something*)

resolverse a (*n./v.*) to "come down to" (*something*), to resolve to (*do something*)

retirarse a (*n./v.*) to retire to (*something / do something*)

romper a (*v.*) to begin (*to do something*)

saber a (*n.*) to taste like/of (*something*)

sentarse a (*n./v.*) to sit down to (*something / doing something*)

someterse a (*n./v.*) to submit oneself to (*something / doing something*)

sonar a (*n.*) to sound like (*something*)

subir a (*n.*) to go up to (*something*), to climb (*something*), to get on (*something*)

tener sabor a (*n.*) to taste like (*something*)

venir a (*n./v.*) to come to (*somewhere / doing something*)

volver a (*n./v.*) to return to (*somewhere / doing something*)

con

aburrirse con (*n.*) to be/get bored with (*someone/something*)

acabar con (*n.*) to finish (*something*), to exhaust (*something*)

amenazar con (*n./v.*) to threaten with (*something / doing something*)

asociarse con (*n.*) to associate with (*someone*), to team up with (*someone*)

asustarse con (*n.*) to be afraid of (*someone/something*)

bastarle a alguien con (*n.*) to have enough of (*something*)

casarse con (*n.*) to marry (*someone*)

comerciar con (*n.*) to trade with (*someone / something* [*business*]), to trade in (*something* [*business*])

conformarse con (*n./v.*) to conform to (*something / doing something*)

contar con (*n.*) to count on (*someone/something*)

contentarse con (*n.*) to content oneself with (*something*)

dar con (*n.*) to come upon (*someone/something*)

disfrutar con (*n.*) to enjoy (*someone/something*)

divertirse con (*n.*) to enjoy (*someone/something*), to have fun with (*someone/something*)

enfadarse con (*n.*) to get mad/angry at (*someone/something*)

enojarse con (*n.*) to get mad/angry at (*someone/something*)

equivocarse con (*n.*) to make a mistake about (*someone*)

espantarse con (*n.*) to become afraid of (*someone/something*)

juntarse con (*n.*) to associate with (*someone*)

limpiar con (*n.*) to clean with (*something*)

meterse con (*n.*) to provoke (*someone/something*)

preocuparse con (*n.*) to worry about (*someone/something*)

romper con (*n.*) to break up with (*someone*), to break off relations with (*someone*)

salir con (*n.*) to go out with (*someone*), to date (*someone*)

soñar con (*n.*) to dream of/about (*someone/something*)

tratarse con (*n.*) to be on good terms with (*someone*), to deal with (*something*)

tropezar con (*n.*) to come upon (*someone/something*)

tropezarse con (*n.*) to bump into (*something*) [*emphatic*]

de

abusar de (*n.*) to take advantage of (*someone/something*)

acabar de (*v.*) to have just (*done something*)

acordarse de (*n./v.*) to remember (*someone/something*), to remember to (*do something*)

alegrarse de (*n./v.*) to be glad (*of something / to do something*)

alejarse de (*n.*) to go away from (*someone/something/somewhere*)

aprovecharse de (*n./v.*) to take advantage of (*someone/something / doing something*)

arrepentirse de (*n./v.*) to repent for (*something / doing something*), to be sorry for (*something / doing something*)

asombrarse de (*n.*) to be astonished at (*something*)

avergonzarse de (*n.*) to be ashamed of (*someone/something*)

brindar a la salud de (*n.*) to toast (*someone*)

burlarse de (*n.*) to make fun of (*someone/something*)

cansarse de (*n./v.*) to get tired of (*someone/something / doing something*)

carecer de (*n.*) to lack (*something*)

cesar de (*v.*) to cease (*doing something*)

conseguir algo de (*n.*) to obtain something from (*someone/something*), to get hold of something from (*someone/something*)

cuidar de (*n.*) to care for (*something*), to take care of (*something*)

deber de (*v.*) to suppose [*conjecture*] (*to be something/someone*), "must be" (*someone/something*)

dejar de (*v.*) to stop (*doing something*)

depender de (*n./v.*) to depend on (*someone/something / doing something*)

encargarse de (*n./v.*) to take charge of (*someone/something / doing something*)

estar encargado de (*n./v.*) to be in charge of (*someone/something / doing something*)

gozar de (*n.*) to enjoy (*something*), to take pleasure in (*something*)

haber de (*v.*) to suppose [*conjecture*] (*to be/do something*)

hablar de (*n./v.*) to talk about (*someone/something / doing something*)

jactarse de (*n./v.*) to brag about (*something / doing something*), to boast of (*something / doing something*)

lastimarse de (*n.*) to feel sorry for (*something*), to complain about (*something*)

librarse de (*n.*) to get rid of (*someone/something*)

maldecir de (*n.*) to speak ill of (*someone/something*)

maravillarse de (*n.*) to marvel at (*someone/something*)

marcharse de (*n.*) to leave from (*somewhere*), to walk away from (*somewhere*)

morir de (*n.*) to die of/from (*something* [*an illness, a situation*])

morirse de (*n.*) to be dying for (*something*)

ocuparse de (*n.*) to pay attention to (*someone/something*), to mind (*someone/something*)

olvidarse de (*n./v.*) to forget (*someone/something / to do something*)

parar de (*v.*) to cease (*doing something*), to stop (*doing something*)

pensar de (*n.*) to think of (*someone/something*), to have an opinion about (*someone/something*)

preciarse de (*n.*) to brag about (*something*), to boast of (*something*)

prescindir de (*n./v.*) to do without (*someone/something / doing something*), to neglect (*someone/something / doing something*)

probar de (*n.*) to sample (*something*), to take a taste of (*something*)

quejarse de (*n./v.*) to complain of/about (*someone/something / doing something*)

salir de (*n.*) to leave from (*somewhere*)

separarse de (*n.*) to leave from (*someone/somewhere*)

servir de (*n.*) to act as (*someone/something*)

sorprenderse de (*n.*) to be surprised at/by (*someone/something*)

terminar de (*v.*) to finish (*doing something*)

tratar de (*v.*) to try to (*do something*)

tratarse de (*n./v.*) to be a question of (*something / doing something*)

en

abdicar en (*n.*) to abdicate to (*someone*)

complacerse en (*n./v.*) to take pleasure in (*something / doing something*)

confiar en (*n./v.*) to trust (*someone/something* [*a situation*] / *doing something*), to confide in (*someone/something* [*a situation*] / *doing something*)

consentir en (*v.*) to consent to (*do something*)

consistir en (*n./v.*) to consist of (*something / doing something*)

convenir en (*n./v.*) to agree to (*something / do something*)

convertirse en (*n.*) to become (*someone/something*), to change into (*someone/something*)

empeñarse en (*n./v.*) to insist on (*something / doing something*)

equivocarse en (*n.*) to make a mistake in (*something*)

esforzarse en (*n./v.*) to try hard in (*something*), to endeavor to (*do something*)

influir en (*n.*) to influence (*someone/something*)

insistir en (*n./v.*) to insist on (*something / doing something*)

interesarse en (*n.*) to be interested in (*someone/something*)

meterse en (*n.*) to become involved in (*something*)

mojarse en (*n.*) to get mixed up in (*something*)

molestarse en (*v.*) to take the trouble to (*do something*)

montar en (*n.*) to ride (*something*)

obstinarse en (*n./v.*) to persist in (*something / doing something*)

ocuparse en (*n./v.*) to be busy with (*something / doing something*)

pararse en (*v.*) to bother to (*do something*)

pensar en (*n./v.*) to think about (*someone/something / doing something*)

persistir en (*n./v.*) to persist in (*something / doing something*)

quedar en (*n./v.*) to agree to (*something / do something*)

recrearse en (*n.*) to amuse oneself with (*something*)

reflexionar en (*n.*) to reflect on (*something*), to think about (*something*)

tardar en (*n./v.*) to delay in (*something*), to take long to (*do something*)

trabajar en (*n.*) to work at (*something*)

vacilar en (*v.*) to hesitate to (*do something*)

para

bastarse para (*v.*) to be self-sufficient in (*doing something*)

estar listo para (*v.*) to be ready to (*do something*)

estar para (*v.*) to be about to (*do something*)

quedarse para (*v.*) to stay to (*do something*)

prepararse para (*n./v.*) to prepare oneself for (*something*), to prepare oneself to (*do something*)

sentarse para (*v.*) to sit down to (*do something*)

servir para (*n./v.*) to be of use for (*something / doing something*)

trabajar para (*n./v.*) to work for (*someone*), to strive to (*do something*)

por

abogar por (*n.*) to plead on behalf of (*someone/something*)

acabar por (*v.*) to end by (*doing something*), to wind up (*doing something*)

apurarse por (*n.*) to be worried by (*someone/something*)

clasificar por (*n.*) to classify in/by (*something*)

esforzarse por (*n./v.*) to strive for (*someone/something*), to strive to (*do something*)

estar por (*v.*) to be inclined to (*do something*)

hacer por (*v.*) to try to (*do something*)

impacientarse por (*n./v.*) to grow impatient for (*someone/something / doing something*)

llorar por (*n./v.*) to cry for/about (*someone/something / doing something*)

luchar por (*n./v.*) to struggle for (*someone/something*), to struggle to (*do something*)

mandar por (*n.*) to send via (*something [mail]*)

mirar por (*n.*) to look after (*something*), to tend to (*something*)

morirse por (*n./v.*) to be dying for (*something*), to be dying to (*do something*)

ofenderse por (*n.*) to be offended by (*something*)

optar por (*n./v.*) to choose (*something / doing something*), to opt for (*something / doing something*)

preocuparse por (*n./v.*) to worry about (*someone/something / doing something*)

rabiar por (*n./v.*) to be crazy about (*someone/something / doing something*)

terminar por (*v.*) to end by (*doing something*)

trabajar por (*n.*) to work for (*someone [as a substitute]*)

votar por (*n.*) to vote for (*someone/something*)

Answer key

Free audio answer key available online and via app. *See the copyright page for details.*

 I   THE PRESENT TENSE

1   Conjugation of regular verbs

1-1   1. Yo canto.   2. Tú cantas.   3. Él canta.   4. Nosotros cantamos.   5. Ellos cantan.   6. Yo pago.
7. Nosotros pagamos la casa.   8. Tú pagas.   9. Ellas pagan.   10. Ella estudia.   11. Él estudia.
12. Yo estudio.   13. Estudiamos.   14. Tú andas. OR Tú caminas.   15. Nosotros andamos. OR
Nosotros caminamos.   16. Yo trabajo.   17. Él trabaja.   18. Ellos trabajan.   19. Trabajamos.   20. Él baila.
21. Yo amo.   22. Tú amas.   23. Ella ama.   24. Nosotros amamos.   25. Ellos aman.   26. Yo practico.
27. Él practica.   28. Ellos entran.   29. Yo miro la casa.   30. Yo miro el jardín.   31. Ellos miran el coche.
32. Ella escucha.   33. Ellas escuchan.   34. Yo escucho.   35. Él compra el coche.   36. Yo compro el perro.
37. Tú compras la casa.   38. Yo hablo con Miguel.   39. Ella paga los libros.   40. Estudiamos español.

1-2   Hola. Mi nombre es Paco. Yo estudio español en la mañana y yo trabajo en un restaurante en la tarde.
Mis amigos hablan español. Yo practico mis lecciones con mis amigos. Ellos hablan rápidamente. Yo no hablo
rápidamente. Mi maestra habla español e inglés. Ella también toca la guitarra y a veces nosotros cantamos
y a veces nosotros bailamos el flamenco. Yo practico el flamenco en mi casa en la noche con un amigo o con
mis amigos. Ellos bailan muy bien. Yo llevo zapatos especiales cuando yo bailo. A veces mi hija Daisy
(Margarita) toca el arpa. Ella toca muy bien. Yo toco el piano. Yo no toco el arpa.

1-3   1. Yo aprendo.   2. Yo bebo.   3. Él bebe.   4. Tú comes.   5. Comemos.   6. Yo comprendo.
7. Yo no comprendo.   8. Ellos comprenden.   9. Tú comprendes.   10. Tú no comprendes.   11. Yo corro.
12. Tú corres.   13. Ella corre.   14. Ellos no corren.   15. Corremos.   16. Yo creo.   17. Yo no creo.
18. Él cree.   19. Debemos.   20. Yo leo.   21. Tú lees.   22. Tú no lees.   23. Él lee.   24. Ella lee.   25. Leemos.
26. Cometo un error.   27. Yo meto.   28. Tú metes.   29. Él mete.   30. Metemos.   31. Ellos meten.
32. Ellas meten.   33. Rompemos.   34. Ellas rompen.   35. Yo rompo.   36. Tú vendes.   37. Vendemos.
38. Yo no vendo.   39. Ella no vende.   40. Aprendemos.

1-4   Yo leo muchos libros. Cuando yo leo un libro, usualmente yo como pizza o yo bebo un vaso de leche o agua.
Yo aprendo mucho de mis libros. Yo también debo mucho dinero a la librería. Mis padres leen libros y revistas,
pero yo leo más. La librería en mi ciudad vende libros, revistas, plumas, lápices, regalos y mucho más. Nosotros
no comemos en la librería, pero a veces bebemos café allí. Mi familia y yo poseemos muchos libros. A veces
un autor comete un error, pero usualmente no.

1-5   1. Abro las ventanas.   2. Ella sufre mucho.   3. Vivimos en los Estados Unidos.   4. Escribes muchas cartas.
5. El niño admite todo.   6. Juan sube la escalera.   7. Descubro un gato en la casa.   8. Muchas personas
sufren.   9. Decidimos.   10. Los unicornios no existen.   11. Ustedes escriben bien.   12. María describe
las arañas.   13. Escribimos muchas cartas.   14. Ellos no asisten a la escuela.   15. María y Juan discuten
el libro.   16. Unes las dos partes.   17. Los chicos describen todo.   18. Cubrís las mesas.   19. Juan no asiste
a la reunión.   20. Recibo regalos para mi cumpleaños.

1-6   Hola. Mi familia y yo vivimos en Habana, Cuba. Mi padre escribe novelas y mi madre trabaja en un banco. Ella decide si una persona recibe dinero del banco. Todo el mundo cree que Cristóbal Colón descubre Cuba en 1492. Unas personas creen que Cristóbal Colón descubre Norteamérica también. Asisto a la escuela cinco días cada semana. Mi hermanita asiste a la escuela solamente tres días cada semana. Sufrimos mucho del calor aquí durante el día, pero en la noche recibimos el aire fresco como un amigo. Cada noche mis amigos y yo caminamos por el Malecón y miramos el mar.

1-7   1. ¿Hablas inglés?   2. ¿Comprendes?   3. ¿Estudiáis mucho?   4. ¿Canta él bien?   5. ¿Vende ella ropa?   6. ¿Trabaja él aquí?   7. ¿Viven ellos allí?   8. ¿Existen los unicornios?   9. ¿Escribe ella libros?   10. ¿Comete él muchos errores?   11. ¿Lees en la biblioteca?   12. ¿Comprende ella?

1-8   1. ¿Dónde vives?   2. ¿Dónde trabajas?   3. ¿Cuándo estudias?   4. ¿Cuándo escribes?   5. ¿Quién comprende?   6. ¿Quién no canta?   7. ¿Por qué baila él?   8. ¿Por qué trabajamos?   9. ¿Qué preparas?   10. ¿Qué miran ustedes?   11. ¿Cómo venden ellos tanto?   12. ¿Cómo lee ella tanto?

1-9   1. ¿Cuál funciona?   2. ¿Cuál necesita agua?   3. ¿Cuáles funcionan?   4. ¿Cuáles necesitan agua?   5. ¿Cuánto dinero paga usted?   6. ¿Cuánto español aprendemos?   7. ¿Cuántos coches compras tú?   8. ¿Cuántos libros vendes?   9. ¿Cuánta agua bebe él?   10. ¿Cuánta verdad posee él?   11. ¿Cuántas personas viven en México?   12. ¿Cuántas ventanas abren ellos?

1-10   Kenny trabaja en un restaurante en Nueva York. Él prepara muchas comidas cada día. Usualmente, él trabaja en la mañana, pero a veces trabaja en la tarde. Kenny no trabaja en la tarde. Sus clientes comen la comida que Kenny prepara y entonces ellos pagan la cuenta. Bob Dylan es su cliente, también Madonna y el escritor Calvin Trillin. Su restaurante no es elegante. La comida no es elegante. Pero, el restaurante es muy popular porque Kenny es fascinante. Su esposa, Eve, también trabaja en el restaurante. Sus cinco hijos trabajan en el restaurante. Kenny prepara muchos tipos de huevos y panqueques y sopas cada día. Kenny cree que cuando sus clientes comen su comida ellos reciben su amor.

2   Ser and estar

2-1   1. Soy de los Estados Unidos.   2. Eres mi amigo/amiga.   3. Él es guapo.   4. Ella es muy interesante.   5. Ellos son astronautas de otro planeta.   6. Sois americanos.   7. Hoy es lunes.   8. Mis calcetines son blancos.   9. Melissa McCarthy es actriz.   10. Él es alto. Ella es alta.   11. Ellos son hombres guapos.   12. ¿De dónde sois?   13. Somos de Chile   14. ¿Qué hora es? Son las diez.   15. ¿Quién eres? ¿Quiénes son ellos?   16. Ellos no son mis amigos.   17. Fido es mi perro y Fufu es tu gato.   18. Las hamburguesas y las papas fritas son muy populares en los Estados Unidos.   19. ¿Qué es esto? Es un zapato.   20. ¿Qué es esto? Es una flor.

2-2   Hola. Mi nombre es Pablo, y mi esposa es Margarita. Somos floristas. Nuestras flores son hermosas. La mayoría de nuestras flores son de Inglaterra, pero algunas de las flores son de otras partes del mundo. Típicamente, los tulipanes son de Holanda y las rosas son de China. Unas flores son simbólicas: Por ejemplo, la margarita blanca es un símbolo de la inocencia, y la azucena es un símbolo de la fe. Yo creo que las flores son maravillosas. Unas flores son rojas y unas son blancas, pero todas son hermosas.

2-3   1. Estoy con Juan. No estoy con Juan.   2. Ella está con Marcos. Ella no está con Marcos.   3. Estoy bien. No estoy feliz.   4. ¿Dónde estás? ¿Dónde está Felipe?   5. Juan está enojado. Ellos están enojados.   6. Juana está de pie pero nosotros estamos sentados.   7. Estoy triste porque no estás aquí.   8. Juana está ansiosa porque no estamos listos.   9. Él está de rodillas porque estamos en la iglesia.   10. Las sillas no están en la cocina.   11. Muchos chicos están en la casa.   12. ¿Por qué estáis aquí?   13. Argentina está en Sudamérica.   14. ¿Están los perros en la sala?   15. Los tomates están verdes.   16. ¡Este pollo está muy bueno!   17. Juan está deprimido.   18. ¿Por qué no estás feliz?   19. Ella está avergonzada.   20. Ellos están de mal humor porque el televisor está roto y por eso están aburridos.

2-4   Hola. ¿Cómo estás? Estoy bien. En realidad, no estoy bien. Estoy en el hospital. Estoy enferma. Mi cara está verde y mis ojos están anaranjados. No estoy cansada. El enfermero está aquí con una jeringa grande. Tengo miedo. Ay, ¡bueno! La jeringa está rota, y por eso tomo una pastilla. Ahora no estoy enferma. Estoy bien, pero el enfermero está enojado porque la jeringa y la cama están rotas. Por eso, estoy sentada en una silla. Mis padres están felices. (Ellos no están felices cuando reciben la cuenta.) La comida aquí está deliciosa. ¿Estoy loca?

2-5   1. estoy 2. soy 3. estás 4. son 5. está 6. eres 7. estamos 8. está 9. sois 10. estás 11. está 12. eres 13. es 14. son 15. están 16. son 17. eres 18. somos 19. está 20. es 21. está 22. está 23. es, Son 24. estáis 25. estoy

2-6 Cuando estoy de mal humor limpio la casa. Limpio cada cuarto y lavo la ropa. Trabajo por muchas horas porque nuestra casa es grande. Unas personas trabajan cuando están de mal humor, y otras leen un libro o comen mucha comida. Vivo con tres personas y una gata. A veces estamos felices y a veces estamos tristes. En otras palabras, somos normales. Somos de la India pero ahora vivimos en Sri Lanka. Nuestra casa está cerca de la costa. Sri Lanka es una isla en el Océano Índico. Sri Lanka exporta mucho té y café. Cuando mi madre prepara el café o el té, está delicioso. Mi padre es médico y mi madre es artista. Ellos son amables. Mi hermana es muy alta. Nuestra gata es negra y gris. ¿De dónde eres tú? ¿Dónde estás ahora?

3   Hay

3-1   1. Hay un perro en el carro.   2. Hay tres tenedores en la mesa.   3. ¿Hay un baño en este edificio?
4. ¿Hay sillas en la sala?   5. No hay agua en el vaso.

3-2   Hola. Vivo en el Palacio Buckingham, la residencia oficial del monarca británico. El palacio está en la ciudad de Westminster. En realidad, trabajo en el Palacio Buckingham. Limpio la cocina. Es una cocina muy grande. Hay muchos platos y vasos porque hay muchas personas y fiestas. El palacio es enorme: Hay cincuenta y dos dormitorios para las personas que viven aquí y para sus invitados. Hay ciento ochenta y ocho dormitorios para las personas que trabajan aquí. (Algunas personas necesitan mucha ayuda.) Hay noventa y dos oficinas y setenta y ocho baños. En total, hay casi seiscientos cuartos aquí. Hay muchas pinturas en el palacio. No hay pinturas de Wallis Simpson donde yo trabajo. Hay muchos visitantes al palacio cada año.

4   Tener

4-1   1. Tengo diez dólares.   2. Tienes mis libros.   3. Ella tiene un diamante.   4. Él tiene los cuchillos y las cucharas.   5. Tenemos una nueva casa.   6. Tenéis muchos amigos.   7. Ellos tienen muchos primos.
8. No tengo el dinero.   9. ¿Quién tiene mis llaves?   10. ¿Por qué tienes un pájaro en tu carro?

4-2   1. Tengo _____ años.   2. Tienes quince años.   3. Sanja tiene sesenta años.   4. Mi coche tiene cuatro años.   5. ¿Cuántos años tienes?   6. ¿Cuántos años tiene el presidente?   7. Esos chicos tienen quince años.
8. Su gato tiene ocho años.   9. Nuestra casa tiene cien años.   10. ¿Cuántos años tienen ellos?

4-3   1. Tengo hambre.   2. Tienes sed.   3. Él tiene frío.   4. Tenemos suerte.   5. Ellos tienen prisa.   6. Tengo mucha hambre.   7. Tienes mucha sed.   8. Él tiene calor.   9. Tengo mucha suerte.   10. Tenéis mucha prisa.
11. Tengo mucho orgullo de mis hijas.   12. Ellos siempre tienen razón.

4-4   1. Tengo mucha hambre.   2. Él tiene sed.   3. Ella tiene mucha suerte.   4. Tengo frío.   5. Él no tiene razón.
6. Ella tiene mucha prisa.   7. Tengo mucho calor.   8. Tengo mucho miedo.   9. Tengo razón.   10. Ellas tienen sueño.

4-5   1. Tengo que leer este libro.   2. Tienes que mirar este programa.   3. Rudolph Nureyev tiene que bailar.
4. Kenny tiene que abrir el restaurante.   5. Tenemos que decidir ahora.   6. Tenéis que escribir cartas de agradecimiento.   7. Ellos tienen que vender su coche.   8. No tengo que comer esta sopa.   9. Tienes que tomar la medicina.   10. Tenemos que comprar el vino para la fiesta.

4-6   Hola. Trabajo en McDonald's. Tengo que trabajar cada viernes y sábado y tengo que llevar un uniforme. El uniforme es blanco y anaranjado y (claro) tiene arcos amarillos en las mangas. Tenemos un menú nuevo hoy, y por eso tengo que estudiar la lista y los precios. Tengo que estar en el restaurante temprano en la mañana. Tenemos veinte mesas en nuestro restaurante. No hay sillas porque tenemos bancos. Los bancos en restaurantes de "comida rápida" son incómodos a propósito: Los clientes "comen y corren" y, por eso, siempre hay espacio para más clientes. Hay McDonald's en casi cada país en el mundo. Cada McDonald's tiene hamburguesas y papas fritas. Vivo en Dublín. Irlanda tiene casi cien McDonald's. Mi gerente tiene veinte años.

5   The personal a

5-1   1. a   2. X   3. a   4. X   5. a   6. X   7. X   8. a   9. X   10. a

5-2   1. Romeo ama a Julieta.   2. Veo a Juan.   3. No creo a María.   4. Escuchamos a Jorge.   5. Buscas a Andrés.
6. Ellos descubren a un ladrón en la casa.   7. ¿A quién amas?   8. ¿Ves a la chica?   9. ¿Le crees al presidente?
10. Esperamos a Silvia.   11. Miro a Marcos y a Teresa.   12. Timoteo ama a Lassie.

6 Common irregular verbs

6-1 1. Doy. 2. Digo. 3. Ellas oyen. 4. Él oye. 5. Haces. 6. Juego. 7. Hago. 8. Veis. 9. Damos.
10. Ella va. 11. Ellos vienen. 12. Él dice. 13. Pones. 14. Pongo. 15. Vemos. 16. Veo. 17. Ellos quieren.
18. Juegas. 19. Salgo. 20. Dices. 21. Oigo. 22. Él quiere. 23. Voy. 24. Ellas juegan.

6-2 *Answers will vary.* 1. Quiero… 2. Normalmente, pongo mi dinero en… 3. Típicamente, vengo a la escuela
a las… 4. Desde la ventana de mi sala, veo… 5. Este año le doy… 6. Cuando estoy enojado/enojada,
digo… 7. Más o menos, voy al cine… 8. Usualmente, voy a… 9. Generalmente, salgo de casa a las…
10. Cuando alguien me dice una mentira…

6-3 *Answers will vary.* 1. Puedo… 2. No puedo… 3. Quiero… 4. Debo… 5. No debo… 6. Puede cantar.
7. Puede tocar el violín. 8. Puede jugar al béisbol. 9. Puede jugar al fútbol. 10. Puede escribir.
11. Puede nadar. 12. Pueden cocinar.

6-4 *Answers will vary.* 1. Hace… 2. Hace… en diciembre. 3. Hace frío. OR Hace viento. OR Hace mal tiempo,
OR Está lloviendo. 4. Hace calor. OR Hace sol. OR Hace buen tiempo. 5. Normalmente, hace…

6-5 1. Babe Ruth juega al béisbol. 2. Wayne Gretzky y Sidney Crosby juegan al hockey. 3. Minnesota Fats juega
al billar. 4. Kylian Mbappé y Lionel Messi juegan al fútbol. 5. Bobby Fischer y Boris Spasky juegan al
ajedrez. 6. Venus y Serena Williams juegan al tenis. 7. Tiger Woods juega al golf. 8. LeBron James y
Brittney Griner juegan al básquetbol. 9. Aaron Rogers y Patrick Mahomes juegan al fútbol americano.
10. Los niños juegan a las damas en una tabla roja y negra.

6-6 1. Voy a practicar. 2. Vas a trabajar. 3. Ella va a mirar la televisión. 4. Vamos a vender el coche.
5. Ellos van a beber la leche. 6. No voy a hacer nada. 7. ¿Qué vas a hacer? 8. ¿Vas a estudiar o mirar
la televisión? 9. No vamos a comprar caramelos. 10. ¿Cuándo vais a jugar al tenis?

6-7 *Answers will vary. All answers should begin with "Voy a" followed by an infinitive.*

6-8 Mañana es mi cumpleaños. Quiero hacer algo especial. Voy a tener una fiesta grande. Todos mis amigos
vienen a la fiesta a las dos. Tengo muchos amigos. Cada amigo/amiga me da un regalo y me dice, "Feliz
Cumpleaños." Les digo, "Muchas gracias." Mi madre va a hacer una torta de chocolate para la fiesta. Ella hace
las mejores tortas—¡ella pone mucho chocolate encima de la torta de chocolate! Oigo a mi madre en la cocina
ahora pero no la veo. Durante mi fiesta vamos a jugar al fútbol en el parque. Puedo ver el parque de mi casa.
Después, vamos a comer pizza y beber limonada. Estoy muy emocionado/emocionada. ¡Quiero tener la fiesta
ahora mismo! Va a ser una fiesta maravillosa.

7 Saber and conocer

7-1 1. Sé tu nombre. 2. Sabes la respuesta. 3. Ella sabe dónde vives. 4. No sabemos por qué él está enojado.
5. ¿Sabes quién tiene el dinero? 6. Ellos no saben nada de mí. 7. ¿Sabe él dónde está María?
8. Sabéis mucho.

7-2 1. Sé que Juan es alto. 2. Sabes que tengo hambre. 3. Ella sabe que tienes sed. 4. ¿Sabes que tengo
veintinueve años? 5. Sabemos que él tiene prisa. 6. Ellos no saben que estoy aquí. 7. ¿Sabéis que hay
culebras en el jardín? 8. Él no sabe que estás en el jardín.

7-3 1. Sé cantar. 2. Sabes hablar español. 3. Ella sabe cocinar muy bien. 4. Él no sabe hablar francés.
5. Gene Kelly y Misty Copeland saben bailar. 6. Sabéis tocar el piano. 7. ¿Sabes esquiar? 8. ¿Quién sabe
abrir esta puerta?

7-4 Juan es mi mecánico. Él sabe mucho de carros y estoy feliz porque yo no sé nada de carros. No, no es
completamente cierto. Yo sé dónde está el tanque de gasolina y sé llenarlo. Sé conducir y sé que no puedo
aparcar enfrente de una estación de bomberos. Juan sabe que él tiene que saber de carros y de la gente,
porque muchas personas saben muy poco de carros.

7-5 1. Conozco a Antonia. 2. Conoces a Isabel. 3. Él conoce a su suegro. 4. Te conocemos. 5. Conocéis
a Juan. 6. Ella conoce a Juana y a Paco. 7. ¿Conoces a mis gatos Fifi y Fufu? 8. Él no me conoce.
9. La conozco. 10. La conoces. 11. Él lo conoce. 12. Nos conoces. 13. Lo conocéis. 14. Ella los conoce.
15. Sí, los conozco. 16. Nadie me conoce aquí.

7-6 1. Yo (no) conozco Chicago. 2. El presidente conoce bien Washington, D.C. 3. El alcalde conoce bien
la ciudad. 4. Dorotea conoce Oz. 5. Ellos no conocen París. 6. ¿Conoces Uganda? 7. Jorge conoce
la selva. 8. El pájaro conoce su árbol.

Free audio answer key available online

7-7   1. El médico conoce bien el cuerpo.   2. El sacerdote conoce bien la Biblia.   3. El peluquero conoce el pelo de sus clientes.   4. LeBron James conoce el básquetbol.   5. La manicurista conoce las uñas de sus clientes. 6. El cocinero conoce la comida de México.   7. El arquitecto conoce la arquitectura de Chicago. 8. El granjero conoce la tierra.

7-8   No sé por qué, pero creo que te conozco. ¿Conoces a mi primo, Enrique? ¿Sí? Pues, entonces tú sabes que su esposa sabe hablar ruso—pero no puede leerlo. Ella tiene muchas fiestas maravillosas porque conoce a todo el mundo y porque sabe cocinar como una cocinera profesional. Yo sé que quieres conocerla. Voy a organizar la presentación.

8   Stem-changing verbs

8-1   1. Yo almuerzo.   2. Tú almuerzas.   3. El perro muerde.   4. Aprobamos.   5. Rogáis.   6. Ellos cuentan el dinero.   7. Muestras la casa.   8. Ella duerme.   9. Resolvemos el problema.   10. Ella envuelve el regalo. 11. Cuelgo el teléfono.   12. Devuelves la camisa.   13. Él muere.   14. El teléfono suena.   15. Encuentro el dinero.   16. Volvemos.   17. Dumbo vuela.   18. Juana tuesta el pan.   19. Rogamos por la paz.   20. Él sueña con un tigre.   21. No recuerdo nada.   22. El libro cuesta diez dólares.   23. Mueves las sillas.   24. Pruebo el café.

8-2   1. Cierro la puerta.   2. Pierdes el juego.   3. Él friega los platos.   4. Te advertimos.   5. Ellos niegan la verdad 6. Él lo siente mucho.   7. Empezáis.   8. Ella me defiende.   9. Hierves el agua.   10. George Santos miente mucho. 11. Consentís.   12. Ella sugiere.   13. Temblamos.   14. Prefiero agua.   15. Él quiere un perro.   16. ¿Entiendes? 17. Él pierde la revista.   18. Ella tropieza con el sofá.   19. Ellos confiesan el delito.   20. El programa comienza. 21. Pienso en la guerra.   22. Enciendes la vela.   23. Convertimos el dinero a dólares.   24. Refiero el caso al profesor.

8-3   1. Compito.   2. Corriges el examen.   3. Él pide ayuda.   4. Ella ríe mucho.   5. Él consigue trabajo. 6. Elegimos al ganador.   7. Freímos las papas.   8. Decís la verdad.   9. Despides al empleado. 10. Pedimos más dinero.   11. Ella gime.   12. Él impide el progreso.   13. Ellos nos dicen la verdad. 14. Te sigo.   15. Nos servís.   16. ¿Quién dice esto?   17. Ella mide cinco pies.   18. Ellos maldicen. 19. Él colige la verdad de los hechos.   20. Compites contra él.   21. Ellos ríen mucho porque están contentos. 22. Ustedes repiten la lección.   23. El sacerdote te bendice.   24. ¿Qué pides?

8-4   Estoy en un avión. Vuelo mucho porque prefiero viajar rápidamente. Vamos a salir en cinco minutos. El/La azafato/azafata cierra la puerta y nos refiere a las instrucciones para emergencias. Algunas personas duermen en el avión y otras muerden sus pañuelos cuando el avión tiembla. Nadie almuerza porque las/los azafatos/azafatas no nos sirven comida. Ellos nos sirven bebidas y cacahuates. ¡¡Somos elefantes?! Cuando mi madre vuela, ella piensa en su familia. Prefiero pensar en el hotel elegante y en la ciudad que voy a visitar. Esta noche voy a dormir en São Paulo.

9   Irregular verb groups

9-1   1. conozco   2. pertenezco   3. parece   4. pertenecen   5. reconozco   6. nacen   7. ofrezco   8. merezco 9. crece   10. aparece

9-2   Soy una celebridad. Aparezco en muchas fiestas y estrenos para películas hechas por otras personas. Conozco a muchas personas, pero es más importante si ellos me reconocen. Creo que pertenezco a la "lista A". No tengo talento ni le ofrezco nada al mundo. Creo que merezco dinero y fama simplemente porque existo. Obedezco todas las leyes de la idiotez.

9-3   *Answers will vary.*   1. Conduzco un coche automático. OR Conduzco un coche de marchas.   2. Sí, produzco mucho trabajo.   3. Sí, traduzco muchas frases en este libro.   4. El panadero produce pan.   5. Sí, introduzco una moneda en el parquímetro.   6. No, normalmente los políticos no reducen los impuestos.

9-4   Conduzco un taxi en la ciudad de Nueva York. Usualmente obedezco las leyes de la ciudad, pero a veces tengo que conducir muy, muy rápidamente (me entiendes, ¿no?). Entonces merezco una propina muy, muy grande (agradezco esta mucho; gracias) y la introduzco en la guantera. Nunca pongo guantes en la guantera porque no hay espacio—está llena de dinero. La mayoría de mis clientes hablan inglés, pero a veces me dicen cosas en otros idiomas, y entonces traduzco lo que me dicen.

9-5   1. Esparzo semillas en el jardín.   2. Venzo al enemigo.   3. Zurzo los calcetines.   4. Ejerzo mucha energía cuando juego al fútbol.   5. Los guerreros vencen a sus enemigos.

9-6 Soy jardinero/jardinera. Cada mañana esparzo las semillas en el jardín. Entonces venzo las malas hierbas y convenzo las moscas y los mosquitos que necesitan volar al jardín de mi vecino. Mi jardín produce muchos vegetales y muchas frutas. Merezco mucha alabanza por mi jardín hermoso.

9-7 1. Protejo a mis hijas.   2. Corrijo mis problemas.   3. El maestro corrige muchos trabajos.   4. A veces finjo estar feliz cuando estoy triste.   5. Escojo a mis amigos con mucho cuidado.   6. Cada cuatro años elegimos a un nuevo líder.   7. Recojo mis calcetines del suelo.   8. Cojo un taxi para el aeropuerto.   9. Exijo mucho de mis empleados.   10. Sumerjo el suéter en agua fría.

9-8 Cada mañana tomo el autobús a la escuela. Cojo el autobús en la esquina de las avenidas Duque y Duquesa. Antes de salir para la escuela, escojo mi ropa para el día y entonces recojo mis libros y mi mochila. Mi mochila protege mis libros. A veces finjo ser astronauta y el autobús es una nave. Otras veces finjo estar enfermo/enferma porque entonces no tengo que ir a la escuela.

9-9 1. traigo   2. rae   3. atrae   4. contrae   5. sustraen

9-10 Soy (una) flor. Soy (un) aster, para ser exacto. Mi jardinero me planta porque atraigo a las abejas. Traigo mucha belleza al jardín. Crezco alto y hermoso en el verano y en el otoño. Muchas personas piensan que soy (una) margarita, pero yo no soy lo que parezco ser. En realidad soy (un) miembro de la familia girasol.

9-11 1. construyo   2. contribuyo   3. fluye   4. huye   5. influyen   6. destruye   7. concluyes   8. constituye   9. incluye   10. contribuyen

9-12 Tengo cinco años. Construyo muchas casas de los bloques de madera que están en mi dormitorio. Unos días mi hermana contribuye muebles de su casa de muñecas a las casas de madera. Al fin del día, cuando es la hora de dormir, las destruyo. Si creo que hay un monstruo en mi closet, huyo del cuarto.

9-13 1. distingo   2. sigue   3. extingo   4. consigo   5. irguen   6. persiguen   7. consigue   8. siguen   9. distinguen   10. sigo   11. consiguen   12. extinguen

9-14 Cuando consigo un aparato nuevo nunca sigo las direcciones. Es demasiado aburrido. Distingo las cosas que necesito entre las muchas piezas y sigo lo que me parece correcto. Algunas veces no tengo razón, y entonces tengo que seguir otra senda. Por ejemplo, si hay un incendio, lo extingo. Tarde o temprano el aparato funciona. (O lo devuelvo a la tienda.) No voy a buscar (un) empleo de mecánico.

10 Reflexive verbs

10-1 1. Me acuesto.   2. Te lavas el pelo.   3. Él se afeita cada mañana.   4. Ella se afeita las piernas.   5. Os despertáis.   6. Ellos se sientan.   7. Ella se va.   8. Me llamo Rex.   9. Te duchas.   10. Nos vestimos.   11. Os dormís.   12. Ella se baña.   13. Me preocupo por el futuro.   14. Uds. se despiertan.   15. Me desvisto en la noche.   16. Te llamas Alicia.   17. Se quita la camisa.   18. Uds. se ven en el espejo.   19. Me siento enfermo/enferma.   20. Te peinas (el pelo).   21. Nos cepillamos los dientes.   22. Ella se duerme.   23. ¿Te duchas?   24. Se llama Horatio.   25. El cerdo se come el maíz.

10-2 Hay dos tipos de personas: Hay alondras (personas de la mañana) y búhos (personas de la noche). Soy alondra. Me despierto—con o sin despertador—a las cinco de la mañana. Me levanto inmediatamente, me cepillo los dientes, me ducho, me lavo el pelo, me seco el pelo, me visto, y me voy al trabajo. Mi hermano es completamente diferente. Él no se despierta hasta el mediodía y no se levanta hasta la una de la tarde. Él es un guarro. Él no se cepilla los dientes, no se lava el pelo, y no se ducha. Cuando se ve en el espejo, creo que en realidad ve a un monstruo. Él nunca se peina. Se enferma mucho y se enoja porque no puede conseguir trabajo cuando está tan sucio.

11 Gustar and similarly formed verbs

11-1 1. Me importa la verdad.   2. No me gustan las arañas.   3. Me duele el estómago.   4. Me sobran los libros.   5. A ella le gusta el otoño.   6. Me parece ridículo.   7. ¡Me encanta tu vestido!   8. Nos sobran diez dólares.   9. Me disgusta tu actitud.   10. Me encanta el helado.   11. Te falta un botón.   12. Nos fascinan estas fotos.   13. A ellos les interesa la película.   14. ¿Qué te importa?   15. Me disgustan sus modales.   16. Me parece egoísta.   17. Esta película me aburre.   18. Ella me molesta.

11-2 Me duele la cabeza y me molesta mucho. Me importa mucho la salud. No me gusta cuando estoy enfermo/enferma. Me encanta cuando me siento bien. Debo tomar medicina, pero me disgusta lo que tengo en el botiquín. Me parece leche vieja y me disgusta. Me fascinan las personas que siempre están sanas. A ellos les encanta la vida y les interesan muchas cosas. ¿Quiénes son ellos? ¿De dónde son ellos?

Free audio answer key available online

12 The present progressive

12-1 1. Estoy buscando un libro bueno.   2. Estás mirando la televisión.   3. Él está tocando el piano.
4. Estamos comiendo pizza y bebiendo limonada.   5. Estáis recibiendo muchos regalos.   6. Uds. están cubriendo los muebles.   7. Estamos almorzando.   8. Estoy pensando en mi mejor amigo/amiga.
9. ¿Qué estás haciendo?   10. ¿Qué está comiendo ella?   11. Ellos están durmiendo.   12. Ella está mintiéndome
OR Ella me está mintiendo.

12-2 1. El río está fluyendo al sur.   2. El cliente no está creyendo al vendedor de coches.   3. No estamos leyendo nada.   4. El presidente no está influyendo a la gente.   5. El odio está destruyendo nuestra sociedad.
6. Romeo está huyendo con Julieta.   7. Ella no está oyendo nada en el sótano.   8. ¿Qué estás leyendo?
9. ¿Quién está trayendo el vino a la fiesta?   10. ¿Por qué están construyendo una casa en las afueras?

12-3 1. durmiendo   2. mintiendo   3. hirviendo   4. sirviendo   5. riendo   6. compitiendo   7. diciendo
8. muriendo   9. siguiendo   10. pidiendo

12-4 1. Estoy estudiándolo.   2. Estás cantándonosla.   3. Él está escribiéndome una carta.
4. ¿Estás escribiéndoles?   5. ¿Por qué están Uds. diciéndome esto?   6. ¿Por qué estás diciéndomelo?
7. Ellos están sentándose.   8. Estamos leyéndolo.   9. Él está mintiéndome.   10. ¿Qué estás dándome?
11. Ellos están siguiéndonos.   12. ¿Qué está leyéndote Lilia?

12-5 Hola. Me llamo Julia. Tengo veintiún años y soy estudiante en una famosa escuela culinaria. No sé por qué estoy aquí; no me gusta cocinar. De hecho, casi todas las cosas en el supermercado me disgustan. Soy vegetariana, pero aquí estoy, preparando pollo, filete y langosta para un grupo de profesores que saben que soy una cocinera terrible. No puedo decir quién tiene más miedo—yo o mis víctimas (hay cinco profesores esperándome en el comedor) que tienen que probar este brebaje. Sé que ellos van a darme una "F" después de comer esta comida. Estoy cortando la carne, pero (estoy) soñando con tocar mi guitarra en frente de una audiencia. Quiero ser (una) música, no (una) cocinera.

 # THE PAST TENSES, THE FUTURE TENSE, THE CONDITIONAL TENSE, AND THE PRESENT AND PAST PERFECT TENSES

13 The preterite tense

13-1 1. Yo compré una camisa ayer.   2. Tú estudiaste anoche.   3. Ella trabajó por dos horas.   4. Nosotros lavamos la ropa anoche.   5. Ellos cantaron cinco canciones.   6. Yo corrí a la esquina.   7. Escribiste una carta.
8. Ella abrió la puerta.   9. No abrimos esas ventanas.   10. Ellos vendieron el carro.   11. Bailamos el tango anoche.   12. Ellos hablaron con el dueño.   13. Me duché esta mañana.   14. Te lavaste el pelo hace dos horas.
15. Ellas se acostaron a las once y media.

13-2 *Answers will vary.*   1. Sí, hablé por teléfono anoche.   2. Compré la camisa en el centro comercial.
3. Comí paella.   4. Recibí flores y colonia.   5. No, hoy no escuché la radio.   6. Sí, tomé café ayer por la mañana.   7. No, no bailé el fin de semana pasado.   8. Sí, estudié español el año pasado.

13-3 Me llamo Cenicientas. Vivo con mi madrastra y mis dos hermanastras. Ellas son muy crueles. Hace dos días, todo el día, trabajé: Limpié la casa, lavé la ropa, preparé las comidas, quité el polvo y barrí los suelos. Ellas miraron la televisión y comieron todo el día. Entonces, a las seis ellas salieron para el baile en el palacio del rey. Lloré por diez minutos y canté una canción. De repente, mi hada madrina apareció en la sala. Me regaló un vestido y unos zapatos y salí para el baile. Entré en el palacio y conocí al príncipe. Inmediatamente nos enamoramos. Bailamos hasta la medianoche y corrí del palacio porque mi noche especial se acabó. Perdí uno de mis zapatos nuevos. Esta tarde, el príncipe llegó con mi zapato. Nos besamos y entonces volamos a Las Vegas y nos casamos. Mi madrina y mis hermanastras se volvieron locas.

13-4 1. Practiqué el piano por una hora.   2. Llegué a las dos.   3. Organicé la fiesta.   4. Empecé a bailar en la mesa.   5. Toqué la guitarra por dos horas en la recepción.   6. Jugué al tenis con el jugador profesional.
7. Saqué veinte fotos de mi gato.   8. Autoricé la compra hace una semana.   9. Clasifiqué la información.
10. Me tropecé con el peldaño de tu casa.   11. Aparqué el carro en el estacionamiento hace tres horas.
12. Nunca destaqué en la clase de inglés por mi pronunciación.   13. Tragué la medicina sin pensar.
14. Pagué la cuenta del gas.   15. Regué las plantas de mi amiga Lola.

13-5 Ayer jugué por una hora y trabajé por dos horas. Jugué a los naipes con mis amigos en la mañana. Después de eso, pagué todas mis cuentas, regué las plantas, practiqué el piano, saqué fotos de mis mascotas, organicé los trastos en el garaje, justifiqué la posesión de los trastos, y recé por un borrador gigante para deshacerme de todo.

13-6 1. Anduve por el parque. 2. Él vino a mi fiesta. 3. Anoche no pude dormir. 4. Ellos tuvieron un accidente el martes pasado. 5. Hicimos las camas esta mañana. 6. ¿Cuándo supiste la respuesta? 7. Estuvisteis aquí (por) no más de diez minutos. 8. Puse la ropa en el armario. 9. ¿Qué hiciste anoche? 10. Ellas tuvieron que trabajar (por) diez horas ayer. 11. Me puse los zapatos. 12. Estuvimos allí (por) media hora. 13. ¿Quién hizo las camas? 14. Ella no vino a la reunión porque tuvo un accidente. 15. Estuve en la tienda (por) veinte minutos y entonces vine aquí.

13-7 Estuve muy triste anoche. Tuve un día horrible en el trabajo. ¡Estuve tan aburrido/aburrida! Llegué a casa a las diez de la noche. Sé que puse mis llaves en el bolsillo, pero no pude encontrarlas. Tuve que llamar a un cerrajero. Fue a mi casa y no llegó hasta la medianoche. Me dormí en la acera.

13-8 1. Yo fui al partido. 2. Yo fui presidente/presidenta del club (por) un año. 3. Él fue a la tienda para comprar huevos. 4. ¿Por qué te fuiste? 5. Ellas no fueron ayer porque fueron la semana pasada. 6. No fuimos a la boda. 7. ¿Fuisteis a la escuela hoy? 8. ¿Quién fue el gran ganador ayer? 9. La fiesta fue terrible. 10. La reunión fue bien. 11. Anita y Pepe fueron novios por dos años pero nunca fueron al cine. 12. Él fue mi mejor amigo por diez años. 13. Fuimos por separado a la misma tienda. 14. ¿Adónde fueron Uds. anoche? 15. ¿Cómo fue la fiesta? ¡Fue un desastre!

13-9 1. Les dije mi nombre a los niños. 2. Me dijiste una mentira. 3. Él trajo el vino a la fiesta. 4. Él dijo que habló con Carlos la semana pasada. 5. Dijimos que no comimos las galletas. 6. La televisión me distrajo. 7. ¿Qué dijeron Uds. a María? 8. ¿Qué le dijiste a ella? 9. Sus modales me atrajeron. 10. ¿Qué dijo él cuando le dijiste que escribiste la carta? 11. No les dije nada. 12. ¿Qué nos trajiste? 13. Ellos no me dijeron la verdad. 14. ¿Te dijo lo que me dijo ayer? 15. El azúcar atrajo a las moscas.

13-10 1. Le di un paquete a Juan ayer. 2. Vi a Juan ayer. 3. Ella me dio un libro. 4. Ella nos vio en el cine. 5. ¿Qué le diste para su cumpleaños? 6. ¿Qué película visteis anoche? 7. Cuando me vieron, me dieron el dinero. 8. Ustedes no nos dieron nada. 9. ¿Viste el gato que Miguel me dio? 10. No vi el regalo que nos dieron.

13-11 Fui a Puerto Rico el enero pasado. ¡Fue maravilloso! Una amiga mía es agente de viajes y cuando me ofreció la oportunidad de ir al Caribe para una semana de sol y diversión—por muy poco dinero—le dije, "¿Cuándo vamos?" El día que salimos, nevó seis pulgadas aquí. Cuando llegamos a San Juan, el sol, el calor y la arena nos saludaron. Tomamos un taxi a nuestro hotel, saqué mi traje de baño de la maleta y fuimos a la playa. Al día siguiente fuimos a El Yunque, la selva tropical, donde anduvimos por horas y vimos muchos pájaros y árboles hermosos. No pude creerlo—¡fue tan hermoso! Al día siguiente fuimos a la Playa Luquillo y nadamos y leímos y nos relajamos. Hicimos esto cada día hasta que—¡ay!—tuvimos que volver a la realidad.

13-12 1. Ella durmió por diez horas. 2. Ellos me mintieron. 3. Él pidió más café. 4. Las cucarachas murieron. 5. Nuestro abogado nos advirtió del peligro. 6. En aquel momento ella prefirió no decir nada. 7. ¿Te advirtieron de tus derechos? 8. Dorothy siguió el camino amarillo de ladrillos. 9. Ellos repitieron la pregunta dos veces. 10. Él le pidió a su jefe un aumento.

13-13 1. Juan no me oyó. 2. Ellas leyeron mi libro dos veces. 3. Los árboles se cayeron durante la tormenta. 4. Tres presos huyeron de la cárcel anoche. 5. Los abastecedores no proveyeron suficiente pan. 6. Los ladrones destruyeron nuestra casa. 7. ¿Leíste mi periódico? 8. Ellos contribuyeron ciento cincuenta dólares el año pasado. 9. El plato huyó con la cuchara. 10. Humpty Dumpty se cayó. 11. Las lágrimas fluyeron de mis ojos. 12. La rama se cayó del árbol. 13. Huyeron de la escena del crimen. 14. Construyeron una casa enorme. 15. ¿Por qué no nos incluyó?

13-14 1. Produje una película el año pasado. 2. Tradujiste bien el documento. 3. Condujimos al teatro. 4. El mago produjo un conejo del sombrero. 5. Condujisteis veinte millas. 6. Traduje esta frase del inglés al español. 7. Condujimos a los chicos a la cafetería. 8. Nos condujeron a la boda. 9. ¿Cuántas páginas tradujiste? 10. ¿Hasta dónde condujiste? 11. Deduje la respuesta. 12. El presidente no redujo los impuestos el año pasado.

13-15 1. V   2. F   3. V   4. F   5. V   6. V   7. V   8. F   9. V   10. F   11. V   12. F

13-16 H. L. Mencken fue un gran escritor. Nació en Baltimore en 1880, donde vivió toda su vida, y murió en 1956. Escribió muchos ensayos sobre la política y las cuestiones sociales, pero su interés principal, creo, fue el lenguaje—en particular, el inglés de los Estados Unidos. Uno de sus libros más conocidos es *El idioma americano,* en el cual Mencken discutió la riqueza de los Estados Unidos y cómo muchos otros idiomas influyeron en este idioma. También produjo una serie de autobiografías y diarios. Leyó toda clase de literatura y poseyó un credo personal muy estricto. Creyó que una persona debe trabajar duro, jugar duro y, sobre todo, pensar.

13-17 1. Conocí a Lisa hace veinticinco años.   2. Él no pudo ver mi punto de vista.   3. Ellos no lo supieron hasta hace quince años.   4. Mi sobrina tuvo un niño el diciembre pasado. OR Mi sobrina tuvo una niña el diciembre pasado.   5. ¿Por qué no quisisteis salir?   6. Él sintió ganar el dinero.   7. Ella quiso salir pero no pudo encontrar sus llaves.   8. Pude pagar las cuentas a tiempo este mes.   9. Nos conocimos en un ascensor. 10. Supe que Juana pudo falsificar mi firma.

13-18 Todo el mundo conoció a Damar Hamlin lunes, el dos de enero, 2023, durante un juego de fútbol americano entre los Bengals de Cincinnati y los Bills de Buffalo (New York). El juego tomó lugar en Cincinnati, Ohio. Damar (de los Bills) de solamente veinticuatro años, tackleo a Tee Higgins (de los Bengals) durante el primer cuarto a las nueve menos cinco de la noche. Todo estuvo normal, pero de repente Damar no pudo levantarse y se cayó. Varios médicos entraron en el campo y lo trataron. Él fue al hospital por ambulancia. Poco después, los telespectadores supieron que Damar tuvo un ataque de corazón y casi murió. Pero él no quiso rendirse, y después de tres días en estado de coma inducido, Damar se despertó. Su progreso continuó y pudo salir del hospital nueve días después.

14 The imperfect tense

14-1 1. Yo estudiaba con Juan.   2. Él trabajaba en un banco.   3. Vivíamos en un apartamento.   4. Ellos escribían notas a sus amigos en clase.   5. Leías muchas revistas.   6. Abríais las ventanas en enero.   7. Yo hacía la cama cada mañana.   8. Mickey Mantle jugaba (al) béisbol para los Yankees.   9. Ellas nos llamaban cada noche.   10. ¿Dónde trabajabas?   11. ¿Dónde vivían ustedes?   12. Él nadaba en nuestra piscina.   13. Marcos era presidente de nuestro club.   14. Yo iba a Ravello, Italia, cada invierno.   15. Invitábamos a todos a nuestras fiestas.

14-2 1. político 2. arquitecto 3. payasos 4. antropóloga 5. detectives 6. escritor 7. pianistas 8. filósofo 9. pintor 10. psiquiatra 11. bailarines 12. explorador

14-3 1. Mi padre era granjero.   2. María tenía un corderito.   3. Llevábamos uniformes a la escuela.   4. Yo estaba avergonzado/avergonzada.   5. La tienda no tenía la camisa que quería.   6. Las ventanas estaban abiertas pero la puerta estaba cerrada.   7. Susana estaba embarazada.   8. Llevabais sombreros ridículos.   9. Jorge era alto y guapo.   10. El gato estaba en el desván.   11. Mi pluma no funcionaba. OR Mi bolígrafo no funcionaba. 12. ¿Dónde estaba el dinero?   13. Yo tenía muchos amigos en el campamento.   14. El gato era blanco y negro. 15. El monstruo tenía dos cabezas.

14-4 Cuando era menor me gustaba mucho la escuela. Mi clase favorita era la ciencia, y siempre soñaba con ser médico/médica. Tenía un "laboratorio" en mi casa. Mezclaba cosas diferentes y esperaba una explosión. Cuando hacía esto, mi madre estaba enojada. A ella le gustaba la casa como era. Mis amigos y yo fingíamos que éramos científicos locos.

14-5 1. Yo fregaba los platos.   2. Nadie escuchaba mientras el político hablaba.   3. Él andaba y yo corría. 4. Ellos escuchaban la radio mientras estudiaban.   5. Intentábamos dormir pero el bebé lloraba. 6. ¿Por qué mirabas la televisión cuando yo estudiaba?   7. Los niños jugaban en el jardín.   8. Vivíamos en una casa de cristal.   9. Vendíais camisetas en la esquina.   10. Yo sufría de un resfriado.   11. Las ranas saltaban cerca del lago.   12. Me duchaba mientras ellas se desayunaban.   13. Carmen preparaba la cena. 14. Pensábamos mucho en ti.   15. Mientras ella explicaba la teoría, todos se iban.

14-6 1. F 2. V 3. V 4. V 5. V 6. F

14-7 1. Yo sabía la respuesta.   2. Juana odiaba el color rojo.   3. ¿Lo conocías? 4. Ellos no me creían. 5. Mi familia me amaba mucho.   6. Estábamos muy tristes por mucho tiempo.   7. Él odiaba a su nuevo jefe. 8. Me gustaba la foto de tu familia.   9. Me gustaban las flores en su jardín.   10. Aunque él me molestaba, lo amaba.   11. Ella se preocupaba mucho por ti.   12. ¿Pensabas en mí?   13. ¿En qué pensabas? 14. ¿Cómo te sentías durante el juicio?   15. Ella no se llevaba bien con su suegra.

14-8 Ayer, cuando caminaba [or iba] a la escuela vi una mariposa. Era enorme. Al principio tenía miedo, pero sólo [or solamente] por un rato porque sabía que las mariposas no son monstruos. Era roja y anaranjada y tenía rayas amarillas. Era hermosa y tenía ojos que me parecían morados. Esta experiencia fue muy extraña.

14-9 1. De niño, Juan miraba la televisión cada día después de la escuela.   2. Cuando vivíamos en Francia, tomábamos vino con cada comida.   3. El año pasado ellos no podían hablar español.   4. ¿Por qué no podías ir al cine conmigo?   5. Cuando yo era joven, miraba debajo de la cama cada noche antes de apagar la luz.   6. Barry Bonds podía jugar al béisbol mejor que Pete Rose.   7. Cuando Juana trabajaba en el banco, tomaba quince tazas de café cada día.   8. Cuando usted era menor, podía recordar las capitales de cada estado.   9. Cuando Juan Smith trabajaba para la CIA, nunca decía a nadie su nombre verdadero.   10. Ellos no podían votar porque no tenían identificación.   11. Tú nunca estabas en casa. ¿Adónde ibas esas noches?   12. No podíamos llamarte porque el teléfono no funcionaba.   13. Para cada fiesta que teníamos, Lisa traía papas fritas y yo traía salsa de tomate.   14. El pan estaba mohoso. No podía comerlo.   15. De niña, Victoria tenía que hacer la cama cada mañana antes de salir para la escuela.

14-10 1. Siempre estudiaba antes de un examen.   2. Él frecuentemente me llamaba después de las diez de la noche.   3. Yo siempre quería tener un piano.   4. Ellos siempre nos engañaban cuando jugábamos a los naipes.   5. Comías allí con frecuencia.   6. A menudo escribíais cartas largas.   7. De vez en cuando enviábamos [OR mandábamos] dinero a la organización.   8. A veces él no ganaba tanto dinero como su esposa.   9. Todo el tiempo que yo estaba allí, nunca decíais nada.   10. Él siempre enviaba una nota de agradecimiento después de recibir un regalo.   11. Ella nunca compraba nada sin cupón.   12. Él nos mentía con frecuencia, pero nunca le decíamos nada.   13. Siempre me preguntaba por qué ella se lavaba las manos tantas veces cada día.   14. Ella nunca estaba feliz. Se quejaba cada día, todo el día. Ella era rara.   15. A veces leíamos y a veces escribíamos en nuestros diarios. De vez en cuando veíamos películas en Netflix.

14-11 1. hablé   2. vivía   3. comió   4. comía   5. fuimos   6. compré   7. llegamos   8. llegó   9. estudiaba   10. estudió   11. comían   12. jugaron   13. era   14. eras   15. fueron

14-12 1. Eran las dos y media cuando me llamaste.   2. María tenía veintidós años cuando compró su primer coche [OR carro].   3. Eran las cuatro y cuarto cuando encontré el dinero.   4. Ellas tenían dieciocho años cuando se graduaron de la escuela secundaria.   5. Eran las cinco menos cinco cuando el árbol se cayó.   6. Trabajábamos duro cuando teníamos quince años.   7. Cuando me levanté eran las seis y cuarto.   8. Aprendí a montar en bicicleta cuando tenía seis años.   9. Eran las cuatro menos cuarto de la mañana cuando sonó el teléfono.   10. Ella tuvo su primera bebé, una niña, cuando tenía cuarenta y un años, y tuvo su segunda hija cuando tenía cuarenta y cuatro (años).   11. No sabíamos que eran las doce y media.   12. Eran las tres de la mañana cuando salieron.   13. ¿Dónde vivías cuando tenías catorce años?   14. ¿Qué hora era cuando terminaste el libro?   15. ¿Cuántos años tenía Juan cuando se casó?

14-13 *Answers will vary.* 1. Eran las once cuando me acosté.   2. Eran las seis cuando me levanté.   3. Tenía cinco años cuando comencé la escuela.   4. Tenía diez años cuando aprendí a montar en bicicleta.   5. Eran las ocho cuando salí de casa.   6. Eran las seis y media cuando volví a casa.   7. Tenía veinte años cuando empecé a estudiar español.   8. Tenía cuatro años cuando aprendí a nadar.

14-14 1. Había una araña debajo de mi cama esta mañana.   2. Había veinte personas en la fiesta.   3. Había una mosca en mi sopa.   4. Había cien preguntas en el examen.   5. Había mucho ruido durante la tormenta.   6. Había quinientas páginas en el libro.   7. No había gasolina en el tanque.   8. No había hojas en los árboles.   9. No había suficiente tiempo para preguntas.   10. Había más mujeres que hombres en la reunión.   11. Había basura en la mesa.   12. Había tanta niebla que no podía conducir [OR manejar].   13. En enero, hacía tanto frío que no había nadie afuera.   14. En el verano había mucha gente por las calles.   15. No había mujeres en ese restaurante.

14-15 Cuando yo era joven, había una exposición de insectos en el zoológico cada verano. Mi familia y yo siempre íbamos. Había un edificio sólo para mariposas, y había diez clases de mariposas volando de un lado a otro. También había un edificio que tenía docenas de insectos. Yo nunca sabía que había tantos insectos. Había información en todas partes. Supe que por cada libra de ser humano, hay doce libras de insectos. También leí que la señorita Muffet verdaderamente existía. Su papá, Thomas Muffet, era un entomólogo que le daba a su hija puré de arañas cuando estaba enferma. ¡Esto era un remedio común para los resfriados hace doscientos años!

14-16 1. Yo iba a comer.   2. ¿Ibas a decirme algo?   3. Él iba a llevar su camisa blanca pero estaba sucia.   4. Íbamos a quitar la nieve.   5. Ellos iban a pasar el día en el campo pero hacía mal tiempo.   6. ¿Cuándo iban (ustedes) a sentarse?   7. Yo iba a acostarme a las diez y media pero había un buen programa en la televisión.   8. ¿Cómo ibas a hacer esto?   9. ¿Por qué iba ella a construir una casa en el bosque?   10. ¿Quién iba a arreglar este grifo?   11. Íbamos a cepillarnos los dientes pero no había pasta de dientes.   12. Yo iba a darle dinero para su cumpleaños.   13. ¿Adónde ibais a enviar este paquete?   14. ¿Cuándo ibas a traernos las flores?   15. ¿Por qué no iba él a llenar los vasos con agua?

14-17 1. Yo estaba comiendo.   2. Estabas estudiando.   3. Dumbo estaba volando.   4. Ella estaba almorzando.   5. Estábamos bebiendo leche.   6. Estabais diciendo la verdad.   7. Ellos estaban acostándose.   8. Ustedes estaban cepillándose el pelo.   9. Yo estaba bañándome.   10. Juan estaba afeitándose.   11. Sofía estaba tocando el piano.   12. Serena estaba jugando al tenis.

14-18 Esta tarde vi el mejor episodio de la *Jueza Judy* mientras almorzaba. Me encanta ese programa. Las demandantes (Shannon y Karen Ann Davenport) demandaban a la demandada (Kelli Filkins) porque Filkins puso un anuncio en eBay para dos teléfonos celulares. Las Davenport querían los teléfonos celulares y le enviaron a Filkins el dinero, pero cuando Filkins recibió su dinero, no les envió los celulares. ¡Ella les envió fotos de los teléfonos celulares! La Juez Judy estuvo enojada, muy enojada en este episodio. La Juez Judy le dijo a Kelli Filkins que ella era una chanchullera. Kelli le dijo a la Juez Judy que no era la culpa suya porque las Davenport no podían leer. Según Filkins, decía "sólo foto." Pero también afirmaba que uno de los teléfonos celulares pesaba 4,7 onzas, y el pedazo de papel no pesaba 4,7 onzas (un pedazo de papel típico pesa 0,16 de una onza). La Juez Judy le dijo a Kelli que si ella vive por cien años, nunca va a tener en todo su cuerpo la inteligencia que la Juez Judy tiene en un dedo, y ¡ella tenía razón! Las Davenport ganaron el caso y Kelli Filkins lo perdió. La Juez Judy falló en favor de las Davenport y dijo que Kelli tuvo que pagarles cinco mil dólares. Este episodio está en YouTube, y ¡tú puedes mirarlo, también!

15 The future tense

15-1 1. compraré   2. correrán   3. abriréis   4. serás   5. estará   6. jugaremos   7. llevará   8. me ducharé   9. llegarán   10. vomitará   11. nevará   12. se acostarán

15-2 1. Te hablaré mañana. OR Hablaré contigo mañana.   2. Ella comprará un carro nuevo el año que viene.   3. Él dormirá hasta mañana por la tarde.   4. Llegaremos a las diez mañana por la noche.   5. ¿A qué hora te acostarás?   6. ¿Cuánto dinero necesitaréis?   7. Ellos se quedarán en un hotel el mes que viene.   8. Nunca nevará en Panamá.   9. ¿Dónde estarás esta noche a las once y media?   10. ¿A qué hora comenzará el programa?   11. No quiero darle el dinero porque sé que él lo perderá.   12. No me quitaré este suéter hasta el verano que viene.   13. Asistiremos a la universidad el otoño que viene.   14. No firmaré esta carta porque no es verdad.   15. Si yo compro este traje en lugar de ése [OR aquél], ahorraré cincuenta dólares.

15-3 *Answers will vary.* 1. Comeré arroz con pollo.   2. ¡Yo seré el próximo presidente!   3. Iré a México.   4. Sí, hablaré español mañana.   5. Estaré en mi oficina.   6. Me acostaré a las diez.   7. Llevaré mis vaqueros.   8. No miraré ningún programa esta semana.   9. España ganará la Copa Mundial el año que viene.   10. Sí, la colgaré antes de acostarme.   11. Mañana me levantaré a las siete.   12. Estudiaré español (por) dos horas.

15-4 Mañana es el primero de enero y por eso trataré de hacer todas las cosas que escribí en mi lista de resoluciones para el año que viene. El año pasado hice diez resoluciones, y por un rato las cumplí, pero una por una falté a mi palabra. Este año, sin embargo, adelgazaré—el año pasado engordé diez libras. Trabajaré más duro—perdí mucho tiempo el año pasado. Leeré más—leí sólo dos libros este año pasado. Iré al gimnasio más a menudo—pertenezco a un club, pero nunca voy. Gastaré menos dinero—iba de compras dos o tres veces cada semana. Andaré o montaré en bicicleta en vez de conducir [OR manejar]—ayer conduje [OR manejé] tres manzanas [OR cuadras] para comprar un periódico—¡qué ridículo! Me quejaré menos—no fui un angelito este año. Finalmente, estudiaré español más. Seré perfecto/perfecta—exactamente como el año pasado.

15-5 1. Me pondré el sombrero.   2. Él deshará este nudo.   3. ¿Te opondrás al presidente?   4. Os abstendréis de fumar por dos semanas.   5. ¿Quién compondrá la música?   6. Nos atendremos a ti.   7. ¿Contendrá este balde toda la pintura?   8. Él rehará su cama más tarde.   9. Supondré que sabes la respuesta.   10. La policía te detendrá si conduces [OR manejas] borracho.   11. Ella mantendrá buenas notas en la universidad.   12. ¿Dónde obtendrás bastante dinero para comprar los muebles nuevos?   13. ¿Convendrán en quedarse conmigo por un rato?   14. Estas vigas no sostendrán una casa.   15. Mañana me abstendré de comer.

15-6 1. haremos   2. pondrán   3. tendrá   4. cabrá   5. sabrá   6. querrá   7. podrán   8. diremos   9. vendréis   10. saldrán   11. valdrá   12. Habrá

15-7 1. Querré ver tus fotos.   2. ¿Dónde pondrás el sofá? Lo pondré en la sala.   3. María hará el vestido de novia.   4. ¿A qué hora vendrán?   5. No podrán ver el barco desde allí.   6. Habrá trescientas tiendas en el nuevo centro comercial.   7. Juan sabrá la respuesta.   8. ¿Cuánto valdrá el coche [OR carro] el año que viene?   9. No habrá ruido durante el programa.   10. ¿Habrá tiempo para hacer preguntas?   11. ¿Podrás llamarme más tarde?   12. Estos martillos nunca cabrán en esa caja.   13. Esta casa valdrá más de dos millones de dólares en cinco años.   14. No le diré tu secreto a nadie.   15. Ellos harán su cheque por quinientos dólares.

15-8 En un par de semanas, renunciaré a este trabajo y comenzaré una nueva vida. Vendí mi casa y compré una camioneta. Anoche puse comida, ropa, mi cámara y una almohada—todo lo que necesitaré—en la camioneta. ¡No puedo creerlo! Dentro de poco ese vehículo será mi hogar. Durante los últimos cinco años ahorré bastante dinero para vivir por diez años. No podré ir a restaurantes elegantes ni comprar trajes de Armani, pero podré viajar. Visitaré nuevos lugares y conoceré a nuevas personas. Siempre soñaba con hacer esto. No seré rico/rica, pero seré feliz. Por primera vez en mi vida, mi realidad y mis sueños serán iguales.

15-9 1. Juan llegará a las diez.   2. ¿Dónde pondrás el cortacésped?   3. Comeremos las pasas de la caja. 4. ¿Cuándo averiguarás si tienes el empleo?   5. Ellos no se acostarán hasta la medianoche.   6. Nunca sabré tocar el violín.   7. De vez en cuando, te visitaré en la cárcel.   8. ¿Cuánto valdrá este anillo en veinte años? 9. ¿Obedecerá usted las leyes de esta ciudad?   10. Nunca nevará en Panamá y nunca lloverá en el desierto. 11. Ellos nos dirán mentiras pero no creeremos nada.   12. ¿Tendrás que viajar mucho? ¿Podrás viajar mucho? 13. Mi coche no cabrá en el garaje. Tendré que dejarlo en la calle.   14. Enterraré el tesoro esta noche; de lo contrario, no estará aquí mañana.   15. El tesoro entero no cabrá en este baúl; tendré que meter los diamantes en mi bolsillo.

16 The conditional tense

16-1 1. Yo comería las galletitas pero estoy a dieta.   2. ¿Se casaría con Juan?   3. ¿Adónde irías?   4. Ellos no vivirían en esa casa porque está embrujada.   5. ¿Entregarían los periódicos a nuestra casa?   6. Si enseño esta clase, seríais mis alumnos.   7. No voy a darles el dinero porque lo perderían.   8. Cambiaríamos las palabras de la canción, pero sería demasiado difícil.   9. Me levantaría pero me duele la pierna.   10. Sé que te darían el dinero que necesitas.   11. ¿Comprarías un carro usado de este hombre?   12. ¿Quién pensaría tal cosa? 13. ¿Por qué no se afeitaría él con esa navaja?   14. ¿Por qué leería alguien esto?   15. Yo no tocaría el piano enfrente de una multitud.

16-2 1. pondría   2. podrías   3. tendría   4. valdría   5. haría   6. cabrían   7. vendríamos   8. Habría 9. dirías   10. diría

16-3 1. Yo vendría a tu fiesta, pero estoy enfermo/enferma.   2. ¿Dónde pondrías estas sillas?   3. Esta pulsera valdría más, pero está rota.   4. ¿Qué diríais a ese hombre?   5. Tendríamos la recepción en nuestra casa, pero no hay suficiente espacio.   6. ¿Crees que Roberto sabría la respuesta?   7. ¿Quién podría hacer tal cosa? 8. Yo querría el carro, pero no es mi elección.   9. Habría dos docenas de huevos en el refrigerador, pero comimos cuatro para el desayuno.   10. ¿Cabrían estos platos en la alacena?   11. ¿Qué harías durante un huracán?   12. Yo no le diría porque él no puede guardar un secreto.   13. Haríamos el cheque, pero no hay suficiente dinero en el banco.   14. No voy a dar estos zapatos a Marcos porque sé que él no podría llevarlos.   15. Yo pondría las flores enfrente de la casa, no atrás.

16-4 Cuando yo era joven, me encantaba leer los cuentos de hadas. Uno de mis personajes favoritos era Aladino porque siempre le concedía a la gente sus fantasías en la forma de tres deseos. ¿Qué haría yo? Primero le pediría un millón de deseos, pero sé que él no haría eso. Por eso, estos son mis tres deseos: 1. Mi gata podría hablar y ella y yo tendríamos conversaciones largas. 2. Nunca tendría que preocuparme por mi peso. Y el deseo más importante es éste: 3. Nadie en el mundo sufriría otro minuto: No habría guerra, no habría hambre, no habría pobreza, no habría tristeza.

17 The present perfect tense

17-1 1. He trabajado.   2. Tú has escuchado.   3. Ella ha bebido la leche.   4. Hemos comprendido.   5. Ellos han recibido un regalo.   6. Hemos vendido la casa.   7. ¿Has mirado la televisión hoy?   8. ¿Dónde han vivido?   9. Me he duchado.   10. Él ha estado conmigo.   11. Usted ha aprendido mucho.   12. ¿Te has cepillado los dientes?   13. Él me ha llamado seis veces.   14. He corrido tres millas.   15. Ella no se ha lavado el pelo.

17-2 1. He leído veinte páginas.   2. Ella ha abierto el libro.   3. ¿Dónde has puesto los platos?   4. El conejo ha muerto.   5. ¿Le has dicho la verdad?   6. ¿Qué has visto?   7. El cocinero ha frito todos los huevos. 8. ¿Qué has hecho hoy?   9. La tienda nos ha provisto de ropa.   10. Ella se ha roto otra uña.   11. ¿Ha resuelto él sus problemas?   12. No hemos dicho nada.   13. El político no nos ha dicho la verdad.   14. ¿Por qué no han vuelto?   15. ¿Qué has hecho para nosotros?

Free audio answer key available online

17-3 1. He tenido el dinero por más de veinte años.   2. Ella ha abierto la ventana y yo he cerrado la puerta. 3. El perro de mi vecino ha ladrado toda la noche, y no he podido dormir.   4. ¿Dónde has puesto tu maleta? 5. ¿Cuántas veces te has cepillado los dientes hoy?   6. ¿Por qué no te has afeitado hoy? ¿Porqué no te has duchado hoy?   7. ¿Por cuántos años has conocido a Carlos?   8. Has llegado tarde cada día [OR todos los días] esta semana.   9. ¿La han visto (ustedes)?   10. Los ladrones han robado nuestras joyas y han roto todas las ventanas.   11. ¿Han vuelto los recién casados de su luna de miel?   12. Tus modales me han atraído.   13. Ellos han demostrado su amor por la música de Beethoven.   14. Si ella es tan rica como me dices, entonces, ¿por qué ha robado el banco?   15. El teléfono ha sonado veinte veces. ¿Por qué no lo has contestado?

17-4 Estoy en el desván de mi abuela. ¡Qué desastre! Ella ha vivido en esta casa por más de ochenta años. Nació aquí, se casó aquí y enterró seis perros y cinco gatos en el patio trasero. ¡Tiene hasta un fregadero de cocina en el rincón! Ella ha guardado todo—desde libros y ropa hasta fotos, muebles y cortinas viejas. Ella me ha dicho muchas veces que yo puedo tener todos los muebles. Ella también le ha dicho a mi hermana que ella puede tener todos los muebles. He estado en este desván en ocasiones innumerables y yo sé que no he visto nada de este siglo. Lo que ella ha guardado no cabría en una tienda de departamentos.

18 The past perfect tense

18-1 1. Yo había pagado la cuenta.   2. Ella había vivido en Texas.   3. Ellos habían perdido todas las cartas. 4. No habíamos recibido una invitación.   5. ¿Habías llevado esos zapatos antes de la boda?   6. Yo había comido todos los dulces antes de descubrir el premio.   7. Habíamos practicado (por) cuatro horas antes del concierto.   8. ¿Por cuánto tiempo habías fumado antes de dejarlo?   9. Ella había vivido en St. Louis antes de mudarse a St. Paul.   10. Habíamos salido por tres años antes de casarnos.   11. Los soldados habían sufrido mucho antes del fin de la guerra.   12. Antes de la fiesta, yo había limpiado la casa de cabo a rabo. 13. Él no había hecho nada antes de la fiesta.   14. Yo nunca había disfrutado del teatro tanto como él. 15. Antes de acostaros, ¿habíais apagado las luces?

18-2 1. Yo no había abierto las ventanas hasta mayo de ese año.   2. Ellos no habían hecho nada.   3. Ella no había visto la película antes del sábado.   4. Todos los árboles habían muerto.   5. No habíamos resuelto los problemas antes de la reunión.   6. Los ladrones habían roto las sillas y las ventanas.   7. ¿Habían cubierto las mesas antes de la tormenta?   8. ¿Dónde habías puesto el dinero?   9. Yo había escrito cincuenta cartas antes de recibir una respuesta.   10. ¿Te habían provisto de bastante información?   11. La comida se había podrido en el refrigerador.   12. Habíamos frito suficientes papas para un ejército.   13. ¿Qué habías hecho para ayudarlos?   14. El perro no había descubierto los huesos debajo de la cama.   15. Los libros se habían caído del estante.

18-3 El príncipe Harry y Meghan Markle se casaron el diecinueve de mayo, 2018. Meghan había sido una actriz y Harry, era, pues, un príncipe. Meghan dio a luz a su hijo, Archie, el seis de mayo, 2019, y después dio a luz a su hija, Lilibet, el cuatro de junio, 2021. Lilibet había sido un apodo de la reina Isabel (Elizabeth) (la abuela de Harry). Aunque ellos eran felices juntos, a Harry y Meghan no les gustaba ser parte de la familia real, y se mudaron primero a Canadá, y después se mudaron a Montecito, California, donde ahora viven. El siete de marzo, 2021, tuvieron una entrevista televisada con Oprah Winfrey en que revelaron su miseria ser miembros activos de la familia real. La entrevista fue explosiva, pero fue apenas el principio. En diciembre, 2022, Harry y Meghan presentaron una serie de seis partes en Netflix, otra vez, compartiendo su miseria. ¡Pero espera! ¡Hay más! En enro, 2023, la memoria de Harry, "Spare," se publicó en que reveló aún más miseria y subterfugio dentro de la familia real. Inmediatamente, fue un éxito de ventas, pero tenía muchos críticos. Muchas personas creen que ellos dijeron demasiado, una y otra vez. Para febrero de 2023, la popularidad de Harry y Meghan había caído dramáticamente. Por años, Harry había sido "el real favorito." Ya no. ¿Qué piensas tú?

III THE IMPERATIVE, THE SUBJUNCTIVE, THE FUTURE AND CONDITIONAL PERFECT TENSES, AND THE PASSIVE VOICE

19 The imperative

19-1 1. ¡Estudia! 2. ¡Trabaja! 3. ¡Mira! 4. ¡Escucha! 5. ¡Lee! 6. ¡Corre! 7. ¡Anda! OR ¡Camina! 8. ¡Baila! 9. ¡Escribe! 10. ¡Decide! 11. ¡Vende! 12. ¡Paga! 13. ¡Sufre! 14. ¡Cuenta! 15. ¡Vuela! 16. ¡Comienza! OR ¡Empieza! 17. ¡Piensa! 18. ¡Duerme! 19. ¡Sigue! OR ¡Continúa! 20. ¡Confiesa!

19-2   1. ¡No mires!   2. ¡No cantes!   3. ¡No estudies!   4. ¡No corras!   5. ¡No pienses!   6. ¡No bebas el agua!
7. ¡No llegues tarde!   8. ¡No practiques ahora!   9. ¡No pagues la cuenta!   10. ¡No organices los papeles!
11. ¡No leas mi diario!   12. ¡No bailes en la mesa!   13. ¡No abras las ventanas!   14. ¡No admitas nada!
15. ¡No creas nada!

19-3   1. ¡Pon el libro aquí!   2. ¡Di la verdad!   3. ¡Haz la cama!   4. ¡Sal de la casa!   5. ¡Ven a la cocina!
6. ¡Sé amable!   7. ¡Ve a la sala!   8. ¡Ten el dinero para mañana!   9. ¡No pongas los zapatos en la mesa!
10. ¡No digas nada!   11. ¡No hagas las camas!   12. ¡No salgas ahora!   13. ¡No vengas mañana!   14. ¡No seas
egoísta!   15. ¡No vayas de compras hoy!   16. ¡No tengas animales en la casa!

19-4   1. ¡Cómpralo!   2. ¡Véndela!   3. ¡Siéntate!   4. ¡Acuéstate!   5. ¡Báñate!   6. ¡Dime un cuento!   7. ¡Ponlo aquí!
8. ¡Vete!   9. ¡Ponlas allí!   10. ¡Déjanos en paz!   11. ¡Dínoslo!   12. ¡Escríbemela!   13. ¡Cántasela!
14. ¡Cómpramelo!   15. ¡Háztelo!

19-5   1. ¡No lo leas!   2. ¡No la bebas!   3. ¡No lo beses!   4. ¡No me digas mentiras!   5. ¡No me mientas!
6. ¡No te vayas!   7. ¡No te levantes!   8. ¡No te duches!   9. ¡No te acuestes!   10. ¡No me odies!
11. ¡No se la des!   12. ¡No se lo digas!   13. ¡No nos lo vendas!   14. ¡No me lo leas!   15. ¡No se la cantes!

19-6   1. ¡Cante!   2. ¡Venda!   3. ¡Cuente!   4. ¡Pague!   5. ¡Corra!   6. ¡Hágalo!   7. ¡Toque el piano!   8. ¡Léalo!
9. ¡Tráigalo aquí!   10. ¡Levántese!   11. ¡Démelo!   12. ¡Dígamelo!   13. ¡No me diga una mentira!
14. ¡No nos espere!   15. ¡No robe el banco!   16. ¡Deme el dinero!   17. ¡Siéntese!   18. ¡Póngalo allí!
19. ¡No lo haga!   20. ¡Dígale un cuento!

19-7   1. ¡Váyase!   2. ¡Sépalo!   3. ¡Sea bueno!   4. ¡No se vaya!   5. ¡No sea mala!   6. ¡No vaya a la fiesta!
7. ¡Sepa todo para mañana!   8. ¡Vaya al frente de la sala!

19-8   1. ¡Trabajen!   2. ¡Piensen!   3. ¡No hagan eso!   4. ¡No salgan!   5. ¡Siéntense!   6. ¡Pónganlos aquí!
7. ¡No me digan nada!   8. ¡Toquen el piano!   9. ¡Jueguen al béisbol!   10. ¡Tráiganme la comida!
11. ¡Díganle el secreto!   12. ¡No se vayan enojadas!   13. ¡Acuéstense!   14. ¡Lávense las manos!
15. ¡Cepíllense los dientes!

19-9   1. ¡Volad!   2. ¡Volved!   3. ¡Venid!   4. ¡Paraos!   5. ¡Corred!   6. ¡Hervid el agua!   7. ¡Dormid!
8. ¡Leedlo!   9. ¡Id a la tienda!   10. ¡Ponedla en la casa!   11. ¡Hacednos un favor!   12. ¡Llegad a las diez!

19-10   1. ¡No comáis!   2. ¡No habléis!   3. ¡No juguéis aquí!   4. ¡No cantéis!   5. ¡No durmáis en el parque!
6. ¡No hirváis el agua!   7. ¡No os durmáis!   8. ¡No salgáis!   9. ¡No toméis el dinero!   10. ¡No me sigáis!
11. ¡No os acostéis!   12. ¡No os vayáis!

19-11   1. ¡Estudiemos!   2. ¡Caminemos!   3. ¡No estudiemos!   4. ¡No comamos!   5. ¡Vendamos el coche!
6. ¡Hagamos algo!   7. ¡No hagamos nada!   8. ¡Almorcemos!   9. ¡Pongamos el perro afuera!
10. ¡Cantémosles!   11. ¡No mintamos!   12. ¡No comencemos ahora!   13. ¡Digamos la verdad!
14. ¡No digamos nada!   15. ¡Comprémoslo!

19-12   1. ¡Sepamos todo!   2. ¡Seamos amables!   3. ¡No vayamos a la fiesta!   4. ¡Vámonos esta noche!
5. ¡No seamos cobardes!   6. ¡Vamos al cine mañana!   7. ¡Seamos personas honradas!   8. ¡No nos vayamos
esta tarde!

20   The present subjunctive

20-1   1. Espero que ella hable conmigo mañana.   2. Quiero que comas el pan.   3. Él quiere que yo escriba una
carta.   4. Rogamos que estés bien.   5. Ellos quieren que lo hagamos.   6. Ella espera que puedas venir
a la fiesta.   7. Ellas sugieren que tú lo hagas.   8. Insisto en que trabajéis.   9. Él pide que estemos aquí
a las nueve.   10. ¿Por qué pides que yo lo haga?   11. Prefiero que no salgamos de casa hasta las cinco.
12. Ella espera que la conozcas.   13. Insistimos en que comas con nosotros.   14. ¿Quieres que yo cuente
el dinero?   15. Ellos sugieren que pongamos los papeles en el gabinete.

20-2   Mañana es el primer día de mi nuevo trabajo. Espero que todo me vaya bien. Mi jefa parece muy amable,
pero prefiero que ella sea más justa que amable. Quiero que entienda que si yo cometo un error (y estoy segura
que cometeré muchos), quiero que ella me lo diga directamente. Antes de que termine la primera semana,
voy a pedirle que me diga lo que piensa de mi desempeño. Si ella sugiere que yo cambie algún aspecto de
mi trabajo, será más fácil hacerlo entonces que después de trabajar allí por unos cuantos meses.

20-3   1. Dudo que ella coma en ese restaurante.   2. No supongo que me digas el nombre del asesino.   3. Ellos no creen que él toque el piano.   4. Ella no está segura de que el café esté listo.   5. No pensamos que los Vikings ganen el partido.   6. Él no está convencido de que yo necesite tanto dinero.   7. ¿Por qué no crees que lo conozcamos?   8. No estamos convencidos de que la luna sea de queso verde.   9. Él duda que ellos sepan la respuesta.   10. Ella no está segura de que siempre digamos la verdad.   11. ¿Por qué no estás convencido/convencida de que yo siempre tenga razón?   12. No parece que él quiera estar aquí.   13. No estoy seguro/segura de que puedas entender esto.   14. Él no cree que yo sea su vecino/vecina.   15. No me imagino que creas mi historia.

20-4   Dudo que Juan sepa que planeamos una fiesta para él. No parece posible que él sea el nuevo presidente de esta compañía y no me imagino que él lo crea tampoco. Dudo que le guste esta nueva posición. No estoy convencido/convencida de que él esté listo para tan gran responsabilidad; en cambio, no supongo que nadie pueda hacerse un gran líder de la noche a la mañana. Quiero que todo le salga bien.

20-5   1. Estoy feliz que seas tan alto/alta.   2. Él está triste que ella sea una persona deshonesta.   3. Estamos encantados que puedas venir a nuestra fiesta.   4. Ellos están enojados que su equipo no gane el torneo.   5. Estás indignado que nuestro equipo pierda cada juego.   6. Estoy frustrado/frustrada que ella siempre esté tarde.   7. Ella está ansiosa que pierdas el dinero.   8. Estoy preocupado/preocupada que ellos me digan más mentiras.   9. Ella está preocupada que yo revele la verdad acerca de ella.   10. Él está triste que ella esté con otro hombre.

20-6   1. Es mejor que comamos en la cocina.   2. Es necesario que les llames mañana.   3. Es preferible que compres los huevos por docenas.   4. Es improbable que estén listos para las cinco.   5. Conviene que tenga un abogado con usted.   6. Es importante que nadie sepa ese secreto.   7. Puede ser que Alicia ya no trabaje aquí.   8. Es ridículo que tantos políticos no digan la verdad.   9. Es imposible que yo esté en dos lugares al mismo tiempo.   10. Es increíble que él hable doce idiomas.   11. Es una lástima que el helado tenga tantas calorías.   12. Ojalá que Juana no cante en la boda.   13. Es fantástico que no tengamos que sentarnos al lado de ellos.   14. Puede ser que Esteban no sea lo que dice que es.   15. Es imposible que me quede en este cuarto por un minuto más.

20-7   Anoche leí por primera vez las reglas y los reglamentos de la compañía donde he trabajado por seis años. Es posible que sea la única persona que ha leído este folleto. Hay tantas reglas absurdas. Por ejemplo, es ridículo que debamos mantener ordenados nuestros escritorios todo el tiempo. Es mejor que una persona tenga la libertad de ser cochino si eso es lo que necesita para trabajar bien. También, es increíble que tengamos que asistir a todas las reuniones, incluso las que no tienen nada que ver con nuestro propio trabajo (nadie asiste a estas reuniones). Es mejor que trabajemos en un escritorio desordenado que asistir a una reunión en una sala de juntas ordenada y voltear los pulgares. ¡Ojalá que nadie imponga estas reglas!

20-8   1. No comeré hasta que tenga hambre.   2. Te escribiré una nota para que recuerdes comprar leche.   3. Te sentirás mejor después (de) que tomes esta medicina.   4. Él no se casará con una mujer a menos que sea inteligente.   5. No podéis cazar a menos que tengáis una licencia.   6. Secaré los platos mientras que los laves.   7. El sacerdote no puede bautizar al bebé antes (de) que lleguen los padrinos.   8. El juego no se acaba hasta que se acabe.   9. Lo creeré cuando lo vea.   10. Él va a leer este libro otra vez en caso de que tengamos una prueba.   11. Él no comerá nada a menos que tenga una servilleta en el regazo.   12. Cada semana ahorro cincuenta dólares para que tenga suficiente dinero para mis vacaciones.   13. Ella nunca estará feliz hasta que sepa conjugar los verbos.   14. Debes cepillarte los dientes antes (de) que salgamos para la consulta del dentista.   15. No podré llevar estos pantalones hasta que pierda diez libras.

20-9   Mi amiga necesitaba un coche, pero no tenía suficiente dinero. Le dije que le prestaría cinco mil dólares, y ella me dijo que me los devolvería dentro del plazo de tres meses. Le di el dinero, ella compró el coche, pero no me devolvió nada. Después de tres meses, le pedí mi dinero y ella me dijo, "Te pagaré cuando consiga un puesto." Pero ella tenía un puesto. Entonces me dijo, "Te pagaré cuando obtenga mi reembolso de impuestos." Ella recibió su reembolso de impuestos. Pero todavía no me pagó nada. Quise mi dinero. Estuve como un perro con un hueso. Entonces ella me dijo, "Te pagaré cuando reciba mi herencia." ¿Pero, nadie murió. Le llevé a los tribunales. Ella le dijo al juez que fue un regalo. El juez no le creyó y le pregunté, "Estás esperando hasta que vuelen los cerdos?" Finalmente, recibí mi dinero, pero he perdido a una amiga.

20-10   1. Buscamos una casa que tenga tres dormitorios.   2. Ella quiere un perro que no ladre.   3. ¿Hay alguien aquí que pueda tocar la guitarra?   4. Necesito una criada que limpie las ventanas.   5. ¿Hay alguien en el mundo que sepa expresarse claramente?   6. Busco un gato que no arañe los muebles.   7. ¿Dónde puedo comprar una camisa que no sea de poliéster?   8. No hay nadie aquí que pueda ayudarte.   9. Para su cumpleaños este año él quiere un loro que hable tres idiomas.   10. Quiero vivir en una ciudad donde no haya crimen.

20-11   Fui de compras con Giralda esta mañana. Nunca más me meteré en esa tortura. ¡Giralda es imposible! Primero, ella quiere un aparcamiento que no esté a más de diez pies de la puerta principal del centro comercial. En esto tardó media hora. Entonces, quiere un vestido que tenga mangas de quita y pon para que pueda llevarlo todo el año. También quiere un collar que parezca algo que llevaría una reina, pero también quiere que este collar cueste menos de diez dólares. Quiere zapatos que tengan joyas en los tacones y quiere guantes que tengan perlitas en las muñecas. En cada tienda le decía a la dependienta exactamente lo que quería y cada dependienta le decía a Giralda que no hay ninguna tienda en ese centro comercial, ni en ningún centro comercial en este planeta, que venda tales artículos. Giralda estaba furiosa y me dijo que no hay nadie en este mundo que entienda su gusto fabuloso.

20-12   1. Quizá [OR Tal vez OR Acaso] él tenga el dinero.   2. Quizá [OR Tal vez OR Acaso] podamos ir.   3. Quizá [OR Tal vez OR Acaso] ellos vivan aquí.   4. Quizá [OR Tal vez OR Acaso] lo conozcas.   5. Quizá [OR Tal vez OR Acaso] ellos compren la casa hoy.   6. Quizá [OR Tal vez OR Acaso] estemos perdidos.   7. Quizá [OR Tal vez OR Acaso] él no sea la persona más inteligente del mundo.   8. Quizá [OR Tal vez OR Acaso] no debáis beber esta leche.   9. Quizá [OR Tal vez OR Acaso] el político no diga la verdad.   10. Quizá [OR Tal vez OR Acaso] el gato tenga sólo ocho vidas.

20-13   A ver. No tengo que trabajar hoy. ¿Qué debo hacer? Tal vez (yo) lea un libro. Tal vez (yo) compre un libro. ¡Tal vez (yo) escriba un libro! Tal vez (yo) vaya al cine. Tal vez (yo) estudie español. Tal vez (yo) remonte una cometa. Tal vez (yo) vuele a la luna. Tal vez (yo) corte el césped. Tal vez (yo) coma un huevo. Tal vez (yo) dé un paseo. Tal vez (yo) saque la basura. Tal vez (yo) no haga nada. ¡Ajá! ¡No haré nada!

20-14   1. Aunque Juana cocine, no me quedaré.   2. Aunque quieran mirar la televisión, no los dejaremos.   3. Aunque me grites, no cambiaré mi idea.   4. Aunque él piense que es un genio, todo el mundo sabe que no lo es.   5. Aunque le ofrezcas mil dólares al policía, todavía te dará una multa.   6. Aunque ignoremos los candidatos, todavía tenemos el derecho de votar.   7. Aunque pongas el gato en el sótano, Bárbara todavía estornudará.   8. Aunque os sintáis enfermos, todavía tenéis que tomar el examen.   9. Aunque des cuerda al reloj cincuenta veces, nunca funcionará.   10. Aunque él sonría todo el tiempo, en su interior es malo.   11. Aunque (yo) sepa la respuesta, no te la diré.   12. Aunque piensen que estoy loco/loca, sé que tengo razón.

20-15   ¡Ay! Alguien llama a la puerta. Estoy mirándolo por la ventana. No se parece a nadie que (yo) conozca. Es posible que sea un político, pero es más probable que sea un vendedor. O tal vez sea el cartero. No— él siempre lleva paquetes. Aunque sea el cartero, no abriré la puerta. Tal vez sea el florista con un ramo de flores para mí. No—los floristas siempre tienen flores. No sé quien pueda ser esta persona. Tal vez sea un representante de Publishers Clearing House porque he ganado diez millones de dólares. No—él tendría ese cheque gigante consigo. No voy a abrir la puerta. Ojalá que el intruso se vaya.

20-16   No hay nadie que pueda cocinar tan bien como mi amiga Catarina. Es fantástico que ella tenga una fiesta este fin de semana porque no he comido una buena comida en mucho tiempo (es decir, desde la última vez que cené en su casa). Espero que ella haga su famosa tarta de manzana otra vez, pero dudo que ella la haga este fin de semana porque la sirvió hace menos de un año y rara vez se repite. Aunque prepare esta delicia, no será lo mismo porque siempre mejora un poquito cada receta cada vez que la usa. Temo que nunca más pruebe esa misma tarta. Quizá le ruegue para que ella me prepare la tarta para mi cumpleaños. Sé que cuando pruebe esa tarta otra vez o estaré en el cielo o en el comedor de Catarina.

21   The imperfect subjunctive

21-1   1. Yo quería que Juan comprara las toallas.   2. Fue una lástima que tuvieras que trabajar el domingo pasado.   3. No había nadie en la clase que hablara francés.   4. Dudábamos que Humpty Dumpty se cayera del muro.   5. Nadie creía que María tuviera un corderito.   6. El señor Clean pidió que nos quitáramos los zapatos antes de entrar en su palacio.   7. ¿Fue necesario que me llamarais en medio de la noche?   8. No estaban seguros de que yo pudiera cuidarme.   9. Ella preparó la cena para que no nos muriéramos de hambre.   10. Limpiamos la casa antes de que llegaran.   11. Ella estudió en caso de que hubiera un examen el día siguiente.   12. Él me rogó que (yo) no pidiera la la langosta porque es tan costosa.   13. No pensamos [OR creímos] que nadie nos oyera.   14. ¿Había alguien allí que supiera todas las capitales de los estados?   15. Pedimos que continuaran sin nosotros.

21-2 1. Ellas no creen que yo hiciera estas galletas.   2. Es improbable que Francis Bacon escribiera estos dramas. 3. No estamos convencidos de que la señorita Muffet tuviera miedo a la araña.   4. Siento que estuvieras enfermo/enferma y que no pudieras venir a nuestra fiesta.   5. No supongo que supieras que ella era la ladrona. 6. No parece que la sirvienta limpiara la casa esta mañana.   7. Ojalá que pagaras las cuentas a tiempo este mes. 8. Puede ser que nadie oyera tu discurso.   9. Él se porta como si tuviera tres años.   10. No creo que él estudiara anoche.   11. Él espera que te lavaras las manos antes de comer.   12. Puede ser que ella no quisiera sacar nuestra foto.   13. Es un milagro que la aerolínea no perdiera tu equipaje.   14. ¿Es posible que dejaras tus llaves en el carro?   15. Es increíble que nacieras el mismo día que yo.

21-3 1. Si yo tuviera un martillo, martillaría en la mañana.   2. Ella no se casaría con él si fuera el último hombre en la Tierra.   3. ¿Qué harías si yo cantara desafinadamente?   4. ¿Si supieras la respuesta, nos la dirías? 5. Si las jirafas no tuvieran los cuellos largos, no podrían comer las hojas.   6. Si no fuera por la gravedad, flotaríamos como burbujas.   7. Los osos no comerían tu comida si la colgaras de un árbol.   8. Si Pinocho no mintiera tanto, la gente lo creería de vez en cuando.   9. Si no hubiera carros, no habría tanta contaminación. 10. Si él no fuera tan perezoso, yo lo contrataría.   11. Si no lloviera, podríamos dar un paseo por el parque. 12. Si no hiciera tanto frío, iría en bicicleta al trabajo.   13. Este anillo valdría mucho más dinero si el diamante fuera genuino.   14. Si mi coche [OR carro] arrancara en este tiempo, sería un milagro.   15. Si los cerdos pudieran volar, ¿adónde irían?

21-4 1. Él habla como si fuera el mismo rey.   2. En tu situación, yo actuaría como si no supiera nada. 3. Ella habla como si fuera la dueña de esta empresa.   4. Bailamos como si fuéramos Fred Astaire y Ginger Rogers.   5. Él gasta dinero como si no hubiera mañana.   6. Te ves como si vieras un fantasma. 7. Él se ve como si perdiera a su mejor amigo.   8. El crítico se ve como si le gustara el drama.   9. Cantas como si tragaras un pájaro [OR un ave].   10. Fue como si no pudiera recordar nada.   11. Él se sintió como si ya la conociera.   12. Ella vivía cada día como si fuera el último.   13. Él me habló como si yo no tuviera cerebro. 14. Ella se veía como si perdiera mucho peso.   15. Fumabas como si fueras una chimenea.

21-5 1. Yo quisiera una limonada fría, por favor.   2. ¿Qué quisieras hacer esta noche?   3. ¿Si pudieras, echarías al correo estas cartas para mí?   4. ¿Si pudieras, me harías un favor?   5. Quisiéramos una habitación con una vista al río.   6. ¿Si pudieras, te moverías un poco a la derecha?   7. ¿Adónde quisieras ir para tu luna de miel?   8. ¿Dónde quisierais cenar mañana por la noche?   9. La reina quisiera hablar.   10. ¿Si pudieras, te callarías, por favor?   11. ¿Qué quisieran hacer esta tarde?   12. Quisiéramos patinar sobre ruedas en el centro comercial.   13. ¿Si pudiera, me prepararía una taza de café?   14. ¿Si pudiera, me llevaría ante su líder? 15. ¿Quisieras comer estos grillos cubiertos de chocolate?

21-6 1. (Yo) quisiera que no estuvieras tan nervioso/nerviosa.   2. Quisiéramos que estuvieras aquí.   3. (Yo) quisiera que hubiera una máquina que pudiera lavar y secar la ropa al mismo tiempo.   4. (Yo) quisiera que no tuvieras que oír esto.   5. Juana quisiera que su esposo no mirara tanta televisión.   6. Los niños siempre quisieran ser mayores y los adultos quisieran ser menores.   7. (Yo) quisiera hablar español con soltura.   8. Él quisiera poder manejar.   9. Él quisiera poder ver a través de las paredes.   10. (Yo) quisiera que no estuviéramos detrás de los caballos en el desfile.   11. (Yo) quisiera ganar más dinero.   12. (Yo) quisiera que nevara.   13. Quisiéramos que se fueran a casa.   14. (Yo) quisiera que no hubiera calorías en el helado.   15. Donald quisiera no tener que pagar impuestos.

21-7 En *El Mago de Oz*, todo el mundo quisiera que su vida fuera diferente. El Espantapájaros quisiera tener un cerebro. El Hombre de Estaño quisiera tener un corazón. El León quisiera ser valiente. Toto quisiera que los monos volantes desaparecieran. El árbol quisiera que la gente no comiera sus manzanas. El Mago quisiera ser mago y la Bruja Malvada quisiera dos cosas: tener los zapatos de Dorotea y poder tolerar mejor el agua. Sobre todo, Dorotea quisiera estar en Kansas.

22 The future perfect tense

22-1 1. En dos semanas, habré vivido aquí (por) cuatro años.   2. Para el año que viene, McDonald's habrá vendido otro mil millones de hamburguesas.   3. Ella no habrá preparado la cena para las cinco y media.   4. ¿Cuándo habrán terminado el trabajo?   5. Nos habremos conocido por doce años este agosto.   6. ¿Habréis planchado vuestros vestidos para esta tarde?   7. ¿Habrás lavado toda esta ropa para esta noche?   8. Él no habrá abierto la farmacia para entonces.   9. Tenemos que ir ahora; si vamos más tarde, ellos ya se habrán ido.   10. Si das toda la comida al perro, la habrá comido toda para mañana.   11. No necesitas preocuparte: Estoy seguro/ segura de que para este momento se lo habrán dicho todo.   12. Supongo que todos se habrán acostado para la medianoche.   13. A este ritmo, habrás frito más patatas [OR papas] que McDonald's para el fin de la semana. 14. Si pierdes esta elección, habrás perdido más elecciones que nadie.   15. Si ganas esta elección, habrás probado que es posible engañar a toda la gente todo el tiempo.

22-2   1. Fernando me habrá enviado estas flores.   2. Él habrá pagado nuestra cuenta. ¡Qué amable!   3. Fido habrá robado estas zapatillas.   4. ¿Adónde se habrá ido mi perrito?   5. Abdul se ve bien enfadado [OR enojado]; Farrah le habrá dicho todo.   6. ¡La cocina huele muy mal! Dorotea habrá preparado la cena otra vez.
7. ¡Eso es una mentira! Lo habrás oído de Roque.   8. ¿Cómo sabe él estas cosas? Él habrá leído mi diario.
9. ¿Cuándo habrá ocurrido esto?   10. Arturo habrá sabido que María quemó todas sus cartas de amor.
11. Habrás sabido que él estaba casado.   12. Habré estado loco/loca para comprar vitaminas por teléfono.
13. Los osos habrán comido nuestra comida.   14. Habrá sido terrible descubrir que las cucarachas eran los dueños verdaderos de tu casa.   15. Ella te habrá dado un falso número de teléfono.

22-3   ¡No puedo creerlo! Para finales de mes habré pagado esta casa completamente. Nunca pensé que esto ocurriría. Creía que o me mudaría o me moriría antes de hacer ese último cheque miserable. Cuando haga ese último cheque, tomando en consideración todo el interés que he pagado, habré comprado esta casa casi tres veces. De ahora en un año, supongo que habré olvidado que el banco tuvo más de esta casa que yo por muchos años y el banco habrá olvidado que yo existí alguna vez. Habré estado loco/loca para creer que una hipoteca de cuarenta años me haría sentir como si fuera un adulto/adulta maduro/madura. Sólo me hizo sentir pobre. En dos años, habré ahorrado miles de dólares y tomado por lo menos dos largas vacaciones. Quisiera estar en Tahití ahora mismo.

23   The conditional perfect tense

23-1   1. Te habría llamado, pero mi teléfono celular no funcionaba.   2. Él habría ido al teatro con nosotros, pero le dolía la cabeza.   3. Sherlock Holmes habría sabido quién robó los diamantes pero no lo contrató.
4. Habríamos invitado a los Jones, pero la última vez que vinieron a nuestra casa, se enfermaron.   5. (Yo) Me habría puesto a dieta, pero no tengo mucha fuerza de voluntad.   6. Yo habría preparado la cena, pero estaba de mal humor.   7. Él habría cambiado la bombilla, pero no había nadie para girar la escalera.   8. Él habría entregado la tarea, pero el perro lo comió.   9. Habríamos comido la comida, pero estaba mohosa.   10. Ellos no habrían hecho nada en esta situación porque son personas débiles y flojas.

23-2   1. ¿Me habrías dicho la respuesta si la supieras?   2. Te habríamos dado un pedazo de torta más grande si no estuvieras a dieta.   3. Él me habría contratado si (yo) hablara español.   4. ¿Habríais ido a la playa si no lloviera?   5. ¿Qué habrías hecho si no tuvieras tu tarjeta de débito?   6. Yo habría comprado el vestido si fuera tamaño más pequeño.   7. Si ella no fuera tan egoísta, te habría ayudado.   8. ¿Me habrías llamado si te diera mi verdadero número de teléfono?   9. Ella no se habría casado con él si él fuera el último hombre en la tierra.   10. Si yo pensara por un momento que me gustaría el libro, lo habría leído.

23-3   1. (Yo) habría llevado el anillo solamente dos o tres veces antes del robo.   2. ¿Dónde habría escondido ella el dinero?   3. Habría sido la una de la mañana cuando sonó el teléfono.   4. Habría sido julio o agosto cuando te conocí porque hacía mucho calor.   5. Nunca habrían conocido a nadie como tú.   6. Habría sido noviembre cuando compré esto porque recuerdo que había pavos en todas partes.   7. ¿Nos habrían mentido?   8. Habría sido un martes cuando nos conocimos porque ese día todo el mundo estaba votando.   9. Habría sido febrero cuando recibí esta carta porque había una tarjeta para el Día de los Enamorados dentro del sobre.
10. No habrían estudiado mucho.   11. Habrían sido las cuatro de la mañana cuando Barbarita regresó de su cita con Ken.   12. Habría sido el cuatro de julio porque yo tenía puesta una camiseta roja, blanca y azul.
13. Habría sido un día de fiesta porque la oficina de correos estaba cerrada.   14. ¿Quién habría dejado esos zapatos en la carretera?   15. ¿Por qué habría puesto Pedro a su esposa dentro de una calabaza?

23-4   Ayer, mientras caminaba [OR estaba caminando] por el parque, encontré una caja llena de dinero. Al principio estuve feliz, porque, pues, ¿quién no estaría feliz en esta situación? Pero después de un rato empecé [OR comencé] a preocuparme, y decidí llevar la caja a la estación de policía. Anoche les pregunté a algunos de mis amigos lo que habrían hecho ellos. John me dijo que habría comprado un coche [OR carro]—había por lo menos diez mil dólares en la caja. Ana me dijo que ella habría donado el dinero a la caridad. Roberto me dijo que él habría dejado sola la caja y habría salido del parque inmediatamente. ¿Qué habrías hecho tú?

24   The present perfect subjunctive

24-1   1. Espero que el gato no haya comido mi carpa dorada.   2. Es improbable que nadie aquí haya conducido [OR manejado] un Rolls Royce.   3. No creo que esas personas en Kalamazoo hayan visto a Elvis Presley.
4. No has vivido hasta que hayas visto el Gran Cañón.   5. ¿Conoces a alguien que haya leído todos los dramas de Shakespeare?   6. El jurado duda que el acusado haya dicho la verdad.   7. Es increíble que nadie haya encontrado el dinero que enterramos [OR habíamos enterrado] en el jardín de casa.   8. Podéis bailar después

de que la banda haya comenzado a tocar.   9. Es un milagro que el banco le haya prestado dinero.   10. Puede ser que ellos nunca hayan aprendido a leer.   11. Es ridículo que yo haya tenido que esperar en esta cola por más de una hora.   12. No podemos ir hasta que todos hayan votado.   13. Esperamos que usted haya gozado de su estancia aquí.   14. ¿Hay alguien en el mundo que no haya leído *The Cat in the Hat*?   15. Busco un estudiante que nunca haya suspendido [OR reprobado] un examen.

24-2   1. No contrataré a nadie que haya conseguido su diploma del Internet.   2. ¿Qué harás después que hayas vencido todos tus temores?   3. Después de que hayamos contado nuestro dinero, lo depositaremos en el banco.   4. El programa comenzará cuando hayan llegado.   5. Él no te dirá nada hasta que le hayas pagado.   6. Tan pronto como hayas puesto la mesa, cenaremos.   7. Traeré una ensalada a la fiesta en caso de que el anfitrión no haya preparado bastante comida.   8. Él no se acostará hasta que se haya cepillado los dientes.   9. Nunca conocerás la verdadera felicidad hasta que hayas aparecido en el *Programa de Oprah Winfrey*.   10. Él nunca podrá correr una milla en cuatro minutos hasta que haya dejado de fumar. 11. ¿Qué haremos después de que hayamos gastado todo nuestro dinero?   12. No beberé leche que haya estado en el mostrador todo el día.   13. No tomaremos ninguna decisión financiera hasta que hayamos pagado los impuestos de este año.   14. El Capitán Kirk irá adónde ningún hombre haya ido antes. 15. Tan pronto como él haya tomado esta medicina, se sentirá mejor.

24-3   "Es formidable que finalmente hayas comenzado a cuidarte mucho, ¿pero qué harás dentro de un año cuando todavía no hayas sido coronada Señorita Universo?" Esto es lo que quiero decir a mi *amiga-enemiga*, Courtney, cuyas delirios son todavía más grandes que su ego.   En la mente confusa de Courtney, ella espera que para el próximo mes, ella haya perdido cincuenta libras, se haya convertido en estrella de cine, y haya ganado un Premio Nobel (ella ganará un Premio Nobel cuando se otorgue uno a la estupidez.)   Ojalá que dentro de un año yo haya terminado esta relación tóxica y haya conocido a alguien digna de mi perfección absoluta.

25   The pluperfect subjunctive

25-1   1. (Yo) no estaba seguro/segura de que ellos me hubieran oído.   2. Juan esperaba que los estudiantes hubieran estudiado la lección.   3. Fue una lástima que el fontanero no hubiera arreglado el desagüe.   4. Les escribimos una carta en caso de que no nos hubieran entendido.   5. ¿Fue posible que ellos nunca hubieran oído de Leo Tolstoy?   6. Actuaban como si nunca se hubieran conocido antes.   7. Él no creyó que yo hubiera dicho tal cosa.   8. Fue improbable que ella hubiera pagado el coche [OR carro] al contado.   9. No había nadie en la fiesta que hubiera viajado alrededor del mundo.   10. (Yo) no creía nunca que ella hubiera sido Miss América. 11. Él se negó a hablar hasta que hubiéramos cerrado las puertas.   12. Le envié un texto en caso de que él todavía no hubiera oído las buenas noticias.   13. Fue trágico que el jardinero—no el mayordomo—lo hubiera hecho. 14. Ella siempre dudaba que él hubiera sido honrado con ella.   15. No había nadie en la casa que se hubiera levantado antes de las diez y media.

25-2   1. Si (yo) hubiera leído este libro antes, no habría hecho [OR cometido] tantos errores en mi vida. 2. Si Bárbara hubiera sabido la verdad acerca de Ken, ¿se habría casado con él?   3. Si nos hubieras advertido de los terremotos, no habríamos construido nuestra casa en este área.   4. Habría sido bueno si hubieras incluido una foto con este artículo.   5. Si me hubieras llamado diez minutos antes, (yo) no habría estado en casa.   6. No sé dónde estaría si no te hubiera conocido.   7. Si hubiera habido una onza de verdad en tu discurso, alguien te habría creído.   8. Si hubieras nacido dos días antes, habríamos tenido el mismo cumpleaños.   9. Si no hubiera habido una nevada ayer, habría habido una hoy.   10. Si hubiéramos sabido que tenías dificultades, te habríamos ofrecido ayuda.   11. Si no me hubieras dado estas manoplas, creo que me habría muerto de frío.   12. Si no hubieras puesto otro sello en esa carta, la oficina de correos no la habría aceptado.   13. Si alguien me hubiera dicho eso, no lo habría creído.   14. Si no hubieras dado a tu carpa dorada tanta comida, no se habría muerto.   15. ¿Cómo se habrían sentido si no hubieras recibido una invitación?

25-3   1. Yo quisiera que él hubiera estudiado más en la escuela secundaria.   2. ¿Quisieras que él hubiera cumplido su palabra?   3. Él quisiera que no hubiera comido tanto.   4. Quisiéramos que nos hubieras dicho que esto sería una fiesta formal.   5. Yo quisiera que no hubiéramos almorzado aquí.   6. Él quisiera que hubiera ahorrado más dinero.   7. Yo quisiera que me hubiera probado estos pantalones antes de comprarlos. 8. Yo quisiera que no hubieras frito estas salchichas en manteca.   9. ¿Quisierais que hubiera habido más variedad en el programa?   10. Yo quisiera que no hubiera llovido en mi desfile.   11. ¿A veces quisieras que hubieras nacido en otro siglo?   12. Yo quisiera que hubiera apagado las luces hace tres horas.   13. Yo quisiera que no hubiera hecho tanto frío.   14. Quisiéramos que nos hubieran dicho algo acerca de las cucarachas en este hotel.   15. Yo quisiera que no hubieras puesto tanta canela en este té.

25-4 Si yo hubiera tenido más cuidado, no estaría en esta oficina disputando esta multa de aparcamiento. Yo pensé que era extraño que hubiera un aparcamiento directamente enfrente del teatro cinco minutos antes de que comenzara el drama pero, ¿quién soy yo para cuestionar tan buena suerte? De hecho, había un letrero que decía "Prohibido Estacionar" a dos pies de mi coche, pero un hombre muy alto estaba de pie enfrente, bloqueando la vista. No, nadie creería eso. Había una mujer vendiendo globos y no pude ver el letrero por los globos, así que si alguien va a tener que pagar esta multa, ella debe pagarla—nadie creerá eso tampoco. La verdad es que me doy cuenta de que si yo le hubiera dicho a alguien alguna de estas historias absurdas, tendría que pagar más de lo que probablemente debo ahora. ¿Dónde está la oficina del cajero?

26 The passive voice

26-1 1. V   2. F   3. V   4. V   5. F   6. V   7. V   8. F   9. V   10. F

26-2 1. vende   2. venden   3. juega   4. juegan   5. mira   6. cultiva   7. cultivan   8. construyen   9. debe   10. puede

26-3 1. Se habla francés.   2. Se habla japonés.   3. Se habla alemán.   4. Se habla portugués.   5. Se hablan suizo, italiano, alemán y francés.   6. Se habla ruso.   7. Se hablan inglés y francés.   8. Se habla inglés.

26-4 1. No se puede comprar un buen puro hoy en día por menos de cinco dólares.   2. Se toma vino blanco con el pollo y el pescado.   3. Se dice que el café colombiano [OR el café de Colombia] es el mejor.   4. Se necesita tener cuidado cuando se maneja en una tormenta de nieve.   5. ¿Cómo se dice "perro" en francés?   6. Se habla portugués en Brasil. [OR En Brasil se habla portugués.]   7. ¿Dónde se escribe que el presidente tiene que ser un hombre?   8. Si se maneja como un loco, te darán una multa.   9. Se dice que el cerdo es más inteligente que el caballo.   10. Siempre se pierde mucho tiempo en estas reuniones.   11. Si se mantiene correctamente, un carro durará veinte años.   12. Nunca se llevan zapatos blancos después del primero de septiembre.   13. Si se hace más ejercicio y se come menos, se adelgazará.   14. ¿Adónde se va en esta ciudad para una buena hamburguesa?   15. Si se puede poner un hombre en la luna, ¿por qué no se puede fabricar un carro que dure más de cinco años?

26-5 1. ¿Cuándo se sacaron estas fotos?   2. ¿Dónde se hizo tu sofá?   3. Se vendía el pan por cinco centavos la barra.   4. Se pintó la casa el año pasado.   5. Había tanto ruido en el restaurante que no se podía pensar.   6. Quería que se entregaran las flores para las cuatro y media.   7. No se podía oír nada; todos hablaban al mismo tiempo.   8. La fiesta fue un desastre. No se había arreglado la sala.   9. Se podía fumar en todas partes; ahora, parece que no se puede fumar en ninguna parte.   10. Se publicará el libro el año que viene.   11. Se descubrió el elemento por casualidad.   12. No se había pintado la casa durante cincuenta años.   13. Se cerrarán las puertas a las once y media.   14. Si se haya visto un castillo, se han visto todos.   15. No se ha vivido hasta que se haya oído a Van Morrison cantar "Gloria."

26-6 1. V   2. F   3. V   4. V   5. F   6. V   7. F   8. V   9. V   10. F   11. F   12. F

26-7 1. El drama *Romeo y Julieta* fue escrito por William Shakespeare.   2. Muchas casas nuevas fueron construidas después de la Segunda Guerra Mundial.   3. Los folletos serán repartidos por voluntarios mañana.   4. Estas galletitas fueron hechas por duendes.   5. El niño consentido fue dado demasiados juguetes por sus padres.   6. Los neumáticos fueron acuchillados por vándalos.   7. La televisión será puesta cuando Juan entre en esta casa.   8. Esta colcha fue cosida completamente a mano.   9. Las puertas serán abiertas y cerradas por guardias armados.   10. La hierba fue sembrada por Martín.   11. Estas cuentas habrían sido pagadas por Juan, pero él perdió el talonario de cheques.   12. Cuando yo era joven, mis clases siempre eran enseñadas por excelentes profesores.   13. Espero que mi casa sea comprada por una persona agradable.   14. Espero que este lío no fuera hecho por ratones.   15. El himno nacional fue cantado por mi vecino antes del partido.

26-8 Después del Super Bowl, el lanzador ganador fue entrevistado por un reportero que le preguntó cómo se sentía. Esto es lo que él dijo: "Pues, se trabaja duro todo el año y se entrena cada día. Claro que se espera algo como esto, pero se sabe que es sólo un sueño, y entonces se ganan muchos partidos, pero sólo porque se tienen estupendos compañeros, y se está verdaderamente feliz. Pero no se está preparado para un día como éste. Se despierta y se sabe que éste es el día más importante de la vida y se piensa que se tiene la oportunidad de ganar, pero no se puede estar demasiado seguro. Por eso, se reza. Y se juega lo mejor posible y se espera que se gane. Y cuando se gana, es lo más maravilloso que se ha sentido en la vida, y cuando se pregunta a bocajarro cómo se siente, se ignora completamente toda la situación y se habla en la voz pasiva."

Spanish-English glossary

NOTE Nouns are marked for gender; verbs are marked for stem changes.

Abbreviations include (*f.*) feminine, (*m.*) masculine, and (*pl.*) plural.

a

a bocajarro point-blank
a este paso at this rate
a menos que unless
a menudo often
a propósito on purpose
a su hora on time
a tiempo on time
a veces at times, sometimes
a ver... let's see ...
abastecedor (*m.*) caterer
abeja (*f.*) bee
abismo (*m.*) abyss
abogado (*m.*) lawyer
abrir to open
abstenerse de + INFINITIVE to abstain from (*doing something*)
abuelo (*m.*) grandfather
aburrido bored, boring
acabarse to end
accidente (*m.*) accident
aceite (*m.*) oil
aceptar to accept
acera (*f.*) sidewalk
acerca de about
acostarse (o > ue) to go to bed
acostumbrarse a to get used to
actitud (*f.*) attitude
actuar to act
acusado (*m.*) defendant, accused
adelgazar to lose weight
adentro inside
admitir to admit
adolescente (*m./f.*) teenager, adolescent
¿adónde? (to) where?
adoptar to adopt
adquirir (i > ie) to acquire, get
adulto (*m.*) adult
advertir (e > ie) to advise, warn
aerolínea (*f.*) airline
aeropuerto (*m.*) airport

afeitar(se) to shave (oneself)
afuera outside
afueras (*fpl.*) suburbs
agente de viajes (*m./f.*) travel agent
agradecer to be thankful
ahora now
ahora mismo right now
ahorita right now
ahorrar to save (*money*)
¡ajá! aha!, that's it!
ajedrez (*m.*) chess
al cine to the movies
al contado in cash
al fin at the end
al lado de next to, next door to
al principio at first, in the beginning
alabanza (*f.*) praise
alacena (*f.*) cabinet
alcanzar to reach (*a goal*)
alejarse to walk away
algo something, anything
alguien someone, somebody, anybody
allí there
almohada (*f.*) pillow
almorzar (o > ue) to eat lunch
almuerzo (*m.*) lunch
alondra (*f.*) lark
alrededor (de) around
amable nice, kind
amar to love
amarillo yellow
amistoso friendly
amor (*m.*) love
andar to walk
anfitrión (*m.*) host
anillo (*m.*) ring
animal (*m.*) **doméstico** pet
anoche last night
antes (de) before, beforehand
año (*m.*) year
apagar to turn off, switch off

311

aparato (*m.*) appliance
aparcamiento (*m.*) parking space, parking lot
aparcar to park
aparecer to appear
apartamento (*m.*) apartment
aprender to learn
aprobar (**o > ue**) to approve
aquí here
araña (*f.*) spider
arañar to scratch
árbol (*m.*) tree
arco (*m.*) arch
área (*f.*) area
arena (*f.*) sand
arete (*m.*) earring
armario (*m.*) closet, cabinet
arpa (*f.*) harp
arquitecto (*m.*) architect
arrancar to start (*engine*)
arreglar to fix, arrange
arroz (*m.*) rice
artículo (*m.*) item, article
asesino (*m.*) murderer
ascensor (*m.*) elevator
asistir a to attend (*something [a function]*)
aster (*m.*) aster
astronauta (*m./f.*) astronaut
atenerse a to depend on, rely on
atleta (*m./f.*) athlete
atraer to attract
atrás back; atrás de behind, in back of
aumento (*m.*) raise, increase
autobús (*m.*) bus
autor/autora (*m./f.*) author
autorizar to authorize
ave (*f.*) bird
avergonzado embarrassed
averiguar to find out
avión (*m.*) airplane
¡ay! alas!
ayer yesterday
ayuda (*f.*) help
ayudar to help
azafata (*m./f.*) flight attendant
azúcar (*m.*) sugar

b

bailar to dance
baile (*m.*) dance, ball
balde (*m.*) pail
básquetbol (*m.*) basketball
bañar(se) to bathe (oneself)
banco (*m.*) bank
banda (*f.*) band
bandera (*f.*) flag
baño (*m.*) bathroom
baraja (*f.*) deck of cards

barco (*m.*) boat
barra (*f.*) loaf; barra de pan loaf of bread
barrer to sweep
bastante enough
bastar to be sufficient, suffice
basura (*f.*) garbage, trash
baúl (*m.*) trunk
bautizar baptize
bebé (*m./f.*) baby
beber to drink
bebida (*f.*) drink
béisbol (*m.*) baseball
Bella Durmiente (*f.*) Sleeping Beauty
bendecir (**e > i**) to bless
besar to kiss
biblioteca (*f.*) library
bicicleta (*f.*) bicycle
bien well
bilingüe bilingual
billar (*m.*) billiards, pool
bloque (*m.*) block
boca (*f.*) mouth
boda (*f.*) wedding
boleto (*m.*) ticket
bolígrafo (*m.*) pen
bolsa (*f.*) purse, pocketbook; bag
bolsillo (*m.*) pocket
bomba (*f.*) bomb; pump
bombero (*m.*) firefighter
bombilla (*f.*) lightbulb
borracho drunk
bosque (*m.*) woods, forest
botiquín (*m.*) medicine cabinet
botón (*m.*) button
bravo brave
brebaje (*m.*) concoction
británico British
broma (*f.*) joke
bruja (*f.*) witch
bueno good
búho (*m.*) owl
burbuja (*f.*) bubble
buscar to look for, search for

c

caballo (*m.*) horse
caber to fit
cabeza (*f.*) head
cacahuate (*m.*) peanut
cada every, each
caer(se) to fall (down)
café (*m.*) coffee; brown
cafeína (*f.*) caffeine
cafetería (*f.*) cafeteria, coffee shop
caja (*f.*) box
calabaza (*f.*) pumpkin
calcetín (*m.*) sock

callarse to be quiet, "shut up"
calle (*f.*) street
calor (*m.*) heat, warmth
caloría (*f.*) calorie
cama (*f.*) bed
cámara (*f.*) camera
cambiar to change
(en) cambio on the other hand
camino (*m.*) road
camioneta (*f.*) van, small truck
camisa (*f.*) shirt
camiseta (*f.*) T-shirt
campamento (*m.*) camp
canción (*f.*) song
candidato (*m.*) candidate
cansado tired
cantar to sing
Caperucita Roja (*f.*) Little Red Riding Hood
capital (*m.*) capital (*wealth*)
capital (*f.*) capital (*city*)
capítulo (*m.*) chapter
carácter (*m.*) character
cárcel (*f.*) jail, prison
carne (*f.*) meat
carpa (*f.*) **dorada** goldfish
carrera (*f.*) career
carretera (*f.*) highway
carta (*f.*) letter, card
casa (*f.*) **de muñecas** dollhouse
casado married
casamiento (*m.*) marriage
casarse con to marry
caso (*m.*) case
castillo (*m.*) castle
catálogo (*m.*) catalogue
cazar to hunt
celebrar to celebrate
celebridad (*f.*) celebrity
cena (*f.*) dinner
cenar to dine, eat dinner
Cenicienta (*f.*) Cinderella
centro (*m.*) center; downtown
centro (*m.*) **comercial** shopping mall
centro (*m.*) **de mesa** centerpiece
cepillar(se) to brush (oneself)
cerdo (*m.*) pig
cerebro (*m.*) brain
ceremonia (*f.*) ceremony
cerrado closed
cerrajero (*m.*) locksmith
cerrar (e > ie) to close, shut
cerveza (*f.*) beer
césped (*m.*) lawn
chanchullero/chanchullera (*m./f.*) scammer
cheque (*m.*) check
chimenea (*f.*) chimney, fireplace
ciencia (*f.*) science

científico/científica (*m./f.*) scientist
cierto certain, true
cigarro (*m.*) cigar
cine (*m.*) movie theater; **al cine** to the movies
cinta (*f.*) ribbon, tape
cita (*f.*) date, appointment
clarificar to clarify
clase (*f.*) class
clasificar to classify
cliente (*m./f.*) client, customer
club (*m.*) club
cochino (*m.*) slob
cocinar to cook
cocinero (*m.*) cook, chef
coger to catch, seize, grab
cola (*f.*) line, tail
colegir (e > i) to deduce
colgar (o > ue) to hang (up)
collar (*m.*) necklace
comedor (*m.*) dining room
comenzar (e > ie) to begin, commence
comer to eat
cometa (*f.*) kite
cometer (un error) to make (a mistake)
cómico funny, comical
comida (*f.*) food, meal
comisión (*f.*) commission
¿cómo? how?
compañero (*m.*) companion, colleague, roommate
compañía (*f.*) company
competir (e > i) to compete
componer to compose
comportarse to act, behave
compra (*f.*) purchase
comprar to buy, purchase
comprender to understand, comprehend
con with
con frecuencia frequently, often
con tal que provided that
conceder to grant
concierto (*m.*) concert
concluir to conclude
concurso (*m.*) contest, game show
conducir to drive, conduct, lead
conejo (*m.*) rabbit
confesar (e > ie) to confess
conjugar to conjugate
conmigo with me
conocer to know (*a person/place*), be familiar with (*a person/place*); to meet
conquistar to conquer
conseguir (e > i) to obtain, get
consentir (e > ie) to consent
constituir to constitute
construir to construct, build
contaminación (*f.*) contamination, pollution
contar (o > ue) to count

contener to contain, hold
contestar to answer
contra against
contraer to contract
contratar to hire, contract
contribuir to contribute
convencer to convince, persuade
convenir en + INFINITIVE to agree to (*do something*)
convertir (en) (e > ie) to convert (into)
corazón (*m.*) heart
corbata (*f.*) necktie
cordero (*m.*) lamb
corregir (e > i) to correct
correo (*m.*) mail
correr to run
cortacésped (*m.*) lawnmower
cortar to cut; **cortar el césped** to mow the lawn
cortés polite, courteous
cortina (*f.*) curtain
cosa (*f.*) thing
costa (*f.*) coast
costar (o > ue) to cost
crecer to grow
credo (*m.*) ethic, creed
creer to believe
criado/criada (*m./f.*) servant; **criada** (*f.*) maid
criar to raise (*children, animals, etc.*)
crimen (*m.*) crime
cristal (*m.*) glass, crystal
crítico (*m.*) critic
cuadra (*f.*) (city) block
cuadro (*m.*) square
¿cuál(es)? which?
cualquier/cualquiera any
cualquier cosa anything
cuando when; **¿cuándo?** when?
¿cuánto/cuánta? how much?
¿cuántos/cuántas? how many?
cuarto (*m.*) room
cubrir to cover
cucaracha (*f.*) cockroach
cuchara (*f.*) spoon
cuchillo (*m.*) knife
cuello (*m.*) neck
cuenta (*f.*) bill
cuento (*m.*) story; **cuento de hadas** fairy tale
cuestión (*f.*) issue, question
cuidado (*m.*) care
cuidar a to care for, take care of (*a person*)
cuidar de to care for (*an animal or thing*)
cuidarse to care for oneself
culebra (*f.*) snake
culinario culinary
culpa (*f.*) fault
cultivar to grow (*plants*)
cumpleaños (*m.*) birthday
cumplido (*m.*) compliment

cumplir to complete; **cumplir la palabra** to keep one's word/promise/resolution
cupón (*m.*) coupon

d

damas (*fpl.*) checkers
dañado broken, damaged
dar to give
dar cuerda a to wind; **dar cuerda a un reloj** to wind a watch
dar un paseo to take a walk
de cabo a rabo from top to bottom
de cualquier forma anyway
de hecho in fact
de lo contrario otherwise
de madera wooden
de niño/niña as a child
de pie standing
de vez en cuando from time to time, once in a while
debajo underneath; **debajo de** under
deber to owe, ought, "should"
deber de + INFINITIVE must (*do something*) [*conjecture*]
decidir to decide
decir (e > i) to say, tell
deducir to deduce, infer
defectuoso defective
defender (e > ie) to defend
dejar to leave (behind), allow
dejar de + INFINITIVE to stop (*doing something*)
delgado thin, slim
demandante (*m./f.*) plaintiff
demandar to sue
demostrar (o > ue) to demonstrate
dentro (de) inside
dependiente (*m.*) clerk
depositar to deposit, put (*money in the bank*)
deprimido depressed
derecha (*f.*) right side; **a la derecha** to the right
derecho (*m.*) right
desafinadamente out of tune
desagüe (*m.*) drain
desaparecer to disappear
desastre (*m.*) disaster
desayuno (*m.*) breakfast
descansar to rest
describir to describe
descubrir to discover
desempeño (*m.*) performance (*on the job*)
deseo (*m.*) wish, desire
desfile (*m.*) parade
deshacer to undo, untie (*a knot*)
desierto (*m.*) desert
deslucir to tarnish, spoil
desordenado messy
despedir (e > i) to fire
despedirse (e > i) to say good-bye; **despedirse de** to say good-bye to

despertador (*m.*) alarm clock
despertarse (**e > ie**) to wake up
después later; **después de** after, afterward; **después de eso** after that
destacar to stand out
destruir to destroy
desván (*m.*) attic
desvestir(se) (**e > i**) to undress (oneself)
detener to detain, stop, arrest
devolver (**o > ue**) to return (*an object*)
día (*m.*) day
diamante (*m.*) diamond
diario (*m.*) diary
diente (*m.*) tooth
dieta (*f.*) diet
difícil difficult, hard
dificultad (*f.*) difficulty
dinero (*m.*) money
dios (*m.*) god
diploma (*m.*) diploma
dirección (*f.*) address; **direcciones** (*fpl.*) directions
dirigir to direct
disco (*m.*) record
disculparse to apologize, pardon oneself
discurso (*m.*) speech
discutir to discuss
disgustar to be repugnant
disolver (**o > ue**) to dissolve
distancia (*f.*) distance
distinguir to distinguish
distinto distinct, different
diversión (*f.*) fun
divorciarse to divorce
divorcio (*m.*) divorce
docena (*f.*) dozen
documento (*m.*) document
dólar (*m.*) dollar
doler (**o > ue**) to be painful
donde where; **¿dónde?** where?
dormir (**o > ue**) to sleep
dormirse (**o > ue**) to fall asleep
drama (*m.*) play, drama
ducha (*f.*) shower
ducharse to take a shower
dudar to doubt
dueño (*m.*) owner
dulce sweet
dulces (*mpl.*) candy
duque (*m.*) duke
duquesa (*f.*) duchess
durante during
durar to last, take time
duro hard

e

e and (*preceding a word beginning with* **i** *or* **hi**)
echar to pour

echar al correo to mail
echar una siesta to take a nap
edificio (*m.*) building
educación (*f.*) education
egoísta selfish, egotistic
ejercer to exert, exercise
ejército (*m.*) army
elección (*f.*) choice, election
elegir (**e > i**) to elect
elemento (*m.*) element
embarazada pregnant
embrujado haunted
empacar to pack
empezar (**e > ie**) to begin
empleado (*m.*) employee
empleo (*m.*) work
en caso de que in case of/that
en ninguna parte nowhere, not anywhere
en ocasiones innumerables on countless occasions
en todas partes everywhere
en vez de instead of
enamorarse to fall in love
encantar to be enchanting
encender (**e > ie**) to light, kindle
encontrarse (**o > ue**) to meet; **encontrarse con** to meet with
encubrir to whitewash, cover up
enemigo (*m.*) enemy
energía (*f.*) energy
enero January
enfermarse to get sick
enfermo sick
enfrente in front; **enfrente de** in front of
engañar to fool, trick, deceive, cheat
engordar to gain weight
enigma (*m.*) puzzle, enigma
enojado angry, mad
enojarse to get angry/mad
ensalada (*f.*) salad
ensayo (*m.*) essay
enseñar to teach
entender (**e > ie**) to understand
entero entire
enterrar (**e > ie**) to bury
entomólogo (*m.*) entomologist
entonces then
entrar to enter; **entrar en** to enter into
entre between, among
entregar to deliver
entrenar to train
entretanto meanwhile
envolver (**o > ue**) to wrap (up)
episodio (*m.*) episode
equipaje (*m.*) equipment; luggage
erguir to erect, lift up
error (*m.*) error, mistake
escalera (*f.*) stairway, staircase; ladder

escena (*f.*) scene
escoger to select
esconder to hide
escribir to write
escritorio (*m.*) desk
escuchar to listen (to)
escuela (*f.*) school; **escuela secundaria** high school
espacio (*m.*) space, room
espalda (*f.*) back
espantapájaros (*m.*) scarecrow
espantar to scare, frighten
esparcir to scatter, spread
espejo (*m.*) mirror
esperar to hope, wait (for)
espía (*m./f.*) spy
esposo/esposa (*m./f.*) husband/wife, spouse
esquiar to ski
esquina (*f.*) corner (*exterior*), street corner
establecer to establish
estación (*f.*) station; **estación de bomberos** fire station
estacionar to park
estado (*m.*) state
Estados Unidos (*m.*) United States
estampilla (*f.*) stamp
estancia (*f.*) stay; habitation
estante (*m.*) shelf
estaño (*m.*) tin
estar to be
estar a dieta to be on a diet
estómago (*m.*) stomach
estornudar to sneeze
estos días these days
estrella (*f.*) star; **estrella de cine** movie star
estreno (*m.*) opening, premiere
estudiante (*m./f.*) student
estudiar to study
estudios (*mpl.*) studies
estupendo great
examen (*m.*) test, examination
exigir to demand
existir to exist
exportar to export
exposición (*f.*) exposition, exhibit
expresarse to express oneself
extinguir to extinguish

f

fallar a favor de to rule in favor of
falsificar to falsify, forge (*one's signature*)
faltar to be lacking, be missing
faltar a su palabra to break one's promise
fama (*f.*) fame
fantasía (*f.*) fantasy
fantasma (*m.*) ghost, phantasm
farmacia (*f.*) pharmacy
fascinar to be fascinating
favor (*m.*) favor

fe (*f.*) faith
felicidad (*f.*) happiness
feliz happy
fiesta (*f.*) party
filete (*m.*) steak
fin de semana (*m.*) weekend
financiero financial
fingir to pretend
firma (*f.*) signature
firmar to sign (one's name)
flor (*f.*) flower
florista (*m./f.*) florist
flotar to float
fluir to flow
folleto (*m.*) pamphlet
fondo (*m.*) bottom, back, background
fontanero (*m.*) plumber
foto (*f.*) photo
frase (*f.*) sentence, phrase
frecuencia frequency; **con frecuencia** frequently, often
frecuentemente frequently, often
fregadero de cocina (*m.*) kitchen sink
fregar (e > ie) to scrub, wash (*dishes*)
freír (e > i) to fry
fresco cool
frío cold
frontera (*f.*) border
fuego (*m.*) fire
fumar to smoke
funcionar to work, run (*machine*)
fútbol (*m.*) soccer; **fútbol americano** (*m.*) football

g

gabinete (*m.*) cabinet
gafas (*fpl.*) de sol sunglasses
galleta (*f.*) cracker
galletita (*f.*) cookie
gana wish, will, need; **tener ganas de** to feel like (*doing something*), be looking forward to (*doing something*)
ganador (*m.*) winner
ganar to win, earn
gasolina (*f.*) gasoline
gastar to spend (*money*)
gemir (e > i) to moan, groan, whine
gente (*f.*) people
gerente (*m./f.*) manager
gigante (*m.*) giant
gimnasio (*m.*) gym, gymnasium
girar to turn
girasol (*m.*) sunflower
gozar de to enjoy
gran great, grand
Gran Cañón (*m.*) Grand Canyon
grande big, large
granja (*f.*) farm
granjero (*m.*) farmer

grave serious
gravedad (*f.*) gravity
grifo (*m.*) faucet, tap
guante (*m.*) glove
guantera (*f.*) glove compartment
guapo handsome
guardar to save; **guardar un secreto** to keep a secret
guarro (*m.*) slob
guerra (*f.*) war
guerrero (*m.*) warrior
guitarra (*f.*) guitar
gustar to like, be pleasing
gusto (*m.*) taste

h

haber to have (*auxiliary*)
habitación (*f.*) room, hotel room
hablar to speak
hacer to make, do
hacer ejercicio to exercise
hacer el papel to play the role
hacer una pregunta to ask a question
hacerse to become
hada madrina (*f.*) fairy godmother
hambre (*f.*) hunger
hamburguesa (*f.*) hamburger
hasta until, even, to
hay there is, there are
hecho (*m.*) fact
hecho por made by
helado (*m.*) ice cream
hermanastra (*f.*) stepsister
hermano (*m.*) brother
hervir (e > ie) to boil
hielo (*m.*) ice
hipoteca (*f.*) mortgage
hogar (*m.*) home
hoja (*f.*) leaf
Holanda Holland
hombre (*m.*) man
homicidio (*m.*) homicide
honrado honest
horno (*m.*) oven, furnace
hotel (*m.*) hotel
hoy today
hueso (*m.*) bone
huevo (*m.*) egg
huir to flee, run away
humano (*m.*) human
húmedo humid
humor (*m.*) humor, mood
huracán (*m.*) hurricane

i

idioma (*m.*) language (*specific*)
idiotez (*f.*) idiocy
iglesia (*f.*) church

ignorar to be ignorant of, ignore
igual equal, same
imaginar(se) to imagine
impedir (e > i) to impede, hinder
imponer to enforce
importar to be important
impuesto (*m.*) tax
incendio (*m.*) fire (*catastrophe*)
incluir to include
incluso including
incómodo uncomfortable
inducir to induce, lead
influir (en) to influence
información (*f.*) information
Inglaterra (*f.*) England
inglés (*m.*) English
inocente innocent
insistir to insist; **insistir en** to insist on
instituir to institute
intentar to try
interés (*m.*) interest
interesar to be interesting
introducir to introduce
intruso (*m.*) intruder
invertir (e > ie) to invest
investigar to investigate
invierno (*m.*) winter
invitación (*f.*) invitation
invitado (*m.*) guest
invitar to invite
ir to go; **ir al cine** to go to the movies; **ir de compras** to go shopping
irse to go away, leave
izquierda left side; **a la izquierda** to the left

j

jardín (*m.*) garden; **jardín de casa** backyard
jardinero (*m.*) gardener
jefe (*m.*) boss, employer
jeringa (*f.*) needle (*syringe*)
jirafa (*f.*) giraffe
joya (*f.*) jewel
juego (*m.*) game
jugar (o > ue) to play (a game); **jugar a los naipes** to play cards
juicio (*m.*) trial
juntos together
jurado (*m.*) jury
justificar to justify
justo fair, just

l

laboratorio (*m.*) laboratory
ladrar to bark
ladrillo (*m.*) brick
ladrón/ladrona (*m./f.*) thief
lago (*m.*) lake

lágrima (*f.*) tear
langosta (*f.*) lobster
lanzador (*m.*) quarterback
largo long
lástima (*f.*) pity, shame
lavar(se) to wash (oneself)
lección (*f.*) lesson
leer to read
lenguaje (*m.*) language
león (*m.*) lion
levantarse to stand up, get up
ley (*f.*) law
libertad (*f.*) freedom, liberty
libra (*f.*) pound
librería (*f.*) bookstore
libro (*m.*) book
licencia (*f.*) license
líder (*m.*) leader
lienzo (*m.*) canvas
limonada (*f.*) lemonade
limpiar to clean, wash
limpio clean
listo ready
llamar a la puerta to be at the door
llamar(se) to call (oneself)
llave (*f.*) key
llegar to arrive
llenar to fill
lleno full
llevar to wear; to carry
llorar to cry
llover to rain
lloviznando drizzling
lluvia (*f.*) rain
lluvioso rainy, wet
lobo (*m.*) wolf
loco crazy, insane
lodo (*m.*) mud
lucir to light up, display
luego later
lugar (*m.*) place
luna (*f.*) moon; **luna de miel** honeymoon
luz (*f.*) light

m

madera (*f.*) wood
madrastra (*f.*) stepmother
maduro mature, ripe
maestro/maestra (*m./f.*) teacher
mago (*m.*) wizard, magician
malas hierbas (*f.*) weeds
maldecir (**e > i**) to curse
maleta (*f.*) suitcase; **maletas** luggage
maletero (*m.*) trunk (*of car*)
malísimo wretched
malo bad, evil
malvado evil, wicked

manejar to drive; to manage; to run (*a machine*)
manga (*f.*) sleeve
mano (*f.*) hand
manopla (*f.*) mitten
manteca (*f.*) lard
mantener to maintain, keep
mantequilla (*f.*) butter
manzana (*f.*) apple; city block
mañana (*f.*) morning
mañana tomorrow
maratón (*m.*) marathon
maravilloso wonderful
margarita (*f.*) daisy
mariposa (*f.*) butterfly
martes (*m.*) Tuesday
martillar to hammer
martillo (*m.*) hammer
más tarde later
mayor older
mayoría (*f.*) majority
mecánico (*m.*) mechanic
medianoche (*f.*) midnight
medicina (*f.*) medicine
medio (*m.*) middle; **en medio** in the middle
mediodía (*m.*) noon, midday
medir (**e > i**) to measure, be long
mejor best
menor younger
menos less
mentir (**e > ie**) to lie, tell a lie
mentira (*f.*) lie
mentiroso (*m.*) liar
mercantilismo (*m.*) mercantilism
merecer to deserve
mes (*m.*) month
mesero (*m.*) waiter
meter to put; **meter en** to put into
meterse en to put oneself through
método (*m.*) method
mientras (que) while
mil (*m.*) thousand
mil millones (*m.*) billion
milagro (*m.*) miracle
milla (*f.*) mile
mirar to watch, look at
mismo same; **lo mismo** the same thing
misterio (*m.*) mystery
mochila (*f.*) backpack
modales (*mpl.*) manners; **buenos modales**
  good manners
modelo (*m./f.*) model
mohoso moldy
mojado wet
molestar to bother, be bothersome
monarca (*m.*) monarch
moneda (*f.*) coin
mono (*m.*) monkey

monstruo (*m.*) monster
montar ride; **montar en bicicleta** to ride a bike
monumento (*m.*) monument
morder (**o** > **ue**) to bite, chew
morir (**o** > **ue**) to die
mosca (*f.*) fly
mosquito (*m.*) mosquito
mostrador (*m.*) counter
mostrar (**o** > **ue**) to show
mover(se) (**o** > **ue**) to move (oneself)
muchas veces many times
mucho a lot, much; **mucho tiempo** a long time;
  por mucho tiempo for a long time
muchos many
mudarse to move, change residence
mueble (*m.*) piece of furniture; **muebles**
  furniture
muerte (*f.*) death
muerto dead
mujer (*m.*) woman
multa (*f.*) fine, (traffic) ticket
multitud (*f.*) crowd
mundo (*m.*) world
muñeca (*f.*) wrist
muro (*m.*) wall (*exterior*)
música (*f.*) music
muy very

n

nacer to be born
nada nothing, not anything
nada menos "all of it"
nadar to swim
nadie nobody, no one
naipes (*m.*) playing cards
nariz (*f.*) nose
navaja (*f.*) razor
nave (*f.*) spaceship
Navidad (*f.*) Christmas
necesitar to need
negar (**e** > **ie**) to deny
nervioso nervous
nevada (*f.*) snowstorm, blizzard
nevar (**e** > **ie**) to snow
niebla (*f.*) fog
nieto (*m.*) grandson, grandchild
nieve (*f.*) snow
ningún, ninguno not any, not a single (one)
noche (*f.*) night
nombre (*m.*) name
nota (*f.*) note; grade; **buenas/malas notas** good/bad
  grades
noticias (*fpl.*) news
novia girlfriend, fiancée, bride
novio boyfriend, fiancé, groom
nublado cloudy
nudo (*m.*) knot

número (*m.*) number; **número de teléfono** telephone
  number
nunca never; **nunca más** never ever

o

o… o… either … or …
obedecer to obey
obtener to obtain, get
océano (*m.*) ocean
ocupado busy
odiar to hate
odio (*m.*) hatred
oficina (*f.*) office; **oficina de correos** post office
ofrecer to offer
oír to hear
ojalá I hope so!, God willing, if only he/it/they/etc. would
ojo (*m.*) eye
oler (**o** > **ue**) to smell; **oler bien/mal** to smell
  good/bad
olimpiadas (*f.*) Olympics
olvidar to forget
onza (*f.*) ounce
oponer to oppose
ordenado neat
organizar to organize
oro (*m.*) gold
oso (*m.*) bear
otoño (*m.*) fall, autumn
otra vez again, another time

p

padrino (*m.*) godfather; **padrinos** godparents
pagar to pay (for)
página (*f.*) page
pájaro (*m.*) bird
palabra (*f.*) word
palacio (*m.*) palace
pan (*m.*) bread
panadería (*f.*) bakery
panadero (*m.*) baker
pantalones (*m.*) pants, slacks
pañuelo (*m.*) handkerchief
papa (*m.*) pope
papa (*f.*) potato; **papas fritas** french fries
papá (*m.*) father
papel (*m.*) paper
paquete (*m.*) package
par pair, couple; **un par de** a couple of
para for
para que so that
para siempre forever
parecer to seem, appear
parecerse a to look like, resemble physically
pared (*f.*) wall (*interior*)
parque (*m.*) park
parte (*f.*) part
participante (*m./f.*) participant, contestant

partido (*m.*) game
partir to leave, depart
pasa (*f.*) raisin
pasta (*f.*) **de dientes** toothpaste
patata (*f.*) potato
patinar to skate
patio atrás (*m.*) backyard
pato (*m.*) duck
pavo (*m.*) turkey
payaso (*m.*) clown
paz (*f.*) peace
pedazo (*m.*) piece
pedir (e > i) to ask for, request
peinarse to comb one's hair
peldaño (*m.*) step, stair
película (*f.*) movie, film
pelo (*m.*) hair
pelota (*f.*) ball (*sports*)
pensar (e > ie) to think; **pensar en** to think about
pequeño small, little
perder (e > ie) to lose; **perder el tiempo** to waste time
perezoso lazy, slothful
periódico (*m.*) newspaper
perla (*f.*) pearl
perlita (*f.*) little pearl
permitir to permit, allow
perseguir (e > i) to pursue, persecute
persona (*f.*) person; **personas** people
personaje (*m.*) character
pertenecer to belong
pesadilla (*f.*) nightmare
pesar to weigh
pescado (*m.*) fish (*prepared*)
peso (*m.*) weight
pez (*m.*) fish (*living*)
pie (*m.*) foot
pierna (*f.*) leg
pijama (*m.*) pajamas
pastilla (*f.*) pill
pintor (*m.*) painter
pintura (*f.*) picture, painting, paint
piscina (*f.*) swimming pool
pistola (*f.*) pistol, gun
placer enjoy, get pleasure from
placer (*m.*) pleasure, enjoyment
plancha (*f.*) iron
planchar to iron
planear to plan
planeta (*m.*) planet
planta (*f.*) plant
plantar to plant
plata (*f.*) silver
plato (*m.*) plate, dish
playa (*f.*) beach
pobreza (*f.*) poverty
poder (o > ue) to be able to, can
policía (*m.*) policeman

policía (*f.*) policewoman; police (force)
política (*f.*) politics
político (*m.*) politician
pollo (*m.*) chicken
Polo Sur (*m.*) South Pole
poner to put, place; **poner un anuncio** to place an ad
ponerse to become, put on (*clothing*), set (*sun*);
    ponerse a dieta to go on a diet
por casualidad by accident, by chance
por ninguna parte not anywhere
por primera vez for the first time
¿por qué? why?
por separado separately
por supuesto of course
por un rato for a while
porque because
poseer to possess
practicar to practice
precio (*m.*) price
preferir (e > ie) to prefer
premio (*m.*) prize
preocuparse to worry; **preocuparse por** to worry about
preparar to prepare
presentación (*f.*) presentation, introduction
prestar to loan, lend
primavera (*f.*) spring
(por) primera vez for the first time
primero first
primo (*m.*) cousin
príncipe (*m.*) prince
probar (o > ue) to prove, test, sample, taste
probarse (o > ue) to try on (*clothing*)
problema (*m.*) problem
producir to produce
profesional (*m./f.*) professional, pro
programa (*m.*) program
progreso (*m.*) progress
prohibido prohibited
promesa (*f.*) promise
prometer to promise
pronunciación (*f.*) pronunciation
propina (*f.*) tip
proteger to protect
proveer to provide
próximo next
prueba (*f.*) quiz
público (*m.*) public, audience
pudrir to rot, spoil
puerta (*f.*) door; **puerta principal** front door
pues well
pues, ... well, ...
pulgada (*f.*) inch
pulgar (*m.*) thumb
pulsera (*f.*) bracelet
punto de vista (*m.*) point of view
puré (*m.*) purée; **puré de patatas** mashed potatoes

q

que that; than
¿qué? what?
quedarse to stay, remain
quedarse de brazos cruzados to twiddle one's thumbs
quejarse to complain; **quejarse de** to complain about
querer (e > ie) to want
queso (*m.*) cheese
quien who; **¿quién?** who(m)?
(de) quita y pon detachable
quitar to remove; **quitar la nieve** to shovel snow;
   quitar el polvo to dust
quitarse to take off, remove (*clothing*)

r

rabia (*f.*) rage
radio (*m./f.*) radio (*apparatus*)
radio (*f.*) radio (station)
raer to scrape, rub off
rama (*f.*) branch
ramo (*m.*) bouquet; **ramo de flores** bouquet of flowers
rana (*f.*) frog
rápidamente fast, quickly, rapidly
rápido fast, rapid
raya (*f.*) stripe
rebaja (*f.*) sale
rebajar de peso to lose weight
recepción (*f.*) reception
recibir to receive
recoger to pick up, gather
reconocer to recognize
recordar (o > ue) to remember, recall
reducir to reduce, cut down
referir (e > ie) to refer
refrigerador (*m.*) refrigerator
regalar to give a gift
regalo (*m.*) gift, present
regar (e > ie) to water (*a plant*)
regla (*f.*) rule
rehacer to redo, remake
reina (*f.*) queen
reír(se) (e > i) to laugh
relajarse to relax
releer to reread
reloj (*m.*) watch, clock
remontar una cometa to fly a kite
renunciar a to quit (*a job, etc.*)
repetir (e > i) to repeat
reportaje (*m.*) report
reprobar (o > ue) to fail
resfriado (*m.*) cold
resolver (o > ue) to solve, resolve
respuesta (*f.*) answer
restaurante (*m.*) restaurant
retraer to bring back, dissuade
reunión (*f.*) meeting
revista (*f.*) magazine

rey (*m.*) king
rezar to pray
rico rich
ridículo ridiculous
rincón (*m.*) corner (*interior*)
río (*m.*) river
riqueza (*f.*) richness, wealth
robar to rob, steal
robo (*m.*) robbery
rodilla knee; **de rodillas** kneeling
rogar (o > ue) to pray, beg
rollo de película (*m.*) film (*camera*)
romper to break
ropa (*f.*) clothing, clothes
roto broken
rubí (*m.*) ruby
rubio blonde
rueda (*f.*) wheel
ruido (*m.*) noise
ruso (*m.*) Russian

s

saber to know information; **saber de** to know about
sacar to take out; **sacar una foto** to take a picture
sacerdote (*m.*) priest
sala (*f.*) living room; **sala de estar** living room;
   sala de juntas boardroom
salchicha (*f.*) sausage
salir to leave; **salir de** to leave from; **salir con** to date
saltar to jump
salud (*f.*) health
sangre (*f.*) blood
secar(se) to dry (oneself)
seco dry
secreto (*m.*) secret
sed (*f.*) thirst
segar (e > ie) to mow (*grass, etc.*)
seguir (e > i) to follow, continue
sello (*m.*) (postage) stamp
selva (*f.*) jungle; **selva tropical** rain forest
semana (*f.*) week
semilla (*f.*) seed
senda (*f.*) path
sentado sitting, seated
sentarse (e > ie) to sit down, be seated
sentir (e > ie) to feel, regret
sentirse (e > ie) to feel
ser to be
Serie (*f.*) **Mundial** World Series
servilleta (*f.*) napkin
servir (e > i) to serve
siempre always
siesta (*f.*) nap
siglo (*m.*) century
siguiente next, following
silla (*f.*) chair
simbolizar to symbolize

símbolo (*m.*) symbol
sin (que) without
sirvienta (*f.*) servant, maid
sobrar to be in surplus, be left over
sobre (*m.*) envelope
sociedad (*f.*) society
sociópata (*m./f.*) sociopath
sofá (*m.*) sofa, couch
sol (*m.*) sun
solamente only
soldado (*m.*) soldier
solo alone
sólo only, just
sombra (*f.*) shade, shadow
sombrero (*m.*) hat
sonar (o > ue) to ring, resound; **sonar a** sound like
sonreír (e > i) to smile
sonrisa (*f.*) smile
soñar (o > ue) to dream; **soñar con** to dream of/about
sopa (*f.*) soup
sostener to sustain, support, uphold
sótano (*m.*) basement
subir to climb, go up
sucio dirty
suegro/suegra (*m./f.*) father-in-law/mother-in-law
suelo (*m.*) floor
sueño (*m.*) dream
suéter (*m.*) sweater
suficiente enough
sufrir to suffer
sugerir (e > ie) to suggest
sumergir to submerge, immerse
supermercado (*m.*) supermarket
supersticioso (*m.*) superstitious person
suponer to suppose, assume
sur (*m.*) south
surgir to surge, spurt
suspender to fail (*a test*)
sustituir to substitute
sustraer to remove, take away

t

tabloide (*m.*) tabloid
tacón (*m.*) heel; **tacón alto** high heel
tal cosa such a thing
talento (*m.*) talent
talla (*f.*) size
tamaño (*m.*) size
también also, too
tampoco not either
tan so
tan pronto como as soon as
tanque (*m.*) tank; **tanque de gasolina** gas tank
tanto/tanta so much, as much; **tanto/tanta como** so much as, as much as
tantos/tantas so many
tardar (en) to take time

tarde (*f.*) afternoon
tarde late; **tarde o temprano** sooner or later
tarea (*f.*) assignment, task, chore
tarjeta (*f.*) card; **tarjeta de débito** debit card
tatuaje (*m.*) tattoo
taza (*f.*) coffee cup, mug
té (*m.*) tea
teatro (*m.*) theater
tela (*f.*) canvas (*painting*)
teléfono (*m.*) telephone
telegrama (*m.*) telegram
televisión (*f.*) television
televisor (*m.*) television
temblar (e > ie) to tremble
temer to fear, suspect, dread
temor (*m.*) fear
temprano early
tenedor (*m.*) fork
tener to have
tener calor to be warm
tener frío to be cold
tener hambre to be hungry
tener miedo to be afraid
tener prisa to be in hurry
tener que + INFINITIVE to have to (*do something*)
tener que ver con to have something/anything to do with
tener razón to be right
tener sed to be thirsty
tener sueño to be sleepy
tener suerte to be lucky
tenis (*m.*) tennis
teoría (*f.*) theory
terminar to finish
terminarse to end
terremoto (*m.*) earthquake
tesoro (*m.*) treasure
tiempo (*m.*) time, weather
tienda (*f.*) store; **tienda de departamentos** department store
tierra (*f.*) land, earth, world
tipo (*m.*) kind, type
toalla (*f.*) towel
tocar to touch; to play (*an instrument*)
(en) todas partes everywhere
todavía still, yet
todo (*m.*) all, everything
todo el año all year long
todo el día all day long
todo el mundo everybody
todos (*m.*) everybody, all
tolerar to tolerate
tomar to take
tomar una decisión to make a decision
tomate (*m.*) tomato
tonto silly, ridiculous
tormenta (*f.*) storm

torta (*f.*) cake
tostar (**o > ue**) to toast
trabajar to work
trabajo (*m.*) work, job; academic paper
traducir to translate
traer to bring
tragar to swallow
traje (*m.*) suit; **traje de baño** bathing suit
trastos (*m.*) junk
tratar de + INFINITIVE to try to (*do something*)
trazar to trace
trágico tragic
triste sad
tristeza (*f.*) sadness
trombón (*m.*) trombone
tropezar con (**e > ie**) to bump into

u

último last, ultimate
único only, one and only, unique
uniforme (*m.*) uniform
unir to unite
universidad (*f.*) university
unos cuantos a few
uña (*f.*) fingernail
uva (*f.*) grape

v

vacaciones (*fpl.*) vacation
vaciar to empty, clean out
vagar to wander, roam
valer to be worth
vampiro (*m.*) vampire
variedad (*f.*) variety
varios several, various
vaso (*m.*) drinking glass; vase
vecindad (*f.*) neighborhood, vicinity
vecino (*m.*) neighbor
vegetal (*m.*) vegetable
vegetariano vegetarian
vehículo (*m.*) vehicle
vela (*f.*) candle
vencer to conquer
vendedor (*m.*) salesperson
vender to sell

venir to come
ventana (*f.*) window
ver(se) to see (oneself)
verano (*m.*) summer
verdad (*f.*) truth
verdadero true, real
vestido (*m.*) dress
vestir(se) (**e > i**) to dress (oneself)
vez (*f.*) time, instance (*pl.* **veces**)
(de) vez en cuando from time to time, once in a while
viajar to travel
viaje (*m.*) trip
víctima (*m./f.*) victim
vida (*f.*) life
vidrio (*m.*) glass
viejo old
viento (*m.*) wind
viga (*f.*) support beam
vigilar to watch over
vino (*m.*) wine
violín (*m.*) violin
vista (*f.*) view
vitamina (*f.*) vitamin
vivir to live
volante flying
volar (**o > ue**) to fly; **volar de un lado a otro** to fly around
voleibol (*m.*) volleyball
volver (**o > ue**) to return
volverse loco to go crazy
vomitar to vomit
votar to vote
voz (*f.*) voice

y

ya already
yacer to lie down

z

zapatear to tap-dance
zapatilla (*f.*) slipper
zapato (*m.*) shoe
zurcir to mend, darn

English-Spanish glossary

NOTE Nouns are marked for gender; verbs are marked for stem changes.

Abbreviations include (*f.*) feminine, (*m.*) masculine, and (*pl.*) plural.

a

a lot mucho
about acerca de
abstain from (*doing something*) abstenerse de +
  INFINITIVE
abyss abismo (*m.*)
accept aceptar
accident accidente (*m.*); **by accident**
  por casualidad
acquire adquirir (i > ie)
act actuar, comportarse
address dirección (*f.*)
admit admitir
adopt adoptar
adult adulto (*m.*)
advise advertir (e > ie)
afraid asustado
(be) afraid tener miedo
after después de; **after that** después de eso
afternoon tarde (*f.*)
afterward después de
again otra vez
against contra
agree to (*do something*) convenir en + INFINITIVE
aha! ¡ajá!
airline aerolínea (*f.*)
airplane avión (*m.*)
airport aeropuerto (*m.*)
alarm clock despertador (*m.*)
alas! ¡ay!
all todo, todos
all day long todo el día
all of it nada menos
all year long todo el año
alone solo
already ya
also también
always siempre
among entre
and y, e (*preceding a word beginning with* i *or* hi)
angry enfadado, enojado

another otro
answer respuesta (*f.*)
answer contestar, responder
any cualquier/cualquiera
(not) any ningún
anything algo, cualquier cosa
anyway de cualquier forma
anywhere en cualquier parte
(not) anywhere en ninguna parte
apartment apartamento (*m.*)
appear aparecer
apple manzana (*f.*)
appliance aparato (*m.*)
appointment cita (*f.*)
approve aprobar (o > ue)
arch arco (*m.*)
architect arquitecto (*m.*)
area área (*f.*)
army ejército (*m.*)
around alrededor (de)
arrange arreglar
arrest detener
arrive llegar
article artículo (*m.*)
as a child de niño/niña
as much tanto; **as much as** tanto como
as soon as tan pronto como
ask (*a question*) preguntar
ask (for) pedir (e > i)
assignment tarea (*f.*)
aster aster (*m.*)
astronaut astronauta (*m./f.*)
at first al principio
at the end al fin
at this rate a este paso
at times a veces
athlete atleta (*m./f.*)
attend asistir (a)
attic desván (*m.*)
attitude actitud (*f.*)
attract atraer

author autor/autora (*m./f.*)
authorize autorizar
autumn otoño (*m.*)

b

baby bebé (*m./f.*)
back espalda (*f.*)
back atrás
background fondo (*m.*)
backpack mochila (*f.*)
backyard jardín (*m.*) de casa, patio (*m.*) atrás
bad malo
bad mood mal humor (*m.*)
bag bolsa (*f.*)
baker panadero (*m.*)
bakery panadería (*f.*)
ball (*dance*) baile (*m.*); (*sports*) pelota (*f.*)
band banda (*f.*)
bank banco (*m.*)
baptize bautizar
bark ladrar
baseball béisbol (*m.*)
basement sótano (*m.*)
basketball básquetbol (*m.*)
bath baño (*m.*)
bathe (oneself) bañar(se)
bathing suit traje de baño (*m.*)
bathroom baño (*m.*)
be (*enduring*) ser; (*location, short-term*) estar
be able to poder (o > ue)
be at the door llamar a la puerta
be ready estar listo
be thankful agradecer
beach playa (*f.*)
beam (*support*) viga (*f.*)
bear oso (*m.*)
because porque
become ponerse, hacerse
bed cama (*f.*)
bee abeja (*f.*)
beer cerveza (*f.*)
before antes
beforehand antes de
beg rogar (o > ue)
begin comenzar (e > ie), empezar (e > ie)
behave comportarse
behind atrás de, detrás de
believe creer
belong pertenecer
best mejor
better mejor
between entre
bicycle bicicleta (*f.*)
big grande, gran
bilingual bilingüe
bill cuenta (*f.*)
billiards billar (*m.*)

billion mil millones (*m.*)
bird ave (*f.*), pájaro (*m.*)
birthday cumpleaños (*m.*)
bite morder (o > ue)
bless bendecir (e > i)
blizzard nevada (*f.*), tormenta (*f.*) de nieve
block (*city*) manzana (*f.*), cuadra (*f.*); (*cube*) bloque (*m.*)
blonde rubio
blood sangre (*f.*)
boardroom sala (*f.*) de juntas
boat barco (*m.*)
boil hervir (e > ie)
bomb bomba (*f.*)
bone hueso (*m.*)
book libro (*m.*)
bookstore librería (*f.*)
border frontera (*f.*)
bored aburrido
boring aburrido
(be) born nacer
boss jefe (*m.*)
bother molestar
bottom fondo (*m.*)
bouquet ramo (*m.*); **bouquet of flowers** ramo de flores
box caja (*f.*)
boyfriend novio (*m.*)
bracelet pulsera (*f.*)
brain cerebro (*m.*)
branch rama (*f.*)
brave bravo, valiente
bread pan (*m.*)
break romper, quebrar
break one's promise faltar a su palabra
breakfast desayuno (*m.*)
brick ladrillo (*m.*)
bride novia (*f.*)
bring traer
bring back retraer, devolver (o > ue)
British británico
broken roto, dañado
brother hermano (*m.*)
brown café, marrón
brush (oneself) cepillar(se)
bubble burbuja (*f.*)
build construir
building edificio (*m.*)
bump into tropezar(se) con (e > ie)
bury enterrar (e > ie)
bus autobús (*m.*)
busy ocupado
butter mantequilla (*f.*)
butterfly mariposa (*f.*)
button botón (*m.*)
buy comprar
by por

c

cabinet alacena (*f.*), armario (*m.*)

cafeteria cafetería (*f.*)

caffeine cafeína (*f.*)

cake torta (*f.*)

call (oneself) llamar(se)

calorie caloría (*f.*)

camera cámara (*f.*)

camp campamento (*m.*)

candidate candidato (*m.*)

candle vela (*f.*)

candy dulces (*m.*), caramelos (*m.*)

canvas (*painting*) tela (*f.*), lienzo (*m.*)

capital (*city*) capital (*f.*); (*wealth*) capital (*m.*)

card tarjeta (*f.*), carta (*f.*)

(playing) cards naipes (*m.*)

care cuidado (*m.*)

care for (*a person*) cuidar a

care for oneself cuidarse

career carrera (*f.*)

case caso (*m.*)

(in) cash al contado

castle castillo (*m.*)

catalogue catálogo (*m.*)

catch coger

caterer abastecedor (*m.*)

celebrate celebrar

center centro (*m.*)

centerpiece centro (*m.*) de mesa

century siglo (*m.*)

ceremony ceremonia (*f.*)

chair silla (*f.*)

change cambio (*m.*)

change cambiar

chapter capítulo (*m.*)

character personaje (*m.*), carácter (*m.*)

cheat engañar

check cheque (*m.*)

checkbook talonario (*m.*) de cheques

checkers damas (*fpl.*)

cheese queso (*m.*)

chef cocinero (*m.*)

chess ajedrez (*m.*)

chicken pollo (*m.*)

chimney chimenea (*f.*)

choice elección (*f.*)

choose elegir (e > i)

chore tarea (*f.*)

Christmas Navidad (*f.*)

church iglesia (*f.*)

cigar cigarro (*m.*), puro (*m.*)

Cinderella Cenicienta (*f.*)

clarify clarificar

class clase (*f.*)

classify clasificar

clean limpio

clean limpiar

clean out vaciar

celebrity celebridad (*f.*)

clerk dependiente (*m.*)

client cliente (*m./f.*)

climb subir

clock reloj (*m.*)

close cerrar (e > ie)

closed cerrado

closet armario (*m.*)

clothes ropa (*f.*)

clothing ropa (*f.*)

cloudy nublado

clown payaso (*m.*)

club club (*m.*)

coast costa (*f.*)

cockroach cucaracha (*f.*)

coffee café (*m.*)

coffee cup taza (*f.*)

coffee shop cafetería (*f.*)

coin moneda (*f.*)

cold resfriado (*m.*)

cold frío

(be) cold tener frío

colleague compañero (*m.*)

comb (one's) hair peinar(se)

come venir

commence comenzar (e > ie)

commission comisión (*f.*)

companion compañero (*m.*)

company compañía (*f.*)

compete competir (e > i)

complain quejarse; complain about quejarse de

complete cumplir

compliment cumplido (*m.*)

compose componer

concert concierto (*m.*)

conclude concluir

concoction brebaje (*m.*)

conduct conducir

confess confesar (e > ie)

conjugate conjugar

conquer conquistar, vencer

consent consentir (e > ie)

constitute constituir

construct construir

contain contener

contamination contaminación (*f.*)

contest concurso (*m.*)

contestant participante (*m./f.*)

continue continuar, seguir (e > i)

contract contratar, contraer

contribute contribuir

convert convertir (e > ie); convert into convertir en

convince convencer

cook cocinar

cookie galletita (*f.*)

corner (*exterior*) esquina (*f.*); (*interior*) rincón (*m.*)

correct corregir (e > i)
cost costar (o > ue)
couch sofá (*m.*)
count contar (o > ue)
counter mostrador (*m.*)
(a) couple of un par de
coupon cupón (*m.*)
courteous cortés
cousin primo (*m.*)
cover cubrir
cover up encubrir
cracker galleta (*f.*)
crime crimen (*m.*)
critic crítico (*m.*)
crowd multitud (*f.*)
cry llorar
crystal cristal (*m.*)
culinary culinario
cup taza (*f.*)
curse maldecir (e > i)
curtain cortina (*f.*)
cut cortar

d

daisy margarita (*f.*)
dance baile (*m.*)
dance bailar
darn zurcir
date fecha (*f.*), cita (*f.*)
date salir con
day día (*m.*)
daydream soñar en (o > ue)
dead muerto
death muerte (*f.*)
debit card tarjeta (*f.*) de débito
deceive engañar
decide decidir
deduce deducir, colegir (e > i)
defeat vencer
defective defectuoso
defend defender (e > ie)
defendant acusado (*m.*)
deliver entregar
demand exigir
demonstrate demostrar (o > ue)
deny negar(se) (e > ie)
depart partir
department store tienda (*f.*) de departamentos
depend depender; **depend on** depender de
deposit depositar
depressed deprimido
describe describir
desert desierto (*m.*)
deserve merecer
desire deseo (*m.*)
desk escritorio (*m.*)
dessert postre (*m.*)

destroy destruir
detachable de quita y pon
detain detener
diamond diamante (*m.*)
diary diario (*m.*)
die morir (o > ue)
diet dieta (*f.*)
diet ponerse a dieta
(be on a) diet estar a dieta, ponerse a dieta
different diferente, distinto
difficult difícil
difficulty dificultad (*f.*)
dine cenar
dining room comedor (*m.*)
dinner cena (*f.*)
diploma diploma (*m.*)
direct dirigir
directions direcciones (*fpl.*)
dirty sucio
disappear desaparecer
disaster desastre (*m.*)
discover descubrir
discuss discutir
dish plato (*m.*)
display lucir
dissolve disolver (o > ue)
dissuade retraer
distance distancia (*f.*)
distinct distinto
distinguish distinguir
divorce divorcio (*m.*)
divorce divorciarse
do hacer
document documento (*m.*)
dollar dólar (*m.*)
dollhouse casa (*f.*) de muñecas
door puerta (*f.*); **front door** puerta principal
doubt duda (*f.*)
doubt dudar
down abajo
downtown centro (*m.*)
dozen docena (*f.*)
drain desagüe (*m.*)
dread temer
dream sueño (*m.*)
dream soñar (o > ue); **dream of** soñar con
dress vestido (*m.*)
dress (oneself) vestir(se) (e > i)
drink bebida (*f.*)
drink beber, tomar
drinking glass vaso (*m.*)
drive conducir, manejar
drizzling lloviznando
drunk borracho
dry seco
dry (oneself) secar(se)
duchess duquesa (*f.*)

duck pato (*m.*)
duke duque (*m.*)
during durante
dust quitar el polvo

e

each cada
early temprano
earn ganar
earring arete (*m.*), pendiente (*m.*)
earth tierra (*f.*)
earthquake terremoto (*m.*)
eat comer
eat breakfast desayunar
eat dinner cenar
eat lunch almorzar (o > ue)
education educación (*f.*)
egg huevo (*m.*)
egoistic egoísta
either ... or ... o... o...
(not) either tampoco
elect elegir (e > i)
election elección (*f.*)
element elemento (*m.*)
elevator ascensor (*m.*)
embarrassed avergonzado
employee empleado (*m.*)
employer jefe (*m.*), empleador (*m.*)
empty vacío
empty vaciar
(be) enchanting encantar
end terminarse, acabarse
enemy enemigo (*m.*)
energy energía (*f.*)
enforce imponer
England Inglaterra (*f.*)
English inglés (*m.*)
enigma enigma (*m.*)
enjoy gozar de
enough bastante, suficiente
enter entrar; **enter into** entrar en
entire entero
entomologist entomólogo (*m.*)
envelope sobre (*m.*)
episode episodio (*m.*)
equal igual
equipment equipaje (*m.*)
erect erguir
error error (*m.*)
essay ensayo (*m.*)
establish establecer
ethic credo (*m.*)
even hasta
every cada
everybody todos (*m.*), todo el mundo
everyone todos (*m.*), todo el mundo
everything todo (*m.*)

everywhere en todas partes, por todas partes
evil malvado
exam examen (*m.*)
exercise hacer ejercicio, ejercer
exert ejercer
exhibit exposición (*f.*)
exist existir
export exportar
express oneself expresarse
extinguish extinguir
eye ojo (*m.*)

f

fail (*a test*) suspender, reprobar (o > ue)
fair justo
fairy godmother hada madrina (*f.*)
fairy tale cuento (*m.*) de hadas
faith fe (*f.*)
fall otoño (*m.*)
fall caer
fall asleep dormirse (o > ue)
fall down caerse
fall in love enamorarse
fame fama (*f.*)
(be) familiar with conocer
fantasy fantasía (*f.*)
farm granja (*f.*)
farmer granjero (*m.*)
(be) fascinating fascinar
fast rápido
father padre (*m.*), papá (*m.*)
father-in-law suegro (*m.*)
faucet grifo (*m.*)
fault culpa (*f.*)
favor favor (*m.*)
fear temor (*m.*)
fear temer, tener miedo de
feel sentir(se) (e > ie)
feel like (*doing something*) tener ganas de +
INFINITIVE
feel sorry sentir (e > ie)
(a) few unos cuantos
fiancé novio (*m.*), prometido (*m.*)
fiancée novia (*f.*), prometida (*f.*)
fill llenar
film (*camera*) película (*f.*), rollo (*m.*) de película
financial financiero
find encontrar (o > ue)
find out averiguar
fine multa (*f.*)
fine bien
fingernail uña (*f.*)
finish terminar
fire fuego (*m.*); (*catastrophic*) incendio (*m.*)
fire despedir (e > i)
fire station estación (*f.*) de bomberos
firefighter bombero (*m.*)

fireplace chimenea (*f.*)
first primero
fish (*living*) pez (*m.*); (*prepared*) pescado (*m.*)
fit caber
fix arreglar
flag bandera (*f.*)
flee huir
flight attendant azafata (*m./f.*)
float flotar
floor suelo (*m.*), piso (*m.*)
florist florista (*m./f.*)
flow fluir
flower flor (*f.*)
fluently con soltura
fly mosca (*f.*)
fly volar (o > ue)
fly a kite remontar una cometa
flying volante
fog niebla (*f.*)
follow seguir (e > i)
following siguiente
food comida (*f.*)
fool engañar
foot pie (*m.*)
football fútbol (*m.*) americano
for para; por
for a while por un rato
for the first time por primera vez
forest bosque (*m.*)
forever para siempre
forge (*a signature*) falsificar
forget olvidar
fork tenedor (*m.*)
freedom libertad (*f.*)
French francés (*m.*)
french fries papas (*f.*) fritas
frequently frecuentemente, con frecuencia
friendly amistoso
frighten espantar
frog rana (*f.*)
from time to time de vez en cuando
from top to bottom de cabo a rabo
fry freír (e > i)
full lleno
fun diversión (*f.*)
funny cómico
furniture muebles (*m.*); **piece of furniture** mueble

g

gain ganar
gain weight engordar
game juego (*m.*), partido (*m.*)
game show concurso (*m.*)
garbage basura (*f.*)
garden jardín (*m.*)
gardener jardinero (*m.*)
gas tank tanque (*m.*) de gasolina

gasoline gasolina (*f.*)
genuine genuino
get obtener, adquirir (i > ie), conseguir (e > i)
get angry enojarse
get mad enojarse
get sick enfermarse
get up levantarse
get used to acostumbrarse
ghost fantasma (*m.*)
giant gigante (*m.*)
gift regalo (*m.*)
giraffe jirafa (*f.*)
girlfriend novia (*f.*)
give dar
give a gift regalar
glass vidrio (*m.*), cristal (*m.*)
(drinking) glass vaso (*m.*)
glove guante (*m.*)
glove compartment guantera (*f.*)
go ir
go away irse
go crazy volverse loco
go to bed acostarse (o > ue)
go to the movies ir al cine
God/god Dios/dios
God willing ojalá
godfather padrino (*m.*)
godparents padrinos (*m.*)
gold oro (*m.*)
good bueno
good mood buen humor (*m.*)
grab coger
grade nota (*f.*); **good/bad grades** buenas/malas notas
grand gran, grande
Grand Canyon Gran Cañón (*m.*)
grandchild nieto (*m.*)
grandfather abuelo (*m.*)
grandson nieto (*m.*)
grant conceder
grape uva (*f.*)
gratify gratificar, satisfacer, complacer
gravity gravedad (*f.*)
great estupendo, gran, grande
groan gemir (e > i)
groom novio (*m.*)
grow crecer, cultivar (*plantas*)
guest invitado (*m.*)
guitar guitarra (*f.*)
gymnasium gimnasio (*m.*)

h

hair pelo (*m.*)
hallway pasillo (*m.*)
hamburger hamburguesa (*f.*)
hammer martillo (*m.*)
hammer martillar

hand mano (*f.*)
(on the other) hand en cambio
handkerchief pañuelo (*m.*)
handsome guapo
hang (up) colgar (o > ue)
happiness felicidad (*f.*)
happy feliz
hard duro; difícil
harp arpa (*f.*)
hat sombrero (*m.*)
hate odiar
hatred odio (*m.*)
haunted embrujado
have tener; haber (*auxiliary*)
have something to do with tener que ver con
have to (*do something*) tener que + INFINITIVE
head cabeza (*f.*)
health salud (*f.*)
hear oír
heart corazón (*m.*)
heel tacón (*m.*); **high heel** tacón alto
help ayuda (*f.*)
help ayudar
here aquí
hide esconder
highway carretera (*f.*), autopista (*f.*)
hinder impedir (e > i)
hire contratar, emplear
hold contener
Holland Holanda
home hogar (*m.*)
homicide homicidio (*m.*)
honest honrado
honeymoon luna (*f.*) de miel
hope (for) esperar
horse caballo (*m.*)
host anfitrión (*m.*)
hotel hotel (*m.*)
how? ¿cómo?
how many? ¿cuántos?
how much? ¿cuánto?
human humano (*m.*)
humid húmedo
humor humor (*m.*)
hunger hambre (*f.*)
(be) hungry tener hambre
hunt cazar
hurricane huracán (*m.*)
(be in a) hurry tener prisa
husband esposo (*m.*)

i

ice hielo (*m.*)
ice cream helado (*m.*)
idiocy idiotez (*f.*)
(be) ignorant of ignorar
imagine imaginar(se)

immerse sumergir
impede impedir (e > i)
(be) important importar
in case (of) en caso de que
in fact de hecho
in front enfrente; **in front of** enfrente de
in the beginning al principio
inch pulgada (*f.*)
include incluir
increase aumentar
induce inducir
influence influir (en)
information información (*f.*)
innocent inocente
insane loco
insert introducir
inside adentro, dentro (de)
insist insistir; **insist on** insistir en
instead (of) en vez de
institute instituir
interest interés (*m.*)
(be) interesting interesar
introduce introducir, presentar
introduction presentación (*f.*)
intruder intruso (*m.*)
invest invertir (e > ie)
investigate investigar
invitation invitación (*f.*)
invite invitar
iron plancha (*f.*)
iron planchar
item artículo (*m.*)

j

jail cárcel (*f.*)
January enero
jewel joya (*f.*)
job trabajo (*m.*)
joke broma (*f.*)
jump saltar
jungle selva (*f.*)
junk trastos (*m.*)
jury jurado (*m.*)
just justo, sólo
justify justificar

k

keep a secret guardar un secreto
key llave (*f.*)
kind tipo (*m.*)
kindle encender (e > ie)
king rey (*m.*)
kiss besar
kitchen sink fregadero (*m.*) de cocina
knee rodilla (*f.*)
kneel estar de rodillas
knife cuchillo (*m.*)

knot nudo (*m.*)
know a person conocer
know information saber; **know about** saber de

l

laboratory laboratorio (*m.*)
(be) lacking faltar
ladder escalera (*f.*)
lake lago (*m.*)
lamb cordero (*m.*)
land tierra (*f.*)
language lenguaje (*m.*); (*specific*) idioma (*m.*)
lard manteca (*f.*)
large grande
lark alondra (*f.*)
last último
last durar
last night anoche
late tarde
later más tarde, luego
laugh reír(se) (e > i)
law ley (*f.*)
lawn césped (*m.*)
lawnmower cortacésped (*m.*)
lawyer abogado (*m.*)
lazy perezoso
lead conducir
leader líder (*m.*)
leaf hoja (*f.*)
learn aprender
leave salir, irse, partir; **leave from** salir dc;
    leave behind dejar
(to the) left a la izquierda
(be) left over sobrar
leg pierna (*f.*)
lemonade limonada (*f.*)
lend prestar
less menos
lesson lección (*f.*)
let's see ... a ver...
letter carta (*f.*)
liar mentiroso (*m.*)
liberty libertad (*f.*)
library biblioteca (*f.*)
license licencia (*f.*)
lie mentira (*f.*)
(tell a) lie mentir (e > ie)
lie down yacer, acostarse (o > ue)
life vida (*f.*)
light luz (*f.*)
light encender (e > ie)
light up lucir
lightbulb bombilla (*f.*)
line cola (*f.*), línea (*f.*)
lion león (*m.*)
listen (to) escuchar
little pequeño, poco

Little Red Riding Hood Caperucita Roja (*f.*)
live vivir
living room sala (*f.*), sala de estar
loaf barra (*f.*); **loaf of bread** barra de pan
loan préstamo (*m.*)
loan prestar
lobster langosta (*f.*)
locksmith cerrajero (*m.*)
long largo
(be) long medir (e > i)
long time mucho tiempo (*m.*)
look (at) mirar
look for buscar
look like parecerse a
lose perder (e > ie)
lose weight adelgazar, rebajar de peso
(a) lot (of) mucho
love amor (*m.*)
love amar
(be) lucky tener suerte
luggage equipaje (*m.*), maletas (*f.*)
lunch almuerzo (*m.*)
lunch almorzar (o > ue)

m

mad enojado
made by hecho por
magazine revista (*f.*)
magician mago (*m.*)
maid criada (*f.*), sirvienta (*f.*)
mail correo (*m.*)
mail echar al correo
maintain mantener
majority mayoría (*f.*)
make hacer
make a decision tomar una decisión
make a mistake cometer un error
mall centro (*m.*) comercial
man hombre (*m.*)
manage manejar
manager gerente (*m./f.*)
manners modales (*mpl.*); **good manners** buenos
    modales
many muchos
marathon maratón (*m.*)
marriage casamiento (*m.*)
married casado
marry casarse con
mashed puré (*m.*)
mature maduro
meal comida (*f.*)
meanwhile entretanto
measure medir (e > i)
meat carne (*f.*)
mechanic mecánico (*m.*)
medicine medicina (*f.*)
medicine cabinet botiquín (*m.*)

meet conocer; encontrarse (o > ue); **meet with** encontrarse con
meeting reunión (*f.*)
mend zurcir
mercantilism mercantilismo (*m.*)
merit merecer
messy desordenado
method método (*m.*)
midday mediodía (*m.*)
middle medio (*m.*); **in the middle** en medio
midnight medianoche (*f.*)
mile milla (*f.*)
miracle milagro (*m.*)
mirror espejo (*m.*)
(be) missing faltar
mistake error (*m.*)
mitten manopla (*f.*)
moan gemir (e > i)
model modelo (*m./f.*)
moldy mohoso
monarch monarca (*m.*)
money dinero (*m.*)
monkey mono (*m.*)
monster monstruo (*m.*)
month mes (*m.*)
monument monumento (*m.*)
mood humor (*m.*)
moon luna (*f.*)
morning mañana (*f.*)
mortgage hipoteca (*f.*)
mosquito mosquito (*m.*)
mother mamá (*f.*), madre (*f.*)
mother-in-law suegra (*f.*)
mouth boca (*f.*)
move (*change residence*) mudarse
move (*oneself*) mover(se) (o > ue)
movie película (*f.*)
movie star estrella (*f.*) de cine
movie theater cine (*m.*)
(to the) movies al cine
mow (*grass, etc.*) cortar, segar (e > ie)
much mucho
mud lodo (*m.*)
murderer asesino (*m.*)
music música (*f.*)
must (*do something*) [*conjecture*] deber de +
    INFINITIVE
mystery misterio (*m.*)

n

name nombre (*m.*)
name nombrar, llamar
nap siesta (*f.*)
napkin servilleta (*f.*)
neat ordenado
neck cuello (*m.*)
necklace collar (*m.*)

necktie corbata (*f.*)
need necesitar
needle (*syringe*) jeringa (*f.*)
neighbor vecino (*m.*)
neighborhood vecindad (*f.*)
nervous nervioso
never nunca; **never ever** nunca más
news noticias (*fpl.*)
newspaper periódico (*m.*)
next próximo, siguiente
next (door) to al lado de
nice amable, simpático
night noche (*f.*)
nightmare pesadilla (*f.*)
no one nadie
nobody nadie
noise ruido (*m.*)
noon mediodía (*m.*)
nose nariz (*f.*)
not any ningún, ninguno
not anything nada
note nota (*f.*)
nothing nada
now ahora
nowhere en ninguna parte
number número (*m.*); **telephone number** número
    de teléfono

o

obey obedecer
obtain obtener, conseguir (e > i)
ocean océano (*m.*)
of de
of course por supuesto
offer ofrecer
office oficina (*f.*); **post office** oficina de correos
often a menudo, frecuentemente, con frecuencia
oil aceite (*m.*)
old viejo
older mayor
Olympics olimpiadas (*f.*)
on countless occasions en ocasiones innumerables
on purpose a propósito
on time a su hora, a tiempo
once una vez
once in a while de vez en cuando
only sólo, solamente, único
open abrir
opening (*premiere*) estreno (*m.*)
oppose oponer
or o
organize organizar
otherwise de lo contrario
ought deber
ounce onza (*f.*)
out of tune desafinadamente
outside afuera

oven horno (*m.*)
owe deber
owl búho (*m.*)
own poseer, tener
owner dueño (*m.*)

p

pack empacar
package paquete (*m.*)
page página (*f.*)
pail balde (*m.*)
(be) painful doler (o > ue)
paint pintura (*f.*)
paint pintar
painter pintor (*m.*)
painting pintura (*f.*), cuadro (*m.*)
pajamas pijama (*m.*)
palace palacio (*m.*)
pamphlet folleto (*m.*)
pants pantalones (*m.*)
paper papel (*m.*); trabajo (*m.*)
parade desfile (*m.*)
pardon oneself disculparse
park parque (*m.*)
park aparcar, estacionar
parking space aparcamiento (*m.*)
part parte (*f.*)
participant participante (*m./f.*)
party fiesta (*f.*)
path senda (*f.*)
pay (for) pagar
peace paz (*f.*)
peanut cacahuate (*m.*)
pearl perla (*f.*); **little pearl** perlita
pen (*ballpoint*) bolígrafo (*m.*); (*fountain*) pluma (*f.*)
people gente (*f.*), personas (*f.*)
performance (*job*) desempeño (*m.*)
permit permitir
persecute perseguir (e > i)
person persona (*f.*)
persuade persuadir, inducir, convencer
pet animal (*m.*) doméstico
pharmacy farmacia (*f.*)
photo foto (*f.*), fotografía (*f.*)
pick up recoger
picture pintura (*f.*), cuadro (*m.*)
piece pedazo (*m.*)
pig cerdo (*m.*)
pill pastilla (*f.*)
pillow almohada (*f.*)
pistol pistola (*f.*)
pity lástima (*f.*)
place lugar (*m.*)
place poner; **place an ad** poner un anuncio
plaintiff demandante (*m./f.*)
plan plan (*m.*)
plan planear

planet planeta (*m.*)
plant planta (*f.*)
plant sembrar (e > ie), plantar
plate plato (*m.*)
play drama (*m.*)
play (*an instrument*) tocar; (*a game*) jugar (u > ue)
play the role hacer el papel
please por favor
please placer
(be) pleasing gustar
plumber fontanero (*m.*)
pocket bolsillo (*m.*)
point punto (*m.*); **point of view** punto de vista
point-blank a bocajarro
police (force) policía (*f.*)
policeman policía (*m.*)
policewoman policía (*f.*)
polite cortés, educado
politician político (*m.*)
politics política (*f.*)
pollution contaminación
pool piscina (*f.*), alberca (*f.*), billar (*m.*)
pope papa (*m.*)
possess poseer
post office oficina (*f.*) de correos
potato patata (*f.*), papa (*f.*)
pound libra (*f.*)
pour echar
poverty pobreza (*f.*)
practice practicar
praise alabanza (*f.*)
pray rezar, rogar (o > ue)
prefer preferir (e > ie)
pregnant embarazada
prepare preparar
present regalo (*m.*)
pretend fingir
price precio (*m.*)
priest sacerdote (*m.*)
prince príncipe (*m.*)
prison prisión (*f.*), cárcel (*f.*)
prize premio (*m.*)
problem problema (*m.*)
produce producir
professional profesional (*m.*)
program programa (*m.*)
progress progreso (*m.*)
prohibited prohibido
promise promesa (*f.*)
promise prometer
pronunciation pronunciación (*f.*)
protect proteger
prove probar (o > ue)
provide proveer
provided that con tal que
pump bomba (*f.*)
pumpkin calabaza (*f.*)

purchase compra (*f.*)
purchase comprar
purse bolsa (*f.*)
pursue perseguir (e > i)
put poner; **put on oneself** ponerse
put into meter en
put oneself through meterse en
puzzle enigma (*m.*)

q

quarterback lanzador (*m.*)
queen reina (*f.*)
question pregunta (*f.*), cuestión (*f.*)
quick rápido
quickly rápidamente
(be) quiet callarse
quit (*a job, etc.*) renunciar a
quiz prueba (*f.*)

r

rabbit conejo (*m.*)
radio (*apparatus*) radio (*m./f.*)
radio (**station**) radio (*f.*)
rage rabia (*f.*)
rain lluvia (*f.*)
rain llover
rain forest selva (*f.*) tropical
rainy lluvioso
raise aumento (*m.*)
raise (*children, animals, etc.*) criar
raisin pasa (*f.*)
razor navaja (*f.*)
reach alcanzar; **reach a goal** alcanzar un objectivo
read leer
ready listo
real verdadero
reality realidad (*f.*)
really realmente, verdaderamente
reception recepción (*f.*)
receive recibir
recognize reconocer
record disco (*m.*)
redo rehacer
reduce reducir
refer referir (e > ie)
refrigerator refrigerador (*m.*)
regret sentir (e > i)
regulation reglamento (*m.*)
relax relajarse
rely on depender de
remain quedarse
remake rehacer
remember recordar
remove remover (o > ue), sustraer; (*clothing*) quitar(se)
repeat repetir (e > i)
report reportaje (*m.*)

(be) repugnant disgustar
request pedir (e > i)
require exigir
reread releer
resolve resolver (o > ue)
rest descansar
restaurant restaurante (*m.*)
return volver (o > ue), regresar
return (*an object*) devolver (o > ue), regresar
ribbon cinta (*f.*)
rice arroz (*m.*)
rich rico
richness riqueza (*f.*)
ride montar; **ride a bike** montar en bicicleta
ridiculous ridículo, tonto
right derecho (*m.*)
(be) right tener razón
(to the) right a la derecha
right now ahora mismo, ahorita
ring anillo (*m.*)
ring sonar (o > ue)
ripe maduro
river río (*m.*)
road camino (*m.*)
roam vagar
rob robar
robbery robo (*m.*)
room cuarto (*m.*), espacio (*m.*), habitación (*f.*)
roommate compañero (*m.*)
rot pudrir
rotten podrido
rub off raer
ruby rubí (*m.*)
rule regla (*f.*)
run correr; (*of a machine*) funcionar; (*a machine*) manejar
rule in favor of fallar a favor de
run away huir
Russian ruso (*m.*)

s

sad triste
sadness tristeza (*f.*)
salad ensalada (*f.*)
sale rebaja (*f.*)
salesperson vendedor (*m.*)
same mismo, igual; **the same** lo mismo, iguales
sample muestra (*f.*)
sample probar (o > ue)
sand arena (*f.*)
sausage salchicha (*f.*)
save guardar; (*a life*) salvar; (*money*) ahorrar
say decir (e > i)
say good-bye despedirse (e > i); **say good-bye to** despedirse de
scammer chanchullero/chanchullera (*m./f.*)
scare espantar

scarecrow espantapájaros (*m.*)
scatter esparcir
scene escena (*f.*)
school escuela (*f.*); **high school** escuela secundaria
science ciencia (*f.*)
scientist científico/científica (*m./f.*)
scrape raer
scratch arañar
scrub fregar (e > ie)
search busca (*f.*), búsqueda (*f.*)
search buscar
seated sentado
secret secreto (*m.*)
see (oneself) ver(se)
seed semilla (*f.*)
seem parecer
seize coger
select escoger
selfish egoísta
sell vender
sentence frase (*f.*)
separately por separado
servant sirviente (*m.*), criado/criada (*m./f.*)
serve servir (e > i)
set (*sun*) poner(se)
several varios
shade sombra (*f.*)
shadow sombra (*f.*)
shame lástima (*f.*)
shave (oneself) afeitar(se)
shelf estante (*m.*)
shoe zapato (*m.*)
shop ir de compras
shopping mall centro (*m.*) comercial
shovel snow quitar la nieve
show mostrar (o > ue)
shower ducha (*f.*)
shower ducharse
shut cerrar (e > ie)
sick enfermo
(get) sick enfermarse
sidewalk acera (*f.*)
sign letrero (*m.*)
sign (*one's name*) firmar
signature firma (*f.*)
silly tonto
silver plata (*f.*)
sing cantar
sister hermana (*f.*)
sit down sentarse (e > ie); **sitting down** sentado
size talla (*f.*), tamaño (*m.*)
skate patín (*m.*)
skate patinar
ski esquiar
sleep dormir (o > ue)
Sleeping Beauty Bella Durmiente (*f.*)
(be) sleepy tener sueño

sleeve manga (*f.*)
slim delgado
slipper zapatilla (*f.*)
slob cochino (*m.*), guarro (*m.*)
small pequeño
smell oler
smile sonrisa (*f.*)
smile sonreír (e > i)
smoke humo (*m.*)
smoke fumar
snake culebra (*f.*)
sneeze estornudar
snow nieve (*f.*)
snow nevar
snowstorm nevada (*f.*), tormenta (*f.*) de nieve
so tan
so many tantos
so much tanto
so that para que
soccer fútbol (*m.*)
society sociedad (*f.*)
sociopath sociópata (*m./f.*)
sock calcetín (*m.*)
sofa sofá (*m.*)
soldier soldado (*m.*)
solve resolver (o > ue)
somebody alguien
someone alguien
something algo
sometimes a veces
song canción (*f.*)
sooner or later tarde o temprano
sound sonar (o > ue); **sound like** sonar a
soup sopa (*f.*)
south sur (*m.*)
South Pole Polo Sur (*m.*)
space espacio (*m.*)
spaceship nave (*f.*)
speak hablar
speech discurso (*m.*)
spend (*money*) gastar
spider araña (*f.*)
spoil pudrir, deslucir
spoon cuchara (*f.*)
spouse esposo/esposa (*m./f.*)
spread esparcir
spring primavera (*f.*)
spurt surgir
spy espía (*m./f.*)
square cuadro (*m.*)
stair peldaño (*m.*)
stairway escalera (*f.*)
(postage) stamp sello (*m.*), estampilla (*f.*)
stand out destacar
stand up levantarse
star estrella (*f.*); **movie star** estrella de cine
start (*engine*) arrancar

state estado (*m.*)
stay estancia (*f.*)
stay quedarse
steak filete (*m.*)
steal robar, hurtar
step peldaño (*m.*)
stepmother madrastra (*f.*)
stepsister hermanastra (*f.*)
still todavía
stomach estómago (*m.*)
stop (*doing something*) dejar de + INFINITIVE
store tienda (*f.*)
storm tormenta (*f.*)
story cuento (*m.*)
street calle (*f.*)
stripe raya (*f.*)
student estudiante (*m./f.*)
studies estudios (*mpl.*)
study estudiar
stumble tropezar (e > ie)
submerge sumergir
substitute sustituir
subtract sustraer
suburbs afueras (*fpl.*)
such tal; **such a thing** tal cosa
sue demandar
suffer sufrir
suffice bastar
sugar azúcar (*m.*)
suggest sugerir (e > ie)
suit traje (*m.*)
suitcase maleta (*f.*)
summer verano (*m.*)
sun sol (*m.*)
sunflower girasol (*m.*)
sunglasses gafas (*fpl.*) de sol
supermarket supermercado (*m.*)
superstitious person supersticioso (*m.*)
support soportar
suppose suponer
(be in) surplus sobrar
sustain soportar
swallow tragar
sweater suéter (*m.*)
sweep barrer
sweet dulce
swim nadar
swimming pool piscina (*f.*)
symbol símbolo (*m.*)
symbolize simbolizar

t

T-shirt camiseta (*f.*)
tabloid tabloide (*m.*)
take tomar
take a picture sacar una foto
take a walk dar un paseo

take care of (*a person*) cuidar a
take off (*clothing*) quitarse
take out sacar
take time durar, tardar (en)
tale cuento (*m.*)
talent talento (*m.*)
talk hablar
tank tanque (*m.*); **gas tank** tanque de gasolina
tap-dance zapatear
tape cinta (*f.*)
tarnish deslucir
task tarea (*f.*)
taste gusto (*m.*)
taste probar (o > ue)
tattoo tatuaje (*m.*)
tax impuesto (*m.*)
tea té (*m.*)
teach enseñar
teacher maestro/maestra (*m./f.*)
tear lágrima (*f.*)
teenager adolescente (*m./f.*)
telegram telegrama (*m.*)
telephone teléfono (*m.*)
television televisión (*f.*), televisor (*m.*)
tell decir (e > i)
tennis tenis (*m.*)
test examen (*m.*)
test probar (o > ue)
thank-you letter carta (*f.*) de agradecimiento
that's it! ¡ajá!
theater teatro (*m.*)
then entonces
theory teoría (*f.*)
there is, there are hay
thief ladrón/ladrona (*m./f.*)
thin delgado, flaco
thing cosa (*f.*)
think pensar (e > ie); **think about** pensar en
thirst sed (*f.*)
(be) thirsty tener sed
thousand mil
thumb pulgar (*m.*)
(traffic) ticket boleto (*m.*), multa (*f.*)
time tiempo (*m.*); vez (*f.*)
(for the first) time por primera vez
(from) time to time de vez en cuando
tin estaño (*m.*)
tip propina (*f.*)
tired cansado
(be) tired estar cansado
toast tostada (*f.*)
toast tostar (o > ue)
today hoy
together juntos
tolerate tolerar
tomato tomate (*m.*)
tomorrow mañana

tonight esta noche
tooth diente (*m.*)
toothpaste pasta (*f.*) de dientes
touch tocar
towel toalla (*f.*)
trace trazar
tragic trágico
train tren (*m.*)
train entrenar
translate traducir
trash basura (*f.*)
travel viajar
travel agent agente (*m./f.*) de viajes
treasure tesoro (*m.*)
tree árbol (*m.*)
tremble temblar (e > ie)
trial juicio (*m.*)
trick engañar
trip viaje (*m.*)
trombone trombón (*m.*)
truck camión (*m.*)
true verdadero, cierto
trunk maletero (*m.*), baúl (*m.*)
truth verdad (*f.*)
try probar (o > ue); try on (*clothing*) probarse
try to (*do something*) tratar de + INFINITIVE, intentar
Tuesday martes (*m.*)
turkey pavo (*m.*)
turn girar
turn off apagar
twiddle one's thumbs quedarse de brazos cruzados

u

ultimate último
uncomfortable incómodo
under debajo de
underneath debajo
understand comprender, entender (e > ie)
undo deshacer
undress (oneself) desvestir(se) (e > i)
uniform uniforme (*m.*)
unique único
unite unir
United States Estados Unidos (*m.*)
university universidad (*f.*)
unless a menos que
until hasta

v

vacation vacaciones (*fpl.*)
valentine tarjeta (*f.*) para el Día de los Enamorados
vampire vampiro (*m.*)
van camioneta (*f.*)
variety variedad (*f.*)
various varios
vase vaso (*m.*)
vegetable vegetal (*m.*)

vegetarian vegetariano
vehicle vehículo (*m.*)
very muy
vicinity vecindad (*f.*)
victim víctima (*m./f.*)
view vista (*f.*)
vitamin vitamina (*f.*)
voice voz (*f.*)
volleyball voleibol (*m.*)
vomit vómito (*m.*)
vomit vomitar
vote votar

w

wait (for) esperar
waiter mesero (*m.*)
wake up despertarse (e > ie)
walk andar, caminar
walk away alejarse
wall (*exterior*) muro (*m.*); (*interior*) pared (*f.*)
wander vagar
want querer (e > ie)
war guerra (*f.*)
(be) warm tener calor
warmth calor (*m.*)
warn advertir (e > ie)
warrior guerrero (*m.*)
wash (oneself) lavar(se)
wash (*dishes*) fregar (e > ie)
waste malgastar
waste time perder (e > ie) el tiempo
watch reloj (*m.*)
watch mirar
watch over vigilar
water agua (*f.*)
water regar (e > ie)
wealth riqueza (*f.*)
wear llevar, usar
wedding boda (*f.*)
weeds malas hierbas (*f.*)
week semana (*f.*)
weekend fin (*m.*) de semana
weigh pesar
weight peso (*m.*)
well bien, pues
well, … pues,…
wet mojado
what? ¿qué?
wheel rueda (*f.*)
when cuando; when? ¿cuándo?
where donde; where? ¿dónde?; (to) where? ¿adónde?
which? ¿cuál(es)?
while mientras (que)
whitewash encubrir
who quien; who? ¿quién?
why? ¿por qué?
wife esposa (*f.*)

win ganar
wind viento (*m.*)
wind dar cuerda a; **wind a watch** dar cuerda a un reloj
window ventana (*f.*)
wine vino (*m.*)
winner ganador (*m.*)
winter invierno (*m.*)
wish deseo (*m.*)
wish desear, querer (e > ie)
witch bruja (*f.*)
with con
with me conmigo
with you contigo
without sin
wizard mago (*m.*)
wolf lobo (*m.*)
woman mujer (*f.*)
wonderful maravilloso
wood madera (*f.*)
wooden de madera
woods bosque (*m.*)

word palabra (*f.*)
work trabajo (*m.*), empleo (*m.*)
work trabajar; (*appliance, machine*) funcionar
world mundo (*m.*)
World Series Serie (*f.*) Mundial
worry preocuparse; **worry about** preocuparse por
(be) worth valer
wrap (up) envolver (o > ue)
wretched malísimo
wrist muñeca (*f.*)
write escribir
(be) wrong no tener razón

y
year año (*m.*)
yellow amarillo
yesterday ayer
yet todavía
young joven
younger menor

About the Author

Dorothy Richmond is a Spanish instructor and author of several Spanish texts and reference works. Titles with McGraw Hill include *Guide to Spanish Suffixes*, *The Big Red Book of Spanish Vocabulary* (coauthor), and the following titles in the Practice Makes Perfect series: *Spanish Verb Tenses* (first–fifth editions), *Spanish Pronouns and Prepositions* (first–fourth editions), *Spanish Vocabulary* (first–fourth editions), *Basic Spanish* (first–third editions), and *Spanish Vocabulary Building with Suffixes*. Ms. Richmond holds degrees in Linguistics, Philosophy, and Educational Administration. She lives in Minneapolis, Minnesota.